Disordered Personalities in Literature

Longman English and Humanities Series
Series Editor: Lee Jacobus, University of
Connecticut, Storrs

Disordered Personalities in
Literature

Charles W. Harwell
University of South Alabama

LONGMAN
NEW YORK AND LONDON

DISORDERED PERSONALITIES IN LITERATURE

Longman Inc., New York
Associated companies, branches, and representatives
throughout the world.

Developmental Editor: Gordon T.R. Anderson
Editorial and Design Supervisors: Joan Matthews and
    Diane Perlmuth
Interior Design: Pencils Portfolio, Inc.
Cover Design: Charles Fellows
Manufacturing and Production Supervisor: Robin B.
    Besofsky
Composition: New Look Typographic Corporation
Printing and Binding: Fairfield Graphics

PS
509
.P45
D5

Library of Congress Cataloging in Publication Data
Main entry under title:
Disordered personalities in literature.
(Longman English and humanities series)
Bibliography: p.
1. Personality, Disorders of—Literary collections.
2. American literature. 3. English literature.
I. Harwell, Charles W., 1934-   II. Series.
PS509.P45D5   820'.803520824   79-26707
ISBN 0-582-28165-2

Manufactured in the United States of America

9 8 7 6 5 4 3 2 1

Acknowledgments

"Counting the Mad" by Donald Justice. Copyright ©1957 by Donald Justice. Reprinted from *The Summer Anniversaries* by permission of Wesleyan University Press.

"Big Blonde" by Dorothy Parker. From *The Portable Dorothy Parker*. Copyright 1929 by Dorothy Parker, © renewed 1957 by Dorothy Parker. Reprinted by permission of Viking Penguin Inc.

"The Addict" by Anne Sexton. From *Live or Die* by Anne Sexton. Copyright ©1966 by Anne Sexton. Reprinted by permission of the Publisher, Houghton Mifflin Company.

"Go Ask Alice." From the book *Go Ask Alice* by Anonymous. ©1971 by Prentice-Hall, Inc. Published by Prentice-Hall, Inc., Englewood Cliffs, New Jersey 07632.

"The Room" by Jean-Paul Sartre. Jean-Paul Sartre, *The Wall*, translated by Lloyd Alexander. Copyright 1948 by New Directions Publishing Corporation. ©1975 by Lloyd Alexander. Reprinted by permission of New Directions.

"Deborah Blau" by Joanne Greenberg. From *I Never Promised You a Rose Garden* by Hannah Green (Joanne Greenberg). Copyright ©1964 by Hannah Green. Reprinted by permission of Holt, Rinehart and Winston, Publishers.

"Silent Snow, Secret Snow" by Conrad Aiken. Reprinted by permission of Brandt & Brandt Literare Agents, Inc. Copyright 1932 by Conrad Aiken. Copyright ©renewed 1960 by Conrad Aiken.

"Desmond" from *Desmond* by John Mortimer, Reprinted by permission of AD Peters & Co Ltd.

"In September It Was Time to See the Doctor," from *The End of the Road*, by John Barth. Reprinted by permission of Doubleday & Company, Inc.

"The Chrysanthemums" by John Steinbeck. From *The Long Valley* by John Steinbeck. Copyright 1938 by John Steinbeck, ©renewed 1966 by John Steinbeck. Reprinted by permission of Viking Penguin Inc.

"The Parson" by Penelope Mortimer, copyright ©1957 by *The New Yorker Magazine* from the book *About Time: An Aspect of an Autobiography* by Penelope Mortimer. Reprinted by permission of Doubleday & Company, Inc.

v

"Woman Poem" by Nikki Giovanni, from *Black Judgement;* copyright ©1968 by Nikki Giovanni, Broadside Press; Detroit, Michigan.

"The Enchanted Doll" by Paul Gallico. "The Enchanted Doll," copyright 1952 by Paul Gallico, from the book *Further Confessions of a Story Teller* by Paul Gallico. Reprinted by permission of Doubleday & Company, Inc.

"Scobie" by Lawrence Durrell. From *Balthazar* by Lawrence Durrell. Copyright,©, 1958 by Lawrence Durrell. Reprinted by permission of the publisher, E.P. Dutton. Reprinted by permission of Faber and Faber Ltd from *Balthazar* by Lawrence Durrell.

"The Strength of God" by Sherwood Anderson. From *Winesburg, Ohio* by Sherwood Anderson. Copyright 1919 by B.W. Heubsch, renewed 1949 by Eleanor Copenhaver Anderson. Reprinted by permission of Viking Penguin Inc.

"Justine" by the Marquis de Sade. Copyright ©1965 by Richard Seaver and Austryn Wainhouse. Reprinted by permission of Grove Press, Inc.

"A Rose for Emily" by William Faulkner. From *Collected Stories of William Faulkner* by William Faulkner. Copyright 1930 renewed 1958 by William Faulkner. Reprinted by permission of Random House, Inc.

"The Jockey" by Carson McCullers. From *Collected Short Stories & the Novel, The Ballad of the Sad Cafe* by Carson McCullers. Copyright 1955 by Carson McCullers. Reprinted by permission of the publisher, Houghton Mifflin Company.

"Paul's Case" by Willa Cather. Reprinted from *Youth and the Bright Medusa*, by Willa Cather, courtesy of Alfred A. Knopf, Inc.

"The Devil Can't Look Back" by John Craig Stewart. Originally published in *The American Mercury*, Vol. LXVII, No. 298. Reprinted by permission of the author.

"A Touch of Marble" by Don S. Potter. Copyright ©1959 by Margaret Mayorga. Reprinted by permission of Margaret Mayorga.

"Little Woman" by Sally Benson. Reprinted by permission; ©1938, 1966 The New Yorker Magazine, Inc.

"The Flyman" by Douglas Woolf. Reprinted by permission of the author.

Contents

For Jennifer

___ Preface

COUNTING THE MAD

Donald Justice

This one was put in a jacket,
This one was sent home
This one was given bread and meat
But would eat none,
And this one cried No No No No
All day long.

This one looked at the window
As though it were a wall,
This one saw things that were not there,
This one things that were,
And this one cried No No No No
All day long.

This one thought himself a bird,
This one a dog,
This one thought himself a man,
An ordinary man,
And cried and cried No No No No
All day long.

Disordered Personalities in Literature is an additional resource for the study of abnormal psychology. The table of contents reflects the most recent nomenclature adopted by the American Psychiatric Association for classifying mental and personality disorders. The introductions sketch the latest diagnostic criteria for the disorders by isolating the specific symptoms of a syndrome. [Both the nomenclature and the diagnostic criteria are taken from the *Diagnostic and Statistical Manual of Mental Disorders* (DSM-III), American Psychiatric Association, 1980.] Although the introductions describe the disorders, they cannot replace a systematic and intensive study of the psychology texts that deal with the various conditions.

The characters who appear in the poems, short stories, and plays are offered as possible examples of the disorders sketched in the introductions. These characters have most of the specific symptoms related to the disorders; therefore, a careful reading permits a provisional diagnosis.

The selections have intrinsic literary merit and provide both an intellectual exercise and an esthetic experience. For example, in Donald Justice's "Counting the Mad," the agony of those who could not cope with the stresses of living outside a hospital is disguised by the nursery-rhyme rhythm. Without using clinical language, Justice depicts violence, frenzy, hallucinations, delusions, and existential despair. He portrays Bedlam in the cadence of Mother Goose.

I am indebted to several members of the Department of English, including Freda Clary, Walter Darring, Genie Hamner, John Stewart, Bob Wilson, and Lowery Varnado, for their suggestions of literature that might be included; to Lloyd Dendinger, Chairman, for his interest and support; to Jim Dorrill and Dan McDonald for their advice and encouragement; to clinical psychologists Cay and Kent Welsh for assistance in classifying some of the selections; and to Barbara Fitzpatrick for assistance in correspondence and manuscript preparation.

I offer a special word of appreciation to Robert L. Spitzer, M.D., Chairman, Task Force on Nomenclature and Statistics, American Psychiatric Association, for reviewing the introductions and offering helpful suggestions.

General Introduction

THE POISON TREE

William Blake

I was angry with my friend:
I told my wrath, my wrath did end.
I was angry with my foe:
I told it not, my wrath did grow.

And I water'd it in fears,
Night and morning with my tears;
And I sunned it with smiles,
and with soft deceitful wiles.

And it grew both day and night,
Till it bore an apple bright;
And my foe beheld it shine,
And he knew that it was mine,

And into my garden stole
When the night had veil'd the pole:
In the morning glad I see
My foe outstretch'd beneath the tree.

Psychology and literature have long been recognized as complementary disciplines. A part of the purpose of each is "to hold, as 't were, the mirror up to nature, to show virtue her own feature, scorn her own image, and the very age and body of the time his form and pressure." Each probes the complexities of human perception, emotion, and behavior; each assesses the impact of environment and personal relationships on an individual. Each contributes, in its own special way, to an understanding of personality.

Abnormal psychology investigates personality and its various disorders by employing as tools a textbook, primary sources (either collected in source books or assigned as collateral reading), case books, and audiovisual aids. The textbook organizes the extensive material of psychology and introduces the basic concepts, methodology, and nomenclature. Primary source readings highlight important concepts in the theorists' own words. Case books focus on a single person whose "case" embodies the abstract concepts. Audiovisual aids enrich the study by providing lectures, taped discussions and interviews, and dramatizations. Using these tools, one may begin to understand personality development, to isolate symptoms within a syndrome, and to classify mental and personality disorders.

While psychology strives for clinical objectivity, literature portrays characters in all their richness and intricacy. The stories, poems, and plays included in this book differ from case studies more in presentation than in theme. For example, the title of Willa Cather's "Paul's Case" (p. 194) is deceptive, for the story is far richer than an objective case study of Schizotypal Personality Disorder. The story portrays a disordered personality that may be schizotypal, but it does so subtly and artistically.

Literature complements psychology by depicting vivid characters whose emotional turmoil may reflect Affective Disorder (Elisa Allen in "The Chrysanthemums," p. 104) or whose behavior points toward Psychosexual Disorder (Miss Emily Grierson in "A Rose For Emily," p.180). In addition, literature often suspends the usual views of the world in order to focus on the unusual perceptions of its characters. For example, Pierre's schizophrenic world (in "The Room" p. 32) and Alice's "drug trips" in "Go Ask Alice," are probably unfamiliar to most people.

Literature presents the fierce emotions that many people experience and some cannot control. For example, William Blake's "The Poison Tree," with which this introduction began, cannot qualify as a case study, because it is too imprecise and metaphorical. This poem does, however, investigate two ways of coping with rage, one positive and the other negative. It illuminates the inner world of a deceitful person and emphasizes the lethal potential of suppressed anger. It also leaves the reader free to speculate as to the cause of the anger, the speaker's specific mental or personality disorder, and the effect of this incident on his subsequent mental health.

The selections that follow contain far more information than this brief poem and serve as authentic pictures of mental or personality disorders. Of course, the authors did not deliberately set out to write pieces that fulfill the DSM-III diagnostic criteria for specific disorders. Rather, they have created one or more fictional characters whose distorted perceptions, intemperate emotions, or peculiar behavior can be examined for evidence of Schizophrenia, Paranoia, Affective Disorders, and the like. Thus the selections can provide practice in diagnosing mental disorders.

If differences of opinion regarding the diagnosis of a specific character's condition arise, these disagreements reveal the difficulty of being precise when dealing with mental disorders. Furthermore, within a selection there may be more than one disordered character. For example, although "The Enchanted Doll" (p. 155) focuses on Essie Nolan's condition, her sister, Rose Callamit, may also be examined to see if she has some personality disorder.

In a chapter on "Freud and Literature" in his *The Liberal Imagination,* Lionel Trilling recounts an anecdote that emphasizes the complementary nature of psychology and literature. He recalls a day in 1926 when Sigmund Freud, the founder of psycholanalysis, was being honored on his seventieth birthday. A speaker greeted Freud as "the discoverer of the unconscious." Freud corrected the speaker, disclaimed the title, and reminded the audience that "The poets and philosophers before me discovered the unconscious; what I discovered was the scientific method by which the unconscious can be studied."

Disordered Personalities in Literature is designed to encourage a continuation of the dialogue between literature and psychology, between the artist's presentation of our inner struggles and the scientist's examination and classification of them.

Disordered Personalities in Literature

Substance Use Disorders

There are many substances that alter individuals' moods or influence their behavior. Among these substances are alcohol, barbiturates, opioids (heroin, morphine, and synthetics with morphine-like action), cocaine, amphetamines ("speed" and "diet pills"), hallucinogens (LSD and mescaline), and cannabis. Individuals who use any of these substances run the risk of either abusing it or becoming dependent on it.

Substance Abuse, one of the subcategories of Substance Use Disorders, involves continuous or episodic use of any of these chemicals for at least a month. During this time, users may experience strained relationships with their family; legal problems, e.g., being ticketed for driving while intoxicated or being arrested for possession of a controlled substance; or occupational difficulties; e.g., absenteeism or inability to perform assigned tasks. In addition to social complications, users often engage in a pattern of pathological usage, e.g., alcoholic blackouts or drug overdose.

Substance Dependence, the other subcategory, is a more severe disorder than Substance Abuse because it incorporates two additional symptoms — tolerance and withdrawal. Users develop physiological tolerance with the prolonged use of the substance, and as a result, they need an ever-increasing amount of the chemical to achieve the desired effect. Furthermore, if users reduce their intake or attempt to stop using the substance, they experience withdrawal symptoms, such as sweating, fatigue, and insomnia. Users of alcohol or cannabis must meet an additional criterion in order to be classified as having Substance Dependence: in addition to tolerance and withdrawal, there must be evidence of social or occupational impairment resulting from usage of either substance.

The following selections depict three women who have Substance Dependence Disorder. Hazel Morse, the "Big Blonde" in Dorothy

Parker's story, suffers from alcoholism; the speaker in Anne Sexton's "The Addict" is dependent on prescription drugs; and Alice, in "Go Ask Alice," is a user of "street drugs." "Go Ask Alice" is an excerpt from the diary kept by an anonymous fifteen-year-old.

Each of these women experiences both the euphoria and the pain associated with Substance Dependence Disorder. Each encounters social complications arising from her substance use. What are some of them? Each has a pattern of pathological usage. How are the patterns similar? Point out evidence of both tolerance and withdrawal symptoms in each woman.

BIG BLONDE

Dorothy Parker

I

Hazel Morse was a large, fair woman of the type that incites some men when they use the word "blonde" to click their tongues and wag their heads roguishly. She prided herself upon her small feet and suffered for her vanity, boxing them in snub-toed, high-heeled slippers of the shortest bearable size. The curious thing about her were her hands, strange terminations to the flabby white arms splattered with pale tan spots — long, quivering hands with deep and convex nails. She should not have disfigured them with little jewels.

She was not a woman given to recollections. At her middle thirties, her old days were a blurred and flickering sequence, an imperfect film, dealing with the actions of strangers.

In her twenties, after the deferred death of a hazy widowed mother, she had been employed as a model in a wholesale dress establishment — it was still the day of the big woman, and she was then prettily colored and erect and high-breasted. Her job was not onerous, and she met numbers of men and spent numbers of evenings with them, laughing at their jokes and telling them she loved their neckties. Men liked her, and she took it for granted that the liking of men was a desirable thing. Popularity seemed to her to be worth all the work that had to be put into its achievement. Men liked you because you were fun, and when they liked you they took you out, and there you were. So, and successfully, she was fun. She was a good sport. Men like a good sport.

No other form of diversion, simpler or more complicated, drew her attention. She never pondered if she might not be better occupied doing something else. Her ideas, or, better, her acceptances, ran right along with those of the other substantially built blondes in whom she found her friends.

When she had been working in the dress establishment some years she met Herbie Morse. He was thin, quick, attractive, with shifting lines about his shiny, brown eyes and a habit of fiercely biting at the skin around his fingers nails. He drank largely; she found that entertaining. Her habitual greeting to him was an allusion to his state of the previous night.

"Oh, what a peach you had," she used to say, through her easy laugh. "I thought I'd die, the way you kept asking the waiter to dance with you."

She liked him immediately upon their meeting. She was enormously amused at his fast, slurreed sentences, his interpolations of apt phreses from vaudeville acts and comic strips; she thrilled at the feel of his lean arm tucked firm beneath the sleeve of her coat; she wanted to touch the wet, flat surface of his hair. He was as promptly drawn to her. They were married six weeks after they had met.

She was delighted at the idea of being a bride; coquetted with it, played upon it. Other offers of marriage she had had, and not a few of them, but it happened that that were all from stout, serious men who had visited the dress establishment as buyers; men from Des Moines and Houston and Chicago and, in her phrase, even funnier places. There was always something immensely comic to her in the thought of living elsewhere than New York. She could not regard as serious proposals that she share a western residence.

She wanted to be married. She was nearing thirty now, and she did not take the years well. She spread and softened, and her darkening hair turned her to inexpert dabblings with peroxide. There were times when she had little flashes of fear about her job. And she had had a couple of thousand evenings of being a good sport among her male acquaintances. She had come to be more conscientious than spontaneous about it.

Herbie earned enough, and they took a little apartment far uptown. There was a Mission-furnished dining-room with a hanging central light globed in liver-colored glass; in the living-room were an "over-stuffed suite," a Boston fern, and a reproduction of the Henner "Magdalene" with the red hair and blue draperies; the bedroom was in gray enamel and old rose, with Herbie's photograph on Hazel's dressing-table and Hazel's likeness on Herbie's chest of drawers..

She cooked — and she was a good cook — and marketed and chatted with the delivery boys and colored laundress. She loved the flat, she loved her life, she loved Herbie. In the first months of their marriage, she gave him all the passion she was ever to know.

She had not realized how tired she was. It was a delight, a new game, a holiday, to give up being a good sport. If her head ached or her arches throbbed, she complained piteously, babyishly. If her mood was quiet, she did not talk. If tears came to her eyes, she let them fall.

She fell readily into the habit of tears during the first year of her marriage.

Even in her good sport days, she had been known to weep lavishly and disinterestedly on occasion. Her behavior at the theater was a standing joke. She could weep at anything in a play—tiny garments, love both unrequited and mutual, seduction, purity, faithful servitors, wedlock, the triangle.

"There goes Haze," her friends would say, watching her. "She's off again."

Wedded and relaxed, she poured her tears freely. To her who had laughed so much, crying was delicious. All sorrows became her sorrows; she was Tenderness. She would cry long and softly over the newspaper accounts of kidnaped babies, deserted wives, unemployed men, strayed cats, heroic dogs. Even when the paper was no longer before her, her mind revolved upon these things and the drops slipped rhythmically over her plump cheeks.

"Honestly," she would say to Herbie, "all the sadness there is in the world when you stop to think about it!"

"Yeah," Herbie would say.

She missed nobody. The old crowd, the people who had brought her and Herbie together, dropped from their lives, lingeringly at first. When she thought of this at all, it was only to consider it fitting. This was marriage. This was peace.

But the thing was that Herbie was not amused.

For a time, he had enjoyed being alone with her. He found the voluntary isolation novel and sweet. Then it palled with a ferocious suddenness. It was as if one night, sitting with her in the steam-heated living-room, he would ask no more; and the next night he was through and done with the whole thing.

He became annoyed by her misty melancholies. At first, when he came home to find her softly tired and moody, he kissed her neck and patted her shoulder and begged her to tell her Herbie what was wrong. She loved that. But time slid by, and he found that there was never anything really, personally, the matter.

"Ah, for God's sake," he would say. "Crabbing again. All right, sit here and crab your head off. I'm going out."

And he would slam out of the flat and come back late and drunk.

She was completely bewildered by what happened to their marriage. First they were lovers; and then, it seemed without transition, they were enemies. She never understood it.

There were longer and longer intervals between his leaving his office and his arrival at the apartment. She went through agonies of picturing him run over and bleeding, dead and covered with a sheet. Then she lost her fears for his safety and grew sullen and wounded. When a person wanted to be with a person, he came as soon as possible. She desperately wanted him to want to be with her; her own hours only marked the time till he would come. It was often nearly nine o'clock before he came home to dinner. Always he had had many drinks, and their effect would die in him, leaving him loud and querulous and bristling for affronts.

He was too nervous, he said, to sit and do nothing for an evening. He boasted, probably not in all truth, that he had never read a book in his life. "What am I expected to do—sit around this dump on my tail all night?" he would ask, rhetorically. And again he would slam out.

She did not know what to do. She could not manage him. She could not meet him.

She fought him furiously. A terrific domesticity had come upon her, and she would bite and scratch to guard it. She wanted what she called "a nice home." She wanted a sober, tender husband, prompt at dinner, punctual at work. She wanted sweet, comforting evenings. The idea of intimacy with other men was terrible to her; the thought that Herbie might be seeking entertainment in other women set her frantic.

It seemed to her that almost everything she read—novels from the drug-store lending library, magazine stories, women's pages in the papers—dealt with wives who lost their husbands' love. She could bear those, at that, better than accounts of neat, companionable marriage and living happily ever after.

She was frightened. Several times when Herbie came home in the evening, he found her determinedly dressed—she had had to alter those of her clothes that were not new, to make them fasten — and rouged.

"Let's go wild tonight, what do you say?" she would hail him. "A person's got lots of time to hang around and do nothing when they're dead."

So they would go out, to chop houses and the less expensive cabarets. But it turned out badly. She could no longer find amusement in watching Herbie drink. She could not laugh at his whimsicalities, she was so tensely counting his indulgences. And she was unable to keep back her remonstrances — "Ah, come on, Herb, you've had enough, haven't you? You'll feel something terrible in the morning."

He would be immediately enraged. All right, crab; crab, crab, crab, crab, that was all she ever did. What a lousy sport she was! There would be scenes, and one or the other of them would rise and stalk out in fury.

She could not recall the definite day that she started drinking, herself. There was nothing separate about her days. Like drops upon a window-pane, they ran together and trickled away. She had been married six months; then a year; then three years.

She had never needed to drink, formerly. She could sit for most of a night at a table where the others were imbibing earnestly and never droop in looks or spirits, nor be bored by the doings of those about her. If she took a cocktail, it was so unusual as to cause twenty minutes or so of jocular comment. But now anguish was in her. Frequently, after a quarrel, Herbie would stay out for the night, and she could not learn from him where the time had been spent. Her heart felt tight and sore in her breast, and her mind turned like an electric fan.

She hated the taste of liquor. Gin, plain or mixtures, made her promptly sick. After experiment, she found that Scotch whisky was best for her. She took it without water, because that was the quickest way to its effect.

Herbie pressed it on her. He was glad to see her drink. They both felt it might restore her high spirits, and their good times together might again be possible.

" 'Atta girl," he would approve her. "Let's see you get boiled, baby."

But it brought them no nearer. When she drank with him, there would be a little while of gaiety and then, strangely without beginning, they would be in a wild quarrel. They would wake in the morning not sure what it had all been about, foggy as to what had been said and done, but each deeply injured and bitterly resentful. There would be days of vengeful silence.

There had been a time when they had made up their quarrels, usually in bed. There would be kisses and little names and assurances of fresh starts .... "Oh, it's going to be great now, Herb. We'll have swell times. I was a crab. I guess I must have been tired. But everything's going to be swell. You'll see."

Now there were no gentle reconciliations. They resumed friendly relations only in the brief magnanimity caused by liquor, before more liquor drew them into new battles. The scenes became more violent. There were shouted invectives and pushes, and sometimes sharp slaps. Once she had a black eye. Herbie was horrified next day at sight of it. He did not go to work; he followed her about, suggesting remedies and heaping dark blame on himself. But after they had had a few drinks— "to pull themselves together" — she made so many wistful references to her bruise that he shouted at her and rushed out and was gone for two days.

Each time he left the place in a rage, he threatened never to come back. She did not believe him, nor did she consider separation. Somewhere in her head or her heart was the lazy, nebulous hope that things would change and she and Herbie settle suddenly into soothing married life. Here were her home, her furniture, her husband, her station. She summoned no alternatives.

She could no longer bustle and potter. She had no more vicarious tears; the hot drops she shed were for herself. She walked ceaselessly about the rooms, her thoughts running mechanically round and round Herbie. In those days began the hatred of being alone that she was never to overcome. You could be by yourself when things were all right, but when you were blue you got the howling horrors.

She commenced drinking alone, little, short drinks all through the day. It was only with Herbie that alcohol made her nervous and quick in offense. Alone, it blurred sharp things for her. She lived in a haze of it. Her life took on a dream-like quality. Nothing was astonishing.

A Mrs. Martin moved into the flat across the hall. She was a great blonde woman of forty, a promise in looks of what Mrs. Morse was to be. They made acquaintance, quickly became inseparable. Mrs. Morse spent her days in the opposite apartment. They drank together, to brace themselves after the drinks of the nights before.

She never confided her troubles about Herbie to Mrs. Martin. The subject was too bewildering to her to find comfort in talk. She let it be assumed that her husband's business kept him much away. It was not regarded as important; husbands, as such, played but shadowy parts in Mrs. Martin's circle.

Mrs. Martin had no visible spouse; you were left to decide for yourself whether he was or was not dead. She had an admirer, Joe, who came to see her almost nightly. Often he brought several friends with him — "The Boys," they were called. The Boys were big, red, good-humored men, perhaps forty-five, perhaps fifty. Mrs. Morse was glad of invitations to join the parties — Herbie was scarcely ever at home at night now. If he did come home, she did not visit Mrs. Martin. An evening alone with Herbie meant inevitably a quarrel, yet she would stay with him. There was always her thin and worthless idea that, maybe, this night, things would begin to be all right.

The Boys brought plenty of liquor along with them whenever they came to Mrs. Martin's. Drinking with them, Mrs. Morse became lively and good-natured and audacious. She was quickly popular. When she had drunk enough to cloud her most recent battle with Herbie, she was excited by their approbation. Crab, was she? Rotten sport, was she? Well, there were some that thought different.

Ed was one the The Boys. He lived in Utica — had "his own business" there, was the awed report — but he came to New York almost every week. He was married. He showed Mrs. Morse the then current photographs of Junior and Sister, and she praised them abundantly and sincerely. Soon it was accepted by the others that Ed was her particular friend.

He staked her when they all played poker; sat next to her and occasionally rubbed his knee against hers during the game. She was rather lucky. Frequently she went home with a twenty-dollar bill or a ten-dollar bill or a handful of crumpled dollars. She was glad of them. Herbie was getting, in her words, something awful about money. To ask him for it brought an instant row.

"What the hell do you do with it?" he would say. "Shoot it all on Scotch?"

"I try to run this house half-way decent," she would retort. "Never thought of that, did you? Oh, no, his lordship couldn't be bothered with that."

Again, she could not find a definite day, to fix the beginning of Ed's proprietorship. It became his custom to kiss her on the mouth when he came in, as well as for farewell, and he gave her little quick kisses of approval all through the evening. She liked this rather more than she disliked it. She never thought of his kisses when she was not with him.

He would run his hand lingeringly over her back and shoulders.

"Some dizzy blonde, eh?" he would say. "Some doll."

One afternoon she came home from Mrs. Martin's to find Herbie in the bedroom. He had been away for several nights, evidently on a prolonged drinking bout. His face was gray, his hands jerked as if they were on wires. On the bed were two old suitcases, packed high. Only her photograph remained on his bureau, and the wide doors of his closet disclosed nothing but coathangers.

"I'm blowing," he said. "I'm through with the whole works. I got a job in Detroit."

She sat down on the edge of the bed. She had drunk much the night before, and the four Scotches she had had with Mrs. Martin had only increased her fogginess.

"Good job?" she said.

"Oh, yeah," he said. "Looks all right."

He closed a suitcase with difficulty, swearing at it in whispers.

"There's some dough in the bank," he said. "The bank book's in your top drawer. You can have the furniture and stuff."

He looked at her, and his forehead twitched.

"God damn it, I'm through, I'm telling you," he cried. "I'm through."

"All right, all right," she said. "I heard you, didn't I?"

She saw him as if he were at one end of a cannon and she at the other. Her head was beginning to ache bumpingly, and her voice had a dreary, tiresome tone. She could not have raised it.

"Like a drink before you go?" she asked.

Again he looked at her, and a corner of his mouth jerked up.

"Cockeyed again for a change, aren't you?" he said. "That's nice. Sure, get a couple of shots, will you?"

She went to the pantry, mixed him a stiff highball, poured herself a couple of inches of whisky and drank it. Then she gave herself another portion and brought the glasses into the bedroom. He had strapped both suitcases and had put on his hat and overcoat.

He took his highball.

"Well," he said, and he gave a sudden, uncertain laugh. "Here's mud in your eye."

"Mud in your eye," she said.

They drank. He put down his glass and took up the heavy suitcases.

"Got to get a train around six," he said.

She followed him down the hall. There was a song, a song that Mrs. Martin played doggedly on the phonograph, running loudly through her mind. She had never liked the thing.

> "Night and daytime,
> Always playtime.
> Ain't we got fun?"

At the door he put down the bags and faced her.

"Well," he said. "Well, take care of yourself. You'll be all right, will you?"

"Oh, sure," she said.

He opened the door, then came back to her, holding out his hand.

" 'By, Haze," he said. "Good luck to you."

She took his hand and shook it.

"Pardon my wet glove," she said.

When the door had closed behind him, she went back to the pantry.

She was flushed and lively when she went into Mrs. Martin's that evening. The Boys were there, Ed among them. He was glad to be in town, frisky and loud and full of jokes. But she spoke quietly to him for a minute.

"Herbie blew today," she said. "Going to live out west."

"That so?" he said. He looked at her and played with the fountain pen clipped to his waistcoat pocket.

"Think he's gone for good, do you?" he asked.

"Yeah," she said. "I know he is. I know. Yeah."

"You going to live on across the hall just the same?" he said. "Know what you're going to do?"

"Gee, I don't know," she said. "I don't give much of a damn."

"Oh, come on, that's no way to talk," he told her. "What you need—you need a little snifter. How about it?"

"Yeah," she said. "Just straight."

She won forty-three dollars at poker. When the game broke up, Ed took her back to her apartment.

"Got a little kiss for me" he asked.

He wrapped her in his big arms and kissed her violently. She was entirely passive. He held her away and looked at her.

"Little tight, honey?" he asked, anxiously. "Not going to be sick, are you?"

"Me?" she said. "I'm swell."

II

When Ed left in the morning, he took her photograph with him. He said he wanted her picture to look at, up in Utica. "You can have that one on the bureau," she said.

She put Herbie's picture in a drawer, out of her sight. When she could look at it, she meant to tear it up. She was fairly successful in keeping her mind from racing around him. Whisky slowed it for her. She was almost peaceful, in her mist.

She accepted her relationship with Ed without question or enthusiasm. When he was away, she seldom thought definitely of him. He was good to her; he gave her frequent presents and a regular allowance. She was even able to save. She did not plan ahead of any day, but her wants were few, and you might as well put money in the bank as have it lying around.

When the lease of her apartment neared its end, it was Ed who suggested moving. His friendship with Mrs. Martin and Joe had become strained over a dispute at poker; a feud was impending.

"Let's get the hell out of here," Ed said. "What I want you to have is a place near the Grand Central. Make it easier for me."

So she took a little flat in the Forties. A colored maid came in every day to clean and to make coffee for her—she was "through with that housekeeping stuff," she said, and Ed, twenty years married to a passionately domestic woman, admired this romantic uselessness and felt doubly a man of the world in abetting it.

The coffee was all she had until she went out to dinner, but alcohol kept her fat. Prohibition she regarded only as a basis for jokes. You could always get all you wanted. She was never noticeably drunk and seldom nearly sober. It required a larger daily allowance to keep her misty-minded. Too little, and she was achingly melancholy.

Ed brought her to Jimmy's. He was proud, with the pride of the transient who would be mistaken for a native, in his knowledge of small, recent restaurants occupying the lower floors of shabby brownstone houses; places where, upon mentioning the name of an habitué friend, might be obtained strange whisky and fresh gin in many of their ramifications. Jimmy's place was the favorite of his acquaintances.

There, through Ed, Mrs. Morse met many men and women, formed quick friendships. The men often took her out when Ed was in Utica. He was proud of her popularity.

She fell into the habit of going to Jimmy's alone when she had no engagement. She was certain to meet some people she knew, and join them. It was a club for her friends, both men and women.

The women at Jimmy's looked remarkably alike, and this was curious, for through feuds, removals, and opportunities of more profitable contacts, the personnel of the group changed constantly. Yet always the newcomers resembled those whom they replaced. They were all big women and stout, broad of shoulder and abundantly breasted, with faces thickly clothed in soft, high-colored flesh. They laughed loud and often, showing opaque and lusterless teeth like squares of crockery. There was about them the health of the big, yet a slight, unwholesome suggestion of stubborn preservation. They might have been thirty-six or forty-five or anywhere between.

They composed their titles of their own first names with their husbands' surnames — Mrs. Florence Miller, Mrs. Vera Riley, Mrs. Lilian Block. This gave at the same time the solidity of marriage and the glamour of freedom. Yet only one or two were actually divorced. Most of them never referred to their dimmed spouses; some, a shorter time separated, described them in terms of great biological interest. Several were mothers, each of an only child — a boy at school somewhere, or a girl being cared for by a grandmother. Often, well on towards morning, there would be displays of Kodak portraits and of tears.

They were comfortable women, cordial and friendly and irrepressibly matronly. Theirs was the quality of ease. Become fatalistic, especially about money matters, they were unworried. Whenever their funds dropped alarmingly, a new donor appeared; this had always happened. The aim of each was to have one man, permanently, to pay all her bills, in return for which she would have immediately given up other admirers and probably would have become exceedingly fond of him; for the affections of all of them were, by now unexacting, tranquil, and easily arranged. This end, however, grew increasingly difficult yearly. Mrs. Morse was regarded as fortunate.

Ed had a good year, increased her allowance and gave her a sealskin coat. But she had to be careful of her moods with him. He insisted upon gaiety. He would not listen to admissions of aches or weariness.

"Hey, listen," he would say, "I got worries of my own, and plenty. Nobody wants to hear other people's troubles, sweetie. What you got to do, you got to be a sport and forget it. See? Well, slip us a little smile, then. That's my girl."

She never had enough interest to quarrel with him as she had with Herbie, but she wanted the privilege of occasional admitted sadness. It was strange. The other women she saw did not have to fight their moods. There was Mrs. Florence Miller who got regular crying jags, and the men sought only to cheer and comfort her. The others spent whole evenings in grieved recitals of worries and ills; their escorts paid them deep sympathy. But she was instantly undesirable when she was low in spirits. Once, at Jimmy's, when she could not make herself lively, Ed had walked out and left her.

"Why the hell don't you stay home and not go spoiling everybody's evening?" he had roared.

Even her slightest acquaintances seemed irritated if she were not conspicuously light-hearted.

"What's the matter with you anyway?" they would say. "Be your age, why don't you? Have a little drink and snap out of it."

When her relationship with Ed had continued nearly three years, he moved to Florida to live. He hated leaving her; he gave her a large check and some shares of a sound stock, and his pale eyes were wet when he said good-by. She did not miss him. He came to New York infrequently, perhaps two or three times a year, and hurried directly from the train to see her. She was always pleased to have him come and never sorry to see him go.

Charley, an acquaintance of Ed's that she had met at Jimmy's, had long admired her. He had always made opportunities of touching her and leaning close to talk to her. He asked repeatedly of all their friends if they had ever heard such a fine laugh as she had. After Ed left, Charley became the main figure in her life. She classified him and spoke of him as "not so bad." There was nearly a year of Charley; then she divided her time between him and Sydney, another frequenter of Jimmy's; then Charley slipped away altogether.

Sydney was a little, brightly dressed, clever Jew. She was perhaps nearest contentment with him. He amused her always; her laughter was not forced.

He admired her completely. Her softness and size delighted him. And he thought she was great, he often told her, because she kept gay and lively when she was drunk.

"Once I had a gal," he said, "used to try and throw herself out of the window every time she got a can on. Jee-zuss," he added, feelingly.

Then Sydney married a rich and watchful bride, and then there was Billy. No — after Sydney came Ferd, then Billy. In her haze, she never recalled how men entered her life and left it. There were no surprises. She had no thrill at their advent, nor woe at their departure. She seemed to be always able to attract men. There was never another as rich as Ed, but they were all generous to her, in their means.

Once she had news of Herbie. She met Mrs. Martin dining at Jimmy's, and the old friendship was vigorously renewed. The still admiring Joe, while on a business trip, had seen Herbie. He had settled in Chicago, he looked fine, he was living with some woman — seemed to be crazy about her. Mrs. Morse had been drinking vastly that day. She took the news with mild interest, as one hearing of the sex peccadilloes of somebody whose name is, after a moment's groping, familiar.

"Must be damn near seven years since I saw him," she commented. "Gee. Seven years."

More and more, her days lost their individuality. She never knew dates, nor was sure of the day of the week.

"My God, was that a year ago!" she would exclaim, when an event was recalled in conversation.

She was tired so much of the time. Tired and blue. Almost everything could give her the blues. Those old horses she saw on Sixth Avenue — struggling and slipping along the car-tracks, or standing at the curb, their heads dropped level with their worn knees. The tightly stored tears would squeeze from her eyes as she teetered past on her aching feet in the stubby, champagne-colored slippers.

The thought of death came and stayed with her and lent her a sort of drowsy cheer. It would be nice, nice and restful, to be dead.

There was no settled, shocked moment when she first thought of killing herself; it seemed to her as if the idea had always been with her. She pounced upon all the accounts of suicides in the newspapers. There was an epidemic of self-killings — or maybe it was just that she searched for the stories of them so eagerly that she found many. To read of them roused reassurance in her; she felt a cozy solidarity with the big company of the voluntary dead.

She slept, aided by whisky, till deep into the afternoons, then lay abed, a bottle and glass at her hand, until it was time to dress to go out for dinner. She was beginning to feel towards alcohol a little puzzled distrust, as toward an old friend who has refused a simple favor. Whisky could still soothe her for most of the time, but there were sudden, inexplicable moments when the cloud fell treacherously away from her, and she was sawed by the sorrow and bewilderment and nuisance of all living. She played voluptuously with the thought of cool, sleepy retreat. She had never been troubled by religious belief and no vision of an after-life intimidated her. She dreamed by day of never again putting on tight shoes, of never having to laugh and listen and admire, of never more being a good sport. Never.

But how would you do it? It made her sick to think of jumping from heights. She could not stand a gun. At the theater, if one of the actors drew a revolver, she crammed her fingers into her ears and could not even look at the stage until after the shot had been fired. There was no gas in her flat. She looked long at the bright blue veins in her slim wrists—a cut with a razor blade, and there you'd be. But it would hurt, hurt like hell, and there would be blood to see. Poison—something tasteless and quick and painless—was the thing. But they wouldn't sell it to you in drugstores, because of the law.

She had few other thoughts.

There was a new man now—Art. He was short and fat and exacting and hard on her patience when he was drunk. But there had been only occasionals for some time before him, and she was glad of a little stability. Too, Art must be away for weeks at a stretch, selling silks, and that was restful. She was convincingly gay with him, though the effort shook her.

"The best sport in the world," he would murmur, deep in her neck. "The best sport in the world."

One night, when he had taken her to Jimmy's, she went into the dressing-room with Mrs. Florence Miller. There, while designing curly mouths on their faces with lip-rouge, they compared experiences of insomnia.

"Honestly," Mrs. Morse said, "I wouldn't close an eye if I didn't go to bed full of Scotch. I lie there and toss and turn and toss and turn. Blue! Does a person get blue lying awake that way!"

"Say, listen, Hazel," Mrs. Miller said, impressively, "I'm telling you I'd be awake for a year if I didn't take veronal. That stuff makes you sleep like a fool."

"Isn't it poison, or something?" Mrs. Morse asked.

"Oh, you take too much and you're out for the count!" said Mrs. Miller. "I just take five grains—they come in tablets. I'd be scared to fool around with it. But five grains, and you cork off pretty."

"Can you get it anywhere?" Mrs. Morse felt superbly Machiavellian.

"Get all you want in Jersey," said Mrs. Miller. "They won't give it to you here without you have a doctor's prescription. Finished? We'd better go back and see what the boys are doing."

That night, Art left Mrs. Morse at the door of her apartment; his mother was in town. Mrs. Morse was still sober, and it happened that there was no whisky left in her cupboard. She lay in bed looking up at the black ceiling.

She rose early, for her, and went to New Jersey. She had never taken the tube, and did not understand it. So she went to the Pennsylvania Station and bought a railroad ticket to Newark. She thought of nothing in particular on the trip out. She looked at the uninspired hats of the women about her and gazed through the smeared window at the flat, gritty scene.

In Newark, in the first drug-store she came to, she asked for a tin of talcum powder, a nailbrush, and a box of veronal tablets. The powder and the brush were to make the hypnotic seem also a casual need. The clerk was entirely unconcerned. "We only keep them in bottles," he said, and wrapped up for her a little glass vial containing ten white tablets, stacked one on another.

She went to another drug-store and bought a face-cloth, an orange-wood stick, and a bottle of veronal tablets. The clerk was also uninterested.

"Well, I guess I got enough to kill an ox," she thought, and went back to the station.

At home, she put the little vials in the drawer of her dressing-table and stood looking at them with a dreamy tenderness.

"There they are, God bless them," she said, and she kissed her finger-tip and touched each bottle.

The colored maid was busy in the living room.

"Hey, Nettie," Mrs. Morse called. "Be an angel will you? Run around to Jimmy's and get me a quart of Scotch."

She hummed while she awaited the girl's return.

During the next few days, whisky ministered to her as tenderly as it had done when she first turned to its aid. Alone, she was soothed and vague, at Jimmy's she was the gayest of the groups. Art was delighted with her.

Then, one night, she had an appointment to meet Art at Jimmy's for an early dinner. He was to leave afterward on a business excursion, to be away for a week. Mrs. Morse had been drinking all the afternoon; while she dressed to go out, she felt herself rising pleasurably from drowsiness to high spirits. But as she came out into the street the effects of the whisky deserted her completely, and she was filled with a slow, grinding wretchedness so horrible that she stood swaying on the pavement, unable for a moment to move forward. It was a gray night with spurts of mean, thin snow, and the streets shone with dark ice. As she slowly crossed Sixth Avenue, consciously dragging one foot past the other, a big, scarred horse pulling a rickety express-wagon crashed to his knees before her. The driver swore and screamed and lashed the beast insanely, bringing the whip back over his shoulder for every blow, while the horse struggled to get a footing on the slippery asphalt. A group gathered and watched with interest.

Art was waiting, when Mrs. Morse reached Jimmy's.

"What's the matter with you, for God's sake?" was his greeting to her.

"I saw a horse," she said. "Gee, I—a person feels sorry for horses. I—it isn't just horses. Everything's kind of terrible, isn't it? I can't help getting sunk."

"Ah, sunk, me eye'" he said. "What's the idea of all the bellyaching? What have you got to be sunk about?"

"I can't help it," she said.

"Ah, help it, me eye," he said. "Pull yourself together, will you? Come on and sit down, and take that face off you."

She drank industriously and she tried hard, but she could not overcome her melancholy. Others joined them and commented on her gloom, and she could do no more for them than smile weakly. She made little dabs at her eyes with her handkerchief, trying to time her movements so they would be unnoticed, but several times Art caught her and scowled and shifted impatiently in his chair.

When it was time for him to go to his train, she said she would leave, too, and go home.

"And not a bad idea, either," he said. "See if you can't sleep yourself out of it. I'll see you Thursday. For God's sake, try and cheer up by then, will you?"

"Yeah," she said. "I will."

In her bedroom, she undressed with a tense speed wholly unlike her usual slow uncertainty. She put on her nightgown, took off her hair-net and passed the comb quickly through her dry, vari-colored hair. Then she took the two little vials from the drawer and carried them into the bathroom. The splintering misery had gone from her, and she felt the quick excitement of one who is about to receive an anticipated gift.

She uncorked the vials, filled a glass with water and stood before the mirror, a tablet between her fingers. Suddenly she bowed graciously to her reflection, and raised the glass to it.

"Well, here's mud in your eye," she said.

The tablets were unpleasant to take, dry and powdery and sticking obstinately half-way down her throat. It took her a long time to swallow all twenty of them. She stood watching her reflection with deep, impersonal interest, studying the movements of the gulping throat. Once more she spoke aloud.

"For God's sake, try and cheer up by Thursday, will you?" she said. "Well, you know what he can do. He and the whole lot of them."

She had no idea how quickly to expect effect from the veronal. When she had taken the last tablet, she stood uncertainly, wondering, still with a courteous, vicarious interest, if death would strike her down then and there. She felt in no way strange, save for a slight stirring of sickness from the effort of swallowing the tablets, nor did her reflected face look at all different. It would not be immediate, then; it might even take an hour or so.

She stretched her arms high and gave a vast yawn.

"Guess I'll go to bed," she said. "Gee, I'm nearly dead."

That struck her as comic, and she turned out the bathroom light and went in and laid herself down in her bed, chuckling softly all the time.

"Gee, I'm nearly dead," she quoted. "That's a hot one!"

III

Nettie, the colored maid, came in late the next afternoon to clean the apartment, and found Mrs. Morse in her bed. But then, that was not unusual. Usually, though, the sounds of cleaning waked her, and she did not like to wake up. Nettie, an agreeable girl, had learned to move softly about her work.

But when she had done the living-room and stolen in to tidy the little square bedroom, she could not avoid a tiny clatter as she arranged the objects on the dressing-table. Instinctively, she glanced over her shoulder at the sleeper, and without warning a sickly uneasiness crept over her. She came to the bed and stared down at the woman lying there.

Mrs. Morse lay on her back, one flabby, white arm flung up, the wrist against her forehead. Her stiff hair hung untenderly along her face. The bed covers were pushed down, exposing a deep square of soft neck and a pink nightgown, its fabric worn uneven by many launderings; her great breasts, freed from their tight confiner, sagged beneath her arm-pits. Now and then she made knotted, snoring sounds, and from the corner of her opened mouth to the blurred turn of her jaw ran a lane of crusted spittle.

"Mis' Morse," Nettie called. "Oh, Mis' Morse! It's terrible late."

Mrs. Morse made no move.

"Mis' Morse," said Nettie. "Look, Mis' Morse. How'm I goin' get this bed made?"

Panic sprang upon the girl. She shook the woman's hot shoulder.

"Ah, wake up, will yuh?" she whined. "Ah, please wake up."

Suddenly the girl turned and ran out in the hall to the elevator door, keeping her thumb firm on the black shiny button until the elderly car and its Negro attendant stood before her. She poured a jumble of words over the boy, and led him back to the apartment. He tiptoed creakingly in to the bedside; first gingerly, then so lustily that he left marks in the soft flesh, he prodded the unconscious woman.

"Hey, there!" he cried, and listened intently, as for an echo.

"Jeez. Out like a light," he commented.

At his interest in the spectacle, Nettie's panic left her. Importance was big in both of them. They talked in quick, unfinished whispers, and it was the boy's suggestion that he fetch the young doctor who lived on the ground floor. Nettie hurried along with him. They looked forward to the limelit moment of breaking their news of something untoward, something pleasurably unpleasant. Mrs. Morse had become the medium of drama. With no ill wish to her, they hoped that her state was serious, that she would not let them down by being awake and normal on their return. A little fear of this determined them to make the most, to the doctor, of her present condition. "Matter of life and death," returned to Nettie from her thin store of reading. She considered startling the doctor with the phrase.

The doctor was in and none too pleased at interruption. He wore a yellow and blue striped dressing-gown, and he was lying on his sofa, laughing with a dark girl, her face scaly with inexpensive powder, who perched on the arm. Half-emptied highball glasses stood beside them, and her coat and hat were neatly hung up with the comfortable implication of a long stay.

Always something, the doctor grumbled. Couldn't let anybody alone after a hard day. But he put some bottles and instruments into a case, changed his dressing-gown for his coat and started out with the Negroes.

"Snap it up there, big boy," the girl called after him. "Don't be all night."

The doctor strode loudly into Mrs. Morse's flat and on to the bedroom, Nettie and the boy right behind him. Mrs. Morse had not moved; her sleep was deep, but soundless, now. The doctor looked sharply at her, then plunged his thumbs into the lidded pits above her eyeballs and threw his weight upon them. A high, sickened cry broke from Nettie.

"Look like he tryin' to push her right on th'ough the bed," said the boy. He chuckled.

Mrs. Morse gave no sign under the pressure. Abruptly the doctor abandoned it, and with one quick movement swept the covers down to the foot of the bed. With another he flung her nightgown back and lifted the thick, white legs, cross hatched with blocks of tiny, iris-colored veins. He pinched them repeatedly, with long, cruel nips, back of the knees. She did not awaken.

"What's she been drinking?" he asked Nettie, over his shoulder.

With the certain celerity of one who knows just where to lay hands on a thing, Nettie went into the bathroom, bound for the cupboard where Mrs. Morse kept her whisky. But she stopped at the sight of the two vials, with their red and white labels, lying before the mirror. She brought them to the doctor.

"Oh, for the Lord Almighty's sweet sake!" he said. He dropped Mrs. Morse's legs, and pushed them impatiently across the bed. "What did she want to go taking that tripe for? Rotten yellow trick, that's what a thing like that is. Now we'll have to pump her out, and all that stuff. Nuisance, a thing like that is; that's what it amounts to. Here, George, take me down in the elevator. You wait here, maid. She won't do anything."

"She won't die on me, will she?" cried Nettie.

"No," said the doctor. "God, no. You couldn't kill her with an ax."

IV

After two days, Mrs. Morse came back to consciousness, dazed at first, then with a comprehension that brought with it the slow, saturating wretchedness.

"Oh, Lord, oh, Lord," she moaned, and tears for herself and for life striped her cheeks.

Nettie came in at the sound. For two days she had done the ugly, incessant tasks in the nursing of the unconscious, for two nights she had caught broken bits of sleep on the living-room couch. She looked coldly at the big, blown woman in the bed.

"What you been tryin' to do, Mis' Morse?" she said. "What kine o'work is that, takin' all that stuff?"

"Oh, Lord," moaned Mrs. Morse, again, and she tried to cover her eyes with her arms. But the joints felt stiff and brittle, and she cried out at their ache.

"Tha's no way to ack, takin' them pills," said Nettie, "You can thank you' stars you heah at all. How you feel now?"

"Oh, I feel great," said Mrs. Morse. "Swell, I feel."

Her hot, painful tears fell as if they would never stop.

"Tha's no way to take on, cryin' like that," Nettie said. "After what you done. The doctor, he says he could have you arrested, doin' a thing like that. He was fit to be tied, here."

"Why couldn't he let me alone?" wailed Mrs. Morse. "Why the hell couldn't he have?"

"Tha's terr'ble, Mis' Morse, swearin' an' talkin' like that," said Nettie, "after what people done for you. Here I ain' had no sleep at all for two nights an' had to give up goin' out to my other ladies!"

"Oh, I'm sorry, Nettie" she said. "You're a peach. I'm sorry I've given you so much trouble. I couldn't help it. I just got sunk. Didn't you ever feel like doing it? When everything looks just lousy to you?"

"I wouldn't think o' no such thing," declared Nettie. "You got to cheer up. Tha's what you got to do. Everybody's got their troubles."

"Yeah," said Mrs. Morse. "I know."

"Come a pretty picture card for you," Nettie said. "Maybe that will cheer you up."

She handed Mrs. Morse a post-card. Mrs. Morse had to cover one eye with her hand, in order to read the message; her eyes were not yet focusing correctly.

It was from Art. On the back of a view of the Detroit Athletic Club he had written: "Greeting and salutations. Hope you have lost that gloom. Cheer up and don't take any rubber nickles. See you on Thursday."

She dropped the card to the floor. Misery crushed her as if she were between great smooth stones. There passed before her a slow, slow pageant of days spent lying in her flat, of evenings at Jimmy's being a good sport, making herself laugh and coo at Art and other Arts; she saw a long parade of weary horses and shivering beggars and all beaten, driven, stumbling things. Her feet throbbed as if she had crammed them into the stubby champagne-colored slippers. Her heart seemed to swell and harden.

"Nettie," she cried, "for heaven's sake pour me a drink, will you?

The maid looked doubtful.

"Now you know, Mis' Morse," she said "you been near daid. I don' know if the doctor he let you drink nothin yet."

"Oh, never mind him," she said. "You get me one, and bring in the bottle. Take one yourself."

"Well," said Nettie.

She poured them each a drink, deferentially leaving hers in the bathroom to be taken in solitude, and brought Mrs. Morse's glass in to her.

Mrs. Morse looked into the liquor and shuddered back from its odor. Maybe it would help. Maybe, when you had been knocked cold for a few days, your very first drink would give you a lift. Maybe whisky would be her friend again. She prayed without addressing a God, without knowing a God. Oh, please, please, let her be able to get drunk, please keep her always drunk.

She lifted the glass.

"Thanks, Nettie'" she said. "Here's mud in your eye."

The maid giggled. "Tha's the way, Mis' Morse," she said. "You cheer up, now."

"Yeah," said Mrs. Morse. "Sure."

THE ADDICT

Anne Sexton

Sleepmonger,
deathmonger,
with capsules in my palms each night,
eight at a time from sweet pharmaceutical bottles
I make arrangements for a pint-sized journey.
I'm the queen of this condition.
I'm an expert on making the trip
and now they say I'm an addict.
Now they ask why.
Why!

Don't they know
that I promised to die!
I'm keeping in practice.
I'm merely staying in shape.
The pills are a mother, but better,
every color and as good as sour balls.
I'm on a diet from death.

Yes, I admit
it has gotten to be a bit of a habit—
blows eight at a time, socked in the eye,
hauled away by the pink, the orange,
the green and the white goodnights.
I'm becoming something of a chemical
mixture.
That's it!

My supply
of tablets
has got to last for years and years.
I like them more than I like me.
Stubborn as hell, they won't let go.
It's a kind of marriage.
It's a kind of war
where I plant bombs inside
of myself.

Yes
I try
to kill myself in small amounts,
an innocuous occupation.
Actually I'm hung up on it.
But remember I don't make too much noise
And frankly no one has to lug me out

and I don't stand there in my winding sheet.
I'm a little buttercup in my yellow nightie
eating my eight loaves in a row
and in a certain order as in
the laying on of hands
or the black sacrament.

It's a ceremony
but like any other sport
it's full of rules.

It's like a musical tennis match where
my mouth keeps catching the ball.
Then I lie on my altar
elevated by the eight chemical kisses.

What a lay me down this is
with two pink, two orange,
two green, two white goodnights.
Fee-fi-fo-fum—
Now I'm borrowed.
Now, I'm done.

GO ASK ALICE

Anonymous

January 24

Oh damn, damn, damn, it's happened again. I don't know whether to
scream with glory or cover myself with ashes and sackcloth, whatever that
means. Anyone who says pot and acid are not addicting is a damn, stupid,
raving idiot, unenlightened fool! I've been on them since July 10, and when
I've been off I've been scared to death to even think of anything that even
looks or seems like dope. All the time pretending to myself that I could take it
or leave it!

All the dumb, idiot kids who think they are only chipping are in reality just
existing from one experience to the other. After you've had it, there isn't
even life without drugs. It's a prodding, colorless, dissonant bare existence. It
stinks. And I'm glad I'm back. Glad! Glad! Glad! I've never had it better than
I had it last night. Each new time is the best time and Chris feels the same
way. Last night when she called and asked me to come over, I knew something terrible had happened. She sounded like she didn't know what to do.
But when I got there and smelled that incredible smell, I just sat down on the
floor of her room with her and cried and smoked. It was beautiful and wonderful and we'd been without it for so long. I'll never be able to express how
really great it is.

Later I called Mother and told her I was spending the night with Chris
because she felt a little depressed. Depressed, No one in the world but a
doper could know the true opposite of depressed.

January 26

Chris feels a little guilty but I'm delighted that we're turned on again, we
belong to the world! The world belongs to us! Poor old George is going to

have to go the way of all squares. He drove by to pick me up for school and I couldn't have been less interested. I don't even need him for a chauffeur anymore.

January 30

I talked to Lane today and he's really amazing. He's got a new connection and he can get me anything I want. So I told him I like uppers best. Who needs to go down when you can go up? Right?

February 6

Life is really unbelievable now. Time seems so endless yet everything goes so fast. I love it!

P.S. Mother's really glad that I'm "in" again. She likes to hear the telephone ringing for me. Isn't that too much!

February 13

Lane was hit last night. I don't know how they found out about him but I guess he was pushing too much too fast to those little teeny boppers of his. I'm just grateful I wasn't there. Being so sweet and innocent and naive, my parents don't let me stay out late on week nights. They are trying to protect me from the big bad bogie man. I'm not really too worried about Lane. He's barely sixteen so they won't give him too much of a problem—probably slap his hands.

February 18

Our supply has dried up somewhat with Lane on good behavior, but Chris and I are very resourceful. Anyway we're managing.

I think I'm going to start taking the pill. It's a lot easier than worrying. I bet the pill is harder to get than drugs—which shows you how screwed up this world really is!

February 23

Dear Diary,

Oh, wow! They raided Chris's house last night while her folks and her aunt were out, but Chris and I played the game. The big blue badge just stood shaking his head while Chris and I swore to our parents it was our very first time and that nothing had really happened. Thank God they arrived while we still had our brains together. I wonder how they knew we were there????

February 24

This is the funniest thing I have ever heard: Mom is worried and hinting that something might have happened to her little baby in those words she can't bring herself use. She wants me to go see Doctor Langley for a check-up, isn't that a laugh?

It took me a while to plead ignorance and innocence with my eyes opened as wide as they would go. I pretended I didn't even know what she was talking about, and do you know, she finally wound up actually feeling guilty for ever even suspecting such a thing.

(?)

We're all on probation, and we are not supposed to see each other and Mom and Dad are sending me to a headshrinker beginning next Monday. I guess that was all part of the bargain to keep me out of court. The rumor is that Lane has been sent away someplace, to a lock-in, dry-out school I think. Actually this was his third bust. I didn't know that. Well, at least he can't think I had anything to do with it since I too got caught up in the drag. At least this is my first charge. I guess actually I'm pretty lucky.

February 27

You'd think I was six years old the way Mom and Dad are watching me. I have to come straight home from school as if I were a baby. This morning when I left Mom's parting words were, "Come straight home after school." Wow! Like I'm going to get stoned at 3:30—it doesn't sound so bad at that.

Later

After dinner I was going to walk down to the drugstore to get some colored pencils to finish my map and as I started out the door Mom called to Tim and told him to go with me. That is really too much! Having my little brother watching me! He didn't like the idea any better than I did. I almost felt like telling him why she wanted him to go with me! It would serve him right. It would serve them all right. I know what I ought to do, I ought to turn him on! Maybe I will! Maybe I'll surprise him with a trip on a piece of candy. Wow! I just wish I could be sure it would be a bummer.

March 1

I'm about to blow. This whole set-up is beginning to bug me until my nerves are all crawling. I can hardly go to the bathroom by myself.

March 2

Today I went to the headshrinker's, a fat ugly little man who doesn't even have enough balls to lose weight. Man, I almost recommended some amphetamines—they'd cut his appetite and give him a blast at the same time. That's probably what he needs, sitting there peering over his glasses waiting for me to tell him some gory details. He's almost worse than anything else that's happened to me.

March 5

Jackie slipped me a couple of co-pilots in English when she passed out the test papers. Tonight after everyone goes to bed I'll get high all by myself. I can hardly wait!

(*)

Like here I am in Denver. When I was high I just walked out and hitch-hiked here, but now it seems crazy quiet and unreal, maybe that's because it's still early. I hope so, I've only got the twenty dollars that I took from Dad's pants, but no source.

(?)

I'm sharing a place with a couple of kids I met, but they think it's kind of dull here so we're going to go to Oregon and see what's happening in Coos Bay. We've got enough acid to keep as all stoned for the next two weeks or forever, and that's all that counts.

March ...

I haven't any clothes except these I had on when I left home and I'm getting so damned dirty I think they've grown on me. It was snowing in Denver, but it's so penetratingly damp here in Oregon it's a hell of a sight worse. I've got a fucking head cold and I feel miserable, and my period has started and I don't have any Tampax. Hell, I wish I had a shot.

(?)

Last night I slept in the park curled under a shrub and today it's drizzling and I can't find any of the kids I came from Denver with. Finally I went into a church and asked the janitor or whatever he was what I should do. He told me to sit here till it stopped raining, then go down to some kind of Salvation Army type place. I guess I have no choice since I know I've got a fever and

---

* There are no dates for the following material. It was recorded on single sheets of paper, paper bags, etc.

I'm dripping wet and so filthy and smelly I can hardly stand myself. I'm trying to use some paper towels from the wash room for Kotex, and man that is some damned inconvenience. Oh, if I only had an upper.

This is a nice church. It's small and quiet and clean. I feel dreadfully out of place here, and I'm beginning to feel so damned lonely I've got to get out of here. Guess I'll try finding the mission or whatever the hell it is in the rain. I just hope I don't lose the bloody goddamned paper towels in the center of some street.

Later

This is really a great place! It really is! They let me have a shower and gave me some clean old square clothes and some Kotex and fed me even though I told them I wouldn't go by their hard stooled rules. They wanted me to stay here a few days and let them contact my parents to work out something so that we could bridge our differences. But my parents aren't about to let me use acid and pot and I'm not about to give them up! This guy was really nice. He is even driving me up to a health clinic to get something for my cold. I really feel lousy, maybe the good doctor will give me something to make me feel better, like wow! Anything! I wish the other old jerk would hurry up doing whatever he is doing so we could go.

It's still the... whatever it is. I met a girl, Doris, in the doctor's waiting room who said I could come share her pad since the couple she lived with and her boyfriend split during the night. Then the doc gave me a shot and a bottle of vitamins, imagine vitamins! He said my body is run down and malnourished, like that of most of the other kids he sees. He really was nice though. He just acted like he cared and told me to come back in a few days. I told him I didn't have any bread and he just laughed and said he'd have been surprised if I had.

(?)

At last the bitchin' rain has quit. Doris and I walked all through Coos Bay. They've really got some shops! I told her about the place Chris and I had opened and Doris wants to get a place when we get a few crumbs, but somehow it doesn't really seem very important anymore. Doris has a whole can of pot so we'll have joints for a long time. We were kind of stoned and everything seemed up even though my ass is still dragging.

(?)

It's good enough to just be alive. I love Coos Bay, and I love acid! The people here, at least here in our section of town, are beautiful. They understand life and they understand me. I can talk like I want and dress like I want and nobody cares. Looking at the posters in the store windows, and even walking around past the Greyhound bus station to watch who is coming in is groovie. We went by a place where they make posters and I'm going to help Doris cover the walls when we get a few crumbs together. We stopped at a Coffee House and the Digger Free Store and the Psychedelic Shop. Tomorrow we're going to see the rest of the sights. Doris has been here a couple of months and she knows everything and everybody. I was amazed when I found out that she was only fourteen. I thought she was a very small and immature eighteen or nineteen.

(?)

Last night Doris was really low. We've run out of pot and money and we're both hungry and the damnable rain has started puking up again. This little one room has only the one burner stove which doesn't seem to give out any heat at all. My ears and sinus cavities (see, I know, I watch TV, or used to) all feel like they've been poured full of concrete, and my chest must surely be bound with a steel band. We'd walk someplace and try to get a free meal or thug something but it's hardly worth the effort in the rain, so I guess we'll just eat noodles and dry cereal again. We've talked about how we hated the tourists and the phonies and the beggars here, but I think I'll go join the ranks tomorrow and try to beg enough bread for a little food and a fix. Doris and I really need both.

(?)

Oh, to be stoned, to have someone tie me off and give me a shot of anything. I've heard paregoric is great. Oh hell, I wish I had enough anything to end the whole shitty mess.

I've been asleep and I don't know if it's the same day or week or year, but who the hell cares anyway?

The goddamned rain is even worse than yesterday. It's like the whole sky is pissing on us. I tried to go out once, but my cold is so bad I was chilled to my ass before I'd even gotten to the goddamned corner, so I came back and went to bed with my clothes on, trying to curl up enough so my body heat would at least keep me from dying. I guess I've got a high fever, because I keep drifting off — that's the only beJesus thing that keeps me from croaking. Oh, I need a fix so bad! I want to scream and pound my head against the wall and climb the damned dusty, faded stringy curtains. I've got to get out of here. I've got to get the hell out of here before I really blow my cool all the way. I'm scared and lonely and I'm as sick as I've ever been in my life.

I tried not to let myself think of home till Doris got started on her screwing life's history, and now I'm really falling apart at the seams. God, if I had enough money I would go back where I came from or at least call. Tomorrow I'll go back to the church and ask them to call my folks. I don't know why I've acted like such an ass when I've always had it so good. Poor Doris has had nothing but shit since she was ten years old. Her mother was married four times by the time Doris was ten and had humped with who knows how many men in between. And when Doris had just turned eleven her current stepfather started having sex with her but good, and the poor little stupid bastard didn't even know what to do about it because he threatened to kill her if she ever told her mother or anyone else. So she put up with the sonofabitch balling her till she was twelve. Then one day when he had hurt her pretty bad she told her gym teacher why she couldn't do the exercises. The teacher had her taken away and put into a juvenile home till they could find a foster home. But even that wasn't much better, because both the teenage brothers gave it to her and later on an older teenage girl tuned her in and turned her on drugs, then took her the homo route. Since then she's pulled down her pants and hopped into bed with anyone who would turn down the covers, or part the bushes. Oh Father, I've got to get out of the cesspool! It's sucking me down and drowning me! I've got to get the hell out of here while I still can. Tomorrow! Tomorrow for sure! After the goddamned rain stops!

(?)

Who the hell cares? At last the goddamned rain has stopped! The sky is as blue as it was ever meant to be, which I gather is unusual for this area. Doris and I are both going to cut out of this asinine assed place. There's going to be a rally in Southern California. Wow! Here we come!

(?)

I'm actually and literally and completely sick to my stomach. I want to puke all over the shitty world. Most of the way down we rode with a big fat assed, baby screwing truck driver who picked us up and got his kicks by physically hurting Doris and watching her cry. When he stopped for gas we both sneaked out even though he had threatened us. Man, what a mother . . . We finally got another ride with some of our kind and while they shared their grass with us it must have been some home grown stuff, because it was so fuckin weak it could barely get us off terra firm.

(?)

The rally itself was great, acid and booze and pot as free as the air. Even now colors are still dripping down over me and the crack in the window is beautiful. This life is beautiful. It's so goddamned beautiful I can hardly stand it. And I'm a glorious part of it! Everybody else is just taking up space. Goddamned stupid people. I'd like to shove life down all their throats and then maybe they'd understand what it's all about.

Near the door a fat girl with long stringy blonde hair is getting to her knees on a green upon green upon purple robe. She's got a guy with her and he has a ring in his nose and multi-colored designs on his shaven head. They keep saying "love" to each other. It's beautiful to watch. Color intermingled with color. People intermingled with people. Color and people intercoursing together.

(?)

I don't know what or when or where or who it is! I only know that I am now a Priestess of Satan trying to maintain after a freak-out to test how free everybody was and to take our vows.

Dear Diary,
   I feel awfully bitched and pissed off at everybody. I'm really confused. I've been the digger here, but now when I face a girl it's like facing a boy. I get all excited and turned-on. I want to screw with the girl, you know, and then I get all tensed-up and scared. I feel goddamned good in a way and goddamned bad in a way. I want to get married and have a family, but I'm afraid. I'd rather be liked by a guy than a girl. I'd rather screw with a guy, but I can't. I guess I've had a bit of a bummer. Sometimes I want one of the girls to kiss me. I want her to touch me, to have her sleep under me, but then I feel terrible. I get guilty and it makes me sick. Then I think of my mother. I think of screaming at her and telling her to make room for me because I'm coming home and I feel like a man. Then I get sick and I just want anybody and I should be out doing my digging. I'm really sick. I'm really way out of it.

Dear Diary,
   It's a thousand light years later, lunar time.
   Everybody's been storytelling except me. I don't have any stories worth telling. All I can do is draw pictures of monsters and internal organs and hate.

(?)

Another day, another blow job. The fuzz has clamped down till the town is mother dry. If I don't give Big Ass a blow he'll cut off my supply. Hell, I'm shaking on the inside more than I'm shaking on the outside. What a bastard world without drugs! The dirty ofay who wants me to lay it on him knows my ass is dragging, but he's doling out the only supply I know about. I'm almost ready to take on the Fat Cats, the Rich Philistines, or even the whole public for one good shot. Goddamn Big Ass makes me do it before he gives me the load. Everybody is just lying around here like they're dead and Little Jacon is yelling, "Mama, Daddy can't come now. He's humping Carla." I've got to get out of this shit hole.

(?)

I don't know what the hell hour or day or even year it is, or even what town. I guess I've had a blackout or they've been passing some bad pills. The girl on the grass beside me is white-faced and Mona Lisa like and she's preggers. I asked her what she was going to do with the baby and she just said, "It will belong to everybody. We'll all share her."

I wanted to go and find someone who's holding, but the baby thing really bugged me. So I asked her for an upper and she just shook her head like a stupid, blank, and I realized that she's completely burned out. Behind that beautiful stoned face is a big dried-up bunch of ashes and she's lying there like a stupid dumb shit who can't do anything.

Well, at least I'm not burned out and I'm not preg. Or maybe I am. I couldn't take the goddamn pill even if I had it. No doper can take the pill because they don't know what the hell day it is. So maybe I am pregnant. So what. There's a pre-med drop out wandering around somewhere who will take care of it. Or maybe some goddamn prick would stomp on me during a freak out and I'd lose it anyway. Or maybe the son-of-a-bitch bomb will go off tomorrow. Who knows?

When I look around here at all the ass draggers, I really think that we are a bunch of gutless wonders. We get pissed off when someone tells us what to do, but we don't know what to do unless some fat bastard tells us. Let somebody else think for us and do for us and act for us. Let them build the roads and the cars and the houses, run the lights and the gas and the water and the sewers. We'll just sit here on our blistered tails with our minds exploding and our hands out. God, I sound like a goddamn Establishmentarian, and I haven't even got a pill to take the taste out of my mouth or drive the bull shit thoughts away.

When?

A raindrop just splashed on my forehead and it was like a tear from heaven. Are the clouds and the skies really weeping over me? Am I really alone in the whole wide gray world? Is it possible that even God is crying for me? Oh no . . . no . . . no . . . I'm losing my mind. Please God, help me.

(?)

I gather from the sky that it is early morning. I've been reading a paper that the wind blew up beside me. It says one girl had her baby in the park, another had a miscarriage and two unidentified boys died during the night from O.D.'s. Oh, how I wish one of them had been me!

Schizophrenic Disorders

Faulty thinking, perceiving, and communicating are symptoms of Schizophrenic Disorders (Schizophrenia).

A schizophrenic may cling to a delusion, a fixed idea that has no basis in fact. The delusion may consist of a belief that one is being controlled by an alien force, that one's thoughts are being monitored, that one is all-powerful or all-knowing, or that one suffers from a debilitating physical ailment. Sometimes the delusion may be a sense of persecution or a feeling of betrayal.

In Schizophrenia, faulty thinking is often accompanied by faulty perceptions in the form of hallucinations, false sensory perceptions that have no basis in concrete external stimuli. For example, schizophrenics think they are being threatened, then they may see or hear the persecutor or rival. Furthermore, they may hear voices conversing or a single voice offering a running commentary on their behavior or thoughts. In either case, what they hear is more complex than single phrases.

Schizophrenics are often illogical, incoherent, or disjointed in their communication, shifting aimlessly from one topic to another. They may be unable to carry on meaningful conversations, sometimes ignoring the rules of effective communication.

Schizophrenics' delusions, hallucinations, or eccentricities in communication are associated with a breakdown in their usual behavior. They may be unable to work or enter into social relationships. In fact, they may be unable to manage their personal hygiene or diet.

The four subtypes of Schizophrenic Disorders are Disorganized (Hebephrenic), Catatonic, Paranoid, and Undifferentiated. In addition to meeting the diagnostic criteria for Schizophrenia sketched above, each subtype includes one or more additional symptoms.

Disorganized Schizophrenia. The two additional symptoms associated with Disorganized Schizophrenia are marked incoherence and inappropriate emotional responses. Incoherence is manifested in speech by a breakdown in grammar, syntax, or diction. Inappropriate emotional responses include outbursts of laughter without apparent reason, grins or grimaces that appear silly, and antics in front of a mirror so that the actors can admire their performances.

Catatonic Schizophrenia. The additional symptom associated with Catatonic Schizophrenia is an excess or a lack of physical activity. The excited catatonics often talk or shout incessantly and incoherently. Their chatter is matched by their frenzied behavior; neither their chatter nor their behavior has a relation to external stimuli. In this excited condition, they may be dangerous to themselves or others. The withdrawn catatonics seem to be unaware of their environment and unresponsive to external stimuli. After a long period of seeming to be in a stupor, they rouse themselves and, without provocation, engage in a violently destructive outburst.

Paranoid Schizophrenia. The additional symptom associated with Paranoid Schizophrenia is a specific delusion. It may be either a delusion of grandeur (an exaggerated concept of one's importance) or a delusion of persecution (a false belief that one is being harassed). Paranoid Schizophrenics may be suspicious, reserved, hostile, or violent. They may be intensely jealous, especially if, in addition to their delusion of presecution, they have hallucinations that have a jealous content.

Undifferentiated Schizophrenia. Undifferentiated Schizophrenia is characterized by pronounced delusions, hallucinations, incoherence, and other symptoms. This classification is used when schizophrenics meet the criteria for more than one of the previous subtypes or do not meet the specific criteria for any one of them.

The three selections that follow seem to portray the world of Schizophrenic Disorders. The nightmarish quality of Pierre's world in "The Room" is almost beyond comprehension. The clinical description in Deborah Blau's medical record hardly does justice to the vividness of her hallucinations. The serenity of Paul Hasleman's secret world in "Silent Snow, Secret Snow" contrasts with his everyday world.

Pierre, Deborah, and Paul experience faulty thinking, perceiving, and communicating. Note examples of each symptom in each character. Give examples of how these symptoms affect the everyday functioning of the characters. Is there enough evidence to assign Pierre, Deborah, or Paul to a subtype of Schizophrenic Disorders? Why or why not?

THE ROOM

Jean-Paul Sartre

Mme. Darbedat held a *rahat-loukoum* between her fingers. She brought it carefully to her lips and held her breath, afraid that the fine dust of sugar that powdered it would blow away. "Just right," she told herself. She bit quickly into its glassy flesh and a scent of stagnation filled her mouth. "Odd how illness sharpens the sensations." She began to think of mosques, of obsequious Orientals (she had been to Algeria for her honeymoon) and her pale lips started in a smile: the *rahat-loukoum* was obsequious too.

Several times she had to pass the palm of her hand over the pages of her book, for in spite of the precaution she had taken they were covered with a thin coat of white powder. Her hand made the little grains of sugar slide and roll, grating on the smooth paper: "That makes me think of Arcachon, when I used to read on the beach." She had spent the summer of 1907 at the seashore. Then she wore a big straw hat with a green ribbon; she sat close to the jetty, with a novel by Gyp or Colette Yver. The wind made swirls of sand rain down upon her knees, and from time to time she had to shake the book, holding it by the corners. It was the same sensation: only the grains of sand were dry while the small bits of sugar stuck a little to the ends of her fingers. Again she saw a band of pearl grey sky above a black sea. "Eve wasn't born yet." She felt herself all weighted down with memories and precious as a coffer of sandalwood. The name of the book she used to read suddenly came back to mind: it was called *Petite Madame,* not at all boring. But ever since an unknown illness had confined her to her room she preferred memories and historical works.

She hoped that suffering, heavy readings, a vigilant attention to her memories and the most exquisite sensations would ripen her as a lovely hothouse fruit.

She thought, with some annoyance, that her husband would soon be knocking at her door. On other days of the week he came only in the evening, kissed her brow in silence and read *Le Temps,* sitting in the armchair across from her. But Thursday was M. Darbedat's *day*: he spent an hour with his daughter, generally from three to four. Before going he stopped in to see his wife and both discussed their son-in-law with bitterness. These Thursday conversations, predictable to their slightest detail, exhausted Mme. Darbedat. M. Darbedat filled the quiet room with his presence. He never sat, but walked in circles about the room. Each of his outbursts wounded Mme. Darbedat like a glass splintering. This particular Thursday was worse than usual: at the thought that it would soon be necessary to repeat Eve's confessions to her husband, and to see his great terrifying body convulse with fury, Mme. Darbedat broke out in a sweat. She picked up a *loukoum* from the saucer, studied it for a while with hesitation, then sadly set it down: she did not like her husband to see her eating *loukoums*.

She heard a knock and started up. "Come in," she said weakly.

M. Darbedat entered on tiptoe. "I'm going to see Eve," he said, as he did every Thursday. Mme. Darbedat smiled at him. "Give her a kiss for me."

M. Darbedat did not answer and his forehead wrinkled worriedly: every Thursday at the same time, a muffled irritation mingled with the load of his digestion. "I'll stop in and see Franchot after leaving her. I wish he'd talk to her seriously and try to convince her."

He had made frequent visits to Dr. Franchot. But in vain. Mme. Darbedat raised her eyebrows. Before, when she was well, she shrugged her shoulders. But since sickness had weighted down her body, she replaced the gestures which would have tired her by plays of emotion in the face: she said *yes* with her eyes, *no* with the corners of her mouth: she raised her eyebrows instead of her shoulders.

"There should be some way to take him away from her by force."

"I told you already it was impossible. And besides, the law is very poorly drawn up. Only the other day Franchot was telling me that they have a tremendous amount of trouble with the families: people who can't make up their mind, who want to keep the patient at home; the doctors' hands are tied. They can give their advice, period. That's all. He would," he went on, "have to make a public scandal or else she would have to ask to have him put away herself."

"And that," said Mme. Darbedat, "isn't going to happen tomorrow."

"No." He turned to the mirror and began to comb his fingers through his beard. Mme. Darbedat looked at the powerful red neck of her husband without affection.

"If she keeps on," said M. Darbedat, "she'll be crazier than he is. It's terribly unhealthy. She doesn't leave his side, she only goes out to see you. She has no visitors. The air in their room is simply unbreathable. She never opens the window because Pierre doesn't want it open. As if you should ask a sick man. I believe they burn incense, some rubbish in a little pan, you'd think it was a church. Really, sometimes I wonder. . . she's got a funny look in her eyes, you know."

"I haven't noticed," Mme. Darbedat said. "I find her quite normal. She looks sad, obviously."

"She has a face like an unburied corpse. Does she sleep? Does she eat? But we aren't supposed to ask her about those things. But I should think that with a fellow like Pierre next to her, she wouldn't sleep a wink all night." He shrugged his shoulders. "What I find amazing is that we, her parents, don't have the right to protect her against herself. Understand that Pierre would be much better cared for by Franchot. There's a big park. And besides, I think," he added, smiling a little, "he'd get along much better with people of his own type. People like that are children, you have to leave them alone with each other; they form a sort of freemasonry. That's where he should have been put the first day and for his own good, I'd say. Of course it's in his own best interest."

After a moment, he added, "I tell you I don't like to know she's alone with Pierre, especially at night. Suppose something happened. Pierre has a very sly way about him."

"I don't know," Mme. Darbedat said, "if there's any reason to worry. He always looked like that. He always seemed to be making fun of the world. Poor boy," she sighed, "to have had his pride and then come to that. He thought he was cleverer than all of us. He had a way of saying 'You're right' simply to end the argument. . . It's a blessing for him that he can't see the state he's in."

She recalled with displeasure the long, ironic face, always turned a little to the side. During the first days of Eve's marriage, Mme. Darbedat asked nothing more than a little intimacy with her son-in-law. But he had discouraged her: he almost never spoke, he always agreed quickly and absentmindedly.

M. Darbedat pursued his idea. "Franchot let me visit his place," he said. "It was magnificent. The patients have private rooms with leather armchairs, if you please, and day-beds. You know, they have a tennis court and they're going to build a swimming pool."

He was planted before the window, looking out, rocking a little on his bent legs. Suddenly he turned lithely on his heel, shoulders lowered, hands in his pockets. Mme. Darbedat felt she was going to start perspiring: it was the same thing every time: now he was pacing back and forth like a bear in a cage and his shoes squeaked at every step.

"Please, please won't you sit down. You're tiring me." Hesitating, she added, "I have something important to tell you."

M. Darbedat sat in the armchair and put his hands on his knees; a slight chill ran up Mme. Darbedat's spine: the time had come, she had to speak.

"You know," she said with an embarrassed cough, "I saw Eve on Tuesday."

"Yes."

"We talked about a lot of things, she was very nice, she hadn't been so confiding for a long time. Then I questioned her a little, I got her to talk about Pierre. Well, I found out," she added, again embarrassed, "that she is *very* attached to him."

"I know that too damned well," said M. Darbedat.

He irritated Mme. Darbedat a little: she always had to explain things in such detail. Mme. Darbedat dreamed of living in the company of fine and sensitive people who would understand her slightest word.

"But I mean," she went on, "that she is attached to him *differently* than we imagined."

M. Darbedat rolled furious, anxious eyes, as he always did when he never completely grasped the sense of an allusion or something new.

"What does that all mean?"

"Charles," said Mme. Darbedat, "don't tire me. You should understand a mother has difficulty in telling certain things."

"I don't understand a damned word of anything you say," M. Darbedat said with irritation. "You can't mean..."

"Yes," she said.

"They're still... now, still...?"

"Yes! Yes! Yes!" she said, in three annoyed and dry little jolts.

M. Darbedat spread his arms, lowered his head and was silent.

"Charles," his wife said, worriedly, "I shouldn't have told you. But I couldn't keep it to myself."

"Our child," he said slowly. "With this madman! He doesn't even recognize her any more. He calls her Agatha. She must have lost all sense of her own dignity."

He raised his head and looked at his wife severely. "You're sure you aren't mistaken?"

"No possible doubt. Like you," she added quickly, "I couldn't believe her and I still can't. The mere idea of being touched by that wretch...So..." she sighed, "I suppose that's how he holds on to her."

"Do you remember what I told you," M. Darbedat said, "when he came to ask for her hand? I told you I thought he pleased Eve *too much*. You wouldn't believe me." He struck the table suddenly, blushing violently. "It's perversity! He takes her in his arms, kisses her and calls her Agatha, selling her on a lot of nonsense about flying statues and God knows what else! Without a word from her! But what in heaven's name's between those two? Let her be sorry for him, let her put him in a sanatorium and see him every day, — fine. But I never thought... I considered her a widow. Listen, Jeannette," he said gravely, "I'm going to speak frankly to you; if she had any sense, I'd rather see her take a lover!"

"Be quiet, Charles!" Mme. Darbedat cried.

M. Darbedat wearily took his hat and the cane he had left on the stool. "After what you've just told me," he concluded, "I don't have much hope left. In any case, I'll have a talk with her because it's my duty."

Mme. Darbedat wished he would go quickly.

"You know," she said to encourage him, "I think Eve is more headstrong than... than anything. She knows he's incurable but she's obstinate, she doesn't want to be in the wrong."

M. Darbedat stroked his beard absently.

"Headstrong? Maybe so. If you're right, she'll finally get tired of it. He's not always pleasant and he doesn't have much to say. When I say hello to him he gives me a flabby handshake and doesn't say a word. As soon as they're alone, I think they go back to his obsessions: she tells me sometimes he screams as though his throat were being cut because of his hallucinations. He sees statues. They frighten him because they buzz. He says they fly around and make fishy eyes at him."

He put on his gloves and continued, "She'll get tired of it, I'm not saying she won't. But suppose she goes crazy before that? I wish she'd go out a little, see the world: she'd meet some nice young man — well, someone like Schroeder, an engineer with Simplon, somebody with a future, she could see him a little here and there and she'd get used to the idea of making a new life for herself."

Mme. Darbedat did not answer, afraid of starting the conversation up again. Her husband bent over her.

"So," he said, "I've got to be on my way."

"Goodbye, Papa," Mme. Darbedat said, lifting her forehead up to him. "Kiss her for me and tell her for me she's a poor dear."

Once her husband had gone, Mme. Darbedat let herself drift to the bottom of the armchair and closed her eyes, exhausted. "What vitality," she thought reproachfully. As soon as she got a little strength back, she quietly stretched out her pale hand and took a *loukoum* from the saucer, groping for it without opening her eyes.

Eve lived with her husband on the sixth floor of an old building on the Rue du Bac. M. Darbedat slowly climbed the 112 steps of the stairway. He was not even out of breath when he pushed the bell. He remembered with satisfaction the words of Mlle. Dormoy: "Charles, for your age, you're simply marvelous." Never did he feel himself stronger and healthier than on Thursday, especially after these invigorating climbs.

Eve opened the door: that's right, she doesn't have a maid. No girls *can* stay with her. I can put myself in their place. He kissed her. "Hello, poor darling."

Eve greeted him with a certain coldness.

"You look a little pale," M. Darbedat said, touching her cheek. "You don't get enough exercise."

There was a moment of silence.

"Is Mamma well?" Eve asked.

"Not good, not too bad. You saw her Tuesday? Well, she's just the same. Your Aunt Louise came to see her yesterday, that pleased her. She likes to have visitors, but they can't stay too long. Aunt Louise came to Paris for that mortgage business. I think I told you about it, a very odd sort of affair. She stopped in at the office to ask my advice. I told her there was only one thing to do: sell. She found a taker, by the way: Bretonnel! You remember Bretonnel. He's retired from business now."

He stopped suddenly: Eve was hardly listening. He thought sadly that nothing interested her any more. It's like the books. Before you had to tear them away from her. Now she doesn't even read any more.

"How is Pierre?"

"Well," Eve said. "Do you want to see him?"

"Of course," M. Darbedat said gaily, "I'd like to pay him a little call."

He was full of compassion for this poor young man, but he could not see him without repugnance. *I detest unhealthy people.* Obviously, it was not Pierre's fault: his heredity was terribly loaded down. M. Darbedat sighed: *All the precautions are taken in vain, you find out those things too late.* No, Pierre was not responsible. But still he had always carried that fault in him; it formed the base of his character; it wasn't like cancer or tuberculosis, something you could always put aside when you wanted to judge a man as he is. His nervous grace, the sublety which pleased Eve so much when he was courting her were the flowers of madness. He was already mad when he married her only you couldn't tell.

It makes you wonder, thought M. Darbedat, *where responsibility begins, or rather, where it ends.* In any case, he was always analysing himself too much, always turned in on himself. But was it the cause or effect of his sickness? He followed his daughter through a long, dim corridor.

"This apartment is too big for you," he said. "You ought to move out."

"You say that every time, Papa," Eve answered, "but I've already told you Pierre doesn't want to leave his room."

Eve was amazing. Enough to make you wonder if she realized her husband's state. He was insane enough to be in a strait-jacket and she respected his decisions and advice as if he still had good sense.

"What I'm saying is for your own good." M. Darbedat went on, somewhat annoyed, "It seems to me that if I were a woman I'd be afraid of these badly lighted old rooms. I'd like to see you in a bright apartment, the kind they're putting up near Auteuil, three airy little rooms. They lowered the rents because they couldn't find any tenants; this would be just the time."

Eve quietly turned the doorknob and they entered the room. M. Darbedat's throat tightened at the heavy odor of incense. The curtains were drawn. In the shadows he made out a thin neck above the back of an armchair: Pierre's back was turned. He was eating.

"Hello, Pierre," M. Darbedat said, raising his voice. "How are we today?"

He drew near him: the sick man was seated in front of a small table: he looked sly.

"I see we had soft boiled eggs," M. Darbedat said, raising his voice higher. "That's good!"

"I'm not deaf," Pierre said quietly.

Irritated, M. Darbedat turned his eyes toward Eve as his witness. But Eve gave him a hard glance and was silent. M. Darbedat realized he had hurt her. Too bad for her. It was impossible to find just the right tone for this boy. He had less sense than a child of four and Eve wanted him treated like a man. M.

Darbedat could not keep himself from waiting with impatience for the moment when all this ridiculous business would be finished. Sick people annoyed him a little — especially madmen because they were wrong. Poor Pierre, for example, was wrong all along the line, he couldn't speak a reasonable word and yet it would be useless to expect the least humility from him, or even temporary recognition of his errors.

Eve cleared away the eggshells and the cup. She put a knife and fork in front of Pierre.

"What's he going to eat now," M. Darbedat said jovially.

"A steak."

Pierre had taken the fork and held it in the ends of his long, pale fingers. He inspected it minutely and then gave a slight laugh.

"I can't use it this time," he murmured, setting it down, "I was warned."

Eve came in and looked at the fork with passionate interest.

"Agatha," Pierre said, "give me another one."

Eve obeyed and Pierre began to eat. She had taken the suspect fork and held it tightly in her hands, her eyes never leaving it; she seemed to make a violent effort. How suspicious all their gestures and relationships are! thought M. Darbedat.

He was uneasy.

"Be careful, Pierre, take it by the middle because of the prongs."

Eve sighed and laid the fork on the serving table. M. Darbedat felt his gall rising. He did not think it well to give in to all this poor man's whims — even from Pierre's viewpoint it was pernicious. Franchot had said: "One must never enter the delirium of a madman." Instead of giving him another fork, it would have been better to have reasoned quietly and made him understand that the first was like all the others.

He went to the serving table, took the fork ostentatiously and tested the prongs with a light finger. Then he turned to Pierre. But the latter was cutting him meat peacefully: he gave his father-in-law a gentle, inexpressive glance.

"I'd like to have a little talk with you," M. Darbedat said to Eve.

She followed him docilely into the salon. Sitting on the couch, M. Darbedat realized he had kept the fork in his hand. He threw it on the table.

"It's much better here," he said.

"I never come here."

"All right to smoke?"

"Of course, Papa," Eve said hurriedly. "Do you want a cigar?"

M. Darbedat preferred to roll a cigarette. He thought eagerly of the discussion he was about to begin. Speaking to Pierre he felt as embarrassed about his reason as a giant about his strength when playing with a child. All his qualities of clarity, sharpness, precision, turned against him; *I must confess it's somewhat the same with my poor Jeannette.* Certainly Mme. Darbedat was not insane, but this illness had... stultified her. Eve, on the other hand, took after her father... a straight, logical nature; discussion with her was a pleasure; *that's why I don't want them to ruin her.* M. Darbedat raised his eyes. Once again he wanted to see the fine intelligent features of his daughter. He was disappointed with this face; once so reasonable and transparent, there was now something clouded and opaque in it. Eve had always been beautiful. M. Darbedat noticed she was made up with great care, almost with pomp. She had blued her eyelids and put mascara on her long lashes. This violent and perfect make-up made a painful impression on her father.

"You're green beneath your rouge," he told her. "I'm afraid you're getting sick. And the way you make yourself up now! You used to be so discreet."

Eve did not answer and for an embarrassed moment M. Darbedat considered this brilliant, worn-out face beneath the heavy mass of black hair. He thought she looked like a tragedian. *I even know who she looks like. That woman... that Roumanian who played* Phèdre *in French at the Mur* d'Orange. He regretted having made so disagreeable a remark: *It escaped me! Better not worry her with little things.*

"Excuse me," he said smiling. "You know I'm an old purist. I don't like all these creams and paints women stick on their face today. But I'm in the wrong. You must live in your time."

Eve smiled amiably at him. M. Darbedat lit a cigarette and drew several puffs.

"My child," he began, "I wanted to talk with you: the two of us are going to talk the way we used to. Come, sit down and listen to me nicely; you must have confidence in your old Papa."

"I'd rather stand," Eve said. "What did you want to tell me?"

"I am going to ask you a single question," M. Darbedat said a little more dryly. "Where will all this lead you?"

"All this?" Eve asked astonished.

"Yes...all this whole life you've made yourself. Listen," he went on, "don't think I don't understand you (he had a sudden illumination) but what you want to do is beyond human strength. You want to live solely by imagination, isn't that it? You don't want to admit he's sick. You don't want to see the Pierre of today, do you? You have eyes only for the Pierre of before. My dear, my darling little girl, it's an impossible bet to win," M. Darbedat continued. "Now I'm going to tell you a story which perhaps you don't know. When we were at Sables-d'Olonne — you were three years old — your mother made the acquaintance of a charming young woman with a superb little boy. You played on the beach with this little boy, you were thick as thieves, you were engaged to marry him. A while later, in Paris, your mother wanted to see this young woman again; she was told he had had a terrible accident. That fine little boy's head was cut off by a car. They told your mother, 'Go and see her, but above all don't talk to her about the death of her child, she *will not* believe he is dead.' Your mother went, she found a half-mad creature: she lived as though her boy was still alive; she spoke to him, she set his place at the table. She lived in such a state of nervous tension that after six months they had to take her away by force to a sanatorium where she was obliged to stay three years. No, my child," M. Darbedat said, shaking his head, "these things are impossible. It would have been better if she had recognized the truth courageously. She would have suffered once, then time would have erased with its sponge. There is nothing like looking things in the face, believe me."

"You're wrong," Eve said with effort. "I know very well that Pierre is..."

The word did not escape. She held herself very straight and put her hands on the back of the armchair: there is something dry and ugly in the lower part of her face.

"So...?" asked M. Darbedat, astonished.

"So...?"

"You...?"

"I love him as he is," said Eve rapidly and with an irritated look.

"Not true," M. Darbedat said forcefully. "It isn't true: you don't love him, you can't love him. You can only feel that way about a healthy, normal person. You pity Pierre, I don't doubt it, and surely you have the memory of three years of happiness he gave you. But don't tell me you love him. I won't believe you."

Eve remained wordless, staring at the carpet absently.

"You could at least answer me," M. Darbedat said coldly. "Don't think this conversation has been any less painful for me than it has for you."

"More than you think."

"Well then, if you love him," he cried, exasperated, "it is a great misfortune for you, for me and for your poor mother because I'm going to tell you something I would rather have hidden from you: before three years Pierre will be sunk in complete dementia, he'll be like a beast."

He watched his daughter with hard eyes: he was angry at her for having compelled him, by stubbornness, to make this painful revelation.

Eve was motionless; she did not so much as raise her eyes.

"I knew."

"Who told you?" he asked stupefied.

"Franchot. I knew six months ago."

"And I told him to be careful with you," said M. Darbedat with bitterness. "Maybe it's better. But under those circumstances you must understand that it would be unpardonable to keep Pierre with you. The struggle you have undertaken is doomed to failure, his illness won't spare him. If there were something to be done, if we could save him by care, I'd say yes. But look: you're pretty, intelligent, gay, you're destroying yourself willingly and without profit. I know you've been admirable, but now it's over... done, you've done your duty and more; now it would be immoral to continue. We also have duties to ourselves, child. And then you aren't thinking about us. You must," he repeated, hammering the words, "send Pierre to Franchot's clinic. Leave this apartment where you've had nothing but sorrow and come home to us. If you want to be useful and ease the sufferings of someone else, you have your mother. The poor woman is cared for by nurses, she needs someone closer to her, and *she,*" he added, "can appreciate what you do for her and be grateful."

There was a long silence. M. Darbedat heard Pierre singing in the next room. It was hardly a song, rather a sort of sharp, hasty recitative. M. Darbedat raised his eyes to his daughter.

"It's no then?"

"Pierre will stay with me," she said quietly. "I get along well with him."

"By living like an animal all day long?"

Eve smiled and shot a glance at her father, strange, mocking and almost gay. *It's true.* M. Darbedat thought furiously, *that's not all they do; they sleep together.*

"You are completely mad," he said, rising.

Eve smiled sadly and murmured, as if to herself, "Not enough so."

"Not enough? I can only tell you one thing, my child. You frighten me."

He kissed her hastily and left. Going down the stairs he thought: *we should send out two strong-arm men who'd take the poor imbecile away and stick him under a shower without asking his advice on the matter.*

It was a fine autumn day, calm and without mystery; the sunlight gilded the faces of the passers-by. M. Darbedat was struck with the simplicity of the faces; some weather-beaten, others smooth, but they reflected all the happiness and care with which he was so familiar.

I know exactly what I resent in Eve, he told himself, entering the Boulevard St. Germain. *I resent her living outside the limits of human nature. Pierre is no longer a human being: in all the care and all the love she gives him she deprives human beings of a little. We don't have the right to refuse ourselves to the world; no matter what, we live in society.*

He watched the faces of the passers-by with sympathy; he loved their clear, serious looks. In these sunlit streets, in the midst of mankind, one felt secure, as in the midst of a large family.

A woman stopped in front of an open-air display counter. She was holding a little girl by the hand.

"What's that?" the little girl asked, pointing to a radio set.

"Mustn't touch," her mother said. "It's a radio; it plays music."

They stood for a moment without speaking, in ecstasy. Touched, M. Darbedat bent down to the little girl and smiled.

2

"He's gone." The door closed with a dry snap. Eve was alone in the salon. *I wish he'd die.*

She twisted her hands around the back of the armchair: she had just remembered her father's eyes. M. Darbedat had bent over Pierre with a competent air; he had said "That's good!" the way someone says when they speak to invalids. He had looked and Pierre's face had been painted in the depths of his sharp, bulging eyes. *I hate him when he looks at him because I think he sees him.*

Eve's hands slid along the armchair and she turned to the window. She was dazzled. The room was filled with sunlight, it was everywhere, in pale splotches on the rug, in the air like a blinding dust. Eve was not accustomed to this diligent, indiscreet light which darted from everywhere, scouring all the corners, rubbing the furniture like a busy housewife and making it glisten. However, she went to the window and raised the muslin curtain which hung against the pane. Just at that moment M. Darbedat left the building; Eve suddenly caught sight of his broad shoulders. He raised his head and looked at the sky, blinking, then with the stride of a young man he walked away. *He's straining himself*, thought Eve, *soon he'll have a stitch in the side.* She hardly hated him any longer: there was so little in that head; only the tiny worry of appearing young. Yet rage took her again when she saw him turn the corner of the Boulevard St. Germain and disappear. *He's thinking about Pierre.* A little of their life had escaped from the closed room and was being dragged through the streets, in the sun, among the people. *Can they never forget about us?*

The Rue de Bac was almost deserted. An old lady crossed the street with mincing steps; three girls passed, laughing. Then men, strong, serious men carrying briefcases and talking among themselves. *Normal people*, thought Eve, astonished at finding such a powerful hatred in herself. A handsome, fleshy woman ran heavily toward an elegant gentleman. He took her in his arms and kissed her on the mouth. Eve gave a hard laugh and let the curtain fall.

Pierre sang no more but the woman on the fourth floor was playing the piano; she played a Chopin Etude. Eve felt calmer; she took a step toward Pierre's room but stopped almost immediately and leaned against the wall in anguish; each time she left the room, she was panic-stricken at the thought of going back. Yet she knew she could live nowhere else: she loved the room. She looked around it with cold curiosity as if to gain a little time: this shadowless, odorless room where she waited for her courage to return. *You'd think it was a dentist's waiting room.* Armchairs of pink silk, the divan, the tabourets were somber and discreet, a little fatherly; man's best friends. Eve imagined those grave gentlemen dressed in light suits, all like the ones she saw at the window, entering the room, continuing a conversation already begun. They did not even take time to reconnoiter, but advanced with firm step to the middle of the room; one of them, letting his hand drag behind him like a wake in passing knocked over cushions, objects on the table, and was never disturbed by their contact. And when a piece of furniture was in their way, these poised men, far from making a detour to avoid it, quietly changed its place. Finally they sat down, still plunged in their conversation, without even glancing behind them. *A living-room for normal people*, thought Eve. She stared at the knob of the closed door and anguish clutched her throat: *I must go back. I never leave him alone so long.* She would have to open the door, then stand for a moment on the threshold, trying to accustom her eyes to the shadow and the room would push her back with all its strength. Eve would have to triumph over this resistance and enter all the way into the heart of the room. Suddenly she wanted violently to see Pierre; she would have liked to make fun of M. Darbedat with him. But Pierre had no need of her; Eve could not foresee the welcome he had in store for her. Suddenly she thought with a sort of pride that she had no place anywhere. *Normal people think I belong with them. But I couldn't stay an hour among them. I need to live out there, on the other side of the wall. But they don't want me out there.*

A profound change was taking place around her. The light had grown old and greying: it was heavy, like the water in a vase of flowers that hasn't been changed since the day before. In this aged light Eve found a melancholy she had long forgotten: the melancholy of an autumn afternoon that was ending. She looked around her, hesitant, almost timid: all that was so far away: there was neither day nor night nor season nor melancholy in the room. She vaguely recalled autumns long past, autumns of her childhood, then suddenly she stiffened: she was afraid of memories.

She heard Pierre's voice. "Agatha! Where are you?"

"Coming!" she cried.

She opened the door and entered the room.

The heavy odor of incense filled her mouth and nostrils as she opened her eyes and stretched out her hands — for a long time the perfume and the gloom had meant nothing more to her than a single element, acrid and heavy, as simple, as familiar as water, air or fire — and she prudently advanced toward a pale stain which seemed to float in the fog. It was Pierre's face: Pierre's clothing (he dressed in black ever since he had been sick) melted in obscurity. Pierre had thrown back his head and closed his eyes. He was handsome. Eve looked at his long, curved lashes, then sat close to him on the low chair. *He seems to be suffering*, she thought. Little by little her eyes grew used to the darkness. The bureau emerged first, then the bed, then Pierre's personal things: scissors, the pot of glue, books, the herbarium which shed its leaves onto the rug near the armchair.

"Agatha?"

Pierre had opened his eyes. He was watching her, smiling. "You know, that fork?" he said. "I did it to frighten that fellow. There was *almost* nothing the matter with it."

Eve's apprehensions faded and she gave a light laugh. "You succeeded," she said, "You drove him completely out of his mind."

Pierre smiled. "Did you see? He played with it a long time, he held it right in his hands. The trouble is," he said, "they don't know how to take hold of things; they grab them."

"That's right," Eve said.

Pierre tapped the palm of his left hand lightly with the index of his right.

"They take with that. They reach out their fingers and when they catch hold of something they crack down on it to knock it out."

He spoke rapidly and hardly moving his lips; he looked puzzled.

"I wonder what they want," he said at last, "that fellow has already been here. Why did they send him to me? If they wanted to know what I'm doing all they have to do is read it on the screen, they don't even need to leave the house. They make mistakes. They have the power but they make mistakes. I never make any, that's my trump card. *Hoffka!*" he said. He shook his long hands before his forehead. "The bitch Hoffka, Paffka! Suffka! Do you want any more?"

"Is it the bell?" asked Eve.

"Yes. It's gone." He went on severely. "This fellow, he's just a subordinate. You know him, you went into the living room with him."

Eve did not answer.

"What did he want?" asked Pierre. "He must have told you."

She hesitated an instant, then answered brutally. "He wanted you locked up."

When the truth was told quietly to Pierre he distrusted it. He had to be dealt with violently in order to daze and paralyze his suspicions. Eve preferred to brutalize him rather than lie: when she lied and he acted as if he believed it she could not avoid a very slight feeling of superiority which made her horrified at herself.

"Lock me up!" Pierre repeated ironically. "They're crazy. What can walls do to me. Maybe they think that's going to stop me. I sometimes wonder if there aren't two groups. The real one, the negro—and then a bunch of fools trying to stick their noses in and making mistake after mistake."

He made his hand jump up from the arm of the chair and looked at it happily.

"I can get through walls. What did you tell them?" he asked, turning to Eve with curiosity.

"Not to lock you up."

He shrugged. "You shouldn't have said that. You made a mistake too... unless you did it on purpose. You've got to call their bluff."

He was silent. Eve lowered her head sadly: *"They grab things!" How scornfully he said that—and he was right. Do I grab things too? It doesn't do any good to watch myself, I think most of my movements annoy him. But he doesn't say anything.* Suddenly she felt as miserable as when she was fourteen and Mme. Darbedat told her, "You don't know what to do with your hands." She didn't dare make a move and just at that time she had an irresistible desire to change her position. Quietly she put her feet under the chair, barely touching the rug. She watched the lamp on the table—the lamp whose base Pierre had painted black—and the chess set. Pierre had left only the black pawns on the board. Sometimes he would get up, go to the table and take the pawns in his hands one by one. He spoke to them, called them Robots and they seemed to stir with a mute life under his fingers. When he set them down, Eve went and touched them in her turn (she always felt somewhat ridiculous about it). They had become little bits of dead wood again but something vague and incomprehensible stayed in them, something like understanding. *These are his things,* she thought. *There is nothing of mine in the room.* She had a few pieces of furniture before; the mirror and the little inlaid dresser handed down from her grandmother and which Pierre jokingly called "*your* dresser." Pierre had carried them away with him; things showed their true face to Pierre alone. Eve could watch them for hours: they were unflaggingly stubborn and determined to deceive her, offering her nothing but their appearance—as they did to Dr. Franchot and M. Darbedat. Yet, she told herself with anguish, *I don't see them quite like my father. It isn't possible for me to see them exactly like him.*

She moved her knees a little: her legs felt as though they were crawling with ants. Her body was stiff and taut and hurt her; she felt it too alive, too demanding. *I would like to be invisible and stay here seeing him without his seeing me. He doesn't need me; I am useless in this room.* She turned her head slightly and looked at the wall above Pierre. Threats were written on the wall. Eve knew it but she could not read them. She often watched the big red roses on the wallpaper until they began to dance before her eyes. The roses flamed in shadow. Most of the time the threat was written near the ceiling, a little to the left of the bed; but sometimes it moved. *I must get up. I can't...I can't sit down any longer.* There were also white discs on the wall that looked like slices of onion. The discs spun and Eve's hands began to tremble: *Sometimes I think I'm going mad. But no,* she thought, *I can't go mad.* I get nervous, *that's all.*

Suddenly she felt Pierre's hand on hers.

"Agatha," Pierre said tenderly.

He smiled at her but he held her hand by the ends of his fingers with a sort of revulsion, as though he had picked up a crab by the back and wanted to avoid its claws.

"Agatha," he said. "I would so much like to have confidence in you."

She closed her eyes and her breast heaved. *I mustn't answer anything, if I do he'll get angry, he won't say anything more.*

Pierre had dropped her hand. "I like you, Agatha," he said, "but I can't understand you. Why do you stay in the room all the time?"

Eve did not answer.

"Tell me why."

"You know I love you," she said dryly.

"I don't believe you," Pierre said, "Why should you love me? I must frighten you: I'm haunted." He smiled but suddenly became serious. "There is a wall between you and me. I see you, I speak to you, but you're on the other side. What keeps us from loving? I think it was easier before. In Hamburg."

"Yes," Eve said sadly. Always Hamburg. He never spoke of their real past. Neither Eve nor he had ever been to Hamburg.

"We used to walk along the canal. There was a barge, remember? The barge was black; there was a dog on the deck."

He made it up as he went along; it sounded false.

"I held your hand. You had another skin. I believed all you told me. Be quiet!" he shouted.

He listened for a moment. "They're coming," he said mournfully.

Eve jumped up. "They're coming? I thought they wouldn't ever come again."

Pierre had been calmer for the past three days; the statues did not come. Pierre was terribly afraid of the statues even though he would never admit it. Eve was not afraid: but when they began to fly, buzzing, around the room, she was afraid of Pierre.

"Give me the ziuthre," Pierre said.

Eve got up and took the ziuthre: it was a collection of pieces of cardboard Pierre had glued together; he used it to conjure the statues. The ziuthre looked like a spider. On one of the cardboards Pierre had written "Power over ambush" and on the other, "Black." On a third he had drawn a laughing face with wrinkled eyes: It was Voltaire.

Pierre seized the ziuthre by one end and looked at it darkly.

"I can't use it any more,"he said.

"Why?"

"They turned it upside down."

"Will you make another?"

He looked at her for a long while. "You'd like me to, wouldn't you," he said between his teeth.

Eve was angry at Pierre. *He's warned every time they come: how does he do it? He's never wrong.*

The ziuthre dangled pitifully from the ends of Pierre's fingers. *He always finds a good reason not use it. Sunday when they came he pretended he'd lost it but I saw it behind the paste pot and he couldn't fail to see it. I wonder if he isn't the one who brings them.* One could never tell if he were completely sincere. Sometimes Eve had the impression that despite himself

Pierre was surrounded by a swarm of unhealthy thoughts and visions. But at other times Pierre seemed to invent them. *He suffers. But how much does he believe in the statues and the negro. Anyhow, I know he doesn't see the statues, he only hears them: when they pass he turns his head away; but he still says he sees them; he describes them.* She remembered the red face of Dr. Franchot: "But my dear madame, all mentally unbalanced persons are liars; you're wasting your time if you're trying to distinguish between what they really feel and what they pretend to feel." She gave a start. *What is Franchot doing here? I don't want to start thinking like him.*

Pierre had gotten up. He went to throw the ziuthre into the wastebasket: *I want to think like you,* she murmured. He walked with tiny steps, on tiptoe, pressing his elbows against his hips so as to take up the least possible space. He came back and sat down and looked at Eve with a closed expression.

"We'll have to put up black wallpaper," he said. "There isn't enough black in this room."

He was crouched in the armchair. Sadly Eve watched his meagre body, always ready to withdraw, to shrink: the arms, legs and head looked like retractable organs. The clock struck six. The piano downstairs was silent. Eve sighed: the statues would not come right away; they had to wait for them.

"Do you want me to turn on the light?"

She would rather not wait for them in darkness.

"Do as you please," Pierre said

Eve lit the small lamp on the bureau and a red mist filled the room. Pierre was waiting too.

He did not speak but his lips were moving, making two dark stains in the red mist. Eve loved Pierre's lips. Before, they had been moving and sensual; but they had lost their sensuality. They were wide apart, trembling a little, coming together incessantly, crushing against each other only to separate again. They were the only living things in this blank face; they looked like two frightened animals. Pierre could mutter like that for hours without a sound leaving his mouth and Eve often let herself be fascinated by this tiny, obstinate movement. *I love his mouth.* He never kissed her any more; he was horrified at contacts; at night they touched him — the hands of men, hard and dry, pinched him all over; the long-nailed hands of women caressed him. Often he went to bed with his clothes on but the hands slipped under the clothes and tugged at his shirt. Once he heard laughter and puffy lips were placed on his mouth. He never kissed Eve after that night.

"Agatha," Pierre said, "don't look at my mouth."

Eve lowered her eyes.

"I am not unaware that people can learn to read lips," he went on insolently.

His hand trembled on the arm of the chair. The index finger stretched out, tapped three times on the thumb and the other fingers curled: this was a spell. *It's going to start,* she thought. She wanted to take Pierre in her arms. Pierre began to speak at the top of his voice in a very sophisticated tone.

"Do you remember São Paulo?"

No answer. Perhaps it was a trap.

"I met you there," he said, satisfied. "I took you away from a Danish sailor. We almost fought but I paid for a round of drinks and he let me take you away. All that was only a joke."

He's lying, he doesn't believe a word of what he says. He knows my name isn't Agatha. I hate him when he lies. But she saw his staring eyes and her rage melted. *He isn't lying,* she thought, *he can't stand it any more. He feels them coming; he's talking to keep from hearing them.* Pierre dug both hands into the arm of the chair. His face was pale; he was smiling.

"These meetings are often strange," he said, "but I don't believe it's by chance. I'm not asking who sent you. I know you wouldn't answer. Anyhow, you've been smart enough to bluff me."

He spoke with great difficulty, in a sharp, hurried voice. There were words he could not pronounce and which left his mouth like some soft and shapeless substance.

"You dragged me away right in the middle of the party, between the rows of black automobiles, but behind the cars there was an army with red eyes which glowed as soon as I turned my back. I think you made signs to them, all the time hanging on my arm, but I didn't see a thing. I was too absorbed by the great ceremonies of the Coronation."

He looked straight ahead, his eyes wide open. He passed his hand over his forehead very rapidly, in one spare gesture, without stopping his talking. He did not want to stop talking.

"It was the Coronation of the Republic," he said stridently, "an impressive spectacle of its kind because of all the species of animals that the colonies sent for the ceremony. You were afraid to get lost among the monkeys. I said among the monkeys," he repeated arrogantly, looking around him, "I could *say among the negroes!* The abortions sliding under the tables, trying to pass unseen, are discovered and nailed to the spot by my Look. The password is silence. To be silent. Everything in place and attention for the entrance of the statues, that's the countersign. Tralala..." he shrieked and cupped his hands to his mouth. "Tralalala, tralalalala!"

He was silent and Eve knew that the statues had come into the room. He was stiff, pale and distrustful. Eve stiffened too and both waited in silence. Someone was walking in the corridor: it was Marie the housecleaner, she had undoubtedly just arrived. Eve thought, *I have to give her money for the gas.* And then the statues began to fly; they passed between Eve and Pierre.

Pierre went "Ah!" and sank down in the armchair, folding his legs beneath him. He turned his face away; sometimes he grinned, but drops of sweat pearled his forehead. Eve could stand the sight no longer, this pale cheek, this mouth deformed by a trembling grimace; she closed her eyes. Gold threads began to dance on the red background of her eyelids; she felt old and heavy. Not far from her Pierre was breathing violently. *They're flying, they're buzzing, they're bending over him.* She felt a slight tickling, a pain in the shoulder and right side. Instinctively her body bent to the left as if to avoid some disagreeable contact, as if to let a heavy, awkward object pass. Suddenly the floor creaked and she had an insane desire to open her eyes, to look to her right, sweeping the air with her hand.

She did nothing: she kept her eyes closed and a bitter joy made her tremble: *I am afraid too,* she thought. Her entire life had taken refuge in her right side. She leaned towards Pierre without opening her eyes. The slightest effort would be enough and she would enter this tragic world for the first time. *I'm afraid of the statues,* she thought. It was a violent, blind affirmation, an incantation. She wanted to believe in their presence with all her strength. She tried to make a new sense, a sense of touch out of the anguish which paralysed her right side. She *felt* their passage in her arm, in her side and shoulder.

The statues flew low and gently; they buzzed. Eve knew that they had an evil look and that eyelashes stuck out from the stone around their eyes; but she pictured them badly. She knew, too, that they were not quite alive but that slabs of flesh, warm scales appeared on their great bodies; the stone peeled from the ends of their fingers and their palms were eaten away. Eve could not *see* all that: she simply thought of enormous women sliding against her, solemn and grotesque, with a human look and compact heads of stone. *They are bending over Pierre* — Eve made such a violent effort that her hands began trembling — *they are bending over me.* A horrible cry suddenly chilled her. They had touched him. She opened her eyes: Pierre's head was in his hands, he was breathing heavily. Eve felt exhausted: *a game,* she thought with remorse; *it was only a game. I didn't sincerely believe it for an instant. And all that time he suffered as if it were real.*

Pierre relaxed and breathed freely. But his pupils were strangely dilated and he was perspiring.

"Did you see them?" he asked.

"I can't see them."

"Better for you. They'd frighten you," he said. "I am used to them."

Eve's hands were still shaking and the blood had rushed to her head. Pierre took a cigarette from his pocket and brought it up to his mouth. But he did not light it:

"I don't care whether I see them or not," he said. "but I don't want them to touch me: I'm afraid they'll give me pimples."

He thought for an instant, then asked, "Did you hear them?"

"Yes," Eve said, "it's like an airplane engine." (Pierre had told her this the previous Sunday.)

Pierre smiled with condescension. "You exaggerate," he said. But he was still pale. He looked at Eve's hands. "Your hands are trembling. That made quite an impression on you, my poor Agatha. But don't worry. They won't come back again before tomorrow." Eve could not speak. Her teeth were chattering and she was afraid Pierre would notice it. Pierre watched her for a long time.

"You're tremendously beautiful," he said, nodding his head. "It's too bad, too bad."

He put out his hand quickly and toyed with her ear. "My lovely devil-woman. You disturb me a little, you are too beautiful: that distracts me. If it weren't a question of recapitulation . . ."

He stopped and looked at Eve with surprise.

"That's not the word . . . it came . . . it came," he said, smiling vaguely. "I had another on the tip of my tongue . . . but this one . . . came in its place. I forget what I was telling you."

He thought for a moment, then shook his head.

"Come," he said, "I want to sleep." He added in a childish voice, "You know, Agatha, I'm tired. I can't collect my thoughts any more."

He threw away his cigarette and looked at the rug anxiously. Eve slipped a pillow under his head.

"You can sleep too," he told her, "they won't be back." . . . *Recapitulation* . . .

Pierre was asleep, a candid, half-smile on his face; his head was turned to one side: one might have thought he wanted to caress his cheek with his shoulder. Eve was not sleepy, she was thoughtful: *Recapitulation.* Pierre had suddenly looked stupid and the word had slipped out of his mouth, long and whitish. Pierre had stared ahead of him in astonishment, as if he had seen the word and didn't recognize it; his mouth was open, soft: something seemed broken in it. He stammered. *That's the first time it ever happened to him: he noticed it, too. He said he couldn't collect his thoughts any more.* Pierre gave a voluptuous little whimper and his hand made a vague movement. Eve watched him harshly: *how is he going to wake up.* It gnawed at her. As soon as Pierre was asleep she had to think about it. She was afraid he would wake up wild-eyed and stammering. *I'm stupid,* she thought, *it can't start before a year; Franchot said so.* But the anguish did not leave her; a year: a winter, a springtime, a summer, the beginning of another autumn. One day his features would grow confused, his jaw would hang loose, he would half open his weeping eyes. Eve bent over Pierre's hand and pressed her lips against it: *I'll kill you before that.*

Translated by Lloyd Alexander

DEBORAH BLAU

Joanne Greenberg

Doctor Fried got up from her chair and went to the window. It faced away from the hospital buildings and over a small garden beyond which lay the grounds where the patients walked. She looked at the report in her hand. Against the weight of three typewritten pages were balanced the lectures she would not be able to give, the writing she would have to neglect, and the counseling of doctors that she would have to refuse if she took this case. She liked working with patients. Their very illness made them examine sanity as few "sane" people could. Kept from loving, sharing, and simple communication, they often hungered for it with a purity of passion that she saw as beautiful.

Sometimes, she thought ruefully, the world is so much sicker than the inmates of its institutions. She remembered Tilda, in the hospital in Germany, at a time when Hitler was on the other side of its walls and not even she could say which side was sane. Tilda's murderous hate, bound down on beds, tube-fed, and drugged into submission, could still fade long enough to let the light in now and then. She remembered Tilda looking up at her, smiling in a travesty of genteel politeness from the canvas-bound bed, and saying, "Oh, do come in, dear Doctor. You are just in time for the patient's soothing tea and the end of the world."

Tilda and Hitler were both gone and now there was more and more to tell the younger doctors who were coming out of the schools with too little experience of life. Is it fair to take private patients when any real improvement may take years, and when thousands and tens of thousands are clamoring, writing, phoning, and begging for help? She laughed, catching in herself the vanity she had once called the doctor's greatest enemy next to his patient's illness. If one by one was good enough for God, it would have to do for her.

She sat down with the folder, opened it, and read it through:

BLAU, DEBORAH F. 16 yrs. PREV. HOSP. None
INITIAL DIAG: SCHIZOPHRENIA.
1. *Testing:* Tests show high (140-150) intelligence, but patterns disturbed by illness. Many questions misinterpreted and overpersonalized. Entire subjective reaction to interview and testing. Personality tests show typically schizophrenic pattern with compulsive and masochistic component.

2. *Interview (Initial):* On admission patient appeared well oriented and logical in her thinking, but as the interview went on, bits of the logic began to fall away and at anything which could be construed as correction or criticism, she showed extreme anxiety. She did everything she

could to impress examiner with her wit, using it as a formidable defense. On three occasions she laughed inappropriately: once when she
claimed that the hospitalization had been brought about by a suicide
attempt, twice with reference to questions about the date of the month.
As the interview proceeded her attitude changed and she began to
speak loudly, giving random happenings in her life which she thought
to be the cause of her illness. She mentioned an operation at the age of
five, the effects of which were traumatic, a cruel babysitter, etc. The
incidents were unrelated, and no pattern appeared in them. Suddenly,
in the middle of recounting an incident, the patient started forward and
said accusingly, "I told you the truth about these things—now are you
going to help me?" It was considered advisable to terminate the interview.

3. *Family History:* Born Chicago, Ill. October, 1932. Breast-fed 8 mos.
One sibling, Susan, born 1937. Father, Jacob Blau, an accountant
whose family had emigrated from Poland 1913. Birth normal. At age 5
patient had two operations for removal of tumor in urethra. Difficult
financial situation made family move in with grandparents in suburb of
Chicago. Situation improved, but father became ill with ulcer and
hypertension. In 1942 war caused move to city. Patient made poor
adjustment and was taunted by schoolmates. Puberty normal physically, but at age 16 patient attempted suicide. There is a long history
hypochondria, but outside of tumor the physical health has been good.

She turned the page and glanced at the various statistical measurements
of personality factors and test scores. Sixteen was younger than any patient
she had ever had. Leaving aside consideration of the person herself, it might
be good to find out if someone with so little life experience could benefit
from therapy and be easier or harder to work with.

In the end it was the girl's age that decided her, and made the report weigh
more heavily than the commitment of doctors' meetings to be attended and
articles to be written.

"*Aber wenn wir*... If we succeed..." she murmured, forcing herself away
from her native tongue, "the good years yet to live..."

Again she looked at the facts and the numbers. A report like this had once
made her remark to the hospital psychologist, "We must someday make a
test to show us where the *health* is as well as the illness."

The psychologist had answered that with hypnotism and the ametyls and
pentothals such information could be obtained more easily.

"I do not think so,"Dr. Fried has answered. "The *hidden* strength is too
deep a secret. But in the end... in the end it is our only ally."

****

For a time — how long by Earth's reckoning Deborah did not know — it was peaceful. The world made few demands so that it seemed once more as if it had been the world's pressures that had caused so much of the agony in Yr. Sometimes she was able to see "reality" from Yr as if the partition between them were only gauze. On such occasions her name became Januce, because she felt like two-faced Janus — with a face on each world. It had been her letting slip this name which had caused the first trouble in school. She had been living by the Secret Calendar (Yr did not measure time as the world did) and had returned to the Heavy Calendar in the middle of the day, and having then that wonderful and omniscient feeling of changing, she had headed a class paper: NOW JANUCE. The teacher had said, "Deborah, what is this mark on your paper? What is this word, Januce?"

And, as the teacher stood by her desk, some nightmare terror coming to life had risen in the day-sane schoolroom. Deborah had looked about and found that she could not see except in outlines, gray against gray, and with no depth, but flatly, like a picture. The mark on the paper was the emblem of coming from Yr's time to Earth's, but, being caught while still in transition, she had to answer for both of them. Such an answer would have been the unveiling of a horror — a horror from which she would not have awakened rationally; and so she had lied and dissembled, with her heart choking her. Such a danger must no more be allowed aloud, and so that night the whole Great Collect had come crowding into the Midworld: gods and demons from Yr and shades from Earth, and they had set up over their kingdoms a Censor to stand between Deborah's speech and actions and to guard the secret of Yr's existence.

Over the years the power of the Censor had grown greater and greater, and it was he who had lately thrust himself into both worlds, so that sometimes no speech and no action escaped him. One whisper of a secret name, one sign written, one slip of light could break into the hidden place and destroy her and both the worlds forever.

On Earth the life of the hospital moved on. Deborah worked in the craft shop, grateful that the world also offered its hiding places. She learned to do basketwork, accepting the instruction in her acerbic and impatient way. She knew that none of the workers liked her. People never had. On the ward a large girl had asked her to play tennis and the shock had sounded down to the last level of Yr. She saw the pencil-doctor a few more times and learned that he was "ward administrator" and the one who gave permission for "privileges" — steps in similitude to the normal world — to get up and go out on the ward, to go to dinner, on the grounds, then out of the hospital itself to the movie or store. Each was a privilege and had a certain connotation of approval that seemed to be expressed in distances. To Deborah he gave permission to walk unrestricted on the grounds, but not outside. Deborah said to the large girl, whose name was Carla, "Well, I'm a hundred square yards sane." If there were such things as man-hours and light-years, surely there was foot-sanity.

Carla said, "Don't worry. You'll get more privileges soon. If you work hard with your doctor, they ease up a little. I just wonder how long I'll have to stay here. It's been three months already." They both thought of the women at the far end of the ward. All of them had been in the hospital for over two years.

"Does anyone ever leave?" Deborah asked. "I mean be well and leave?"

"I don't know," said Carla.

They asked a nurse.

"I don't know," she said, "I haven't been here that long."

There was a groan from Lactamaeon, the black god, and a derisive laugh from the Collect, which were the massed images of all of the teachers and relatives and schoolmates standing eternally in secret judgment and giving their endless curses.

Forever, crazy girl! Forever, lazy girl!

Later, one of the little student nurses came to where Deborah was lying, looking at the ceiling.

"It's time to get up now," she said in the wavering and frightened voice of her inexperience. There was a new group of these students working out their psychiatric training in this place. Deborah sighed and got up dutifully, thinking: She is astounded at the haze of craziness with which I fill a room.

"Come on now," the student said. "The doctor is going to see you. She's one of the heads here and a very famous doctor, too, so we must hurry, Miss Blau."

"If she's that good, I'll wear my shoes," Deborah replied, watching the young woman's expression widen with surprise and her face fight with its look of disapproval. She must have been told not to show anything so strong as anger or fear or amusement.

"You really should be grateful," the student said. "You're very lucky to get to see her at all."

"Known and loved by madmen the world over," Deborah said. "Let's go."

The nurse unlocked the ward door and then the stairway door, and they went down to the lower floor, which was open, and out of the back of the building. The nurse pointed to a green-shuttered white house—a small-town, oak-lined-streets type of white house—standing incongruously just inside the hospital grounds. They went to the front door and rang. After a while a tiny, gray-haired, plump little woman answered the door. "We're from Admissions. Here she is," the nurse said.

"Can you come back for her in an hour?" the little woman said to the student.

"I'm supposed to wait."

"Very well."

As Deborah stepped through the door, the Censor began to thrum his warnings: *Where is the doctor? Is she watching from behind a door somewhere?* The little housekeeper motioned toward a room.

"Where is the doctor?" Deborah said, trying to stop the rapid juxtaposition of walls and doors.

"I am the doctor," the woman said. "I thought you knew. I am Dr. Fried."

Anterrabae laughed, falling and falling in his darkness. *What a disguise!* And the Censor growled, *Take care... take care.*

They went into a sunny room and the Housekeeper-Famous-Doctor turned, saying, "Sit down. Make yourself comfortable." There came a great exhaustion and when the doctor said, "Is there anything you want to tell me?" a great gust of anger, so that Deborah stood up quickly and said to her and to Yr and to the Collect and to the Censor, "All right—you'll ask me questions and I'll answer them—you'll clear up my 'symptoms' and send me home...*and what will I have then?*"

The doctor said quietly, "If you did not really want to give them up, you wouldn't tell me." A rope of fear pulled its noose about Deborah. "Come, sit down. You will not have to give up anything until you are ready, and then there will be something to take its place."

Deborah sat down, while the Censor said in Yri: *Listen, Bird-one; there are too many little tables in here. The tables have no defense against your clumsiness.*

"Do you know why you are here?" the doctor said.

"Clumsiness. Clumsiness is first and then we have a list: lazy, wayward, headstrong, self-centered, fat, ugly, mean, tactless, and cruel. Also a liar. That category includes subheads: (a) False blindness, imaginary pains causing real doubling-up, untrue lapses of hearing, lying leg injuries, fake dizziness, and unproved and malicious malingerings; (b) Being a bad sport. Did I leave out unfriendliness?...Also unfriendliness."

In the silence where the dust motes fell through the sun shaft, Deborah thought that she had perhaps spoken her true feelings for the first time. If these things were so, so be it, and she would leave this office at least having stated her tiredness and disgust at the whole dark and anguish-running world.

The doctor said simply, "Well, that seems to be quite a list. Some of these, I think, are not so, but we have a job cut out for us."

"To make me friendly and sweet and agreeable and happy in the lies I tell."

"To help you to get well."

"To shut up the complaints."

"To end them, where they are the products of an upheaval in your feelings."

The rope tightened. Fear was flowing wildly in Deborah's head, turning her vision gray. "You're saying what they all say—phony complaints about nonexistent sicknesses."

"It seems to me that I said that you are very sick, indeed."

"Like the rest of them here?" It was as near as she dared go, already much too near the black places of terror.

"Do you mean to ask me if I think you belong here, if yours is what is called a mental illness? Then the answer is yes. I think you are sick in this way, but with your very hard work here and with a doctor's working hard with you, I think you can get better."

As bald as that. Yet with the terror connected with the hedged-about, circled-around word "crazy," the unspoken word that Deborah was thinking about now, there was a light coming from the doctor's spoken words, a kind of light that shone back on many rooms of the past. The home and the school and all of the doctors' offices ringing with the joyful accusation: There Is Nothing The Matter With You. Deborah had known for years and years that there was more than a little the matter—something deeply and gravely the matter, more even than the times of blindness, intense pain, lameness, terror, and the inability to remember anything at all might indicate. They had always said, "There is nothing the matter with you, if you would only..." Here at last was a vindication of all the angers in those offices.

The doctor said, "What are you thinking about? I see your face relax a little."

"I am thinking about the difference between a misdemeanor and a felony."

"How so?"

"The prisoner pleads guilty to the charge of not having acute something-itis and accepts the verdict of guilty of being nuts in the first degree."

"Perhaps in the second degree," the doctor said, smiling a little. "Not entirely voluntary nor entirely with forethought."

Deborah suddenly recalled the picture of her parents standing very single and yet together on the other side of the shatter-proof locked door. Not aforethought, this thing, but more than a little with malice.

Deborah became aware of the nurse moving about in the other room as if to let them know that the time was up.

The doctor said, "If it's all right with you, we will make another appointment and begin our talks, because I believe that you and I, if we work like the devil together, can beat this thing. First, I want to tell you again that I will not pull away symptoms or sickness from you against your will."

Deborah shied away from the commitment, but she allowed her face a very guarded "yes," and the doctor saw it. They walked from the office with Deborah striving assiduously to act as if she were somewhere else, elaborately unconcerned with this present place and person.

"Tomorrow at the same time," the doctor told the nurse and the patient.

"She can't understand you," Deborah said, "Charon spoke in Greek."

Dr. Fried laughed a little and then her face turned grave. "Someday I hope to help you see this world as other than a Stygian hell."

They turned and left, and Charon, in white cap and striped uniform, guided the removed spirit toward the locked ward. Dr. Fried watched them walking back to the large building and thought: Somewhere in that precocity and bitterness and somewhere in the illness, whose limits she could not yet define, lay a hidden strength. It was there and working; it had sounded in the glimmer of relief when the fact of the sickness was made plain, and most of all in the "suicide attempt," the cry of a mute for help, and the statement, bold and dramatic as adolescents and the still-fighting sick must always make it, that the game was over and the disguising ended. The fact of this mental illness was in the open now, but the disease itself had roots still as deeply hidden as the white core of a volcano whose slopes are camouflaged in wooded green. Somewhere, even under the volcano itself, was the buried seed of will and strength. Dr. Fried sighed and went back to her work.

"This time . . .this time can I only call it forth!" she sighed, lapsing into the grammar of her native tongue.

SILENT SNOW, SECRET SNOW
Conrad Aiken

Just why it should have happened, or why it should have happened just when it did, he could not, of course, possibly have said; nor perhaps would it even have occurred to him to ask. The thing was above all a secret, something to be preciously concealed from Mother and Father; and to that very fact it owed an enormous part of its deliciousness. It was like a peculiarly beautiful trinket to be carried unmentioned in one's trouser pocket — a rare stamp, an old coin, a few tiny gold links found trodden out of shape on the path in the park, a pebble of carnelian, a sea shell distinguishable from all others by an unusual spot or stripe — and, as if it were any one of these, he carried around with him everywhere a warm and persistent and increasingly beautiful sense of possession. Nor was it only a sense of possession — it was also a sense of protection. It was as if, in some delightful way, his secret gave him a fortress, a wall behind which he could retreat into heavenly seclusion. This was almost the first thing he had noticed about it — apart from the oddness of the thing itself — and it was this that now again, for the fiftieth time, occurred to him, as he sat in the little schoolroom. It was the half-hour for geography. Miss Buell was revolving with one finger, slowly, a huge terrestrial globe which had been placed on her desk. The green and yellow continents passed and repassed, questions were asked and answered, and now the little girl in front of him, Deirdre, who had a funny little constellation of freckles on the back of her neck, exactly like the Big Dipper, was standing up and telling Miss Buell that the equator was the line that ran round the middle.

Miss Buell's face, which was old and grayish and kindly, with gray stiff curls beside the cheeks, and eyes that swam very brightly, like little minnows, behind thick glasses, wrinkled itself into a complication of amusements.

"Ah! I see. The earth is wearing a belt, or a sash. Or someone drew a line round it!"

"Oh no — not that — I mean — "

In the general laughter, he did not share, or only a very little. He was thinking about the Arctic and Antarctic regions, which of course, on the globe, where white. Miss Buell was now telling them about the tropics, the jungles, the steamy heat of equatorial swamps, where the birds and butterflies, and even the snakes, were like living jewels. As he listened to these things, he was already, with a pleasant sense of half-effort, putting his secret between himself and the words. Was it really an effort at all? For effort implied something voluntary, and perhaps even something one did not especially want; whereas this was distinctly pleasant, and came almost of its own accord. All he needed to do was to think of that morning, the first one, and then of all the others—

But it was all so absurdly simple! It had amounted to so little. It was nothing, just an idea — and just why it should have become so wonderful, so permanent, was a mystery — a very pleasant one, to be sure, but also, in an amusing way, foolish. However, without ceasing to listen to Miss Buell, who had now moved up to the north temperate zones, he deliberately invited his memory of the first morning. It was only a moment or two after he had waked up — or perhaps the moment itself. But was there, to be exact, an exact moment? Was one awake all at once? or was it gradual? Anyway, it was after he had stretched a lazy hand up towards the headrail, and yawned, and then relaxed again among his warm covers, all the more grateful on a December morning, that the thing had happened. Suddenly, for no reason, he had thought of the postman, he remembered the postman. Perhaps there was nothing so odd in that. After all, he heard the postman almost every morning in his life — his heavy boots could be heard clumping round the corner at the top of the little cobbled hill-street, and then, progressively nearer, progressively louder, the double knock at each door, the crossings and re-crossings of the street, till finally the clumsy steps came stumbling across to the very door, and the tremendous knock came which shook the house itself.

(Miss Buell was saying, "Vast wheat-growing areas in North America and Siberia."

Deirdre had for the moment placed her left hand across the back of her neck.)

But on this particular morning, the first morning, as he lay there with his eyes closed, he had for some reason *waited* for the postman. He wanted to hear him come round the corner. And that was precisely the joke—he never did. He never came. He never had come — *round the corner* — again. For when at last the steps *were* heard, they had already, he was quite sure, come a little down the hill, to the first house; and even so, the steps were curiously different—they were softer, they had a new secrecy about them, they were muffled and indistinct; and while the rhythm of them was the same, it now said a new thing—it said peace, it said remoteness, it said cold, it said sleep. And he had understood the situation at once — nothing could have seemed simpler — there had been snow in the night, such as all winter he had been longing for; and it was this which had rendered the postman's first footsteps inaudible, and the later ones faint. Of course! How lovely! And even now it must be snowing—it was going to be a snowy day—the long white ragged lines were drifting and sifting across the street, across the faces of the old houses, whispering and hushing, making little triangles of white in the corners between cobblestones, seething a little when the wind blew them over the ground to a drifted corner; and so it would be all day, getting deeper and deeper and silenter and silenter.

(Miss Buell was saying, "Land of perpetual snow.")

All this time, of course (while he lay in bed), he had kept his eyes closed, listening to the nearer progress of the postman, the muffled footsteps thumping and slipping on the snow-sheathed cobbles; and all the other sounds— the double knocks, a frosty far-off voice or two, a bell ringing thinly and softly as if under a sheet of ice — had the same slightly abstracted quality, as if removed by one degree from actuality — as if everything in the world had been insulated by snow. But when at last, pleased, he opened his eyes, and turned towards the window, to see for himself this long-desired and now so clearly imagined miracle — what he saw instead was brilliant sunlight on a roof; and when, astonished, he jumped out of bed and stared down into the street, expecting to see the cobbles obliterated by the snow, he saw nothing but the bare bright cobbles themselves.

Queer, the effect this extraordinary surprise had had upon him — all the following morning he had kept with him a sense of snow falling about him, a secret screen of new snow between himself and the world. If he had not dreamed such a thing—and how could he have dreamed it while awake?— how else could one explain it? In any case, the delusion had been so vivid as to affect his entire behavior. He could not now remember whether it was on the first or the second morning—or was it even the third?—that his mother had drawn attention to some oddness in his manner.

"But my darling"—she had said at the breakfast table—"what has come over you? You don't seem to be listening..."

And how often that very thing had happened since!

(Miss Buell was now asking if anyone knew the difference between the North Pole and the Magnetic Pole. Deirdre was holding up her flickering brown hand, and he could see the four white dimples that marked the knuckles.)

Perhaps it hadn't been either the second or third morning — or even the fourth or fifth. How could he be sure? How could he be sure just when the delicious *progress* had become clear? Just when it had really *begun?* The intervals weren't very precise....All he now knew was, that at some point or other — perhaps the second day, perhaps the sixth — he had noticed that the presence of the snow was a little more insistent, the sound of it clearer; and, conversely, the sound of the postman's footsteps more indistinct. Not only could he not hear the steps come around the corner, he could not even hear them at the first house. It was below the first house that he heard them; and then, a few days later, it was below the second house that he heard them; and a few days later again, below the third. Gradually, gradually, the snow was becoming heavier, the sound of its seething louder, the cobblestones more and more muffled. When he found, each morning, on going to the window, after the ritual of listening, that the roofs and cobbles were as bare as ever, it made no difference. This was, after all, only what he had expected. It was even what pleased him, what rewarded him: the thing was his own, belonged to no one else. No one else knew about it, not even his mother and father. There, outside, were the bare cobbles; and here, inside, was the snow. Snow growing heavier each day, muffling the world, hiding the ugly, and deadening increasingly — above all — the steps of the postman.

"But, my darling" — she said at the luncheon table — "what has come over you? You don't seem to listen when people speak to you. That's the third time I've asked you to pass your plate...."

How was one to explain this to Mother? or to Father? There was, of course, nothing to be done about it: nothing. All one could do was to laugh embarrassedly, pretend to be a little ashamed, apologize, and take a sudden and somewhat disingenuous interest in what was being done or said. The cat had stayed out all night. He had a curious swelling on his left cheek — perhaps somebody had kicked him, or a stone had struck him. Mrs. Kempton was or was not coming to tea. The house was going to be house cleaned, or "turned out," on Wednesday instead of Friday. A new lamp was provided for his evening work — perhaps it was eyestrain which accounted for this new and so peculiar vagueness of his — Mother was looking at him with amusement as she said this, but with something else as well. A new lamp? A new lamp. Yes, Mother, No, Mother, Yes, Mother. School is going very well. The geometry is very easy. The history is very dull. The geography is very interesting — particularly when it takes one to the North Pole. Why the

North Pole? Oh, well, it would be fun to be an explorer. Another Peary or Scott or Shackleton. And then abruptly he found his interest in the talk at an end, stared at the pudding on his plate, listened, waited and began once more — ah, how heavenly, too, the first beginnings — to hear or feel — for could he actually hear it? — the silent snow, the secret snow.

(Miss Buell was telling them about the search for the Northwest Passage, about Hendrik Hudson, the *Half Moon.*)

This had been, indeed, the only distressing feature of the new experience; the fact that it so increasingly had brought him into a kind of mute misunderstanding, or even conflict, with his father and mother. It was as if he were trying to lead a double life. On the one hand, he had to be Paul Hasleman, and keep up the appearance of being that person—dress, wash, and answer intelligently when spoken to — ; on the other, he had to explore this new world which had been opened to him. Nor could there be the slightest doubt — not the slightest — that the new world was the profounder and more wonderful of the two. It was irresistible. It was miraculous. Its beauty was simply beyond anything— beyond speech as beyond thought— utterly incommunicable. But how then, between the two worlds, of which he was thus constantly aware, was he to keep a balance? One must get up, one must go to breakfast, one must talk with Mother, go to school, do one's lessons— and, in all this, try not to appear too much of a fool. But if all the while one was also trying to extract the full deliciousness of another and quite separate existence, one which could not easily (if at all) be spoken of—how was one to manage? How was one to explain? Would it be safe to explain? Would it be absurd? Would it merely mean that he would get into some obscure kind of trouble?

These thoughts came and went, came and went, as softly and secretly as the snow; they were not precisely a disturbance, perhaps they were even a pleasure; he liked to have them; their presence was something almost palpable, something he could stroke with his hand, without closing his eyes, and without ceasing to see Miss Buell and the schoolroom and the globe and the freckles on Deirdre's neck; nevertheless he did in a sense cease to see, or to see the obvious external world, and substituted for this vision the vision of snow, the sound of snow, and the slow, almost soundless, approach of the postman. Yesterday, it had been only at the sixth house that the postman had become audible; the snow was much deeper now, it was falling more swiftly and heavily, the sound of its seething was more distinct, more soothing, more persistent. And this morning, it had been — as nearly as he could figure—just above the seventh house—perhaps only a step or two above; at most, he had heard two or three footsteps before the knock had sounded.... And with each such narrowing of the sphere, each nearer approach of the limit at which the postman was first audible, it was odd how sharply was increased the amount of illusion which had to be carried into the ordinary business of daily life. Each day, it was harder to get out of bed, to go to the window, to look out at the — as always — perfectly empty and snowless street. Each day it was more difficult to go through the perfunctory motions of greeting Mother and Father at breakfast, to reply to their questions, to put his books together and go to school. And at school, how extraordinarily hard to conduct with success simultaneously the public life and the life that was secret! There were times when he longed — positively ached — to tell everyone about it — to burst out with it — only to be checked almost at once by a far-off feeling as of some faint absurdity which was inherent in it — but *was* it absurd? — and more importantly by a sense of mysterious power in his very secrecy. Yes; it must be kept secret. That, more and more, became clear. At whatever cost to himself, whatever pain to others——

(Miss Buell looked straight at him, smiling, and said "Perhaps we'll ask Paul. I'm sure Paul will come out of his daydream long enough to be able to tell us. Won't you Paul?" He rose slowly from his chair, resting one hand on the brightly varnished desk, and deliberately stared through the snow toward the blackboard. It was an effort, but it was amusing to make it. "Yes," he said slowly, "It was what we now call the Hudson River. This he thought to be the Northwest Passage. He was disappointed." He sat down again, and as he did so Deirdre half turned in her chair and gave him a shy smile, of approval and admiration.)

At whatever pain to others.

This part of it was very puzzling, very puzzling. Mother was very nice, and so was Father. Yes, that was all true enough. He wanted to be nice to them, to tell them everything — and yet, was it really wrong of him to want to have a secret place of his own?

At bed-time, the night before, Mother had said, "If this goes on my lad, we'll have to see a doctor, we will! We can't have our boy — " But what was it she had said? "Live in another world"? "Live so far away"? The word "far" had been in it, he was sure, and then Mother had taken up a magazine again and laughed a little but with an expression which wasn't mirthful. He had felt sorry for her....

The bell rang for dismissal. The sound came to him through long curved parallels of falling snow. He saw Deirdre rise, and had himself risen almost as soon — but not quite as soon — as she.

2

On the walk homeward, which was timeless, it pleased him to see through the accompaniment, or counterpoint, of snow, the items of mere externality on his way. There were many kinds of brick in the sidewalks, and laid in many kinds of patterns. The garden walls, too, were various, some of wooden palings, some of plaster, some of stone. Twigs of bushes leaned over the walls: the little hard green winter-buds of lilac, on gray stems, sheathed and fat; other branches very thin and fine and black and desiccated. Dirty sparrows huddled in the bushes, as dull in color as dead fruit left in leafless trees. A single starling creaked on a weather vane. In the gutter, beside a drain, was a scrap of torn and dirty newspaper, caught in a little delta of filth; the word ECZEMA appeared in large capitals, and below it was a letter from Mrs. Amelia D. Cravath, 2100 Pine Street, Fort Worth, Texas, to the effect that after being a sufferer for years she had been cured by Caley's Ointment. In the little delta, beside the fan-shaped and deeply runneled continent of brown mud, were lost twigs, descended from their parent trees, dead matches, a rusty horse-chestnut burr, a small concentration of sparkling gravel on the lip of the sewer, a fragment of eggshell, a streak of yellow sawdust which had been wet and now was dry and congealed, a brown pebble, and a broken feather. Farther on was a cement sidewalk, ruled into geometrical parallelograms, with a brass inlay at one end commemorating the contractors who had laid it, and halfway across, an irregular and random series of dog-tracks, immortalized in synthetic stone. He knew these well, and always stepped on them; to cover the little hollows with his own foot had always been a queer pleasure; today he did it once more, but perfunctorily and detachedly, all the while thinking of something else. That was a dog, a long time ago, who had made a mistake and walked on the cement while it was still wet. He had probably wagged his tail, but that hadn't been recorded. Now, Paul Hasleman, aged twelve, on his way home from school, crossed the same river, which in the meantime had frozen into rock. Homeward through the snow, the snow falling in bright sunshine. Homeward?

Then came the gateway with the two posts surmounted by egg-shaped stones which had been cunningly balanced on their ends, as if by Columbus, and mortared in the very act of balance; a source of perpetual wonder. On the brick wall just beyond, the letter H had been stenciled, presumably for some purpose. H? H.

The green hydrant, with a little green-painted chain attached to the brass screw-cap.

The elm tree, with the great gray wound in the bark, kidney-shaped, into which he always put his hand—to feel the cold but living wood. The injury, he had been sure, was due to the gnawings of a tethered horse. But now it deserved only a passing palm, a merely tolerant eye. There were more important things. Miracles. Beyond the thoughts of trees, mere elms. Beyond the thoughts of sidewalks, mere stone, mere brick, mere cement. Beyond the thoughts even of his own shoes, which trod these sidewalks obediently bearing a burden — far above — of elaborate mystery. He watched them. They were not very well polished; he had neglected them, for a very good reason: they were one of the many parts of the increasing difficulty of the daily return to daily life, the morning struggle. To get up, having at last opened one's eyes, to go to the window, and discover no snow, to wash, to dress, to descend the curving stairs to breakfast——

At whatever pain to others, nevertheless, one must persevere in severance, since the incommunicability of the experience demanded it. It was desirable, of course, to be kind to Mother and Father, especially as they seemed to be worried, but it was also desirable to be resolute. If they should decide—as appeared likely—to consult the doctor, Doctor Howells, and have Paul inspected, his heart listened to through a kind of dictaphone, his lungs, his stomach—well, that was all right. He would go through with it. He would give them answer for question, too — perhaps such answers as they hadn't expected? No. That would never do. For the secret world must, at all costs, be preserved.

The bird-house in the apple tree was empty — it was the wrong time of year for wrens. The little round black door had lost its pleasure. The wrens were enjoying other houses, other nests, remoter trees. But this too was a notion which he only vaguely and grazingly entertained—as if, for the moment, he merely touched an edge of it; there was something further on, which was already assuming a sharper importance; something which already teased at the corners of his eyes, teasing also at the corner of his mind. It was funny to think that he so wanted this, so awaited it—and yet found himself enjoying this momentary dalliance with the bird-house, as if for a quite deliberate postponement and enhancement of the approaching pleasure. He was aware of his delay, of his smiling and detached and now almost uncomprehending gaze at the little bird-house; he knew what he was going to look at next: it was his own little cobbled hill-street, his own house, the little river at the bottom of the hill, the grocer's shop with the cardboard man in the window—and now, thinking of all this, he turned his head, still smiling, and looking quickly right and left through the snow-laden sunlight.

And the mist of snow, as he had foreseen, was still on it—a ghost of snow falling in the bright sunlight, softly and steadily floating and turning and pausing, soundlessly meeting the snow that covered, as with a transparent mirage, the bare bright cobbles. He loved it — he stood still and loved it. Its beauty was paralyzing — beyond all words, all experience, all dream. No fairy story he had ever read could be compared with it — none had ever given him this extraordinary combination of ethereal loveliness with a something else, unnameable, which was just faintly and deliciously terrifying. What was this thing? As he thought of it, he looked upward toward his own bedroom window, which was open—and it was as if he looked straight into the room and saw himself lying half awake in his bed. There he was—at this very instant he was still perhaps actually there—more truly there than standing here at the edge of the cobbled hill-street, with one hand lifted to shade his eyes against the snow-sun. Had he indeed ever left his room, in all this time? since that very first morning? Was the whole progress still being enacted there, was it still the same morning, and himself not yet wholly awake? And even now, had the postman not yet come round the corner?...

This idea amused him, and automatically, as he thought of it, he turned his head and looked toward the top of the hill. There was, of course, nothing there — nothing and no one. The street was empty and quiet. And all the more because of its emptiness it occurred to him to count the houses — a thing which, oddly enough, he hadn't before thought of doing. Of course, he had known there weren't many—many, that is, on his own side of the street, which were the ones that figured in the postman's progress—but nevertheless it came as something of a shock to find that there were precisely six, above his own house — his own house was the seventh.

Six!

Astonished, he looked at his own house — looked at the door, on which was the number thirteen—and then realized that the whole thing was exactly and logically and absurdly what he ought to have known. Just the same, the realization gave him abruptly, and even a little frighteningly, a sense of hurry. He was being hurried—he was being rushed. For—he knit his brow— he couldn't be mistaken — it was just above the *seventh* house, his *own* house, that the postman had first been audible this very morning. But in that case—in that case—did it mean that tomorrow he would hear nothing? The knock he had heard must have been the knock of their own door. Did it mean—and this was an idea which gave him a really extraordinary feeling of surprise — that he would never hear the postman again? — that tomorrow morning the postman would already have passed the house, in a snow so deep as to render his footsteps completely inaudible? That he would have made his approach down the snow-filled street so soundlessly, so secretly, that he, Paul Hasleman, there lying in bed, would not have waked in time, or waking, would have heard nothing?

But how could that be? Unless even the knocker should be muffled in the snow— frozen tight, perhaps?...But in that case—

A vague feeling of disappointment came over him; a vague sadness as if he felt himself deprived of something which he had long looked forward to, something much prized. After all this, all this beautiful progress, the slow delicious advance of the postman through the silent and secret snow, the knock creeping closer each day, and the footsteps nearer, the audible compass of the world thus daily narrowed, narrowed, narrowed, as the snow soothingly and beautifully encroached and deepened, after all this, was he to be defrauded of the one thing he had so wanted—to be able to count, as it were, the last two or three solemn footsteps, as they finally approached his own door? Was it all going to happen, at the end, so suddenly? or indeed, had it already happened? with no slow and subtle gradations of menace, in which he could luxuriate?

He gazed upward again, toward his own window which flashed in the sun; and this time almost with a feeling that it would be better if he *were* still in bed, in that room; for in that case this must still be the first morning, and there would be six more mornings to come — or, for that matter, seven or eight or nine — how could he be sure? — or even more.

3

After supper, the inquisition began. He stood before the doctor, under the lamp, and submitted silently to the usual thumpings and tappings.

"Now will you please say 'Ah!'?"

"Ah!"

"Now again, please, if you don't mind."

"Ah!"

"Say it slowly, and hold it if you can——"

"Ah-h-h-h-h-h —— "

"Good."

How silly all this was. As if it had anything to do with his throat! Or his heart, or lungs!

Relaxing his mouth, of which the corners, after all this absurd stretching, felt uncomfortable, he avoided the doctor's eyes, and stared toward the fireplace, past his mother's feet (in gray slippers) which projected from the green chair, and his father's feet (in brown slippers) which stood neatly side by side on the hearth rug.

"Hm. There is certainly nothing wrong there . . .?"

He felt the doctor's eyes fixed upon him, and, as if merely to be polite, returned the look, but with a feeling of justifiable evasiveness.

"Now, young man, tell me — do you feel all right?"

"Yes, sir, quite all right."

"No headaches? no dizziness?"

"No, I don't think so."

"Let me see. Let's get a book, if you don't mind — yes, thank you, that will do splendidly — and now, Paul, if you'll just read it, holding it as you would normally hold it —— "

He took the book and read:

"And another praise have I to tell for this the city our mother, the gift of a great god, a glory of the land most high; the might of horses, the might of young horses, the might of the sea . . . .For thou, son of Cronus, our lord Poseidon, hath throned herein this pride, since in these roads first thou didst show forth the curb that cures the rage of steeds. And the shapely oar, apt to men's hands, hath a wondrous speed on the brine, following the hundred-footed Nereids . . . .O land that art praised above all lands, now is it for thee to make those bright praises seen in deeds."

He stopped, tentatively, and lowered the heavy book.

"No — as I thought — there is certainly no superficial sign of eyestrain."

Silence thronged the room, and he was aware of the focused scrutiny of the three people who confronted him . . . .

"We could have his eyes examined — but I believe it is something else."

"What could it be?" That was his father's voice.

"It's only the curious absent-mindedness—" This was his mother's voice. In the presence of the doctor, they both seemed irritatingly apologetic.

"I believe it is something else. Now Paul — I would like very much to ask you a question or two. You will answer them, won't you — you know I'm an old, old friend of yours, eh? That's right . . ."

His back was thumped twice by the doctor's fat fist — then the doctor was grinning at him with false amiability, while with one fingernail he was scratching the top button of his waistcoat. Beyond the doctor's shoulder was the fire, the fingers of flame making light prestidigitation against the sooty fireback, the soft sound of their random flutter the only sound.

"I would like to know — is there anything that worries you?"

The doctor was again smiling, his eyelids low against the little black pupils, in each of which was a tiny white bead of light. Why answer him? why answer him at all? "At whatever pain to others" — but it was all a nuisance, this necessity for resistance, this necessity for attention; it was as if one had been stood up on a brilliantly lighted stage, under a great round blaze of spotlight as if one were merely a trained seal, or a performing dog, or a fish, dipped out of an aquarium and held up by the tail. It would serve them right if he were merely to bark or growl. And meanwhile, to miss these last few precious hours, these hours of which each minute was more beautiful than the last, more menacing — ! He still looked, as if from a great distance, at the beads of light in the doctor's eyes, at the fixed false smile, and then, beyond, once more at his mother's slippers, his father's slippers, the soft flutter of the fire. Even here, even amongst these hostile presences, and in this arranged light, he could see the snow, he could hear it — it was in the corners of the room, where the shadow was deepest, under the sofa, behind the half-opened door which led to the dining room. It was gentler here, softer, its seethe the quietest of whispers, as if, in deference to a drawing room, it had quite deliberately put on its "manners"; it kept itself out of sight, obliterated itself, but distinctly with an air of saying, "Ah, but just wait! Wait till we are alone together! Then I will begin to tell you something new! Something white! something cold! something sleepy! something of cease, and peace, and the long bright curve of space! Tell them to go away, Banish them. Refuse to speak. Leave them, go upstairs to your room, turn out the light and get into bed — I will go with you, I will be waiting for you, I will tell you a better story than Little Kay of the Skates, or The Snow Ghost — I will surround your bed, I will close the windows, pile a deep drift against the door, so that none will ever again be able to enter. Speak to them!..." It seemed as if the little hissing voice came from a slow white spiral of falling flakes in the corner by the front window— but he could not be sure. He felt himself smiling, then, and said to the doctor, but without looking at him, looking beyond him still——

"Oh no, I think now——"

"But are you sure, my boy?"

His father's voice came softly and coldly then — the familiar voice of silken warning.

"You needn't answer at once, Paul— remember we're trying to help you — think it over and be quite sure, won't you?"

He felt himself smiling again, at the notion of being quite sure. What a joke! As if he weren't so sure that reassurance was no longer necessary, and all this cross-examination a ridiculous farce, a grotesque parody! What could they know about it? these gross intelligences, these humdrum minds so bound to the usual, the ordinary? Impossible to tell them about it! Why, even now, even now, with the proof so abundant, so formidable, so imminent, so appallingly present here in this very room, could they believe it? — could even his mother believe it? No — it was only too plain that if anything were said about it, the merest hint given, they would be incredulous— they would laugh — they would say "Absurd!" — think things about him which weren't true. . . .

"Why no, I'm not worried — why should I be?"

He looked then straight at the doctor's low-lidded eyes, looked from one of them to the other, from one bead of light to the other, and gave a little laugh.

The doctor seemed to be disconcerted by this. He drew back in his chair, resting a fat white hand on either knee. The smile faded slowly from his face.

"Well, Paul!" he said, and paused gravely, "I'm afraid you don't take this quite seriously enough. I think you perhaps don't quite realize — don't quite realize —" He took a deep quick breath and turned, as if helplessly, at a loss for words, to the others. But Mother and Father were both silent— no help was forthcoming.

"You must surely know, be aware, that you have not been quite yourself, of late? Don't you know that? . . ."

It was amusing to watch the doctor's renewed attempt at a smile, a queer disorganized look, as of confidential embarrassment.

"I feel all right, sir," he said, and again gave the little laugh.

"And we're trying to help you." The doctor's tone sharpened.

"Yes, sir, I know. But why? I'm all right. I'm just *thinking,* that's all."

His mother made a quick movement forward, resting a hand on the back of the doctor's chair.

"Thinking?" she said. "But my dear, about what?"

This was a direct challenge — and would have to be directly met. But before he met it, he looked again into the corner by the door, as if for reassurance. He smiled again at what he saw, at what he heard. The little spiral was still there, still softly whirling, like the ghost of a white kitten chasing the ghost of a white tail, and making as it did so the faintest of whispers. It was all right! If only he could remain firm, everything was going to be all right.

"Oh, about anything, about nothing — you know the way you do!"

"You mean — daydreaming?"

"Oh, no — thinking!"

"But thinking about what?"

"Anything."

He laughed a third time — but this time, happening to glance upward toward his mother's face, he was appalled at the effect his laughter seemed to have upon her. Her mouth had opened in an expression of horror. . . .This was too bad! Unfortunate! He had known it would cause pain, of course — but he hadn't expected it to be quite so bad as this. Perhaps — perhaps if he just gave them a tiny gleaming hint —— ?

"About the snow," he said.

"What on earth!" This was his father's voice. The brown slippers came a step nearer on the hearth-rug.

"But my dear, what do you mean?" This was his mother's voice.

The doctor merely stared.

"Just snow, that's all. I like to think about it."

"Tell us about it, my boy."

"But that's all it is. There's nothing to tell. You know what snow is?"

This he said almost angrily, for he felt that they were trying to corner him. He turned sideways so as no longer to face the doctor, and the better to see the inch of blackness between the window-sill and the lowered curtain — the cold inch of beckoning and delicious night. At once he felt better, more assured.

"Mother — can I go to bed, now, please? I've got a headache."

"But I thought you said——"

"It's just come. It's all these questions —! Can I, Mother?"

"You can go as soon as the doctor has finished."

"Don't you think this thing ought to be gone into thoroughly, and now?" This was Father's voice. The brown slippers again came a step nearer, the voice was the well-known "punishment" voice, resonant and cruel.

"Oh, what's the use, Norman——"

Quite suddenly, everyone was silent. And without precisely facing them, nevertheless he was aware that all three of them were watching him with an extraordinary intensity — staring hard at him — as if he had done something monstrous, or was himself some kind of monster. He could hear the soft irregular flutter of the flames; the cluck-click-cluck-click of the clock; far and faint, two sudden spurts of laughter from the kitchen, as quickly cut off as begun; a murmur of water in the pipes; and then, the silence seemed to deepen, to spread out, to become world-long and world-wide, to become timeless and shapeless, and to center inevitably and rightly, with a slow and sleepy but enormous concentration of all power, on the beginning of a new sound. What this new sound was going to be, he knew perfectly well. It might begin with a hiss, but it would end with a roar — there was no time to lose — he must escape. It mustn't happen here —

Without another word, he turned and ran up the stairs.

4

Not a moment too soon. The darkness was coming in long white waves. A prolonged sibilance filled the night — a great seamless seethe of wild influence went abruptly across it — a cold low humming shook the windows. He shut the door and flung off his clothes in the dark. The bare black floor was like a little raft tossed in waves of snow, almost overwhelmed, washed under whitely, up again, smothered in curled billows of feather. The snow was laughing; it spoke from all sides at once; it pressed closer to him as he ran and jumped exulting into his bed.

"Listen to us!" it said. "Listen! We have come to tell you the story we told you about. You remember? Lie down. Shut your eyes, now — you will no longer see much — in this white darkness who could see, or want to see? We will take the place of everything.... Listen——"

A beautiful varying dance of snow began at the front of the room, came forward and then retreated, flattened out toward the floor, then rose fountain-like to the ceiling, swayed, recruited itself from a new stream of flakes which poured laughing in through the humming window, advanced again, lifted long white arms. It said peace, it said remoteness, it said cold — it said ——

But then a gash of horrible light fell brutally across the room from the opening door — the snow drew back hissing — something alien had come into the room — something hostile. This thing rushed at him, clutched at him, shook him — and he was not merely horrified, he was filled with such a loathing as he had never known. What was this? this cruel disturbance? this act of anger and hate? It was as if he had to reach up a hand toward another world for any understanding of it — an effort of which he was only barely capable. But of that other world he still remembered just enough to know the exorcising words. They tore themselves from his other life suddenly ——

"Mother! Mother! Go away! I hate you!"

And with that effort, everything was solved, everything became all right: the seamless hiss advanced once more, the long white wavering lines rose and fell like enormous whispering sea-waves, the whisper becoming louder, the laughter more numerous.

"Listen!" it said. "We'll tell you the last, the most beautiful and secret story—shut your eyes—it is a very small story—a story that gets smaller and smaller — it comes inward instead of opening like a flower — it is a flower becoming a seed—a little cold seed—do you hear? We are leaning closer to you —— "

The hiss was now becoming a roar — the whole world was a vast moving screen of snow — but even now it said peace, it said remoteness, it said cold, it said sleep.

___ Paranoid Disorders

Individuals with a Paranoid Disorder cling to a belief that they are being persecuted or that their affections are being betrayed, even though there is no evidence for either delusion. Unlike schizophrenics, they have no hallucinations accompanying their delusions. Their delusions may not interfere with either their job or their intellectual functioning, but social and marital relationships are often impaired.

If the paranoids' delusions involve persecution, they feel they are being conspired against, followed, harassed, or cheated by other people. They may exaggerate an innocent social slight until it becomes the nucleus of their delusional system.

If the paranoids' delusions involve having their affections betrayed, they seek "evidence" that will confirm this belief, and they manage to find it. They will accept no other explanation for their "evidence"; it justifies their delusional system.

Either delusion feeds anger, resentment, and suspicion of others, often a particular person. When the delusion is fully developed into a system, these suppressed emotions may erupt into violence.

Paranoia and Shared Paranoid Disorder are two of the three Paranoid Disorders. (The third, Scute Paranoid Disorder, rarely becomes chronic and is usually seen in people who change their living accommodations or working conditions.) In Paranoia, the delusion (whether it springs from feelings of persecution or jealousy) develops gradually until it becomes a well-established system. As the system develops, there is no evidence of thought disorder. When the contents of the system are expressed in emotions and dehavior that follow logically from the delusion, Paranoia is revealed.

In Shared Paranoid Disorder *(Folie à deux),* one person accepts as valid the delusion of a close friend of spouse who has Paranoia. He or she shares the belief of being persecuted or betrayed, and the delusion becomes a full-fledged system. However, if the person without the initial disorder is separated from the Paranoid person, the delusional system diminishes or disappears.

Readers must participate in "My Last Duchess" because it is a dramatic monologue. They must try to hear the tone of voice that the Duke of Ferrara uses as he describes his dead wife to a marriage broker who represents the father of the Duke's next Duchess. Readers must try to see what the Duke and the agent see and feel what they feel. "The Cask of Amontillado" is less subtle than "My Last Duchess," but readers must remain involved. Through their involvement, readers should be able to identify the delusion in both selections, find specific evidence of logical thinking within each delusional system, and point out how the characters' emotions and behavior are consistent with their delusions.

Paranoia

MY LAST DUCHESS
Robert Browning
FERRARA

That's my last Duchess painted on the wall,
Looking as if she were alive, I call
That piece a wonder, now: Frà Pandolf's hands
Worked busily a day, and there she stands
Will't please you sit and look at her? I said
"Frà Pandolf" by design, for never read
Strangers like you that pictured countenance,
The depth and passion of its earnest glance,
But to myself they turned (since none puts by
The curtain I have drawn for you, but I)
And seemed as they would ask me, if they durst,
How such a glance came there; so, not the first
Are you to turn and ask thus Sir, 'twas not
Her husband's presence only, called that spot
Of joy into the Duchess' cheek: perhaps
Frà Pandolf chanced to say "Her mantle laps
Over my lady's wrist too much," or "Paint
Must never hope to reproduce the faint
Half-flush that dies along her throat": such stuff
Was courtesy, she thought, and cause enough
For calling up that spot of joy. She had
A heart — how shall I say? — too soon made glad,
Too easily impressed; she liked whate'er
She looked on, and her looks went everywhere.
Sir, 'twas all one! My favor at her breast,

The dropping of the daylight in the West,
The bough of cherries some officious fool
Broke in the orchard for her, the white mule
She rode with round the terrace — all and each
Would draw from her alike the approving speech,
Or blush, at least. She thanked men — good! but thanked
Somehow — I know not how — as if she ranked
My gift of a nine-hundred-years-old name
With anybody's gift. Who'd stoop to blame
This sort of trifling? Even had you skill
In speech — (which I have not) — to make your will
Quite clear to such an one, and say, "Just this
Or that in you disgusts me; here you miss,
Or there exceed the mark" — and if she let
Herself be lessoned so, nor plainly set
Her wits to yours, forsooth, and made excuse.
— E'en then would be some stooping, and I choose
Never to stoop. Oh sir, she smiled, no doubt,
Whene'er I passed her; but who passed without
Much the same smile? This grew; I gave commands;
Then all smiles stopped together. There she stands
As if alive. Will't please you rise? We'll meet
The company below, then. I repeat,
The Count your master's known munificence
Is ample warrant that no just pretense
Of mine for dowry will be disallowed;
Though his fair daughter's self, as I avowed
At starting, is my object. Nay, we'll go
Together down, sir. Notice Neptune, though,
Taming a sea horse, thought a rarity,
Which Claus of Innsbruck cast in bronze for me!

THE CASK OF AMONTILLADO

Edgar Allan Poe

The thousand injuries of Fortunato I had borne as I best could, but when he ventured upon insult I vowed revenge. You, who so well know the nature of my soul, will not suppose, however, that I gave utterance to a threat. At length I would be avenged; this was a point definitively settled—but the very definitiveness with which it was resolved precluded the idea of risk. I must not only punish but punish with impunity. A wrong is unredressed when retribution overtakes its redresser. It is equally unredressed when the avenger fails to make himself felt as such to him who has done the wrong.

It must be understood that neither by word nor deed had I given Fortunato cause to doubt my good will. I continued, as was my wont, to smile in his face, and he did not perceive that my smile *now* was at the thought of his immolation.

He had a weak point—this Fortunato—although in other regards he was a man to be respected and even feared. He prided himself upon his connoisseurship in wine. Few Italians have the true virtuoso spirit. For the most part their enthusiasm is adopted to suit the time and opportunity, to practice imposture upon the British and Austrian *millionaires*. In painting and gemmary, Fortunato, like his countrymen, was a quack, but in the matter of old wines he was sincere. In this respect I did not differ from him materially; — I was skillful in the Italian vintages myself, and bought largely whenever I could.

It was about dusk, one evening during the supreme madness of the carnival season, that I encountered my friend. He accosted me with excessive warmth, for he had been drinking much. The man wore motley. He had on a tight-fitting parti-striped dress, and his head was surmounted by the conical cap and bells. I was so pleased to see him that I thought I should never have done wringing his hand.

I said to him— "My dear Fortunato, you are luckily met. How remarkably well you are looking to-day. But I have received a pipe of what passes for Amontillado, and I have my doubts."

"How?" said he. "Amontillado? A pipe? Impossible! And in the middle of the carnival!"

"I have my doubts," I replied; "and I was silly enough to pay the full Amontillado price without consulting you in the matter. You were not to be found, and I was fearful of losing a bargain."

"Amontillado!"

"I have my doubts."

"Amontillado!"

"And I must satisfy them."

"Amontillado!"

"As you are engaged, I am on my way to Luchrest' If any one has a critical turn it is he. He will tell me——"

"Luchresi cannot tell Amontillado from Sherry."

"And yet some fools will have it that his taste is a match for your own."

"Come, let us go."

"Whither?"

"To your vaults."

"My friend, no; I will not impose upon your good nature. I perceive you have an engagement. Luchresi——"

"I have no engagement; — come."

"My friend, no. It is not the engagement, but the severe cold with which I perceive you are afflicted. The vaults are insufferably damp. They are encrusted with nitre."

"Let us go, nevertheless. The cold is merely nothing. Amontillado! You have been imposed upon. And as for Luchresi, he cannot distinguish Sherry from Amontillado."

Thus speaking, Fortunato possessed himself of my arm; and putting on a mask of black silk and drawing a *roquelaire* closely about my person, I suffered him to hurry me to my palazzo.

There were no attendants at home; they had absconded to make merry in honor of the time. I had told them that I should not return until the morning, and had given them explicit orders not to stir from the house. These orders were sufficient, I well knew, to insure their immediate disappearance, one and all, as soon as my back was turned.

I took from their sconces two flambeaux, and giving one to Fortunato, bowed him through several suites of rooms to the archway that led into the vaults. I passed down a long and winding staircase, requesting him to be cautious as he followed. We came at length to the foot of the descent, and stood together upon the damp ground of the catacombs of the Montresors.

The gait of my friend was unsteady, and the bells upon his cap jingled as he strode.

"The pipe," said he.

"It is farther on," said I; "but observe the white web-work which gleams from these cavern walls."

He turned towards me, and looked into my eyes with two filmy orbs that distilled the rheum of intoxication.

"Nitre?" he asked at length.

"Nitre," I replied. "How long have you had that cough?"

"Ugh! ugh! ugh! — ugh! ugh! ugh! — ugh! ugh! ugh! — ugh! ugh! ugh! — ugh! ugh! ugh!"

My poor friend found it impossible to reply for many minutes.

"It is nothing," he said, at last.

"Come," I said, with decision, "we will go back; your health is precious. You are rich, respected, admired, beloved; you are happy, as once I was. You are a man to be missed. For me it is no matter. We will go back; you will be ill, and I cannot be responsible. Besides, there is Luchresi——"

"Enough," he said; "the cough is a mere nothing; it will not kill me. I shall not die of a cough."

"True — true," I replied; "and, indeed, I had no intention of alarming you unnecessarily — but you should use all proper caution. A draught of this Medoc will defend us from the damps."

Here I knocked off the neck of a bottle which I drew from a long row of its fellows that lay upon the mould.

"Drink," I said, presenting him the wine.

He raised it to his lips with a leer. He paused and nodded to me familiarly, while his bells jingled.

"I drink," he said, "to the buried that repose around us."

"And I to your long life."

He again took my arm and we proceeded.

"These vaults," he said, "are extensive."

"The Montresors," I replied, "were a great and numerous family."

"I forget your arms."

"A huge human foot d'or, in a field azure; the foot crushes a serpent rampant whose fangs are imbedded in the heel."

"And the motto?"

"Nemo me impune lacessit."

"Good!" he said.

The wine sparkled in his eyes and the bells jingled. My own fancy grew warm with the Medoc. We had passed through long walls of piled skeletons, with casks and puncheons intermingling, into the inmost recesses of the catacombs. I paused again, and this time I made bold to seize Fortunato by an arm above the elbow.

"The nitre!" I said; "see, it increases. It hangs like moss upon the vaults. We are below the river's bed. The drops of moisture trickle among the bones. Come, we will go back ere it is too late. Your cough ——"

"It is nothing," he said; "let us go on. But first, another draught of the Medoc."

I broke and reached him a flacon of De Grâve. He emptied it at a breath. His eyes flashed with a fierce light. He laughed and threw the bottle upwards with a gesticulation I did not understand.

I looked at him in surprise. He repeated the movement—a grotesque one.

"You do not comprehend?" he said.

"Not I," I replied.

"Then you are not of the brotherhood."

"How?"

"You are not of the masons."

"Yes, yes," I said; "yes, yes."

"You? Impossible! A mason?"

"A mason," I replied.

"A sign," he said, "a sign."

"It is this," I answered, producing from beneath the folds of my *roquelaire* a trowel.

"You jest," he exclaimed, recoiling a few paces. "But let us proceed to the Amontillado."

"Be it so," I said, replacing the tool beneath the cloak and again offering him my arm. He leaned upon it heavily. We continued our route in search of the Amontillado. We passed through a range of low arches, descended, passed on, and descending again, arrived at a deep crypt, in which the foulness of the air caused our flambeaux rather to glow than flame.

At the most remote end of the crypt there appeared another less spacious. Its walls had been lined with human remains, piled to the vault overhead, in the fashion of the great catacombs of Paris. Three sides of this interior crypt were still ornamented in this manner. From the fourth side the bones had been thrown down, and lay promiscuously upon the earth, forming at one point a mound of some size. Within the wall thus exposed by the displacing of the bones, we perceived a still interior crypt or recess, in depth about four feet, in width three, in height six or seven. It seemed to have been constructed for no especial use within itself, but formed merely the interval between two of the colossal supports of the roof of the catacombs, and was backed by one of their circumscribing walls of solid granite.

It was in vain that Fortunato, uplifting his dull torch, endeavored to pry into the depth of the recess. Its termination the feeble light did not enable us to see.

"Proceed," I said; "herein is the Amontillado. As for Luchresi——"

"He is an ignoramus," interrupted my friend, as he stepped unsteadily forward, while I followed immediately at his heels. In an instant he had reached the extremity of the niche, and finding his progress arrested by the rock, stood stupidly bewildered. A moment more and I had fettered him to the granite. In its surface were two iron staples, distant from each other about two feet, horizontally. From one of these depended a short chain, from the other a padlock. Throwing the links about his waist, it was but the work of a few seconds to secure it. He was too much astounded to resist. Withdrawing the key I stepped back from the recess.

"Pass your hand," I said, "over the wall; you cannot help feeling the nitre. Indeed it is *very* damp. Once more let me *implore* you to return. No? Then I must positively leave you. But I will first render you all the little attentions in my power."

"The Amontillado!" ejaculated my friend, not yet recovered from his astonishment.

"True," I replied; "the Amontillado."

As I said these words I busied myself among the pile of bones of which I have before spoken. Throwing them aside, I soon uncovered a quantity of building stone and mortar. With these materials and with the aid of my trowel, I began vigorously to wall up the entrance of the niche.

I had scarcely laid the first tier of the masonry when I discovered that the intoxication of Fortunato had in great measure worn off. The earliest indication I had of this was a low moaning cry from the depth of the recess. It was *not* the cry of a drunken man. There was then a long and obstinate silence. I laid the second tier, and the third, and the fourth; and then I heard the furious vibration of the chain. The noise lasted for several minutes, during which, that I might hearken to it with the more satisfaction, I ceased my labors and sat down upon the bones. When at last the clanking subsided, I resumed the trowel, and finished without interruption the fifth, the sixth, and the seventh tier. The wall was now nearly upon a level with my breast. I again paused, and holding the flambeaux over the mason-work, threw a few feeble rays upon the figure within.

A succession of loud and shrill screams, bursting suddenly from the throat of the chained form, seemed to thrust me violently back. For a brief moment I hesitated, I trembled. Unsheathing my rapier, I began to grope with it about the recess; but the thought of an instant reassured me. I placed my hand upon the solid fabric of the catacombs, and felt satisfied. I reapproached the wall. I replied to the yells of him who clamored. I re-echoed, I aided, I surpassed them in volume and in strength. I did this, and the clamorer grew still.

It was now midnight, and my task was drawing to a close. I had completed the eighth, the ninth, and the tenth tier. I had finished a portion of the last and the eleventh; there remained but a single stone to be fitted and plastered in. I struggled with its weight; I placed it partially in its destined position. But now there came from out the niche a low laugh that erected the hairs upon my head. It was succeeded by a sad voice, which I had difficulty in recognizing as that of the noble Fortunato. The voice said —

"Ha! ha! ha! — he! he! he! — a very good joke, indeed — an excellent jest. We will have many a rich laugh about it at the palazzo — he! he! he! — over our wine — he! he! he!"

"The Amontillado!" I said.

"He! he! he! — he! he! he! — yes, the Amontillado. But is it not getting late? Will not they be awaiting us at the palazzo — the Lady Fortunato and the rest? Let us be gone."

"Yes," I said, "let us be gone."

"For the love of God, Montresor!"

"Yes," I said, "for the love of God!"

But to these words I hearkened in vain for a reply. I grew impatient. I called aloud —

"Fortunato!"

No answer. I called again —

"Fortunato!"

No answer still. I thrust a torch through the remaining aperture and let it fall within. There came forth in return only a jingling of the bells. My heart grew sick; it was the dampness of the catacombs that made it so. I hastened to make an end of my labor. I forced the last stone into its position; I plastered it up. Against the new masonry I re-erected the old rampart of bones. For the half of a century no mortal has disturbed them. *In pace requiescat!*

___ Affective Disorders

In all Affective Disorders, there is a disturbance of mood not attributable to to any other physical or mental disorder. Mood refers to a prolonged emotion that affects one's perceptions of and responses to the world; it generally involves either depression or elation. The disturbance of mood is accompanied by a full or partial depressive or manic syndrome. These syndromes have symptoms that tend to occur together.

DSM—III divides Affective Disorders into Major Affective Disorders (in which there is a full depressive or manic syndrome), other Specific Affective Disorders (in which there is only a partial depressive or manic syndrome), and Atypical Affective Disorders. Other classifications group these disorders in various categories including Affective, Personality, and Neurotic Disorders.

Major Affective Disorders

Bipolar Disorder, Manic

Major Affective Disorders include Bipolar Disorder and Major Depression (more common and less severe than Bipolar Disorder). Bipolar Disorder is distinguished from Major Depression by the presence of one or more manic episodes. In DSM-III, the category of Manic Disorder is omitted. Instead, when there has been one or more manic episodes, with or without a major depressive episode, the classification Bipolar Disorder is used.

Manic episode. Individuals who have a manic episode will be more elated, expansive, or irritable than usual. If their mood is elation, they describe themselves as feeling particularly good, intensely cheerful, and completely happy. If their mood is expansive, they are unselectively

80

enthusiastic about themselves, others (even strangers), and their environment. If their mood is irritable, they may feel thwarted at every turn. Regardless of the mood, individuals who experience a manic episode exhibit certain traits. They may be hyperactive without considering the harmful potentials in the activity, e.g., reckless driving or sexual indiscretions. Their attention span is often short; their speech generally becomes louder and more rapid than usual. Their thoughts may race from one topic to another, thus making conversation difficult. They may have unreasonable ideas of their own abilities. They may even have a decreased need for sleep.

In John Mortimer's "Desmond," Emma Grant seems to be experiencing a manic episode. In addition to reading carefully Emma's monologue, one should pay close attention to stage directions dealing with her movements and inflections. How can her mood be described? What are some specific examples of other traits that point toward Bipolar Disorder, Manic?

DESMOND

John Mortimer

Characters
EMMA GRANT

Scene:

> A large dining room in a London house with a hatch through to the kitchen. Modern furniture. Slab-of-marble table. Abstract paintings. All over the place are photographs of Desmond – Desmond, perhaps thirty but looking younger and more boyish; Desmond skiing; Desmond diving; Desmond on a horse; Desmond in a white dinner jacket caught in a flash of light. Desmond on water-skis, skin-diving or just looking beautiful.
>
> The table is laid for lunch for two. At one end, a full battery of knives and forks, decanters, glasses – at the other, a plate on which there are two biscuits and a glass full of some cloudy chemical substance. The places are laid at each end of the table so that there is a long space of cold marble between them.
>
> Emma Grant is fussing round the room, opening cigarette boxes. She finds a cigarette, searches for a match. She is very thin and elegant and in her forties, though dressed as if she were younger. She is in an extremely nervous state. She finds a lighter. Then, picks up a card from the mantelpiece, holds it close to read it. Feels for her glasses; puts them on to read.

EMMA GRANT: "Joanna Waterhouse, 2 Appleby Court. Kensington 7568. I love you, rabbit." *(She puts down the card, goes to the phone, starts to dial, thinks better of it and puts the phone down again)* No, Miss Waterhouse, I'm not going to put you off, much as you'd be relieved to hear from me that lunch is unavoidably postponed because I've run out of courage. I mean, it's got to be *faced up to*. We've got to discuss this whole thing like a couple of civilized people...well, one-and-a-half civilized people. I'm not all that civilized this morning. No sleep. That's the real trouble...no sleep. *(She yawns)* It's all been like a sort of dream...*(She moves away from the phone)* Well, we've done quite well so far. A calm and controlled phone call after breakfast. "It that Miss Waterhouse? Oh, this is Emma Grant. Desmond's wife. Yes, the one whose weekly articles are standing in the way of his being a genius. Didn't he tell you that? He usually does. No, I don't think we've met. In fact, you've been rather kept from me; even to the extent of being whisked down the fire escape when I got back early from the paper. Desmond found that a very flattering incident. It made him feel like Casanova's memoirs." "Look," I said, "Why don't you come to lunch, Miss Waterhouse — I mean, if you really want to marry my husband why don't we discuss this like two civilized people?" And she said, "How lovely! Thanks for asking me." Such nice party manners. Now I wonder what Mrs. Mac's dreamt up for you to eat? I mean, what would be really suitable. *(She goes to the hatch, pulls it open and shouts through it)* Mrs. Mac! What are we giving our little visitor to eat? *(Without waiting for a reply, she bangs the hatch shut again and says very angrily:)* You know what I think you need? Nursery cooking! Builds up the puppy fat! Polishes up the little white milk teeth! Something inoffensive. Bread and butter, macaroni and cheese, frozen peas, tapioca in a brown overcoat and eat it up and help the poor soldiers at the front! That's a thought, Miss Waterhouse. When you were being made to eat up your tapioca, *I* was a poor soldier at the front. A poor bloody lieutenant with khaki bloomers and portable typewriter, sending home human interest stories about our brave boys in battle dress. And you ate up your tapioca pudding. Just to help me! Dear little Miss Watermouse! Thank you so much. *(She opens the lid of a dish and sniffs)* Steak and kidney pie! Yellow crust and thick gravy and...*(She lifts up another lid)*...new potatoes. Butter and parsley. *(She puts down the lid. Then, goes to the mantlepiece, stubs out her cigarette in an ashtray; coughs)* What's for afters? Wait and see, Miss Watermouse dear! Treacle tart with Devonshire cream, bread and Stilton and Irish coffee. You're going to do a great job today for the poor soldiers! *(She takes a cigarette out of the box and puts it in her mouth)* Steak and kidney pie! You live dangerously, don't you little Miss....All right! I know your name. Miss Waterhouse. Miss Joanna Waterhouse. *(She lights her cigarette)* Watermouse is what I *choose* to call you! *(A clock over the mirror chimes)* I'd better collect my thoughts. Collect my poor, bloody scattered thoughts! *(She looks at herself critically in the mirror, feels her neck, puts down her cigarette and takes off her glasses)* I bet *you* don't wear glasses. They're a sign of surrender, according to Desmond. Like gray hair and wrinkles 'round the neck and taking off your shoes in the cinema and going to bed at eight-thirty with a poached egg and *Panorama*. And neither Desmond nor I *could* surrender. Not while our war was on. *(She looks in the mirror again and straightens up. Starts to address herself in the manner of a general addressing his troops on the field of battle)* Well, this is it. I'm very much afraid that at 00.10 hours the enemy's going to hit us with all he's got, which is a nineteen-year-old blonde, with a daddy in the Stock Exchange and a frightfully sweet pony and a really super flat just off Ken. High Street in which the enemy has now established his temporary headquarters...*(Her voice changes, becomes serious)* Oh, it's not funny...it's not funny. All the same, better have a plan! *(She picks up her cigarette, goes to her place at the table, sits down, leans her elbow on the table and talks as if her guest were at the other end)* I shall say...I think I shall say...*(Serious, intense)* Dear Joanna—do you mind if I call you Miss Waterhouse? *(She smiles for a moment, then goes on seriously)* I shall talk to her seriously. I shall say... Seriously, Miss Waterhouse. Seriously, Joanna. Look here, love, I shall say, with all due respect...What the hell, I mean what the *hell* do you know about life? Shall I tell you something, darling? Let me tell you, at your sort of age I'd risen from being a cub reporter on the old Derby Echo, which I'd joined at fifteen-and-a-half, covering murders and garden parties, to be put in sole charge of the best women's page in Fleet Street, and I had the finest editor in the world die in my own divan bed in The Boltons on a night when he was meant to be in Morocco with Mister Winston Churchill, no less. Could I now tell you that I've built up a readership so world-wide that I get approximately fifty letters a day, and am syndicated in the North American continent simply because I see life through eyes clear and disillusioned, without fear or favor ...that is, on any occasion when I haven't lost my damned glasses! And may I say that I've been through four wars, not counting marriage with Desmond, and have on my left breast the scar caused by the fragments of a bottle of Pernod shot out of my hands in the old Bar Neptune in Algiers! And what have *you* been through Miss Waterhouse, dear, apart from chickenpox and a nasty toss at the gym? So what do *you* know about *life!* *(Pause)* And don't think *he's* averse from any of all that either, will you? Don't think Desmond actually turns his nose up at the free champagne, and Presidential Class Trans-Atlantic Air Lines, or he doesn't enjoy mentioning that we were at Kensington Palace in the course of conversation. And what can *you* offer him to take the place of all that? The Richmond Horse Show? Miss Waterhouse. Dear, dear Miss Waterhouse—do you happen to know what you're taking on? I mean...now at this present moment he may be all, being very gentle and sweet; he may be remembering your birthday and sending you red roses on *my* account and bringing you back a bottle of perfume he crept out and bought in Paris when I was in the Manager's office, adding up the bill. But it won't last. It can't possible last! I shall say... *(Pause. She is thoughful; becomes less angry)* I shan't say *any* of that. Sounds revolting, my life story in the *Ladies' Home Journal* as told to Joanna Watermouse. Miss Waterhouse. Miss Waterhouse, *may* I call you Joanna? Joanna, you look like a sensible and sensitive girl — that's how you look to me. I mean, that's what's so very marvelous about today. Everyone gets to know so much more so quickly. I bet nothing shocks you, does it? Undoubtedly you've seen it all — in your area of Surrey? Death and drugs all 'round Guildford as we read in the papers. Nothing shocks you — not even what you may be doing to me. I mean, you mature so young nowadays. To be totally honest with you — I lost, my virginity at the age of twenty-three. And even then it was a kind of mistake. A man came up to me at a dance and he said "You're Hermione, aren't you? Come out to the Humber. I understand you do that sort of thing..." Well, I wasn't Hermione, and I didn't, but — can you believe it? — I didn't even have the courage to tell him, and so I went. It was appalling! I never really knew what it was like, not till I met Desmond. Honestly, I didn't ask you to lunch to get your sympathy. Nothing like that. I asked you... *(Pause; she frowns)* I asked you because naturally he wouldn't come. Oh, he'll leave all that sort of thing to you, sacking the char, ringing up the bank manager. I tell you... if a washer comes off the tap he'll leave home and not come back until you've had a man to fix it. So... this is a message for him really. Oh love, you see it's the *War!* Tell him *that's* what he's gong to miss. Will you tell him that? Life's going to be very dull and uneventful for him without it. Desmond was never much of a reporter. When I first met him he was at Queen Charlotte's Ball for the *Diary,* and he was sitting on the stairs surrounded by a lot of stupid girls like — oh not like you in the least, except they all had puppy fat and baby blue eyes, and teeth just out of braces — and he was saying, "This is the sort of occasion that keeps England great." And I was coming down the stairs with a perfectly nice osteopath, whom I might just've well've married, come to think of it, and I happened to say, "What a bloody silly remark that was." And Desmond looked up at me and said, "Move over girls, here comes my Mother." We danced then. And arranged our future battles. Look, why don't you have a drink? *(She gets up and goes to the sideboard, pours gin from a decanter)* Why don't you have a nice, great big gin and oh... an enormous gin and tonic! *(When she has poured it, she looks at it)* I can't, you see. In this sort of war you've got to keep your wits about you. Besides, if I drank this it'd land me with great big impossible calories which Desmond would object to. In fact, he'd probably ...that sounds funny, I was going to say in fact, he'd probably leave home... You think you know what's happening, don't you? You think he's fallen in love with you. I tell you. It's part of the campaign. It's what he enjoys. Part of the battle with me. You know how I found out, don't you? Your name and address written on his membership card to Dolly's with "I love you, rabbit" written underneath it. Well, the point is, he left it on the table by my bed. Oh, he pretended to have forgotten it. He pretended he'd made an awful mistake — but that's what you are in our lives. His secret weapon. "Rabbit!" What a thing to call anyone! "Rabbit!" We keep each other going you see, we keep each other up to the mark. If it weren't for him...God knows what'd happen to me. I think...I think I'd become old quite suddenly. I think...well, I'd just let myself go, wouldn't I? I'd put on calories. I'd go out to lunch and say, "Forget the cottage cheese salad—I'll have the joint and two vegs, with apple tart to follow." I'd start the day with bacon and eggs and muffins! I don't know...can you *still* get muffins? Desmond saved me from that. Of course he's younger than I am, and so beautiful. He keeps me up to the mark. I mean because of him when I get back from the paper we go to all these places. Last night we went to one. *(She yawns again)*...The Electric Current. Psychedelic lighting and a group dressed as corpses. I'd never really know about life...*(She yawns again)*...if it weren't for Desmond. I tell you, I'd be propped up in bed with a tray full of eggs and toast, watching Robin Day on the problems of Ethiopia. *(She yawns)* I'm afraid I'm not making much sense...We didn't get back till five and then he carefully dropped the information on his way to the bathroom. So we fought till nine, and then he left banging the door, and I went to the paper and rang you and ordered lunch. What I want to know is — are you strong enough for it, Miss Waterhouse? You can't relax, you see...you can't relax at all! *(She picks up the drink and looks at it)* "One gin," he'll tell you, "is as good as a three-course meal and if you want to go about looking like a prolapsed district nurse, don't blame me, darling." So you'll have to be careful now; I should warn you, Joanna. You'll be on guard all the time with Desmond. *(She picks up the drink and suddenly finishes it)* You'll never be able to drink things like that. *(She goes to her place and sits down disconsolately)* Swedish slimming biscuits, that's what you'll live on! A whole day's meal packed in a nourishing square inch. *(She bites)* With the flavor of medicated sawdust! And to wash it down...sugar-free, slimline, vitamin souped-up, health-kick barley water! We must keep ourselves beautiful for Desmond. Desmond's is a world without a stomach...He's flat, of course. Flat as an ironing board! Kept like that by lifting dumbbells in the garage, and water-skiing on Ruislip reservoir and...oh, he's taken you, hasn't he? He took care to tell me that, just because I'm afraid of drowning and I feel ridiculous in a rubber suit. But there's more treats in store for you, Joanna. Great long workouts in private gyms with Bach on the Hi-Fi and cups of coffee and gray-haired inquisitors tanned from the sunray lamp, saying, "Only another quarter-of-an-hour on the rack for you, Mrs. Grant. We don't want to waste your fifty-guinea subscription, do we?" You know what they're trying to stamp out in that little torture chamber, don't you? The heresy we might any of us grow old! *(She pours herself another drink and knocks it back)* That was the calorie equivalent of three enormous Christmas dinners! *(She goes back to the mantelpiece and picks up her glasses and puts them on. She goes back to the dishes on the heater, lifts the lid off the steak and kidney pie and sniffs)* I'd forgotten the experience of steak and kidney! *(She breaks off a bit of crust, starts to nibble at it)* Thank God, Desmond's kept me away from any such temptations! You know what I am? Forty-four at the very best is what I am, and if it wasn't for Desmond I'd know nothing about contemporary life, I'd never have been jumping up and down all night with my head split in two with psychedelic music. I'd have been alone and lonely, all last evening, eating sausages and mash and turning the pages of my library book over with a fork. *(Almost absent-mindedly, she picks up a plate from the sideboard and begins to spoon steak and kidney pie onto it)* I'd've stretched out all across the bed at night and in the morning I'd've gone down in my dressing gown, covered in cigarette ash, to make scrambled eggs and come back and eat them and listen to Housewives' Choice with crumbs all over the eiderdown. You know what? Without Desmond there'd be no obligation . . .no obligation at all. *(She takes the plate of food with her and goes back to her place at the table. She takes a big greedy bite of pie-crust and pours a glass of wine to wash it down)* Look here, Miss Waterhouse. Look here, Joanna...Desmond's part of my life, of course. I've kept up with him man and boy now for ten years, fighting and dieting and seeing he got all the sun he deserved, and changed his motorcar regularly, and every year we've got younger...and thinner...and smaller it seems to me. And now we're just slips of things, just a couple of kids trembling on the brink of middle age... and of course it's been wonderful, but...*(She tears off a bit of bread, starts to butter it lavishly)* This is what I'm trying to say...*(She bites into the bread)* If you *really* care about Desmond...look here, I've thought this over very carefully and if you really want to take him on...*I'm not going to stand in your way.* I wouldn't be so selfish. *(She wipes her mouth, then raises her glass)* Good afternoon, Miss Waterhouse! Good luck, Desmond! Give my love to everyone at the gym. I shan't be seeing them any more. *(She kicks off her shoes, leans back in her chair. She seems, for a moment, entirely happy. The phone on the sideboard rings. For a moment, she sits still, smiling, not answering it. Then, she gets up, and still smiling happily, picks up the phone)* Yes...yes, this is Emma Grant. Who? Joanna...Well, it's a good thing you rang as a matter of fact. I feel...I feel I can save us a lot of trouble. I've been thinking and honestly, this morning I was really being dreadfully turgid, wasn't I? I mean, there wasn't any reason to ring you up as if you'd committed some *crime.* I really think the way you and Desmond feel about each other is a hundred-percent understandable. Given the fact that for all practical purposes he's still about *eighteen,* and you're the extremely bright and attractive character that I'm willing to bet you are. So...there's honestly no need for you to come over here and for us to thrash 'round and 'round just as if we really hated each other, when all I want to say is, be happy because you deserve it. *(She looks round guiltily at the table)* Also, something seems to have happened to your lunch. *(She listens to the telephone. Her smile fades)* Desmond feels *what? Guilty!* Well, that's ridiculous. I mean, I've got the paper and oh...all sorts of things I'm going to have time for that I never did before...Well, like cooking. I said like...sleep and library books and the study of British Regional Food and...No, tell him he's not to feel guilty! Let me...let me speak to him. Of course he's there! Oh, I know. The number of times I've told people on the telephone he's just gone out while he's stood beside the instrument making signals. *(Pause. She's appalled)* He's *what?* He's on his way back here...You decided you couldn't do a thing like that to me...you couldn't ruin...a wonderful relationship! Joanna...Miss Waterhouse...Don't ring off! No! Listen to me! Listen to me! Please...*(She stands for a moment and listens to the dead phone)* She's gone. Miss Watermouse has left us. Desmond. Poor old Desmond. We're left with each other. *(She looks round the room and then goes to the doors of the hatch, opens them and shouts through)* Mrs. Mac! Mrs. Mac! Come and take away all this food. For God's sake, Mrs. Mac, please come and remove the steak and kidney pie! *(She moves away from the hatch and looks, almost bewildered at the room)* What have I eaten...oh, whatever have I eaten? I must've gone mad! From tomorrow...We'll do it *together.* From tomorrow, nothing but hot water...with a little lemon juice. *(She goes to the mirror, pulls off her glasses, looks at her face)* The district nurse! I was getting quite fond of her. All right, Desmond. All right, you bastard! I know, she'll have to go! *(She pulls a lipstick out of her handbag and quickly starts to redo her make-up)* Won't we *ever* rest? *(She pauses a moment at the sound of a door opening somewhere in the house. She starts to speak, brightly, as if she were ten years younger)* Not that I'm tired, darling. I'm *not* tired, honestly! *(Her lips are on now. She turns towards the opening door of the room, smiles brilliantly and apparently with perpetual inexhaustible youth)* Welcome home!

Curtain

Bipolar Disorder, Depressed

Individuals who have experienced one or more manic episodes (p. 81) and are currently, or most recently, experiencing a major depressive episode are diagnosed as having Bipolar Disorder, Depressed.

Major depressive episode. Individuals who are experiencing a major depressive episode may describe their mood as sad, depressed, low, discouraged, or blue. In all these descriptions, they are announcing their unhappiness or inability to enjoy themselves. They may have lost interest in almost everything, and they gain little enjoyment from their usual pleasures. Regardless of how they express their mood, individuals experiencing a major depressive episode have certain other symptoms. They may find both their appetite and sleep patterns disturbed. They may complain of fatigue; their movements and thinking may be slower than usual. They often have feelings of excessive or inappropriate guilt. Sometimes they may even wish for death or attempt suicide.

John Barth depicts Jacob Horner sometime after his recovery from a major depressive episode. As Jacob recalls the episode, it should be easy to identify his essential mood and certain related symptoms. In addition to noting the evidence used to classify Jacob's condition, one should enjoy the Doctor's explanation of the various imaginative therapies that he uses to treat his patients.

IN SEPTEMBER
IT WAS TIME
TO SEE THE DOCTOR
John Barth

In September it was time to see the Doctor again: I drove out to the Remobilization Farm one morning during the first week of the month. Because the weather was fine, a number of the Doctor's other patients, quite old men and women, were taking the air, seated in their wheel chairs or in the ancient cane chairs along the porch. As usual, they greeted me a little suspiciously with their eyes; visitors of any sort, but particularly of my age, were rare at the farm, and were not welcomed cordially. Ignoring their stony glances, I went inside to pay my respects to Mrs. Dockey, the receptionist-nurse. I found her in consultation with the Doctor himself.

"Good day, Horner," the Doctor beamed.

"Good morning, sir. Good morning, Mrs. Dockey."

That large, masculine woman nodded shortly without speaking—her custom — and the Doctor told me to wait for him in the Progress and Advice Room, which, along with the dining room, the kitchen, the reception room, the bathroom, and the Treatment Room constituted the first floor of the old frame house. Upstairs the partitions between the original bedrooms had been removed to form two dormitories, one for the men and one for the women. The Doctor had his own small bedroom upstairs too, and there were two bathrooms. I did not know at the time where Mrs. Dockey slept, or whether she slept at the farm at all. She was a most uncommunicative woman.

I had first met the Doctor quite by chance — a fortunate chance — on the morning of March 17, 1951, in what passes for the grand concourse of the Pennsylvania Railroad Station in Baltimore. It happened to be the day after my twenty-eighth birthday, and I was sitting on one of the benches in the station with my suitcase beside me. I was in an unusual condition: I couldn't move. On the previous day I had checked out of my room in the apartment hotel owned by the university. I had roomed there since September of the year before, when, half-heartedly, I matriculated as a graduate student and began work on the degree that I was scheduled to complete the following June.

But on March 16, my birthday, with my oral examination passed but my master's thesis not even begun, I packed my suitcase and left the room to take a trip somewhere. Because I have learned to be not much interested in causes and biographies, I ascribe this move to simple birthday despondency, a phenomenon sufficiently familiar to enough people so that I need not explain it further. Birthday despondency, let us say, had reminded me that I had no self-convincing reason for continuing for a moment longer to do any of the things that I happened to be doing with myself as of seven o'clock in the evening of March 16, 1951. I had thirty dollars and some change in my pocket: when my suitcase was filled I hailed a taxi, went to Pennsylvania Station, and stood in the ticket line.

"Yes?" said the ticket agent when my turn came.

"Ah — this will sound theatrical to you," I said with some embarrassment, "but I have thirty dollars or so to take a trip on. Would you mind telling me some of the places I could ride to from here for, say, twenty dollars?"

The man showed no surprise at my request. He gave me an understanding if unsympathetic look and consulted some sort of rate scales.

"You can go to Cincinnati, Ohio," he declared. "You can go to Crestline, Ohio. And let's see, now — you can go to Dayton, Ohio. Or Lima, Ohio. That's a nice town. I have some of my wife's people up around Lima, Ohio. Want to go there?"

"Cincinnati, Ohio," I repeated, unconvinced. "Crestline, Ohio; Dayton, Ohio; and Lima, Ohio. Thank you very much. I'll make up my mind and come back."

So I left the ticket window and took a seat on one of the benches in the middle of the concourse to make up my mind. And it was there that I simply ran out of motives, as a car runs out of gas. There was no reason to go to Cincinnati, Ohio. There was no reason to go to Crestline, Ohio. Or Dayton, Ohio; or Lima, Ohio. There was no reason, either, to go back to the apartment hotel, or for that matter to go anywhere. There was no reason to do anything. My eyes, as Winckelmann said inaccurately of the eyes of the

Greek statues, were sightless, gazing on eternity, fixed on ultimacy, and when that is the case there is no reason to do anything—even to change the focus of one's eyes. Which is perhaps why the statues stand still. It is the malady *cosmopsis*, the cosmic view, that afflicted me. When one has it, one is frozen like the bullfrog when the hunter's light strikes him full in the eyes, only with cosmopsis there is no hunger, and no quick hand to terminate the moment—there's only the light.

Shortsighted animals all around me hurried in and out of doors leading down to tracks; trains arrived and departed. Women, children, salesmen, soldiers, and redcaps hurried across the concourse toward immediate destinations, but I sat immobile on the bench. After a while Cincinnati, Crestline, Dayton, and Lima dropped from my mind, and their place was taken by that test pattern of my consciousness, *Pepsi-Cola hits the spot,* intoned with silent oracularity. But it, too, petered away into the void, and nothing appeared in its stead.

If you look like a vagrant it is difficult to occupy a train-station bench all night long, even in a busy terminal, but if you are reasonably well dressed, have a suitcase at your side, and sit erect, policemen and railroad employees will not disturb you. I was sitting in the same place, in the same position, when the sun struck the grimy station windows next morning, and in the nature of the case I suppose I would have remained thus indefinitely, but about nine o'clock a small dapper fellow in his fifties stopped in front of me and stared directly into my eyes. He was bald, dark-eyed, and dignified, a Negro, and wore a graying mustache and a trim tweed suit to match. The fact that I did not stir even the pupils of my eyes under his gaze is an index to my condition, for ordinarily I find it next to impossible to return the stare of a stranger.

"Weren't you sitting here like this last night?" he asked me sharply. I did not reply. He came close, bent his face down toward mine, and moved an upthrust finger back and forth about two inches from my eyes. But my eyes did not follow his finger. He stepped back and regarded me critically, then suddenly snapped his fingers almost on the point of my nose. I blinked involuntarily, although my head did not jerk back.

"Ah," he said, and regarded me again. "Does this happen to you often, young man?"

Perhaps because of the brisk assuredness of his voice, the no welled up in me like a belch. And I realized as soon as I deliberately held my tongue (there being in the last analysis no reason to answer his question at all) that as of that moment I was artificially prolonging what had been a genuine physical immobility. Not to choose at all is unthinkable: what I had done before was simply choose not to act, since I had been at rest when the situation arose. Now, however, it was harder—"more of a choice"—to hold my tongue than to croak out something that filled my mouth, and so after a moment I said, "No."

Then, of course, the trance was broken. I was embarrassed, and rose quickly and stiffly from the bench to leave.

"Where will you go?" my examiner asked with a smile.

"What?" I frowned at him. "Oh — get a bus home, I guess. See you around."

"Wait." His voice was mild, but entirely commanding. I stopped. "Won't you have coffee with me? I'm a physician, and I'd be interested in discussing your case with you."

"I don't have any case," I said awkwardly. "I was just — sitting there for a minute or so."

"No. I saw you there last night at ten o'clock when I came in from New York," the doctor said. "You were sitting in the same position. You *were* paralyzed, weren't you?"

I laughed shortly. "Well, if you want to call it that, but there's nothing wrong with me. I don't know what came over me."

"Of course you don't, but I do. My specialty is various sorts of physical immobility. You're lucky I came by this morning."

"Oh, you don't understand ——"

"I brought you out of it, didn't I?" he said cheerfully. "Here." He took a fifty-cent piece from his pocket and handed it to me — I accepted it before I realized what he'd done. "I can't go into that lounge over there. Get two cups of coffee for us and we'll sit here for a minute and decide what to do."

"No, listen, I ——"

"Why not?" he laughed. "Go on, now. I'll wait here."

Why not, indeed?

"I have my own money," I protested lamely, offering him his fifty-cent piece back, but he waved me away and lit a cigar.

"Now hurry up," he ordered calmly, around the cigar. "Move fast, or you might get stuck again. Don't think of anything but the coffee I've asked you to get."

"All right." I turned and walked with dignity toward the lounge, just off the concourse.

"Fast!" the doctor laughed behind me. I flushed, and impulsively quickened my step.

While I waited for the coffee I tried to feel the curiosity about my invalidity and my rescuer that it seemed appropriate I should feel, but I was too weary in mind and body to wonder at anything. I do not mean to suggest that my condition had been unpleasant — it was entirely anesthetic in its advanced stage, and even a little bit pleasant in its inception — but it was fatiguing, as a over-long sleep is fatiguing, and one had the same reluctance to throw it off that one has to finally get out of bed when one has slept around the clock. Indeed, as the Doctor had warned (it was at this time, not knowing my benefactor's name, that I began to think of him with a capital D), to slip back into immobility at the coffee counter would have been extremely easy: I felt my mind begin to settle into rigidity, and only the clerk's peremptory "Thirty cents, please," brought me back to action — luckily, because the Doctor could not have entered the white lounge to help me. I paid the clerk and took the paper cups of coffee back to the bench.

"Good," the Doctor said. "Sit down."

I hesitated. I was standing directly in front of him.

"Here!" he laughed. "On this side! You're like the donkey between two piles of straw!"

I sat where ordered and we sipped our coffee. I rather expected to be asked questions about myself, but the Doctor ignored me.

"Thanks for the coffee," I said uncertainly. He glanced at me impassively for a moment, as though I were a hitherto silent parrot who had suddenly blurted a brief piece of nonsense, and then he returned his attention to the crowd in the station.

"I have one or two calls to make yet before we catch the bus," he announced without looking at me. "Won't take long. I wanted to see if you were still here before I left town."

"What do you mean, catch the bus?"

"You'll have to come over to the farm — my Remobilization Farm over near Wicomico — for a day or so, for observation," he explained coldly. "You don't have anything else to do, do you?"

"Well, I should get back to the university, I guess. I'm a student."

"Oh," he chuckled. "Might as well forget about that for a while. You can come back in a few days if you want to."

"Say, you know, really, I think you must have a misconception about what was wrong with me a while ago. I'm not a paralytic. It's all just silly, really. I'll explain it to you if you want to hear it."

"No, you needn't bother. No offense intended, but the things you think are important probably aren't even relevant at all. I'm never very curious about my patients' histories. Rather not hear them, in fact—just clutters things up. It doesn't much matter what caused it anyhow, does it?" He grinned. "My farm's like a nunnery in that respect—I never bother about why my patients come there. Forget about causes; I'm no psychoanalyst."

"But that's what I mean, sir," I explained, laughing uncomfortably. "There's nothing physically wrong with me."

"Except that you couldn't move," the Doctor said. "What's your name?"

"Jacob Horner. I'm a graduate student up at Johns Hopkins——"

"Ah, ah," he warned. "No biography, Jacob Horner." He finished his coffee and stood up. "Come on, now, we'll get a cab. Bring your suitcase along."

"Oh, wait now!"

"Yes?"

I fumbled for protests: the thing was absurd.

"Well — this is absurd."

"So?"

I hesitated, blinking, wetting my lips.

"Think, think!" the Doctor said brusquely.

My mind raced like a car engine when the clutch is disengaged. There was no answer.

"Well, I — are you sure it's all right?" I had no idea what my question signified.

The Doctor made a short, derisive sound (a sort of "Huf!") and turned away. I shook my head — at the same moment aware that I was watching myself act bewildered — and then fetched up my suitcase and followed after him, out to the line of taxicabs at the curb.

Thus began my *alliance* with the Doctor. He stopped first at an establishment on North Howard Street, where he ordered two wheel chairs, three pairs of crutches, and certain other apparatus for the farm, and then at a pharmaceutical supply house on South Paca Street, where he also made some sort of order. Then we went to the W.B.&A. bus terminal on Howard and Redwood streets and took the Red Star bus to the Eastern Shore. The Doctor's Mercury station wagon was parked at the Wicomico bus depot; he drove to the little settlement of Vineland, about three miles south of Wicomico, turned off onto a secondary road, and finally drove up a long, winding dirt lane to the Remobilization Farm, an aged but clean-painted white clapboard house in a clump of oaks on a knoll overlooking some creek or other. The patients on the porch, senile men and women, welcomed the Doctor with querulous enthusiasm, and he returned their greeting. Me they regarded with open suspicion, if not hostility, but the Doctor made no explanation of my presence — for that matter, I should have been hard put to explain it myself.

Inside I was introduced to the muscular Mrs. Dockey and taken to the Progress and Advice Room for my first interview. I waited alone in that clean room, bare, but not really clinical-looking — just an empty white room in a farmhouse — for some ten minutes, and then the Doctor entered and took his seat very much in front of me. He had donned a white medical-looking jacket and appeared entirely official and competent.

"I'll make a few things clear very quickly, Jacob," he said, leaning forward with his hands on his knees and rolling his cigar around in his mouth between sentences. "The farm, as you can see, is designed for the treatment of paralytics. Most of my patients are old people, but you musn't infer from that that this is a nursing home for the aged. It's not. Perhaps you noticed when we drove up that my patients like me. It has happened several times in the past that for one reason or another I have seen fit to change the location of the farm. Once it was outside of Troy, New York; another time near Fond du Lac, Wisconsin; another time near Biloxi, Mississippi. And we've been other places, too. Nearly all the patients I have on the farm now have been with me at least since Fond du Lac, and if I should have to move tomorrow to Helena, Montana, or Far Rockaway, most of them would go with me, and not because they haven't anywhere else to go. But don't think I have an equal love for them. They're just more or less interesting problems in immobility, for which I find it satisfying to work out therapies. I tell this to you, but not to them, because your problem is such that this information is harmless. And for that matter, you've no way of knowing whether anything I've said or will say is the truth, or just a part of my general therapy for you. You can't even tell whether your doubt in this matter is an honestly founded doubt or just a part of your treatment: access to the truth, Jacob, even belief that there is such a thing, is itself therapeutic or antitherapeutic, depending on the problem. The reality of your problem itself is all that you can be sure of."

"Yes, sir."

"Why do you say that?" the Doctor asked.

"Say what?"

" 'Yes, sir.' Why do you say 'Yes, sir'?"

"Oh—I was just acknowledging what you said before."

"Acknowledging the truth of what I said or merely the fact that I said it?"

"Well," I hesitated, flustered. "I don't know, sir."

"You don't know whether to say you were acknowledging the truth of my statements, when actually you weren't, or to say you were simply acknowledging that I said something, at the risk of offending me by the implication that you don't agree with any of it. Eh?"

"Oh, I agree with *some* of it," I assured him.

"What parts of it do you agree with? Which statements?"

"I don't know: I guess——" I searched my mind hastily to remember even one thing that he'd said. He regarded my floundering coldly for a minute and then went on as if the interruption hadn't occurred.

"Agapotherapy—devotion therapy—is often useful with older patients," he said. "One of the things that work toward restoring their mobility is devotion to some figure, a doctor or other kind of administrator. It keeps their allegiances from becoming divided. For that reason I'd move the farm occasionally even if other circumstances didn't make it desirable. It does them good to decide to follow me. Agapotherapy is one small therapy in a great number, some consecutive, some simultaneous, which are exercised on the patients. No two patients have the same schedule of therapies, because no two people are ever paralyzed in the same way. The authors of medical textbooks," he added with some contempt, "like everyone else, can reach generality only by ignoring enough particularity. They speak of paralysis, and the treatment of paralytics, as though one read the textbook and then followed the rules for getting paralyzed properly. There is no such thing as *paralysis*, Jacob. There is only paralyzed Jacob Horner. And I don't *treat* paralysis: I schedule therapies to mobilize John Doe or Jacob Horner, as the case may be. That's why I ignore you when you say you aren't paralyzed as the people out on the porch are paralyzed. I don't treat your paralysis: I treat paralyzed you. Please don't say, 'Yes, sir.' "

The urge to acknowledge is almost irresistible, but I managed to sit silent and not even nod.

"There are several things wrong with you, I think. I daresay you don't know the seating capacity of the Cleveland Municipal Stadium, do you?"

"*What?*"

The Doctor did not smile. "You suggest that my question is absurd, when you have no grounds for knowing whether it is or not—you obviously heard me and understood me. Probably you want to delay my learning that you *don't* know the seating capacity of Cleveland Municipal Stadium, since your vanity would be ruffled if the question *weren't* absurd, and even if it were. It makes no difference whether it is or not, Jacob Horner: it's a question asked you by your doctor. Now, is there any ultimate reason why the Cleveland Stadium shouldn't seat fifty-seven thousand, four hundred eighty-eight people?"

"None that I can think of," I grinned.

"Don't pretend to be amused. Of course there's not. Is there any reason why it shouldn't seat eighty-eight thousand, four hundred seventy-five people?"

"No, sir."

"Indeed not. Then as far as Reason is concerned its seating capacity could be almost anything. Logic will never give you the answer to my question. Only Knowledge of the World will answer it. There's no ultimate reason at all why the Cleveland Stadium should seat exactly seventy-seven thousand, seven hundred people, but it happens that it does. There's no reason in the long run why Italy shouldn't be shaped like a sausage instead of a boot, but that doesn't happen to be the case. *The world is everything that is the case*, and what the case is is not a matter of logic. If you don't simply *know* how many people can sit in the Cleveland Municipal Stadium, you have no real reason for choosing one number over another, assuming you can make a choice at all—do you understand? But if you have some Knowledge of the World you may be able to say, 'Seventy-seven thousand, seven hundred,' just like that. No choice is involved."

"Well," I said, "you'd still have to choose whether to answer the question or not, or whether to answer it correctly, even if you knew the right answer, wouldn't you?"

The Doctor's tranquil stare told me my question was somehow silly, though it seemed reasonable enough to me.

"One of the things you'll have to do," he said dryly, "is buy a copy of the *World Almanac* for 1951 and begin to study it scrupulously. This is intended as a discipline, and you'll have to pursue it diligently, perhaps for a number of years. Informational Therapy is one of a number of therapies we'll have to initiate at once."

I shook my head and chuckled genially. "Do all your patients memorize the *World Almanac*, Doctor?"

I might as well not have spoken.

"Mrs. Dockey will show you to your bed," the Doctor said, rising to go. "I'll speak to you again presently." At the door he stopped and added, "One, perhaps two, of the older men may attempt familiarities with you at night up in the dormitory. They're on Sexual Therapy, and I find it useful and convenient in their cases to suggest homosexual affairs rather than heterosexual ones. But unless you're accustomed to that sort of thing I don't think you should accept their advances. You should keep your life as un-complicated as possible, at least for a while. Reject them gently, and they'll go back to each other."

There was little I could say. After a while Mrs. Dockey showed me my bed in the men's dormitory. I was not introduced to my roommates, nor did I introduce myself. In fact (though since then I've come to know them better), during the three days that I remained at the farm not a dozen words were exchanged between us, much less homosexual advances. When I left they were uniformly glad to see me go.

The Doctor spent two or three one-hour sessions with me each day. He asked me virtually nothing about myself; the conversations consisted mostly of harangues against the medical profession for its stupidity in matters of paralysis, and imputations that my condition was the result of defective character and intelligence.

"You claim to be unable to choose in many situations," he said once. "Well, I claim that the inability is only theoretically inherent in situations, when there's no chooser. Given a particular chooser, it's unthinkable. So, since the inability *was* displayed in your case, the fault lies not in the situation but in the fact that there was no chooser. Choosing is existence: to the extent that you don't choose, you don't exist. Now, everything we do must be oriented toward choice and action. It doesn't matter whether this action is more or less reasonable than inaction; the point is that it is its opposite."

"But why should anyone prefer it?" I asked.

"There's no reason why you should prefer it," he said, "and no reason why you shouldn't. One is a patient simply because one chooses a condition that only therapy can bring one to, not because any one condition is inherently better than another. All my therapies for a while will be directed toward making you conscious of your existence. It doesn't matter whether you act constructively or even consistently, so long as you act. It doesn't matter to the case whether your character is admirable or not, so long as you think you have one."

"I don't understand why you should choose to treat anyone, Doctor," I said.

"That's my business, not yours."

And so it went. I was charged, directly or indirectly, with everything from intellectual dishonesty and vanity to nonexistence. If I protested, the Doctor observed that my protests indicated my belief in the truth of his statements. If I only listened glumly, he observed that my glumness indicated my belief in the truth of his statements.

"All right, then," I said at last, giving up. "Everything you say is true. All of it is the truth."

The Doctor listened calmly. "You don't know what you're talking about," he said. "There's no such thing as truth as you conceive it."

These apparently pointless interviews did not constitute my only activity at the farm. Before every meal the other patients and I were made to perform various calisthenics under the direction of Mrs. Dockey. For the older patients these were usually very simple — perhaps a mere nodding of the head or flexing of the arms — although some of the old folks could execute really surprising feats: one gentleman in his seventies was an excellent rope climber, and two old ladies turned agile somersaults. For each Mrs. Dockey prescribed different activities; my own special prescription was to keep some sort of visible motion going all the time. If nothing else, I was constrained to keep a finger wiggling or a foot tapping, say, during mealtimes, when more involved movements would have made eating difficult. And I was told to rock from side to side in my bed all night long: not an unreasonable request, as it happened, for I did this habitually anyhow, even in my sleep — a habit carried over from childhood.

"Motion! Motion!" the Doctor would say, almost exalted. "You must be always *conscious* of motion!"

There were special diets and, for many patients, special drugs. I learned of Nutritional Therapy, Medicinal Therapy, Surgical Therapy, Dynamic Therapy, Informational Therapy, Conversational Therapy, Sexual Therapy, Devotional Therapy, Occuptional and Preoccupational Therapy, Virtue and Vice Therapy, Theotherapy and Atheotherapy — and later, Mythotherapy, Philosophical Therapy, Scriptotherapy, and many, many other therapies practiced in various combinations and sequence by the patients. Everything, to the Doctor, is either therapeutic, anti-therapeutic, or irrelevant. He is a kind of super-pragmatist.

At the end of my last session — it had been decided that I was to return to Baltimore experimentally, to see whether and how soon my immobility might recur — the Doctor gave me some parting instructions.

"It would not be well in your particular case to believe in God," he said.

"Religion will only make you despondent. But until we work out something for you it will be useful to subscribe to some philosophy. Why don't you read Sartre and become an existentialist? It will keep you moving until we find something more suitable for you. Study the *World Almanac:* it is to be your breviary for a while. Take a day job, preferably factory work, but not so simple that you are able to think coherently while working. Something involving sequential operations would be nice. Go out in the evenings; play cards with people. I don't recommend buying a television set just yet. If you read anything outside the *Almanac,* read nothing but plays — no novels or non-fiction. Exercise frequently. Take long walks, but always to a previously determined destination, and when you get there, walk right home again, briskly. And move out of your present quarters; the association is unhealthy for you. Don't get married or have love affairs yet: if you aren't courageous enough to hire prostitutes, then take up masturbation temporarily. Above all, act impulsively: don't let yourself get stuck between alternatives, or you're lost. You're not that strong. If the alternatives are side by side, choose the one on the left; if they're consecutive in time, choose the earlier. If neither of these applies, choose the alternative whose name begins with the earlier letter of the alphabet. These are the principles of Sinistrality, Antecedence, and Alphabetical Priority — there are others, and they're arbitrary, but useful. Good-by."

"Good-by, Doctor," I said, a little breathless, and prepared to leave.

"If you have another attack, contact me as soon as you can. If nothing happens, come back in three months. My services will cost you ten dollars a visit — no charge for this one. I have a limited interest in your case, Jacob, and in the vacuum you have for a self. That *is* your case. Remember, keep moving all the time. Be *engagé.* Join things."

I left, somewhat dazed, and took the bus back to Baltimore. There, out of it all, I had a chance to attempt to decide what I thought of the Doctor, the Remobilization Farm, the endless list of therapies, and my own position. One thing seemed fairly clear: the Doctor was operating either outside the law or on its very fringes. Sexual Therapy, to name only one thing, could scarcely be sanctioned by the American Medical Association. This doubtless was the reason for the farm's frequent relocation. It was also apparent that he was a crank — though perhaps not an ineffective one — and one wondered whether he had any sort of license to practice medicine at all. Because — his rationalization aside — I was so clearly different from his other patients, I could only assume that he had some sort of special interest in my case: perhaps he was a frustrated psychoanalyst. At worst he was some combination of quack and prophet — Father Divine, Sister Kenny, and Bernarr Mac-Fadden combined (all of them quite effective people), with elements of faith healer and armchair Freud thrown in — running a semi-legitimate rest home for senile eccentrics; and yet one couldn't easily laugh off his forcefulness, and his insights frequently struck home. As a matter of fact, I was unable to make any judgment one way or the other about him or the farm or the therapies.

A most extraordinary Doctor. Although I kept telling myself that I was just going along with the joke, I actually did move down to East Chase Street; I took a job as an assembler on the line of the Chevrolet factory out on Broening Highway, where I operated an air wrench that bolted leaf springs on the left side of Chevrolet chassis, and I joined the U.A.W. I read Sartre but had difficulty deciding how to apply him to specific situations (How did existentialism help one decide whether to carry one's lunch to work or buy it in the factory cafeteria? I had no head for philosophy). I played poker with my fellow assemblers, took walks from Chase Street down to the waterfront and back, and attended B movies. Temperamentally I was already pretty much of an atheist most of the time, and the proscription of women was a small burden, for I was not, as a rule, heavily sexed. I applied Sinistrality, Antecedence, and Alphabetical Priority religiously (though in some instances I found it hard to decide which of those devices best fitted the situation). And every quarter for the next two years I drove over to the Remobilization Farm for advice. It would be idle for me to speculate further on why I assented to this curious alliance, which more often than not is insulting to me — I presume that anyone interested in causes will have found plenty to pick from by now in this account.

I left myself sitting in the Progress and Advice Room, I believe, in September of 1953, waiting for the Doctor. My mood on this morning was an unusual one; as a rule I am almost "weatherless" the moment I enter the farmhouse, and I suppose that weatherlessness is the ideal condition for receiving advice, but on this morning, although I felt unemotional, I was not without weather. I felt dry, clear, and competent, for some reason or other — quite sharp and not a bit humble. In meteorological terms, my weather was *sec Supérieur*.

"How are you these days, Horner?" the Doctor asked affably as he entered the room.

"Just fine, Doctor," I replied breezily. "How's yourself?"

The Doctor took his seat, spread his knees, and regarded me critically, not answering my question.

"Have you begun teaching yet?"

"Nope. Start next week. Two sections of grammar and two of composition."

"Ah." He rolled his cigar around in his mouth. He was studying me, not what I said. "You shouldn't be teaching composition."

"Can't have everything," I said cheerfully, stretching my legs out under his chair and clasping my hands behind my head. "It was that or nothing, so I took it." The Doctor observed the position of my legs and arms.

"Who is this confident fellow you've befriended?" he asked. "One of the other teachers? He's terribly sure of himself!"

I blushed: it occurred to me that I *was* imitating Joe Morgan. "Why do you say I'm imitating somebody?"

"I didn't," the Doctor smiled. "I only asked who was the forceful fellow you've obviously met."

"None of your business, sir."

"Oh, my. Very good. It's a pity you can't take over that manner consistently—you'd never need my services again! But you're not stable enough for that yet, Jacob. Besides, you couldn't act like him when you're in his company, could you? Anyway I'm pleased to see you assuming a role. You do it, evidently, in order to face up to me: a character like your friend's would never allow itself to be insulted by some crank with his string of implausible therapies, eh?"

"That's right, Doctor," I said, but much of the fire had gone out of me under his analysis.

"This indicates to me that you're ready for Mythotherapy, since you seem to be already practicing it without knowing it, and therapeutically, too. But it's best you be aware of what you're doing, so that you won't break down through ignorance. Some time ago I told you to become an existentialist. Did you read Sartre?"

"Some things. Frankly I really didn't get to be an existentialist."

"No? Well, no matter now. Mythotherapy is based on two assumptions: that human existence precedes human essence, if either of the two terms really signifies anything; and that a man is free not only to choose his own essence but to change it at will. Those are both good existentialist premises, and whether they're true or false is of no concern to us — they're *useful* in your case."

He went on to explain Mythotherapy.

"In life," he said, "there are no essentially major or minor characters. To that extent, all fiction and biography, and most historiography, are a lie. Everyone is necessarily the hero of his own life story. *Hamlet* could be told from Polonius's point of view and called *The Tragedy of Polonius, Lord Chamberlain of Denmark.* He didn't think he was a minor character in anything, I daresay. Or suppose you're an usher in a wedding. From the groom's viewpoint he's the major character; the others play supporting parts, even the bride. From your viewpoint, though, the wedding is a minor episode in the very interesting history of *your* life, and the bride and groom both are minor figures. What you've done is choose to *play the part* of a minor character: it can be pleasant for you to *pretend to be* less important than you know you are, as Odysseus does when he disguises as a swineherd. And every member of the congregation at the wedding sees himself as the major character, condescending to witness the spectacle. So in this sense fiction isn't a lie at all, but a true representation of the distortion that everyone makes of life.

"Now, not only are we the heroes of our own life stories—we're the ones who conceive the story, and give other people the essences of minor characters. But since no man's life story as a rule is ever one story with a coherent plot, we're always reconceiving just the sort of hero we are, and consequently just the sort of minor roles that other people are supposed to play. This is generally true. If any man displays almost the same character day in and day out, all day long, it's either because he has no imagination, like an actor who can play only one role, or because he has an imagination so comprehensive that he sees each particular situation of his life as an episode in some grand over-all plot, and can so distort the situations that the same type of hero can deal with them all. But this is most unusual.

"This kind of role-assigning is myth-making, and when it's done consciously or unconsciously for the purpose of aggrandizing or protecting your ego — and it's probably done for this purpose all the time — it becomes Mythotherapy. Here's the point: an immobility such as you experienced that time in Penn Station is possible only to a person who for some reason or other has ceased to participate in Mythotherapy. At that time on the bench you were neither a major nor a minor character: you were no character at all. It's because this has happened once that it's necessary for me to explain to you something that comes quite naturally to everyone else. It's like teaching a paralytic how to walk again.

"Now many crises in people's lives occur because the hero role that they've assumed for one situation or set of situations no longer applies to some new situation that comes up, or—the same thing in effect—because they haven't the imagination to distort the new situation to fit their old role. This happens to parents, for instance, when their children grow older. If the new situation is too overpowering to ignore, and they can't find a mask to meet it with, they may become schizophrenic—a last-resort mask—or simply shattered. All questions of integrity involve this consideration, because a man's integrity consists in being faithful to the script he's written for himself.

"I've said you're too unstable to play any one part all the time—you're also too unimaginative—so for you these crises had better be met by changing scripts as often as necessary. This should come naturally to you; the important thing for you is to realize what you're doing so you won't get caught without a script, or with the wrong script in a given situation. You did well, for example, for a beginner, to walk in here so confidently and almost arrogantly a while ago, and assign me the role of a quack. But you must be able to change masks at once if by some means or other I'm able to make the one you walked in with untenable. Perhaps — I'm just suggesting an offhand possibility—you could change to thinking of me as The Sagacious Old Men-

tor, a kind of Machiavellian Nestor, say, and yourself as The Ingenuous But
Promising Young Protégé, a young Alexander, who someday will put all
these teachings into practice and far outshine the master. Do you get the
idea? Or—this is repugnant,but it could be used as a last resort—The Silently
Indignant Young Man, who tolerates the ravings of a Senile Crank but who
will leave this house unsullied by them. I call this repugnant because if you
ever used it you'd cut yourself off from much that you haven't learned yet.

"It's extremely important that you learn to assume these masks
wholeheartedly. Don't think there's anything behind them: *ego* means *I*
and *I* means *ego*, and the ego by definition is a mask. Where there's no ego
— this is you on the bench—there's no *I*. If you sometimes have the feeling
that your mask is *insincere* — impossible word! — it's only because one of
your masks is incompatible with another. You mustn't put on two at a time.
There's a source of conflict, and conflict between masks, like absence of
masks, is a source of immobility. The more sharply you can dramatize your
situation, and define your own role and everybody else's role, the safer
you'll be. It doesn't matter in Mythotherapy for paralytics whether your role
is major or minor, as long as it's clearly conceived, but in the nature of things
it'll normally always be major. Now say something."

I could not.

"Say something!" the doctor ordered. "Move! Take a role!"

I tried hard to think of one, but I could not.

"Damn you!" the Doctor cried. He kicked back his chair and leaped upon
me, throwing me to the floor and pounding me roughly.

"Hey!" I hollered, entirely startled by his attack. "Cut it out! What the
hell!" I struggled with him and, being both larger and stronger than he, soon
had him off me. We stood facing each other warily, panting from the exer-
tion.

"You watch that stuff!" I said belligerently. "I could make plenty of trouble
for you if I wanted to, I'll bet!"

"Anything wrong?" asked Mrs. Dockey, sticking her head into the room. I
would not want to tangle with her.

"No, not now," the Doctor smiled, brushing the knees of his white trousers. "A little Pugilistic Therapy for Jacob Horner. No trouble." She closed
the door.

"Shall we continue our talk?" he asked me, his eyes twinkling. "You were
speaking in a manly way about making trouble."

But I was no longer in a mood to go along with the whole ridiculous
business. I'd had enough of the old lunatic for this quarter.

"Or perhaps you've had enough of The Old Crank for today, eh?"

"What would the sheriff in Wicomico think of this farm?" I grumbled
uncomfortably. "Suppose the police were sent out to investigate Sexual
Therapy?"

The Doctor was unruffled by my threats.

"Do you intend to send them?" he asked pleasantly.

"Do you think I wouldn't?"

"I've no idea," he said, still undisturbed.

"Do you dare me to?"

This question, for some reason or other, visibly upset him: he looked at me sharply.

"Indeed I do not," he said at once. "I'm sure you're quite able to do it. I'm sorry if my tactic for mobilizing you just then made you angry. I did it with all good intent. You *were* paralyzed again, you know."

"Horseshit!" I sneered. "You and your paralysis!"

"You *have* had enough for today, Horner!" the Doctor said. He too was angry now. "Get out! I hope you get paralyzed driving sixty miles an hour on your way home!" He raised his voice. "Get out of here, you damned moron!"

His obviously genuine anger immediately removed mine, which after the first instant had of course been only a novel mask.

"I'm sorry, Doctor," I said. "I won't lose my temper again."

We exchanged smiles.

"Why not?" he laughed. "It's both therapeutic and pleasant to lose your temper in certain situations." He relit his cigar, which had been dropped during our scuffle. "Two interesting things were demonstrated in the past few minutes, Jacob Horner. I can't tell you about them until your next visit. Good-by, now. Don't forget to pay Mrs. Dockey."

Out he strode, cool as could be, and few moments later out strode I: A Trifle Shaken, But Sure Of My Strength.

Bipolar Disorder, Mixed

Individuals with Bipolar Disorder, Mixed have had at least one manic episode (p. 81) and usually also a major depressive episode (p. 88). The initial episode is usually manic and relatively brief; it is immediately followed by a major depressive episode, also relatively brief.

In "The Chrysanthemums, "John Steinbeck portrays a day in the life of Elisa Allen, who seems to experience both a manic and a depressive episode. What contributes to Elisa's elated mood? What symptoms of a manic episode are evident? What triggers her depression? What symptoms of a major depressive episode are present?

THE CHRYSANTHEMUMS

John Steinbeck

The high grey-flannel fog of winter closed off the Salinas Valley from the sky and from all the rest of the world. On every side it sat like a lid on the mountains and made of the great valley a closed pot. On the broad, level land floor the gang plows bit deep and left the black earth shining like metal where the shares had cut. On the foothill ranches across the Salinas River, the yellow stubble fields seemed to be bathed in pale cold sunshine, but there was no sunshine in the valley now in December. The thick willow scrub along the river flamed with sharp and positive yellow leaves.

It was a time of quiet and of waiting. The air was cold and tender. A light wind blew up from the southwest so that the farmers were mildly hopeful of a good rain before long; but fog and rain did not go together.

Across the river, on Henry Allen's foothill ranch there was little work to be done, for the hay was cut and stored and the orchards were plowed up to receive the rain deeply when it should come. The cattle on the higher slopes were becoming shaggy and rough-coated.

Elisa Allen, working in her flower garden, looked down across the yard and saw Henry, her husband, talking to two men in business suits. The three of them stood by the tractor shed, each man with one foot on the side of the little Fordson. They smoked cigarettes and studied the machine as they talked.

Elisa watched them for a moment and then went back to her work. She was thirty-five. Her face was lean and strong and her eyes were as clear as water. Her figure looked blocked and heavy in her gardening costume, a man's black hat pulled low down over her eyes, clod-hopper shoes, a fig-ured print dress almost completely covered by a big corduroy apron with four big pockets to hold the snips, the trowel and scratcher, the seeds and the knife she worked with. She wore heavy leather gloves to protect her hands while she worked.

She was cutting down the old year's chrysanthemum stalks with a pair of short and powerful scissors. She looked down toward the men by the tractor shed now and then. Her face was eager and mature and handsome; even her work with the scissors was over-eager, over-powerful. The chrysan-themum stems seemed too small and easy for her energy.

She brushed a cloud of hair out of her eyes with the back of her glove, and left a smudge of earth on her cheek in doing it. Behind her stood the neat white farm house with red geraniums close-banked around it as high as the windows. It was a hard-swept looking little house, with hard-polished win-dows, and a clean mud-mat on the front steps.

Elisa cast another glance toward the tractor shed. The strangers were get-ting into their Ford coupe. She took off a glove and put her strong fingers

down into the forest of new green chrysanthemum sprouts that were growing around the old roots. She spread the leaves and looked down among the
close-growing stems. No aphids were there, no sowbugs or snails or cut-
worms. Her terrier fingers destroyed such pests before they could get
started.

Elisa started at the sound of her husband's voice. He had come near
quietly, and he leaned over the wire fence that protected her flower garden
from cattle and dogs and chickens.

"At it again," he said. "You've got a strong new crop coming."

Elisa straightened her back and pulled on the gardening glove again.
"Yes. They'll be strong this coming year." In her tone and on her face there
was a little smugness.

"You've got a gift with things," Henry observed. "Some of those yellow
chrysanthemums you had this year were ten inches across. I wish you'd
work out in the orchard and raise some apples that big."

Her eyes sharpened. "Maybe I could do it, too. I've a gift with things, all
right. My mother had it. She could stick anything in the ground and make it
grow. She said it was having planters' hands that knew how to do it."

"Well, it sure works with flowers," he said.

"Henry, who were those men you were talking to?"

"Why, sure, that's what I came to tell you. They were from the Western
Meat Company. I sold those thirty head of three-year-old steers. Got nearly
my own price, too."

"Good," she said. "Good for you."

"And I thought," he continued, "I thought how it's Saturday afternoon,
and we might go into Salinas for dinner at a restaurant, and then to a picture
show — to celebrate, you see."

"Good," she repeated. "Oh, yes. That will be good."

Henry put on his joking tone. "There's fights tonight. How'd you like to go
to the fights?"

"Oh, no," she said breathlessly. "No, I wouldn't like fights."

"Just fooling, Elisa. We'll go to a movie. Let's see. It's two now. I'm going
to take Scotty and bring down those steers from the hill. It'll take us maybe
two hours. We'll go in town about five and have dinner at the Cominos
Hotel. Like that?"

"Of course I'll like it. It's good to eat away from home."

"All right, then. I'll go get up a couple of horses."

She said, "I'll have plenty of time to transplant some of these sets, I
guess."

She heard her husband calling Scotty down by the barn. And a little later
she saw the two men ride up the pale yellow hillside in search of the steers.

There was a little square sandy bed kept for rooting the chrysanthemums.
With her trowel she turned the soil over and over, and smoothed it and

patted it firm. Then she dug ten parallel trenches to receive the sets. Back at the chrysanthemum bed she pulled out the little crisp shoots, trimmed off the leaves of each one with her scissors and laid it on a small orderly pile.

A squeak of wheels and plod of hoofs came from the road. Elisa looked up. The country road ran along the dense bank of willows and cottonwoods that bordered the river, and up this road came a curious vehicle, curiously drawn. It was an old spring-wagon, with a round canvas top on it like the cover of a prairie schooner. It was driven by an old bay horse and a little grey-and-white burro. A big stubble-bearded man sat between the cover flaps and drove the crawling team. Underneath the wagon, between the hind wheels, a lean and rangy mongrel dog walked sedately. Words were painted on the canvas, in clumsy, crooked letters. "Pots, pans, knives, sisors, lawn mores, Fixed." Two rows of articles, and the triumphantly definitive "Fixed" below. The black paint had run down in little sharp points beneath each letter.

Elisa, squatting on the ground, watched to see the crazy, loose-jointed wagon pass by. But it didn't pass. It turned into the farm road in front of her house, crooked old wheels skirling and squeaking. The rangy dog darted from between the wheels and ran ahead. Instantly the two ranch shepherds flew out at him. Then all three stopped, and with stiff and quivering tails, with taut straight legs, with ambassadorial dignity, they slowly circled, sniffing daintily. The caravan pulled up to Elisa's wire fence and stopped. Now the newcomer dog, feeling outnumbered, lowered his tail and retired under the wagon with raised hackles and bared teeth.

The man on the wagon seat called out, "That's a bad dog in a fight when he gets started."

Elisa laughed. "I see he is. How soon does he generally get started?"

The man caught up her laughter and echoed it heartily. "Sometimes not for weeks and weeks," he said. He climbed stiffly down, over the wheel. The horse and donkey drooped like unwatered flowers.

Elisa saw that he was a very big man. Although his hair and beard were greying, he did not look old. His worn black suit was wrinkled and spotted with grease. The laughter had disappeared from his face and eyes the moment his laughing voice ceased. His eyes were dark, and they were full of the brooding that gets in the eyes of teamsters and of sailors. The calloused hands he rested on the wire fence were cracked, and every crack was a black line. He took off his battered hat.

"I'm off my general road, ma'am," he said. "Does this dirt road cut over across the river to the Los Angeles highway?"

Elisa stood up and shoved the thick scissors in her apron pocket. "Well, yes, it does, but it winds around and then fords the river. I don't think your team could pull through the sand."

He replied with some asperity, "It might surprise you what them beasts can pull through."

"When they get started?" she asked.

He smiled for a second. "Yes. When they get started."

"Well," said Elisa, "I think you'll have time if you go back to the Salinas road and pick up the highway there."

He drew a big finger down the chicken wire and made it sing. "I ain't in any hurry, ma'am. I go from Seattle to San Diego and back every year. Takes all my time. About six months each way. I aim to follow nice weather."

Elisa took off her gloves and stuffed them in the apron pocket with the scissors. She touched the under edge of her man's hat, searching for fugitive hairs. "That sounds like a nice kind of a way to live," she said.

He leaned confidentially over the fence. "Maybe you noticed the writing on my wagon. I mend pots and sharpen knives and scissors. You got any of them things to do?"

"Oh, no," she said quickly. "Nothing like that." Her eyes hardened with resistance.

"Scissors is the worst thing," he explained. "Most people just ruin scissors trying to sharpen 'em, but I know how. I got a special tool. It's a little bobbit kind of thing, and patented. But it sure does the trick."

"No. My scissors are all sharp."

"All right, then. Take a pot," he continued earnestly, "a bent pot, or a pot with a hole. I can make it like new so you don't have to buy no new ones. That's a saving for you."

"No," she said shortly. "I tell you I have nothing like that for you to do."

His face fell to an exaggerated sadness. His voice took on a whining undertone. "I ain't had a thing to do today. Maybe I won't have no supper tonight. You see I'm off my regular road. I know folks on the highway clear from Seattle to San Diego. They save their things for me to sharpen up because they know I do it so good and save them money."

"I'm sorry," Elisa said irritably. "I haven't anything for you to do."

His eyes left her face and fell to searching the ground. They roamed about until they came to the chrysanthemum bed where she had been working. "What's them plants, ma'am?"

The irritation and resistance melted from Elisa's face. "Oh, those are chrysanthemums, giant whites and yellows. I raise them every year, bigger than anybody around here."

"Kind of a long-stemmed flower? Looks like a quick puff of colored smoke?" he asked.

"That's it. What a nice way to describe them."

"They smell kind of nasty till you get used to them," he said.

"It's a good bitter smell," she retorted, "not nasty at all."

He changed his tone quickly. "I like the smell myself."

"I had ten-inch blooms this year," she said.

The man leaned farther over the fence. "Look. I know a lady down the road a piece, has got the nicest garden you ever seen. Got nearly every kind of flower but no chrysanthemums. Last time I was mending a copper-bottom washtub for her (that's a hard job but I do it good), she said to me, "If you ever run acrost some nice chrysanthemums I wish you'd try to get me a few seeds. That's what she told me."

Elisa's eyes grew alert and eager. "She couldn't have known much about chrysanthemums. You can raise them from seed, but it's much easier to root the little sprouts you see there."

"Oh," he said. "I s'pose I can't take none to her, then."

"Why yes you can," Elisa cried. "I can put some in damp sand, and you can carry them right along with you. They'll take root in the pot if you keep them damp. And then she can transplant them."

"She'd sure like to save some, ma'am. You say they're nice ones?"

"Beautiful," she said. "Oh, beautiful." Her eyes shone. She tore off the battered hat and shook out her dark pretty hair. "I'll put them in a flower pot, and you can take them right with you. Come into the yard."

While the man came through the picket fence Elisa ran excitedly along the geranium-bordered path to the back of the house. And she returned carrying a big red flower pot. The gloves were forgotten now. She kneeled on the ground by the starting bed and dug up the sandy soil with her fingers and scooped it into the bright new flower pot. Then she picked up the little pile of shoots she had prepared. With her strong fingers she pressed them into the sand and tamped around them with her knuckles. The man stood over her. "I'll tell you what to do," she said. "You remember so you can tell the lady."

"Yes, I'll try to remember."

"Well, look. These will take root in about a month. Then she must set them out, about a foot apart in good rich earth like this, see?" She lifted a handful of dark soil for him to look at. "They'll grow fast and tall. Now remember this. In July tell her to cut them down, about eight inches from the ground."

"Before they bloom?" he asked.

"Yes, before they bloom." Her face was tight with eagerness. "They'll grow right up again. About the last of September the buds will start."

She stopped and seemed perplexed. "It's the budding that takes the most care," she said hesitantly. "I don't know how to tell you." She looked deep into his eyes, searchingly. Her mouth opened a little, and she seemed to be listening. "I'll try to tell you," she said. "Did you ever hear of planting hands?"

"Can't say I have, ma'am."

"Well, I can only tell you what if feels like. It's when you're picking off the buds you don't want. Everything goes right down into your finger-tips. You watch your fingers work. They do it themselves. You can feel how it is. They

pick and pick the buds. They never make a mistake. They're with the plant. Do you see? Your fingers and the plant. You can feel that, right up your arm. They know. They never make a mistake. You can feel it. When you're like that you can't do anything wrong. Do you see that? Can you understand that?"
passionately.

The man's eyes narrowed. He looked away self-consciously. "Maybe I know," he said. "Sometimes in the night in the wagon there ——"

Elisa's voice grew husky. She broke in on him. "I've never lived as you do, but I know what you mean. When the night is dark—why, the stars are sharp-pointed, and there's quiet. Why, you rise up and up! Every pointed star gets driven into your body. It's like that. Hot and sharp and—lovely."

Kneeling there, her hand went out toward his legs in the greasy black trousers. Her hesitant fingers almost touched the cloth. Then her hand dropped to the ground. She crouched low like a fawning dog.

He said, "It's nice, just like you say. Only when you don't have no dinner, it ain't."

She stood up then, very straight, and her face was ashamed. She held the flower pot out to him and placed it gently in his arms. "Here. Put it in your wagon, on the seat, where you can watch it. Maybe I can find something for you to do."

At the back of the house she dug in the can pile and found two old and battered aluminum saucepans. She carried them back and gave them to him. "Here, maybe you can fix these."

His manner changed. He became professional. "Good as new I can fix them." At the back of his wagon he set a little anvil, and out of an oily tool box dug a small machine hammer. Elisa came through the gate to watch him while he pounded out the dents in the kettles. His mouth grew sure and knowing. At a difficult part of the work he sucked his under-lip.

"You sleep right in the wagon?" Elisa asked.

"Right in the wagon, ma'am. Rain or shine I'm dry as a cow in there."

"It must be nice," she said. "It must be very nice. I wish women could do such things."

"It ain't the right kind of a life for a woman."

Her upper lip raised a little, showing her teeth. "How do you know? How can you tell?" she said.

"I don't know, ma'am," he protested. "Of course I don't know. Now here's your kettles, done. You don't have to buy no new ones."

"How much?"

"Oh, fifty cents'll do. I keep my prices down and my work good. That's why I have all them satisfied customers up and down the highway."

Elisa brought him a fifty-cent piece from the house and dropped it in his hand. "You might be surprised to have a rival some time. I can sharpen scissors, too. And I can beat the dents out of little pots. I could show you what a woman might do."

He put his hammer back in the oily box and shoved the little anvil out of sight. "It would be a lonely life for a woman, ma'am, and a scarey life, too, with animals creeping under the wagon all night." He climbed over the singletree, steadying himself with a hand on the burro's white rump. He settled himself in the seat, picked up the lines. "Thank you kindly, ma'am," he said. "I'll do like you told me; I'll go back and catch the Salinas road."

"Mind," she called, "if you're long in getting there, keep the sand damp."

"Sand, ma'am? ... Sand? Oh sure. You mean around the chrysanthemums. Sure I will." He clucked his tongue. The beasts leaned luxuriously into their collars. The mongrel dog took his place between the back wheels. The wagon turned and crawled out the entrance road and back the way it had come, along the river.

Elisa stood in front of her wire fence watching the slow progress of the caravan. Her shoulders were straight, her head thrown back, her eyes half-closed, so that the scene came vaguely into them. Her lips moved silently, forming the words "Good-bye—good-bye." Then she whispered, "That's a bright direction. There's a glowing there." The sound of her whisper startled her. She shook herself free and looked about to see whether anyone had been listening. Only the dogs had heard. They lifted their heads toward her from their sleeping in the dust, and then stretched out their chins and settled asleep again. Elisa turned and ran hurriedly into the house.

In the kitchen she reached behind the stove and felt the water tank. It was full of hot water from the noonday cooking. In the bathroom she tore off her soiled clothes and flung them into the corner. And then she scrubbed herself with a little block of pumice, legs and thighs, loins and chest and arms, until her skin was scratched and red. When she had dried herself she stood in front of a mirror in her bedroom and looked at her body. She tightened her stomach and threw out her chest. She turned and looked over her shoulder at her back.

After a while she began to dress, slowly. She put on her newest under-clothing and her nicest stockings and the dress which was the symbol of her prettiness. She worked carefully on her hair, pencilled her eyebrows and rouged her lips.

Before she was finished she heard the little thunder of hoofs and the shouts of Henry and his helper as they drove the red steers into the corral. She heard the gate bang shut and set herself for Henry's arrival.

His step sounded on the porch. He entered the house calling, "Elisa, where are you?"

"In my room, dressing. I'm not ready. There's hot water for your bath. Hurry up. It's getting late."

When she heard him splashing in the tub, Elisa laid his dark suit on the bed, and shirt and socks and tie beside it. She stood his polished shoes on the floor beside the bed. Then she went to the porch and sat primly and stiffly down. She looked toward the river road where the willow-line was still yellow with frosted leaves so that under the high grey fog they seemed a thin band of sunshine. This was the only color in the grey afternoon. She sat unmoving for a long time. Her eyes blinked rarely.

Henry came banging out of the door, shoving his tie inside his vest as he came. Elisa stiffened and her face grew tight. Henry stopped short and looked at her. "Why — why, Elisa. You look so nice!"

"Nice? You think I look nice? What do you mean by 'nice'?"

Henry blundered on. "I don't know. I mean you look different, strong and happy."

"I am strong? Yes, strong. What do you mean 'strong'?"

He looked bewildered. "You're playing some kind of a game," he said helplessly. "It's a kind of a play. You look strong enough to break a calf over your knee, happy enough to eat it like a watermelon."

For a second she lost her rigidity. "Henry! Don't talk like that. You didn't know what you said." She grew complete again. "I'm strong," she boasted. "I never knew before how strong."

Henry looked down toward the tractor shed, and when he brought his eyes back to her, they were his own again. "I'll get out the car. You can put on your coat while I'm starting."

Elisa went into the house. She heard him drive to the gate and idle down his motor, and then she took a long time to put on her hat. She pulled it here and pressed it there. When Henry turned the motor off she slipped into her coat and went out.

The little roadster bounced along on the dirt road by the river, raising the birds and driving the rabbits into the brush. Two cranes flapped heavily over the willow-line and dropped into the river-bed.

Far ahead on the road Elisa saw a dark speck. She knew.

She tried not to look as they passed it, but her eyes would not obey. She whispered to herself sadly, "He might have thrown them off the road. That wouldn't have been much trouble, not very much. But he kept the pot," she explained. "He had to keep the pot. That's why he couldn't get them off the road."

The roadster turned a bend and she saw the caravan ahead. She swung full around toward her husband so she could not see the little covered wagon and the mismatched team as the car passed them.

In a moment it was over. The thing was done. She did not look back. She said loudly, to be heard above the motor, "It will be good, tonight, a good dinner."

"Now you're changed again," Henry complained. He took one hand

from the wheel and patted her knee. "I ought to take you in to dinner of-
tener. It would be good for both of us. We get so heavy out on the ranch."

"Henry," she asked, "could we have wine at dinner?"

"Sure we could. Say! That will be fine."

She was silent for a while; then she said, "Henry, at those prize fights, do
the men hurt each other very much?"

"Sometimes a little, not often. Why?"

"Well, I've read how they break noses, and blood runs down their chests.
I've read how the fighting gloves get heavy and soggy with blood."

He looked around at her. "What's the matter, Elisa? I didn't know you
read things like that." He brought the car to a stop, then turned to the right
over the Salinas River bridge.

"Do any women ever go to the fights?" she asked.

"Oh, sure, some. What's the matter, Elisa? Do you want to go? I don't
think you'd like it, but I'll take you if you really want to go."

She relaxed limply in the seat. "Oh, no. No. I don't want to go. I'm sure I
don't." Her face was turned away from him. "It will be enough if we can
have wine. It will be plenty." She turned up her coat collar so he could not
see that she was crying weakly — like an old woman.

Other Specific Affective Disorders

Cyclothymic Disorder

DSM-III recognizes two Other Specific Affective Disorders: Cyclothymic Disorder and Dysthymic Disorder (p.121).

Individuals with Cyclothymic Disorder experience numerous periods
during which both manic (p. 81) and depressive (p. 88) symptoms
affect them. Their episodes of mania and depression are relatively mild,
but they recur with some degree of regularity. This fact explains the
name *Cyclothymia*—*cycle*, circle; *thymis*, mind or temperament—regularly alternating periods of elation and depression usually unrelated to
external circumstances.

The unnamed Parson in Penelope Mortimer's story seems to have
Cyclothymic Disorder because he regularly experiences episodes of
elation and depression. Incidents of elation and its attendant symptoms
as well as incidents of depression with its accompanying symptoms
should be noted.

THE PARSON

Penelope Mortimer

He was a short, very heavy man — obese, although oddly thin in the face and with square hands, flat-tipped fingers, no flesh between the knuckles. A narrow, flat forehead that with the years grew higher, although he never appeared to become bald; eyebrows that jutted out enormously long, curly and wiry, and small eyes beneath all this tangle as sharp as terriers', but blue. They were never tender or glazed with sentiment.

His nose became larger and bonier as his forehead grew higher. As he grew older, as his face sank away from it, this nose like the prow of Methodism rising out of a receding sea. The eyes might blaze, the eyebrows bristle, the forehead soar ever more lofty, but the nose was of chapel and sin. Around the bridge, it had a pinched look of virtue and condemnation.

A long upper lip, which might have been taken off a comedian; and a mouth that changed with time more than any other feature, starting off wide and broad-lipped and ending as a thin line, an opening slit for food or, almost nonexistent, clamped around a cigarette.

All this head, with its contradictions and discrepancies, rode too large for the short heavy body. His back view, in suspended gray flannels and shirtsleeves, digging, weeding, mowing a lawn, was the rear of a squat old elephant — the same vast, solid gray folds ending in short, tubular legs, the same lumbering quality.

And yet he was deft. Until he became ill and crazy and clumsy, he could make or mend most things. He played chess in a series of vicious jabs, pouncing the pieces down, grunting, puffing great blasts of smoke, and usually winning — his one intellectual achievement.

He was a clergyman for one reason only — there was nothing else he could possibly have been. As a small boy, bullied and teased by six sisters and four brothers, he sat under the nursery table chanting, "Mama, Papa, all the children are disagreeable except me...." God shone a compassionate eye through the silk tassels on the green serge cloth that covered the table, disregarded the ten clever goody-goodies, and picked him out. He began preaching — a stocky, timid, bombastic little boy shouting of Hell-fire in the front parlor while his brothers sneered and his sisters tittered and his father played the harmonium. As a reward, his grandmother would give him lollipops, lovingly slipped from her tongue onto his. The only color in the house was the white of the girls' petticoats whisking round dark corners.

He went to various schools, but he learned nothing. He was beaten, put in the attic, kept on bread and water. This made him cry, convinced him that he was a sinner, but made him even more stupid. At sixteen, hair slicked down from a center parting, stiff-collared, in hound's-tooth check, he was taken away from school and bound as an apprentice in his father's printing firm. The other apprentices were disagreeable; he clung firmly to God and became a preacher in the local Wesleyan chapel, flaying the nodding bonnets with his great new voice, guiltily and savagely in love with a girl called Maisie. Maisie, a bobbish little rich girl of fifteen, was frightened and ran away; she never married, but for sixty years kept, transfixed, her startled giggle, her look of petrified alarm.

He might have gone on like this for some years, but his father died; the printing firm collapsed. He enrolled in the Methodist Theological College at Putney.

It was a ghastly mistake. Black-suited, forced to attend long lectures on the Roman Baptismal creed, to puzzle his way through Athanasius and Marcellus and the Cappadocians, to battle with the theory of enhypostasia and Socinianism and kenosis, to listen to pale young men with clammy hands discussing Theodore of Mopsuestia and the laws of ecclesiastical polity—all this was the nearest thing to Hell he had ever known. God moved away from him and hid in a cloud of unknowing. For the first time in his life, with the agony of a child who sees his father pinching the maid's bottom, he had Doubts. He wept and prayed, but it was no good. The College expelled him for failing all his examinations. He thought, as he walked slowly away with his Gladstone bag and his Bible, of walking straight on into the placid river. Instead, he became a Unitarian.

He could preach again,and when he was preaching he could convince himself of anything. He shook his square hands, howled, and whispered; his huge, resonant voice shook the corrugated-iron roofs of dismal chapels, stroked the souls of girls in village halls. But afterward, alone in his lodgings, he suffered. Preaching, although he worked as hard as he knew how to on his sermons, didn't take up much time. He had begun to read Nietzsche and, almost more furtively, H. G. Wells; he had heard, uneasily, of "Man and Superman," and the phrase "life-force" began to creep into his sermons. The idea of Life, which had nothing to do with living, had begun to take the place of God, who had shown Himself to have nothing to do with religion. "Life is Love!" he bawled to a startled congregation. Pinch-mouthed, severely buttoning their gloves, they asked him to leave. He packed his "Zarathustra" and went.

What to do with him now? He was twenty-eight, uneducated, unqualified, tormented by sins he hadn't committed and unable to understand the ones he had, tremendously ambitious without the slightest talent for success, full of urges and yearning and pains of the soul, frightening and frightened and altogether a mess. The family gave him a piece of land in the middle of Manitoba and sent him off, with a younger brother, to Canada. Perhaps, as the ship heaved off into the Liverpool fog, they thought they had seen the last of him.

He never found the piece of land. Perhaps he didn't really look. He took various trains in the hope of finding it, but always ended up sitting on his box in some desolate way station, waiting for a train to take him back to Winnipeg. After several of these excursions, he gave up and took a job in a printing firm. It was cold, barbaric. Everyone was disagreeable, and he spent hours every night reading Browning out loud to himself in order to keep his accent pure. Away from any form of organized religion, his doubts were calmed; the longer he stayed a printer, the firmer his faith became. After a year of it, he wrote home for his passage money. His cold, ink-stained fingers could hardly hold the pen. "I know," he wrote, "that God intends me for the Ministry."

His mother flew into one of her rages, whistled "Worthy Is the Lamb" under her breath, and sent her daughters cowering to their rooms. But she was lonely. All her sons had left her and, with this one exception, were living brash and ungodly lives, both in jail and out. One was company-promoting in Sydney, another was razing Kanaka villages to the ground for the hell of it and living with a native girl who played the mouth organ and filled his shoes with sugar, another had just killed a lumberman in an argument and temporarily disappeared. She sent the passage money.

So he came home, chilly, chastened, and full of hope. He would study, he would do what he was told. Somebody must want him; somebody must recognize his ability. As he set foot on English soil at Liverpool, he felt that one blast of his voice would be enough. "Why," bishops would ask each other, "has he been neglected so long?"

Six months later, in a tweed hat and knickerbockers, he was bicycling about the lanes of Wiltshire, his heavy head bent low over the handle bars, his stout legs numbly pedalling. He was an itinerant preacher again. Browning went with him everywhere and his text was always the same: "'Tis not what man does that exalts him, but what man would do." He read "Saul" aloud, with great passion, in the drawing rooms of the local gentry. One of their daughters, a handsome, strong-willed, ailing woman of thirty-five, fell in love with him. They married at eight o'clock one morning in a thick fog, walking to the chapel through muddy fields and going off to a disastrous honeymoon in lodgings at Eastbourne.

Marriage, far from calming him, goaded him to a kind of fury. He had always been violently, if furtively, conscious of sex; now, legitimately sexual, he became intoxicated with the idea that the world was more or less equally divided into men and women. Free love and the life-force and the emancipation of women all whirled together in his innocent brain, causing an extraordinary chaos in which women were exactly like men and yet were at the same time accessible. His heart gave out under the strain. He became ill. His wife had a nervous breakdown. The Wesleyans turned him out. His in-laws,

stern materialists who believed devoutly in success, refused to have anything to do with him. There seemed, this time, no way out.

But, of course, there was. All his life he had been beating his head against
the narrow limits of Nonconformity. The Church of England, that great,
placid, unshakable compromise, loomed calm and radiant over the horizon.
Why had he never thought of it before? The gracious, socially acceptable
vicarages; the brown, book-lined studies where even a heretic could sleep
undisturbed; the great cathedrals that could ring with his reading of Isaiah, of
which he was rightly proud; and, above all, the limitless scope for a man of
talent. Revived, with passionate energy and pin-bright faith, he went off to
Lambeth Palace and the Archbishop of Canterbury.

The first question he was asked was whether he had any money. None.
Oxford or Cambridge? Neither. Who would speak for him? No one. A
fortnight later, a letter came from the Palace, signed with one spidery name;
he was not, it was thought, suitable for the Church of England.

Now it was a case of do or die. Browning was no longer any use to him;
neither was life-force. He was well into his thirties, and God was passing him
by. He badgered, he pestered, he wrote long, impassioned letters. For the
first time in his life he worked, swallowing great chunks of doctrine and not
daring to think how uneasily it lay. The end—the study with its armchair and
the mellow peal of bells—was all that mattered. When at last they accepted
him, he wept for joy, although with the appearance of awful grief. Once in
the Church, he knew, nothing short of murder or flagrant adultery would get
him out.

They gave him the job of curate in a parish in the East End of London. His
residence was a little slum house next to the gasworks; lascars prowled the
streets at night and the church was a grimy great place with a sparse scattering of old women who wanted to take the weight off their feet and get away
for an hour or two from their drunken husbands. He found himself looking
with hostile envy at the local Catholic priest, but, of course, it was too late for
that. He applied himself to the business of visiting the sick, who were very
sick, and whom he found very disagreeable.

However, London had something to be said for it. He went, having carefully removed his dog collar, to a private performance of "Mrs. Warren's
Profession;" he got to know a few vaguely literary personalities—the humble outer fringe of the Café Royal world; he began to write himself, pouring
out his untidy feelings on Life and sex and God in dull, pompous sentences
to which his wife listened with an expression of hopeless martyrdom that
eventually became permanent. For her, as a curate's wife, there had begun
the lifelong task of keeping up appearances; she did this with increasing skill,
but once alone with her husband she became quite silent, an industrious
shadow, locked and bolted against attack.

They were now secure. He was still fairly young, his great energy still untapped. The ideas pullulating inside him were still unexpressed; an East End curacy was hardly enough. He began looking around for something more alive, something with more scope.

He was offered a village that consisted of a cozy huddle of cottages under a gentle, sheltering hill. The squire's eighteenth-century mansion faced serenely away from the church, in its wilderness of moon daisies. The vicarage stood quiet in the sun, protected by a high pink wall — a great house full of dark passages and damp stone, mellow with dust and the smell of rotting apples. There was no sound but the swing of milk pails carried on their wooden yoke, the clop of a tired horse, the hum of a fat bee in the honeysuckle. It was hard to keep awake, and a beautiful place to die in — the Church of England at its best.

He burst in like a lion, scattering teacups and raising the warm dust. For the first time in his life, he felt a sense of power. "Yes, Vicar," the villagers said. "Of course, Vicar." They pulled their forelocks, and the squire raised his hat.

" 'The voice of him that crieth in the wilderness, Prepare ye the way of the Lord, make straight in the desert a highway...' " He was back in form again. The church shook with Isaiah, and the moon daisies were scythed down. He had a son and two hundred and fifty pounds a year, he had a study with an armchair, and six days off a week. There was only one thing missing. He no longer believed in God.

It was a terrible realization. Not only did he not believe in God, he didn't believe in the Thirty-nine Articles, the Virgin Birth, the idea of the Trinity, the Resurrection, the sanctity of marriage, or the conception of original sin. They had all, in the security and promise of his new life, deserted him.

He began desperately to try to fill the great gap. His faith in Life became almost fanatic; loving Life and living Love — it was comprehensive, unanswerable. If anyone was foolish enough to ask him exactly what it meant, his eyes blazed more fiercely than ever, he flung his arms wide and shouted, "You ask me what Life means? Life! Life speaks for itself!"

But he had to find some more practical expression for it. The villagers seemed smugly content with their uninspired existence, and those whom he buried were undeniably dead. He persuaded the squire that what was needed was a village club, a place where they could come together as a community and live a little. He helped to build it, slapping on the cement — braces straining over his great shoulders — singing at the top of his voice. It was a very ugly building, a gabled and stuccoed monstrosity among the thatched cottges and rosy brick, but when it was finished the villagers obediently used it, playing slow games of billiards and watching with delight the children of the local gentry making fools of themselves on the overelaborate stage. It was finished, and a great hopelessness came over him as he looked at it, a great hatred of his parishioners who shambled about its clean and empty rooms. It was not enough and they were not enough. There must be something more — but what?

He was now forty-six and his wife was over fifty. His son had been followed, painfully, after five intervening years, by a daughter. In order to make ends meet, his wife had started a small residential school that she called, with a hankering after sweetness, The Little People's Garden. The vicarage was overrun with children and governesses, beans growing on blotting paper, and jam jars of catkins. He took to living in an old Army hut at the bottom of the garden, where he was waited on by a surly manservant, who occasionally took notes to the house, asking the children to tea. He began sleeping in the afternoons, waking with a start to a black world of sin and atonement, the ghostly roaring of his own voice. But the sun poured lazily down through the apple trees and there was nothing to do — hours and days of nothing to do. He had a few weeks of keeping hens, who were given incredible incubators and runs of revolutionary design. One by one, they died. Two savage dogs, whom he christened Loyalty and Verity, took over the runs. They devoured the drawing-room curtains while everyone was in church, and shortly afterward the runs were empty. Their enormous collars, together with their leads and a whistle on a leather thong, hung about for some time and then were thrown by children into the tall nettles.

He still filled the church with his voice, bellowing at the deaf squire and the old women, who had heard him a thousand times, but it was becoming an effort. He would often break off after five minutes, abruptly mutter the names of Father, Son and Holy Ghost, and stamp out of the pulpit. The sense of futility made him physically ill. Unable to deafen himself with ideas, he had begun to listen to the ticking of the clock, the almost inaudible snapping of decay. There was still, perhaps, time to get out.

But, of course, he couldn't get out. the Church had him trapped as effectively as if he were behind bars. He exchanged his village for an amorphous jumble of suburban streets with identical houses crammed with office girls and bank clerks. The vicarage overlooked the railway line and shuddered all night with the crash and scream of shunting cars. He started a youth club and preached his splendid, meaningless sermons to huge congregations of children—fifteen-year-old girls, who loved him, and adolescent boys with nothing better to do. "Life!" he shouted at them desperately. "Believe in Life!" He grasped the edge of the pulpit, the tears ran down his face, he laughed, he flung his spectacles into the congregation, narrowly missing his wife, who was sitting, suffering tortures of embarrassment and misery, in the front pew. When it was all over, he would go home and play the piano — loud, frustrated, unskillful chords — or shut himself in his study and sit doing nothing until, mercifully, he fell asleep.

He began toying with theosophy, anthroposophy, spiritualism. His wife, perhaps out of loneliness, had always had a very reasonable relationship with ghosts, and this, at least — the need for something mysterious in a life spent cutting up small pieces of bread for Communion, or carrying cans of water from the kitchen tap to the font, or footing the bill for sacramental wine — they had in common. For a short while, it drew them together, but whereas she was content not to believe very much, his craving for belief grew greater as the possibility of satisfying it grew less. He could by now believe ten contradictory theories at the same time, and they tossed around in his soul like dead leaves, never settling, useless, whispering in the emptiness. The day he discovered Communism, he believed, with great gratitude, that he was saved.

Once again his energy soared. Reckless, enthusiastic, he devoted a whole issue of the parish magazine to supporting the Soviet persecution of the Church. Christ, he argued, was a Communist anyway. Nobody understood it. He was amazed. At last, after so much searching, he believed he had found the true meaning of Christianity. Did the Church of England not care for Christianity? Apparently it didn't. He was advised to go north, where, it was hoped, he might sink into oblivion.

The square, gloomy house in Lancashire rose like a fortress out of a forest of dripping shrubs — laurel and rhododendron, privet and yew. The cotton mills and foundries glowed like Hell under a steel sky, and the huge church, built in memory of the Napoleonic Wars, echoed like a tomb for the few living souls who crept inside it.

Wearily, with the resignation of a man who has been through this move many times before, he started a youth club. He was over fifty—the prime, he insisted aggressively, of life — and so heavy that it became increasingly difficult for him to move about. He went everywhere by car, hunched over the wheel, saluting his parishioners with a gesture that was half gracious, half insulting. For days at a time, he sat in his study — the same desk, the same armchair, the same glass-fronted bookshelves—speaking to no one, scribbling away at some new work that was to enlighten the world, or trying to crowd out the emptiness with bits of Bertrand Russell, a few predigested scraps of Einstein, populating his desert with Ethel Mannin, A.S. Neill, Rudolf Steiner, Mme. Blavatsky, Krafft-Ebing. Every Saturday, in a hushed house, he wrote what he thought was a new sermon, but they were all the same, a torment of words disgorged to a slowly dwindling congregation. His voice was still remarkable, but it had nothing to say. Like Fowler, Graham Greene's character in "The Quiet American," he longed for the existence of someone to whom he could say he was sorry. There was no one. For the first time in over twenty years, he brought the photograph of his mother out of his drawer, and set it between his watch and his collar box on the bedroom mantelpiece.

One day, while conducting a funeral service, he stumbled and fell into the open grave. Climbing out, cumbersome and horrified and ashamed, his surplice streaked with mud, he knew that everything was really over. He was not even afraid of death. It was no more than a hole in the ground, a box in the earth. He apologized, finished the service, and went home. There was nothing else he could do.

His searching now had the desperation of a man finally cornered, without sanctuary. He became a nudist. But in the colony where he went for a vacation he found nothing among the dripping trees but a group of elderly ladies dressed in spectacles, knitting scarves for their less enlightened relatives. At this time, he weighed over sixteen stone, and there was much of him to suffer. He spent one wretched night in the chalet he had booked for three weeks, and came home. The next morning, as dawn burst over the cotton mills, he was to be seen wandering naked about the shrubbery, a great, pale, disconsolate shape in the gritty light, looking for something irretrievably lost.

At the age of sixty, already an old man, he drifted west, to Somerset, setting up his desk, his armchair, his bookshelves in yet another study, laboriously climbing the stairs of a new pulpit, looking down from it on the same faces, the same bowed heads, the same expressions of patient boredom. The Church of England had fulfilled its promise; he was still alive, his children had been educated, he was sure of a pension, however small. With a sort of awkward gratitude, he tried to do his best. He started a youth club. He introduced religious film shows into the church. Some forgotten superstition, stirring again at last, prevented him from putting the screen on the altar, which, since the church was small, was the obvious place. He fixed it up between the choir stalls, and the congregation peered intently, uncomprehending, at the vast shadows, vaguely Oriental in appearance, that flickered, unfocussed, between the damp Norman pillars. The electrical part of the apparatus was unreliable, and to prevent himself from getting severe shocks he wore thick crepe-soled shoes under his surplice. But the films disgusted him. He gave them up, and the congregation, temporarily doubled, died away. He sat longer and longer in his study, the room thick with smoke, Elgar or Sibelius blaring from the record-player, a novel from the local library propped inside a mildewed tome on psychology or ethics. He gave up writing, gave up sending his manuscripts away. He gave up composing sermons and extemporized, meandering on about Life while the children fidgeted and the two old women yawned behind gloved hands and his wife, now years younger than he, thought briskly about something else.

Sometimes, like a man stirring in his sleep, he began to think that he must move, must change, must get out of it all. But the thought was never finished. His eyes closed, Sibelius played on unheeded, soft mounds of ash fell on his darned gray pullover. When he woke, it was time for another meal. In silence, they ate scantily, shovelling in the careless food. The house crumbled and peeled round them, unmended, uncared for. He gave up having his daily bath, came down from his cold ascetic bedroom at the top of the house to the luxurious spare room, with its great mahogany furniture and brass fire irons and little pots of dried lavender. An old, sick clergyman, he would have done better to die and be buried with honor and a rural dean in attendance. Instead, for the last time, the removal van came and took away the desk, the armchair, the bookshelves. The Church thanked him and sent him out into the world with six pounds a week and a few cordial letters of good wishes. For the first time in fifty years, Sunday became a day like any other.

He sat in a ground-floor room in North London; the room faced south and the identical rooms opposite, the identical front gardens with neat little curly girls in white socks carefully riding their tricycles on the paths. For over a year, the old man sat at his desk in this room, with the city sun pouring through the William Morris curtains.

God knows what passed through his mind. Meals came and were eaten. He was pitifully hungry, but they said he must lose weight — dandelion coffee and starch-reduced rolls — and he was beyond complaining. The days merged into months, interrupted only by the absurd celebration of sleep, when he went from the desk to the bed and sat upright, differently dressed, observing darkness.

Finally, without knowing it, he died. The nurse, to whom he was just a dead old man, bustled through her routine and left him tidy, unpillowed, slightly askew on the bed. The sun poured on through the faded linen, slanted over the leather-topped desk, with its little brass nameplate, the useless books.

The letters of condolence began to arrive. "He is passing," they said, "through the Gateway to a far, far greater happiness in that Glorious Kingdom beyond...truly thankful that his sufferings are over and now he knows, and has found what he longed for....Perhaps he is happier now....It will be a relief not to have to feel sorry for him any more, for now he has found Truth...." There was no confirmation and no denial. Already he existed only as a set of ideas, shifting and fading. They could do what they liked with him. There was no way in which he could speak for himself.

Dysthymic Disorder

The term *dysthymia* is derived from the prefix *dys*, which means "faulty" or "bad," and *thymis*, which means "mind" or "temperament." It can be defined as despondency.

Individuals with Dysthymic Disorder (sometimes called Depressive

Neurosis) have lost interest in or derive little pleasure from their usual activities or pastimes. This depression has lasted, in a relatively mild form, for at least two years, although there may have been periods in which the individuals' moods were normal.

During the depressive periods, individuals with Dysthymic Disorder may exhibit a variety of symptoms. For example, they may experience a change in sleeping patterns; they may feel tired all the time and move more slowly than usual. They may become socially withdrawn, preoccupied, and less talkative than when they are not depressed. Their attitude toward the past may be tinged with guilt because of certain activities, and their attitude toward the future may be pessimistic. They may have recurring thoughts about death.

The speaker in Nikki Giovanni's "Woman Poem" seems to have Dysthymic Disorder. She identifies both her mood and the symptoms associated with it. What are some of the specific conditions that contribute to this woman's despondency?

The Reverend Mr. Hooper in Nathaniel Hawthorne's "The Minister's Black Veil" dons a mask that dramatically rveals his mood. What incidents suggest Dysthymic Disorder? Why did he put the veil on? One should remember that Pastor Hooper's death-bed explanation seems to be a justification based on years of reflection, a justification based on the results of wearing the veil but not the initial reason for donning it.

WOMAN POEM
Nikki Giovanni

you see, my whole life
is tied up
to unhappiness
its father cooking breakfast
and me getting fat as a hog
or having no food
at all and father proving
his incompetence
again
i wish i knew how it would feel
to be free

its having a job
they won't let you work
or no work at all

castrating me
(yes it happens to women too)

its a sex object if you're pretty
and no love
or love and no sex if you're fat
get back fat black woman be a mother
grandmother strong thing but not woman
gameswoman romantic woman love needer
man seeker dick eater sweat getter
fuck needing love seeking woman

its a hole in your shoe
and buying lil sis a dress
and her saying you shouldn't
when you know
all too well—that you shouldn't

but smiles are only something we give
to properly dressed social workers
not each other
only smiles of i know
your game sister
which isn't really
a smile

joy is finding a pregnant roach
and squashing it
not finding someone to hold
let go get off get back don't turn
me on you black dog
how dare you care
about me
you ain't got no good sense
cause i ain't shit you must be lower
than that to care

its a filthy house
with yesterday's watermelon
and monday's tears
cause true ladies don't
know how to clean

its intellectual devastation
of everybody
to avoid emotional commitment
"yeah honey i would've married
him but he didn't have no degree"

its knock-kneed mini skirted
wig wearing died blond mamma's scar
born dead my scorn your whore
rough heeled broken nailed powdered
face me
whose whole life is tied
up to unhappiness
cause its the only
for real thing
i
know

THE MINISTER'S BLACK VEIL

Nathaniel Hawthorne

The sexton stood in the porch of Milford meeting-house pulling lustily at the bell-rope. The old people of the village came stooping along the street. Children with bright faces tript merrily beside their parents, or mimicked a graver gait in the conscious dignity of their Sunday clothes. Spruce bachelors looked sidelong at the pretty maidens, and fancied that the Sabbath sunshine made them prettier than on week-days. When the throng had mostly streamed into the porch, the sexton began to toll the bell, keeping his eye on the Reverend Mr. Hooper's door. The first glimpse of the clergyman's figure was the signal for the bell to cease its summons.

"But what has good Parson Hooper got upon his face?" cried the sexton in astonishment.

All within hearing immediately turned about, and beheld the semblance of Mr. Hooper pacing slowly in his meditative way towards the meeting-house. With one accord they started, expressing more wonder than if some strange minister were coming to dust the cushions of Mr. Hooper's pulpit.

"Are you sure it is our parson?" inquired Goodman Gray of the sexton.

"Of a certainty it is good Mr. Hooper," replied the sexton. "He was to have exchanged pulpits with Parson Shute, of Westbury; but Parson Shute sent to excuse himself yesterday, being to preach a funeral sermon."

The cause of so much amazement may appear sufficiently slight. Mr.

Hooper, a gentlemanly person of about thirty, though still a bachelor, was dressed with due clerical neatness, as if a careful wife had starched his band, and brushed the weekly dust from his Sunday's garb. There was but one thing remarkable in his appearance. Swathed about his forehead, and hanging down over his face so low as to be shaken by his breath, Mr. Hooper had on a black veil. On a nearer view it seemed to consist of two folds of crape, which entirely concealed his features except the mouth and chin, but probably did not intercept his sight farther than to give a darkened aspect to all living and inanimate things. With this gloomy shade before him, good Mr. Hooper walked onward at a slow and quiet pace, stooping somewhat and looking on the ground, as is customary with abstracted men, yet nodding kindly to those of his parishioners who still waited on the meeting-house steps. But so wonderstruck were they that his greeting hardly met with a return.

"I can't really feel as if good Mr. Hooper's face was behind that piece of crape," said the sexton.

"I don't like it," muttered an old woman, as she hobbled into the meeting-house. "He has changed himself into something awful only by hiding his face."

"Our parson has gone mad!" cried Goodman Gray, following him across the threshold.

A rumor of some unaccountable phenomenon had preceded Mr. Hooper into the meeting-house, and set all the congregation astir. Few could refrain from twisting their heads towards the door; many stood upright and turned directly about; while several little boys clambered upon the seats, and came down again with a terrible racket. There was a general bustle, a rustling of the women's gowns and shuffling of the men's feet, greatly at variance with that hushed repose which should attend the entrance of the minister. But Mr. Hooper appeared not to notice the perturbation of his people. He entered with an almost noiseless step, bent his head mildly to the pews on each side, and bowed as he passed his oldest parishioner, a white-haired great-grandsire, who occupied an armchair in the centre of the aisle. It was strange to observe how slowly this venerable man became conscious of something singular in the appearance on the pastor. He seemed not fully to partake of the prevailing wonder till Mr. Hooper had ascended the stairs, and showed himself in the pulpit face to face with his congregation except for the black veil. That mysterious emblem was never once withdrawn. It shook with his measured breath as he gave out the psalm; it threw its obscurity between him and the holy page a he read the Scriptures; and while he prayed, the veil lay heavily on his uplifted countenance. Did he seek to hide it from the dread Being whom he was addressing?

Such was the effect of this simple piece of crape that more than one woman of delicate nerves was forced to leave the meeting-house. Yet perhaps the pale-faced congregation was almost as fearful a sight to the minister as his black veil to them.

Mr. Hooper had the reputation of a good preacher, but not an energetic one: he strove to win his people heavenward by mild, persuasive influences, rather than to drive them thither by the thunders of the Word. The sermon which he now delivered was marked by the same characteristics of style and manner as the general series of his pulpit oratory. But there was something either in the sentiment of the discourse itself, or in the imagination of the auditors, which made it greatly the most powerful effort that they had ever heard from their pastor's lips. It was tinged rather more darkly than usual with the gentle gloom of Mr. Hooper's temperament. The subject had reference to secret sin, and those sad mysteries which we hide from our nearest and dearest, and would fain conceal from our own consciousness, even forgetting that the Omniscient can detect them. A subtle power was breathed into his words. Each member of the congregation, the most innocent girl, and the man of hardened breast, felt as if the preacher had crept upon them behind his awful veil, and discovered their hoarded iniquity of deed or thought. Many spread their clasped hands on their bosoms. There was nothing terrible in what Mr. Hooper said, at least, no violence; and yet, with every tremor of his melancholy voice the hearers quaked. An unsought pathos came hand in hand with awe. So sensible were the audience of some unwonted attribute in their minister, that they longed for a breath of wind to blow aside the veil, almost believing that a stranger's visage would be discovered, though the form, gesture, and voice were those of Mr. Hooper.

At the close of the service the people hurried out with indecorous confusion, eager to communicate their pent-up amazement, and conscious of lighter spirits the moment they lost sight of the black veil. Some gathered in little circles, huddled closely together, with their mouths all whispering in the centre; some went homeward alone, wrapt in silent meditation; some talked loudly, and profaned the Sabbath-day with ostentatious laughter. A few shook their sagacious heads, intimating that they could penetrate the mystery; while one or two affirmed that there was no mystery at all, but only that Mr. Hooper's eyes were so weakened by the midnight lamp as to require a shade. After a brief interval, forth came good Mr. Hooper also, in the rear of his flock. Turning his veiled face from one group to another, he paid due reverence to the hoary heads, saluted the middle-aged with kind dignity, as their friend and spiritual guide, greeted the young with mingled authority and love, and laid his hands on the little children's heads to bless them. Such was always his custom on the Sabbath-day. Strange and bewildered looks repaid him for his courtesy. None, as on former occasions, aspired to the honor of walking by their pastor's side. Old Squire Saunders, doubtless by an accidental lapse of memory, neglected to invite Mr. Hooper to his table, where the good clergyman had been wont to bless the food almost every

Sunday since his settlement. He returned, therefore, to the parsonage, and, at the moment of closing the door, was observed to look back upon the people, all of whom had their eyes fixed upon the minister. A sad smile gleamed faintly from beneath the black veil, and flickered about his mouth, glimmering as he disappeared.

"How strange," said a lady, "that a simple black veil, such as any woman might wear on her bonnet, should become such a terrible thing on Mr. Hooper's face!"

"Something must surely be amiss with Mr. Hooper's intellects," observed her husband, the physician of the village. "But the strangest part of the affair is the effect of this vagary, even on a sober-minded man like myself. The black veil, though it covers only our pastor's face, throws its influence over his whole person, and makes him ghostlike from head to foot. Do you not feel it so?"

"Truly do I," replied the lady; "and I would not be alone with him for the world. I wonder he is not afraid to be alone with himself!"

"Men sometimes are so," said her husband.

The afternoon service was attended with similar circumstances. At its conclusion, the bell tolled for the funeral of a young lady. The relatives and friends were assembled in the house, and the more distant acquaintances stood about the door, speaking of the good qualities of the deceased, when their talk was interrupted by the appearance of Mr. Hooper, still covered with his black veil. It was now an appropriate emblem. The clergyman stepped into the room where the corpse was laid, and bent over the coffin to take a last farewell of his deceased parishioner. As he stooped, the veil hung straight down from his forehead, so that, if her eyelids had not been closed for ever, the dead maiden might have seen his face. Could Mr. Hooper be fearful of her glance, that he so hastily caught back the black veil? A person who watched the interview between the dead and living scrupled not to affirm that, at the instant when the clergyman's features were disclosed, the corpse had slightly shuddered, rustling the shroud and muslin cap, though the countenance retained the composure of death. A superstitious old woman was the only witness of this prodigy. From the coffin Mr. Hooper passed into the chamber of the mourners, and thence to the head of the staircase, to make the funeral prayer. It was a tender and heart-dissolving prayer, full of sorrow, yet so imbued with celestial hopes that the music of a heavenly harp, swept by the fingers of the dead, seemed faintly to be heard among the saddest accents of the minister. The people trembled, though they but darkly understood him, when he prayed that they, and himself, and all of mortal race, might be ready, as he trusted this young maiden had been, for the dreadful hour that should snatch the veil from their faces. The bearers went heavily forth, and the mourners followed, saddening all the street, with the dead before them, and Mr. Hooper in the black veil behind.

"Why do you look back?" said one in the procession to his partner.

"I had a fancy," replied she, "that the minister and the maiden's spirit were walking hand in hand."

"And so had I at the same moment," said the other.

That night the handsomest couple in Milford village were to be joined in wedlock. Though reckoned a melancholy man, Mr. Hooper had a placid cheerfulness for such occasions which often excited a sympathetic smile where livelier merriment would have been thrown away. There was no quality of his disposition which made him more beloved than this. The company at the wedding awaited his arrival with impatience, trusting that the strange awe which had gathered over him throughout the day would now be dispelled. But such was not the result. When Mr. Hooper came, the first thing that their eyes rested on was the same horrible black veil, which had added deeper gloom to the funeral, and could portend nothing but evil to the wedding. Such was its immediate effect on the guests, that a cloud seemed to have rolled duskily from beneath the black crape and dimmed the light of the candles. The bridal pair stood up before the minister. But the bride's cold fingers quivered in the tremulous hand of the bridegroom, and her deathlike paleness caused a whisper that the maiden who had been buried a few hours before was come from her grave to be married. If ever another wedding were so dismal, it was that famous one where they tolled the wedding knell. After performing the ceremony, Mr. Hooper raised a glass of wine to his lips, wishing happiness to the new-married couple, in a strain of mild pleasantry that ought to have brightened the features of the guests, like a cheerful gleam from the hearth. At that instant, catching a glimpse of his figure in the looking-glass, the black veil involved his own spirit in the horror with which it overwhelmed all others. His frame shuddered — his lips grew white — he spilt the untasted wine upon the carpet — and rushed forth into the darkness. For the earth, too, had her black veil.

The next day the whole village of Milford talked of little else than Parson Hooper's black veil. That, and the mystery concealed behind it, supplied a topic for discussion between acquaintances meeting in the street, and good women gossiping at their open windows. It was the first item of news that the tavern-keeper told to his guests. The children babbled of it on their way to school. One imitative little imp covered his face with an old black handkerchief, thereby so affrighting his playmates that the panic seized himself, and he well-nigh lost his wits by his own waggery.

It was remarkable that, of all the busybodies and impertinent people in the parish, not one ventured to put the plain question to Mr. Hooper, wherefore he did this thing. Hitherto, whenever there appeared the slightest call for such interference, he had never lacked advisers, nor shown himself averse to be guided by their judgment. If he erred at all, it was by so painful a degree of self-distrust that even the mildest censure would lead him to consider an indifferent action as a crime. Yet, though so well acquainted with this amiable weakness, no individual among his parishioners chose to make the black veil a subject of friendly remonstrance. There was a feeling of dread, neither plainly confessed nor carefully concealed, which caused each to shift the responsibility upon another, till at length it was found expedient to send a deputation of the church, in order to deal with Mr. Hooper about the mystery before it should grow into a scandal. Never did an embassy so ill discharge its duties. The minister received them with friendly courtesy, but became silent after they were seated, leaving to his visitors the whole burden of introducing their important business. The topic, it might be supposed, was obvious enough. There was the black veil swathed round Mr. Hooper's forehead, and concealing every feature above his placid mouth, on which at times they could perceive the glimmering of a melancholy smile. But that piece of crape, to their imagination, seemed to hang down before his heart, the symbol of a fearful secret between him and them. Were the veil but cast aside they might speak freely of it, but not till then. Thus they sat a considerable time, speechless, confused, and shrinking uneasily from Mr. Hooper's eye, which they felt to be fixed upon them with an invisible glance. Finally, the deputies returned abashed to their constituents, pronouncing the matter too weighty to be handled, except by a council of the churches, if indeed it might not require a general synod.

But there was one person in the village unappalled by the awe with which the black veil had impressed all beside herself. When the deputies returned without an explanation, or even venturing to demand one, she, with the calm energy of her character, determined to chase away the strange cloud that appeared to be settling round Mr. Hooper, every moment more darkly than before. As his plighted wife, it should be her privilege to know what the black veil concealed. At the minister's first visit, therefore, she entered upon the subject with a direct simplicity which made the task easier both for him and her. After he had seated himself she fixed her eyes steadfastly upon the veil, but could discern nothing of the dreadful gloom that had so overawed the multitude: it was but a double fold of crape, hanging down from his forehead to his mouth, and slightly stirring with his breath.

"No," said she aloud, and smiling, "there is nothing terrible in this piece of crape, except that it hides a face which I am always glad to look upon. Come, good sir, let the sun shine from behind the cloud. First lay aside your black veil: then tell me why you put it on."

Mr. Hooper's smile glimmered faintly.

"There is an hour to come," said he, "when all of us shall cast aside our veils. Take it not amiss, beloved friend, if I wear this piece of crape till then."

"Your words are a mystery too," returned the young lady. "Take away the veil from them at least."

"Elizabeth, I will," said he, "so far as my vow may suffer me. Know, then, this veil is a type and a symbol, and I am bound to wear it ever, both in light and darkness, in solitude and before the gaze of multitudes, and as with strangers, so with my familiar friends. No mortal eye will see it withdrawn. This dismal shade must separate me from the world: even you, Elizabeth, can never come behind it!"

"What grievous afflication hath befallen you," she earnestly inquired, "that you should thus darken your eyes for ever?"

"If it be a sign of mourning," replied Mr. Hooper, "I, perhaps, like most other mortals, have sorrows dark enough to be typified by a black veil."

"But what if the world will not believe that it is the type of an innocent sorrow?" urged Elizabeth. "Beloved and respected as you are, there may be whispers that you hide your face under the consciousness of secret sin. For the sake of your holy office, do away with this scandal!"

The color rose into her cheeks as she intimated the nature of the rumors that were already abroad in the village. But Mr. Hooper's mildness did not forsake him. He even smiled again — that same sad smile, which always appeared like a faint glimmering of light proceeding from the obscurity beneath the veil.

"If I hide my face for sorrow, there is cause enough," he merely replied; "and if I cover it for secret sin, what mortal might not do the same?"

And with this gentle but unconquerable obstinacy did he resist all her entreaties. At length Elizabeth sat silent. For a few moments she appeared lost in thought, considering, probably, what new methods might be tried to withdraw her lover from so dark a fantasy, which, if it had no other meaning, was perhaps a symptom of mental disease. Though of a firmer character than his own, the tears rolled down her cheeks. But in an instant, as it were, a new feeling took the place of sorrow: her eyes were fixed insensibly on the black veil, when, like a sudden twilight in the air, its terrors fell around her. She arose, and stood trembling before him.

"And do you feel it then at last?" said he mournfully.

She made no reply, but covered her eyes with her hand, and turned to leave the room. He rushed forward and caught her arm.

"Have patience with me, Elizabeth!" cried he passionately. "Do not desert me, though this veil must be between us here on earth. Be mine, and hereafter there shall be no veil over my face, no darkness between our souls! It is but a mortal veil — it is not for eternity! Oh! you know not how lonely I am, and how frightened, to be alone behind my black veil. Do not leave me in this miserable obscurity for ever!"

"Lift the veil but once and look me in the face," said she.

"Never! It cannot be!" replied Mr. Hooper.

"Then, farewell!" said Elizabeth.

She withdrew her arm from his grasp and slowly departed, pausing at the door to give one long, shuddering gaze, that seemed almost to penetrate the mystery of the black veil. But even amid his grief Mr. Hooper smiled to think that only a material emblem had separated him from happiness, though the horrors which it shadowed forth must be drawn darkly between the fondest of lovers.

From that time no attempts were made to remove Mr. Hooper's black veil, or, by a direct appeal, to discover the secret which it was supposed to hide. By persons who claimed a superiority to popular prejudice it was reckoned merely an eccentric whim, such as often mingles with the sober actions of men otherwise rational, and tinges them all with its own semblance of insanity. But with the multitude good Mr. Hooper was irreparably a bugbear. He could not walk the streets with any peace of mind, so conscious was he that the gentle and timid would turn aside to avoid him, and that others would make it a point of hardihood to throw themselves in his way. The impertinence of the latter class compelled him to give up his customary walk at sunset to the burial-ground; for when he leaned pensively over the gate, there would always be faces behind the grave-stones peeping at his black veil. A fable went the rounds that the stare of the dead people drove him thence. It grieved him to the very depth of his kind heart to observe how the children fled from his approach, breaking up their merriest sports while his melancholy figure was yet afar off. Their instinctive dread caused him to feel more strongly than aught else that a preternatural horror was interwoven with the threads of the black crape. In truth, his own antipathy to the veil was known to be so great that he never willingly passed before a mirror, nor stooped to drink at a still fountain, lest in its peaceful bosom he should be affrighted by himself. This was what gave plausibility to the whispers, that Mr. Hooper's conscience tortured him for some great crime too horrible to be entirely concealed, or otherwise than so obscurely intimated. Thus from beneath the black veil there rolled a cloud into the sunshine, an ambiguity of sin or sorrow, which enveloped the poor minister, so that love or sympathy could never reach him. It was said that ghost and fiend consorted with him there. With self-shudderings and outward terrors he walked continually in its shadow, groping darkly within his own soul, or gazing through a medium that saddened the whole world. Even the lawless wind, it was believed, respected his dreadful secret and never blew aside the veil. But still good Mr. Hooper sadly smiled at the pale visages of the worldly throng as he passed by.

Among all its bad influences, the black veil had the one desirable effect of making its wearer a very efficient clergyman. By the aid of his mysterious emblem — for there was no other apparent cause — he became a man of awful power over souls that were in agony for sin. His converts always regarded him with a dread peculiar to themselves, affirming, though but figuratively, that, before he brought them to celestial light, they had been with him behind the black veil. Its gloom, indeed, enabled him to sympathize with all dark affections. Dying sinners cried aloud for Mr. Hooper, and would not yield their breath till he appeared; though ever, as he stooped to whisper consolation, they shuddered at the veiled face so near their own. Such were the terrors of the black veil, even when Death had bared his visage! Strangers came long distances to attend service at his church, with the mere idle purpose of gazing at his figure, because it was forbidden them to behold his face. But many were made to quake ere they departed! Once, during Governor Belcher's administration, Mr. Hooper was appointed to preach the election sermon. Covered with his black veil, he stood before the chief magistrate, the council, and the representatives, and wrought so deep an impression that the legislative measures of that year were characterized by all the gloom and piety of our earliest ancestral sway.

In this manner Mr. Hooper spent a long life, irreproachable in outward act, yet shrouded in dismal suspicions; kind and loving, though unloved, and dimly feared; a man apart from men, shunned in their health and joy, but ever summoned to their aid in mortal anguish. As years wore on, shedding their snows above his sable veil, he acquired a name throughout the New England churches, and they called him Father Hooper. Nearly all his parishioners who were of mature age when he was settled had been borne away by many a funeral: he had one congregation in the church, and a more crowded one in the church-yard; and having wrought so late into the evening, and done his work so well, it was now good Father Hooper's turn to rest.

Several persons were visible by the shaded candlelight in the death-chamber of the old clergyman. Natural connections he had none. But there was the decorously grave though unmoved physician, seeking only to mitigate the last pangs of the patient whom he could not save. There were the deacons, and other eminently pious members of his church. There, also, was the Reverend Mr. Clark, of Westbury, a young and zealous divine, who had ridden in haste to pray by the bedside of the expiring minister. There was the nurse, no hired handmaiden of death, but one whose calm affection had endured thus long in secrecy, in solitude, amid the chill of age, and would not perish, even at the dying hour. Who, but Elizabeth! And there lay the hoary head of good Father Hooper upon the death-pillow, with the black veil still swathed about his brow and reaching down over his face, so that each more difficult gasp of his faint breath caused it to stir. All through life that piece of crape had hung between him and the world: it had separated him from cheerful brotherhood and woman's love, and kept him in that saddest of all prisons, his own heart; and still it lay upon his face, as if to deepen the gloom of his darksome chamber, and shade him from the sunshine of eternity.

For some time previous his mind had been confused, wavering doubtfully between the past and the present, and hovering forward, as it were, at intervals, into the indistinctness of the world to come. There had been feverish turns, which tossed him from side to side, and wore away what little strength he had. But in his most convulsive struggles, and in the wildest vagaries of his intellect, when no other thought retained its sober influence, he still showed an awful solicitude lest the black veil should slip aside. Even if his bewildered soul could have forgotten, there was a faithful woman at his pillow, who, with averted eyes, would have covered that aged face, which she had last beheld in the comeliness of manhood. At length the death-stricken old man lay quietly in the torpor of mental and bodily exhaustion, with an imperceptible pulse, and breath that grew fainter and fainter, except when a long, deep, and irregular inspiration seemed to prelude the flight of his spirit.

The minister of Westbury approached the bedside.

"Venerable Father Hooper," said he, "the moment of your release is at hand. Are you ready for the lifting of the veil that shuts in time from eternity?"

Father Hooper at first replied merely by a feeble motion of his head; then, apprehensive, perhaps, that his meaning might be doubtful, he exerted himself to speak.

"Yea," said he, in faint accents, "my soul hath a patient weariness until that veil be lifted."

"And is it fitting," resumed the Reverend Mr. Clark, "that a man so given to prayer, of such a blameless example, holy in deed and thought, so far as mortal judgment may pronounce; is it fitting that a father in the church should leave a shadow on his memory, that may seem to blacken a life so pure? I pray you, my venerable brother, let not this thing be! Suffer us to be gladdened by your triumphant aspect, as you go to your reward. Before the veil of eternity be lifted, let me cast aside this black veil from your face!"

And thus speaking, the Reverend Mr. Clark bent forward to reveal the mystery of so many years. But exerting a sudden energy that made all the beholders stand aghast, Father Hooper snatched both his hands from beneath the bed-clothes, and pressed them strongly on the black veil, resolute to struggle if the minister of Westbury would contend with a dying man.

"Never!" cried the veiled clergyman. "On earth, never!"

"Dark old man!" exclaimed the affrighted minister, "with what horrible crime upon your soul are you now passing to the judgment?"

Father Hooper's breath heaved, it rattled in his throat; but with a mighty effort, grasping forward with his hands, he caught hold of life, and held it back till he should speak. He even raised himself in bed; and there he sat, shivering with the arms of death around him, while the black veil hung down, awful, at the last moment, in the gathered terrors of a lifetime. And yet the faint, sad smile, so often there, now seemed to glimmer from its obscurity, and linger on Father Hooper's lips.

"Why do you tremble at me alone?" cried he, turning his veiled face round the circle of pale spectators. "Tremble also at each other! Have men avoided me, and women shown no pity, and children screamed and fled, only for my black veil? What but the mystery which it obscurely typifies has made this crape so awful? When the friend shows his inmost heart to his friend; the lover to his best beloved; when man does not vainly shrink from the eye of his Creator, loathsomely treasuring up the secret of his sin; then deem me a monster, for the symbol beneath which I have lived, and die! I look around me, and, lo! on every visage a black veil!"

While his auditors shrank from one another in mutual affright, Father Hooper fell back upon his pillow, a veiled corpse, with a faint smile lingering on the lips. Still veiled, they laid him in his coffin, and a veiled corpse they bore him to the grave. The grass of many years has sprung up and withered on that grave, the burial-stone is moss-grown, and good Mr. Hooper's face is dust; but awful is still the thought that it mouldered beneath the black veil!

___ Anxiety Disorders

Anxiety Disorders (sometimes called Neuroses or Neurotic Disorders) have as their dominant feature some form of anxiety or fear of a potentially hostile environment. Anxiety manifests itself physiologically in an increased heart rate, disturbed breathing, trembling, and sweating. Psychologically, anxiety expresses itself as an uncomfortable feeling of impending doom accompanied by an overwhelming sense of powerlessness and prolonged feelings of tension.

This classification includes Phobic Disorders, in which the dominant feature is irrational fear and avoidance of some specific type of stimulus or situation; Panic Disorder, characterized by recurrent, intense anxiety attacks; Generalized Anxiety Disorder, which has as its essential feature a period of at least one month of persistent generalized anxiety; and Obsessive Compulsive Disorder.

Obsessive Compulsive Disorder

People with Obsessive Compulsive Disorder are excessively perfectionistic, overly conscientious, and extremely inhibited. Their obsession (a persistent irrational idea that cannot be eliminated from consciousness by logical effort) invades their consciousness, thereby impairing their thinking. Their compulsion (an uncontrollable impulse to perform an act again and again) is equally stress-producing. They may not recognize that the repetitive activity is used to avoid unacceptable ideas. They may resent and resist the demands the compulsion makes on their time and energy. But their efforts to stop are futile. If they quit doing the activity, anxiety usually follows.

Owen Warland, in Nathaniel Hawthorne's "The Artist of the Beautiful," may have Obsessive Compulsive Disorder. What is Owen's obsession? How does this obsession impair his thinking? Why is his obsession irrational? What is his compulsion? How does Owen's obsessive compulsive behavior intefere with his relationships?

135

THE ARTIST OF THE BEAUTIFUL

Nathaniel Hawthorne

An elderly man, with his pretty daughter on his arm, was passing along the street, and emerged from the gloom of the cloudy evening into the light that fell across the pavement from the window of a small shop. It was a projecting window; and on the inside were suspended a variety of watches, pinchbeck, silver, and one or two of gold, all with their faces turned from the streets, as if churlishly disinclined to inform the wayfarers what o'clock it was. Seated within the shop, sidelong to the window, with his pale face bent earnestly over some delicate piece of mechanism on which was thrown the concentrated lustre of a shade lamp, appeared a young man.

"What can Owen Warland be about?" muttered old Peter Hovenden, himself a retired watchmaker, and the former master of this same young man whose occupation he was now wondering at. "What can the fellow be about? These six months past I have never come by his shop without seeing him just as steadily at work as now. It would be a flight beyond his usual foolery to seek for the perpetual motion; and yet I know enough of my old business to be certain that what he is now so busy with is no part of the machinery of a watch."

"Perhaps, father," said Annie, without showing much interest in the question, "Owen is inventing a new kind of timekeeper. I am sure he has ingenuity enough."

"Poh, child! He has not the sort of ingenuity to invent anything better than a Dutch toy," answered her father, who had formerly been put to much vexation by Owen Warland's irregular genius. "A plague on such ingenuity! All the effect that ever I knew of it was to spoil the accuracy of some of the best watches in my shop. He would turn the sun out of its orbit and derange the whole course of time, if, as I said before, his ingenuity could grasp anything bigger than a child's toy!"

"Hush, father! He hears you!" whispered Annie, pressing the old man's arm. "His ears are as delicate as his feelings; and you know how easily disturbed they are. Do let us move on."

So Peter Hovenden and his daughter Annie plodded on without further conversation, until in a by-street of the town they found themselves passing the open door of a blacksmith's shop. Within was seen the forge, now blazing up and illuminating the high and dusky roof, and now confining its lustre to a narrow precinct of the coal-strewn floor, according as the breath of the bellows was puffed forth or again inhaled into its vast leathern lungs. In the intervals of brightness it was easy to distinguish objects in remote corners of the shop and the horseshoes that hung upon the wall; in the momentary gloom the fire seemed to be glimmering amidst the vagueness of uninclosed space. Moving about in this red glare and alternate dusk was the figure of the blacksmith, well worthy to be viewed in so picturesque an aspect of light and shade, where the bright blaze struggled with the black night, as if each would have snatched his comely strength from the other. Anon he drew a white-hot bar of iron from the coals, laid it on the anvil, uplifted his arm of might, and was soon enveloped in the myriads of sparks which the strokes of his hammer scattered into the surrounding gloom.

"Now, that is a pleasant sight," said the old watchmaker. "I know what it is to work in gold; but give me the worker in iron after all is said and done. He spends his labor upon a reality. What say you, daughter Annie?"

"Pray don't speak so loud, father," whispered Annie, "Robert Danforth will hear you."

"And what if he should hear me?" said Peter Hovenden. "I say again, it is a good and a wholesome thing to depend upon main strength and reality, and to earn one's bread with the bare and brawny arm of a blacksmith. A watchmaker gets his brain puzzled by his wheels within a wheel, or loses his health or the nicety of his eyesight, as was my case, and finds himself at middle age, or a little after, past labor at his own trade and fit for nothing else, yet too poor to live at his ease. So I say once again, give me main strength for my money. And then, how it takes the nonsense out of a man! Did you ever hear of a blacksmith being such a fool as Owen Warland yonder?"

"Well said, uncle Hovenden!" shouted Robert Danforth from the forge, in a full deep, merry voice, that made the roof re-echo. "And what says Miss Annie to that doctrine? She, I suppose, will think it a genteeler business to tinker up a lady's watch than to forge a horsehoe or make a gridiron."

Annie drew her father onward without giving him time to reply.

But we must return to Owen Warland's shop, and spend more meditation upon his history and character than either Peter Hovenden, or probably his daughter Annie, or Owen's old school-fellow, Robert Danforth, would have thought due to so slight a subject. From the time that his little fingers could grasp a penknife, Owen had been remarkable for a delicate ingenuity which sometimes produced pretty shapes in wood, principally figures of flowers and birds, and sometimes seemed to aim at the hidden mysteries of mechanism. But it was always for purposes of grace, and never with any mockery of the useful. He did not, like the crowd of schoolboy artisans, construct little windmills on the angle of a barn or watermills across the neighboring brook. Those who discovered such peculiarity in the boy as to think it worth their while to observe him closely, sometimes saw reason to suppose that he was attempting to imitate the beautiful movements of Nature as exemplified in the flight of birds or the activity of little animals. It seemed, in fact, a new development of the love of the beautiful, such as might have made him a poet, a painter, or a sculptor, and which was completely refined from all utilitarian coarseness as it could have been in either of the fine arts. He looked with singular distaste at the stiff and regular processes of ordinary machinery. Being once carried to see a steam-engine, in the expectation that his intuitive comprehension of mechanical principles would be gratified, he turned pale and grew sick, as if something monstrous and unnatural had been presented to him. This horror was partly owing to the size and terrible energy of the iron laborer; for the character of Owen's mind was microscopic, and tended naturally to the minute, in accordance with his diminutive frame and the marvellous smallness and delicate power of his fingers. Not that his sense of beauty was thereby diminished into a sense of prettiness. The beautiful idea has no relation to size, and may be as perfectly developed in a space too minute for any but microscopic investigation as within the ample verge that is measured by the arc of the rainbow. But, at all events, this characteristic minuteness of his objects and accomplishments made the world even more incapable than it might otherwise have been of appreciating Owen Warland's genius. The boy's relatives saw nothing better to be done — as perhaps there was not — than to bind him apprentice to a watchmaker, hoping that his strange ingenuity might thus be regulated and put to utilitarian purpose.

Peter Hovenden's opinion of his apprentice has already been expressed. He could make nothing of the lad. Owen's apprehension of the professional mysteries, it is true, were inconceivably quick; but he altogether forgot or despised the grand object of a watchmaker's business, and cared no more for the measurement of time than if it had been merged into eternity. So long, however, as he remained under his old master's care, Owen's lack of sturdiness made it possible, by strick injunctions and sharp oversight, to restrain his creative eccentricity within bounds, but when his apprenticeship was served out, and he had taken the little shop which Peter Hovenden's failing eyesight compelled him to relinquish, then did people recognize how unfit a person was Owen Warland to lead old blind Father Time along his daily course. One of his most rational projects was to connect a musical operation with the machinery of his watches, so that all the harsh dissonances of life might be rendered tuneful, and each fitting moment fall into the abyss of the past in golden drops of harmony. If a family clock was intrusted to him for repair, — one of those tall, ancient clocks that have grown nearly allied to human nature by measuring out the lifetime of many generations, — he would take upon himself to arrange a dance or funeral procession of figures across its venerable face, representing twelve mirthful or melancholy hours. Several freaks of this kind quite destroyed the young watchmaker's credit with that steady and matter-of-fact class of people who hold the opinion that time is not to be trifled with, whether considered as the medium of advancement and prosperity in this world or preparation for the next. His custom rapidly diminished — a misfortune, however, that was probably reckoned among his better accidents by Owen Warland, who was becoming more and more absorbed in a secret occupation which drew all his science and manual dexterity into itself, and likewise gave full employment to the characteristic tendencies of his genius. This pursuit had already consumed many months.

After the old watchmaker and his pretty daughter had gazed at him out of the obscurity of the street, Owen Warland was seized with a fluttering of the nerves, which made his hand tremble too violently to proceed with such delicate labor as he was now engaged upon.

"It was Annie herself!" murmured he. "I should have known it, by this throbbing of my heart, before I heard her father's voice. Ah, how it throbs! I shall scarcely be able to work again on this exquisite mechanism to-night. Annie! dearest Annie! thou shouldst give firmness to my heart and hand, and not shake them thus; for if I strive to put the very spirit of beauty into form and give it motion, it is for thy sake alone. O throbbing heart, be quiet! If my labor be thus thwarted, there will come vague and unsatisfied dreams which will leave me spiritless to-morrow."

As he was endeavoring to settle himself again to his task, the shop door opened and gave admittance to no other than the stalwart figure which Peter Hovenden had paused to admire, as seen amid the light and shadow of the blacksmith's shop. Robert Danforth had brought a little anvil of his own manufacture, and peculiarly constructed, which the young artist had recently bespoken. Owen examined the article and pronounced it fashioned according to his wish.

"Why, yes," said Robert Danforth, his strong voice filling the shop as with the sound of a bass viol, "I consider myself equal to anything in the way of my own trade; though I should have made but a poor figure at yours with such a fist as this," added he, laughing, as he laid his vast hand beside the delicate one of Owen. "But what then? I put more main strength into one blow of my sledge hammer than all that you have expended since you were a 'prentice. Is not that the truth?"

"Very probably," answered the low and slender voice of Owen. "Strength is an earthly monster. I make no pretensions to it. My force, whatever there may be of it, is altogether spiritual."

"Well, but, Owen, what are you about?" asked his old school-fellow, still in such a hearty volume of tone that it made the artist shrink, especially as the question related to a subject so sacred as the absorbing dream of his imagination. "Folks do say that you are trying to discover the perpetual motion."

"The perpetual motion? Nonsense!" replied Owen Warland, with a movement of disgust; for he was full of little petulances. "It can never be discovered. It is a dream that may delude men whose brains are mystified with matter, but not me. Besides, if such a discovery were possible, it would not be worth my while to make it only to have the secret turned to such purposes as are now effected by steam and water power. I am not ambitious to be honored with the paternity of a new kind of cotton machine."

"That would be droll enough!" cried the blacksmith, breaking out into such an uproar of laughter that Owen himself and the bell glasses on his work-board quivered in unison. "No, no Owen! No child of yours will have iron joints and sinews. Well, I won't hinder you any more. Good night, Owen, and success, and if you need any assistance, so far as a downright blow of hammer upon anvil will answer the purpose, I'm your man."

And with another laugh the man of main strength left the shop.

"How strange it is," whispered Owen Warland to himself, leaning his head upon his hand, "that all my musings, my purposes, my passion for the beautiful, my consciousness of power to create it, — a finer, more ethereal power, of which this earthly giant can have no conception, — all, all, look so vain and idle whenever my path is crossed by Robert Danforth! He would drive me mad were I to meet him often. His hard, brute force darkens and confuses the spiritual element within me; but I, too, will be stong in my own way. I will not yield to him."

He took from beneath a glass a piece of minute machinery, which he set in the condensed light of his lamp, and looking intently at it through a magnifying glass, proceeded to operate with a delicate instrument of steel. In an instant, however, he fell back in his chair and clasped his hands, with a look of horror on his face that made its small features as impressive as those of a giant would have been.

"Heaven! What have I done?" exclaimed he. "The vapor, the influence of that brute force, — it has bewildered me and obscured my perception. I have made the very stroke — the fatal stroke — that I have dreaded from the first. It is all over — the toil of months, the object of my life. I am ruined!"

And there he sat, in stange despair, until his lamp flickered in the socket and left the Artist of the Beautiful in darkness.

Thus it is that ideas, which grow up within the imagination and appear so lovely to it and of a value beyond whatever men call valuable, are exposed to be shattered and annihilated by contact with the practical. It is requisite for the ideal artist to possess a force of character that seems hardly compatible with its delicacy; he must keep his faith in himself while the incredulous world assails him with its utter disbelief; he must stand up against mankind and be his own sole disciple, both as respects his genius and the objects to which it is directed.

For a time Owen Warland succumbed to this severe but inevitable test. He spent a few sluggish weeks with his head so continually resting in his hands that the towns-people had scarcely an opportunity to see his countenance. When at last it was again uplifted to the light of day, a cold, dull, nameless change was perceptible upon it. In the opinion of Peter Hovenden, however, and that order of sagacious understandings who think that life should be regulated, like clockwork, with leaden weights, the alteration was entirely for the better. Owen now, indeed, applied himself to business with dogged industry. It was marvellous to witness the obtuse gravity with which he would inspect the wheels of a great old silver watch; thereby delighting the owner, in whose fob it had been worn till he deemed it a portion of his own life, and was accordingly jealous of its treatment. In consequence of the good report thus acquired, Owen Warland was invited by the proper authorities to regulate the clock in the church steeple. He succeeded so admirably in this matter of public interest that the merchants gruffly acknowledged his merits on 'Change; the nurse whispered his praises as she gave the potion in the sick-chamber; the lover blessed him at the hour of appointed interview; and the town in general thanked Owen for the punctuality of dinner time. In a word, the heavy weight upon his spirits kept everything in order, not merely within his own system, but wheresoever the iron accents of the church clock were audible. It was a circumstance, though minute, yet characteristic of his present state, that, when employed to engrave names or initials on silver spoons, he now wrote the requisite letters in the plainest possible style, omitting a variety of fanciful flourishes that had heretofore distinguished his work in this kind.

One day, during the era of this happy transformation, old Peter Hovenden came to visit his former apprentice.

"Well, Owen," said he, "I am glad to hear such good accounts of you from all quarters, and especially from the town clock yonder, which speaks in your commendation every hour of the twenty-four. Only get rid altogether of your nonsensical trash about the beautiful, which I nor nobody else, nor yourself to boot, could ever understand, — only free yourself of that, and your success in life is as sure as daylight. Why, if you go on in this way, I should even venture to let you doctor this precious old watch of mine, though, except my daughter Annie, I have nothing else so valuable in the world."

"I should hardly dare touch it, sir," replied Owen, in a depressed tone; for he was weighed down by his old master's presence.

"In time," said the latter, — "in time, you will be capable of it."

The old watchmaker, with the freedom naturally consequent on his former authority, went on inspecting the work which Owen had in hand at the moment, together with other matters that were in progress. The artist, meanwhile, could scarcely lift his head. There was nothing so antipodal to his nature as this man's cold, unimaginative sagacity, by contact with which everything was converted into a dream except the densest matter of the physical world. Owen groaned in spirit and prayed fervently to be delivered from him.

"But what is this?" cried Peter Hovenden abruptly, taking up a dusty bell glass, beneath which appeared a mechanical something, as delicate and minute as the system of a butterfly's anatomy. "What have we here? Owen! Owen! there is witchcraft in these little chains, and wheels, and paddles. See! with one pinch of my finger and thumb I am going to deliver you from all future peril."

"For Heaven's sake," screamed Owen Warland, springing up with wonderful energy, "as you would not drive me mad, do not touch it! The slightest pressure of your finger would ruin me forever."

"Aha, young man! And is it so?" said the old watchmaker, looking at him with just enough of penetration to torture Owen's soul with the bitterness of worldly criticism. "Well, take your own course; but I warn you again that in this small piece of mechanism lives your evil spirit. Shall I exorcise him?"

"You are my evil spirit," answered Owen, much excited, — "you and the hard, coarse world! The leaden thoughts and the despondency that you fling upon me are my clogs, else I should long ago have achieved the task that I was created for."

Peter Hovenden shook his head, with the mixture of contempt and indignation which mankind, of whom he was partly a representative, deem themselves entitled to feel towards all simpletons who seek other prizes than the dusty one along the highway. He then took his leave, with an uplifted finger and a sneer upon his face that haunted the artist's dreams for many a night afterwards. At the time of his old master's visit, Owen was probably on the point of taking up the relinquished task; but, by this sinister event, he was thrown back into the state whence he had been slowly emerging.

But the innate tendency of his soul had only been accumulating fresh vigor during its apparent sluggishness. As the summer advanced he almost totally relinquished his business, and permitted Father Time, so far as the old gentleman was represented by the clocks and watches under his control, to stray at random through human life, making infinite confusion among the train of bewildered hours. He wasted the sunshine, as people said, in wandering through the woods and fields and along the banks of streams. There, like a child, he found amusement in chasing butterflies or watching the motions of water insects. There was something truly mysterious in the intentness with which he contemplated these living playthings as they sported on the breeze or examined the structure of an imperial insect whom he had imprisoned. The chase of butterflies was an apt emblem of the ideal pursuit in which he had spent so many golden hours; but would the beautiful idea ever be yielded to his hand like the butterfly that symbolized it? Sweet, doubtless, were these days, and congenial to the artist's soul. They were full of bright conceptions, which gleamed through his intellectual world as the butterflies gleamed through the outward atmosphere, and were real to him, for the instant, without the toil, and perplexity, and many disappointments of attempting to make them visible to the sensual eye. Alas that the artist, whether in poetry, or whatever other material,. may not content himself with the inward enjoyment of the beautiful, but must chase the flitting mystery beyond the verge of his ethereal domain, and crush its frail being in seizing it with material grasp. Owen Warland felt the impulse to give external reality to his ideas as irresistibly as any of the poets or painters who have arrayed the world in a dimmer and fainter beauty, imperfectly copied from the richness of their visions.

The night was now his time for the slow progress of re-creating the one idea to which all his intellectual activity referred itself. Always at the approach of dusk he stole into the town, locked himself within his shop, and wrought with patient delicacy of touch for many hours. Sometimes he was startled by the rap of the watchman, who, when all the world should be asleep, had caught the gleam of lamplight through the crevices of Owen Warland's shutters. Daylight, to the morbid sensibility of his mind, seemed to have an intrusiveness that interfered with his pursuits. On cloudy and inclement days, therefore, he sat with his head upon his hands, muffling, as it were, his sensitive brain in a mist of indefinite musings; for it was a relief to escape from the sharp distinctness with which he was compelled to shape out his thoughts during his nightly toil.

From one of these fits of torpor he was aroused by the entrance of Annie Hovenden, who came into the shop with the freedom of a customer, and also with something of the familiarity of a childish friend. She had worn a hole through her silver thimble, and wanted Owen to repair it.

"But I don't know whether you will condescend to such a task," said she, laughing, "now that you are so taken up with the notion of putting spirit into machinery."

"Where did you get that idea, Annie?" said Owen, starting in surprise.

"Oh, out of my own head," answered she, "and from something that I heard you say, long ago, when you were but a boy and I a little child. But come; will you mend this poor thimble of mine?"

"Anything for your sake, Annie," said Owen Warland, — "anything, even were it to work at Robert Danforth's forge."

"And that would be a pretty sight!" retorted Annie, glancing with imperceptible slightness at the artist's small and slender frame. "Well, here is the thimble."

"But that is a strange idea of yours," said Owen, "about the spiritualization of matter."

And then the thought stole into his mind that this young girl possessed the gift to comprehend him better than all the world besides. And what a help and strength it would be to him in his lonely toil if he could gain the sympathy of the only being whom he loved! To persons whose pursuits are insulated from the common business of life — who are either in advance of mankind or apart from it — there comes a sensation of moral cold that makes the spirit shiver as it if had reached the frozen solitudes around the pole. What the prophet, the poet, the reformer, the criminal, or any other man with human yearnings, but separated from the multitude by a peculiar lot, might feel, poor Owen felt.

"Annie," cried he, growing pale as death at the thought, "how gladly would I tell you the secret of my pursuit! You, methinks, would estimate it rightly. You, I know, would hear it with a reverence that I must not expect from the harsh material world."

"Would I not? to be sure I would!" replied Annie Hovenden, lightly laughing. "Come; explain to me quickly what is the meaning of this little whirligig, so delicately wrought that it might be a plaything for Queen Mab. See! I will put it in motion."

"Hold!" exclaimed Owen, "hold!"

Annie had but given the slightest possible touch, with the point of a needle, to the same minute portion of complicated machinery which has been more than once mentioned, when the artist seized her by the wrist with a force that made her scream aloud. She was affrighted at the convulsion of intense rage and anguish that writhed across his features. The next instant he let his head sink upon his hands.

"Go, Annie," murmured he; "I have deceived myself, and must suffer for it. I yearned for sympathy and thought, and fancied, and dreamed that you might give it me; but you lack the talisman, Annie, that should admit you into my secrets. That touch has undone the toil of months and the thought of a lifetime! It was not your fault, Annie; but you have ruined me!"

Poor Owen Warland! He had indeed erred, yet pardonably; for if any human spirit could have sufficiently reverenced the processes so sacred in his eyes, it must have been a woman's. Even Annie Hovenden, possibly, might not have disappointed him had she been enlightened by the deep intelligence of love.

The artist spent the ensuing winter in a way that satisfied any persons who had hitherto retained a hopeful opinion of him that he was, in truth, irrevocably doomed to inutility as regarded the world, and to an evil destiny on his own part. The decease of a relative had put him in possession of a small inheritance. Thus freed from the necessity of toil, and having lost the steadfast influence of a great purpose, — great, at least, to him, — he abandoned himself to habits from which it might have been supposed the mere delicacy of his organization would have availed to secure him. But when the ethereal portion of a man of genius is obscured, the earthly part assumes an influence the more uncontrollable, because the character is now thrown off the balance to which Providence had so nicely adjusted it, and which, in coarser natures, is adjusted by some other method. Owen Warland made proof of whatever show of bliss may be found in riot. He looked at the world through the golden medium of wine, and contemplated the visions that bubble up so gayly around the brim of the glass, and that people the air with shapes of pleasant madness, which so soon grow ghostly and forlorn. Even when this dismal and inevitable change had taken place, the young man might still have continued to quaff the cup of enchantments, though its vapor did but shroud life in gloom and fill the gloom with spectres that mocked at him.

There was a certain irksomeness of spirit, which, being real, and the deepest sensation of which the artist was now conscious, was more intolerable than any fantastic miseries and horrors that the abuse of wine could summon up. In the latter case he could remember, even out of the midst of his trouble, that all was but a delusion; in the former, the heavy anguish was his actual life.

From this perilous state he was redeemed by an incident which more than one person witnessed, but of which the shrewdest could not explain or conjecture the operation on Owen Warland's mind. It was very simple. On a warm afternoon of spring, as the artist sat among his riotous companions with a glass of wine before him, a splendid butterfly flew in at the open window and fluttered about his head.

"Ah," exclaimed Owen, who had drank freely, "are you alive again, child of the sun and playmate of the summer breeze, after your dismal winter's nap? Then it is time for me to be at work!"

And, leaving his unemptied glass upon the table, he departed and was never known to sip another drop of wine.

And now, again, he resumed his wanderings in the woods and fields. It might be fancied that the bright butterfly, which had come so spirit-like into the window as Owen sat with the rude revellers, was indeed a spirit commissioned to recall him to the pure, ideal life that had so etherealized him among men. It might be fancied that he went forth to seek this spirit in its sunny haunts; for still, as in the summer time gone by, he was seen to steal gently up wherever a butterfly had alighted, and lose himself in contemplation of it. When it took flight his eyes followed the winged vision, as if its airy track would show the path to heaven. But what could be the purpose of the unseasonable toil, which was again resumed, as the watchman knew by the lines of lamplight through the crevices of Owen Warland's shutters? The towns-people had one comprehensive explanation of all these singularities. Owen Warland had gone mad! How universally efficacious — how satisfactory, too, and soothing to the injured sensibility of narrowness and dulness — is this easy method of accounting for whatever lies beyond the world's most ordinary scope! From St. Paul's days down to our poor little Artist of the Beautiful, the same talisman had been applied to the elucidation of all mysteries in the words or deeds of men who spoke or acted too wisely or too well. In Owen Warland's case the judgment of his towns-people may have been correct. Perhaps he was mad. The lack of sympathy — that contrast between himself and his neighbors which took away the restraint of example — was enough to make him so. Or possibly he had caught just so much of the ethereal radiance as served to bewilder him, in an earthly sense, by its intermixture with the common daylight.

One evening, when the artist had returned from a customary ramble and had just thrown the lustre of his lamp on the delicate piece of work so often interrupted, but still taken up again, as if his fate were embodied in its mechanism, he was surprised by the entrance of old Peter Hovenden. Owen never met this man without a shrinking of the heart. Of all the world he was most terrible, by reason of a keen understanding which saw so distinctly what it did see, and disbelieved so uncompromisingly in what it could not see. On this occasion the old watchmaker had merely a gracious word or two to say.

"Owen my lad," said he, "we must see you at my house to-morrow night."

The artist began to mutter some excuse.

"Oh, but it must be so," quoth Peter Hovenden, "for the sake of the days when you were one of the household. What, my boy! don't you know that my daughter Annie is engaged to Robert Danforth? We are making an entertainment, in our humble way, to celebrate the event."

"Ah!" said Owen.

That little monosyllable was all he uttered; its tone seemed cold and unconcerned to an ear like Peter Hovenden's; and yet there was in it the stifled outcry of the poor artist's heart, which he compressed within him like a man holding down an evil spirit. One slight outbreak, however, imperceptible to the old watchmaker, he allowed himself. Raising the instrument with which he was about to begin his work, he let it fall upon the little system of machinery that had, anew, cost him months of thought and toil. It was shattered by the stroke!

Owen Warland's story would have been no tolerable representation of the troubled life of those who strive to create the beautiful, if, amid all other thwarting influences, love had not interposed to steal the cunning from his head. Outwardly he had been no ardent or enterprising lover; the career of his passion had confined its tumults and vicissitudes so entirely within the artist's imagination that Annie herself had scarcely more than a woman's intuitive perception of it; but, in Owen's view, it covered the whole field of his life. Forgetful of the time when she had shown herself incapable of any deep response, he had persisted in connecting all his dreams of artistical success with Annie's image; she was the visible shape in which the spiritual power that he worshipped, and on whose altar he hoped to lay a not unworthy offering, was made manifest to him. Of course he had deceived himself; there were no such attributes in Annie Hovenden as his imagination had endowed her with. She, in the aspect which she wrote to his inward vision, was as much a creature of his own as the mysterious piece of mechanism would be were it ever realized. Had he become convinced of his mistake through the medium of successful love, — had he won Annie to his bosom, and there beheld her fade from angel into ordinary woman, — the disappointment might have driven him back, with concentrated energy, upon his sole remaining object. On the other hand, had he found Annie what he fancied, his lot would have been so rich in beauty that out of its mere redundancy he might have wrought the beautiful into many a worthier type than he had toiled for; but the guise in which his sorrow came to him, the sense that the angel of his life had been snatched away and given to a rude man of earth and iron, who could neither need nor appreciate her ministrations, — this was the very perversity of fate that makes human existence appear too absurd and contradictory to be the scene of one other hope or one other fear. There was nothing left for Owen Warland but to sit down like a man that had been stunned.

He went through a fit of illness. After his recovery his small slender frame assumed an obtuser garniture of flesh than it had ever before worn. His thin cheeks became round; his delicate little hand, so spiritually fashioned to achieve fairy task-work, grew plumper than the hand of a thriving infant. His aspect had a childishness such as might have induced a stranger to pat him on the head—pausing, however, in the act, to wonder what manner of child was here. It was if the spirit has gone out of him, leaving the body to flourish in a sort of vegetable existence. Not that Owen Warland was idiotic. He could talk, and not irrationally. Somewhat of a babbler, indeed, did people begin to think him; for he was apt to discourse at wearisome length of marvels of mechanism that he had read about in books, but which he had learned to consider as absolutely fabulous. Among them he enumerated the Man of Brass, constructed by Albertus Magnus, and the Brazen Head of Friar Bacon; and coming down to later times, the automata of a little coach and horses, which it was pretended had been manufactured for the Dauphin of France; together with an insect that buzzed about the ear like a living fly, and yet was but a contrivance of minute steel springs. There was a story, too, of a duck that waddled and quacked, and ate; though, had any honest citizen purchased it for dinner, he would have found himself cheated with the mere mechanical apparition of a duck.

"But all these accounts," said Owen Warland, "I am now satisified are mere impositions."

Then, in a mysterious way, he would confess that he once thought differently. In his idle and dreamy days he had considered it possible, in a certain sense, to spiritualize machinery, and to combine with the new species of life and motion thus produced a beauty that should attain to the ideal which Nature has proposed to herself in all her creatures, but has never taken pains to realize. He seemed, however, to retain no very distinct perception either of the process of achieving this object or of the design itself.

"I have thrown it all aside now," he would say, "It was a dream such as young men are always mystifying themselves with. Now that I have acquired a little common sense, it makes me laugh to think of it."

Poor, poor and fallen Owen Warland! These were the symptoms that he had ceased to be an inhabitant of the better sphere that lie unseen around us. He had lost his faith in the invisible, and now prided himself, as such unfortunates invariably do, in the wisdom which rejected much that even his eye could see, and trusted confidently in nothing but what his hand could touch. This is the calamity of men whose spiritual part dies out of them and leaves the grosser understanding to assimilate them more and more to the things of which alone it can take cognizance; but in Owen Warland the spirit was not dead nor passed away; it only slept.

How it woke again is not recorded. Perhaps the torpid slumber was broken by a convulsive pain. Perhaps, as in a former instance, the butterfly came and hovered about his head and reinspired him, — as indeed this creature of the sunshine had always a mysterious mission for the artist, — reinspired him with the former purpose of his life. Whether it were pain or happiness that thrilled through his veins, his first impulse was to thank Heaven for rendering him again the being of thought, imagination, and keenest sensibility that he had long ceased to be.

"Now for my task," said he, "Never did I feel such strength for it as now."

Yet, strong as he felt himself, he was incited to toil the more diligently by an anxiety lest death should surprise him in the midst of his labors. This anxiety, perhaps, is common to all men who set their hearts upon anything so high, in their own view of it, that life becomes of importance only as conditional to its accomplishment. So long as we love life for itself, we seldom dread the losing it. When we desire life for the attainment of an object, we recogize the frailty of its texture. But, side by side with this sense of insecurity, there is a vital faith in our invulnerability to the shaft of depth while engaged in any task that seems assigned by Providence as our proper thing to do, and which the world would have cause to mourn for should we leave it unaccomplished. Can the philosopher, big with the inspiration of an idea that is to reform mankind, believe that he is to be beckoned from this sensible existence at the very instant when he is mustering his breath to speak the word of light? Should he perish so, the weary ages may pass away — the world's, whose life sand may fall, drop by drop — before another intellect is prepared to develop the truth that might have been uttered then. But history affords many an example where the most precious spirit, at any particular epoch manifested in human shape, has gone hence untimely, without space allowed him, so far as mortal judgment could discern, to perform his mission on the earth. The prophet dies, and the man of torpid heart and sluggish brain lives on. The poet leaves his song half sung, or finishes it, beyond the scope of mortal ears, in a celestial choir. The painter — as Allston did — leaves half his conception on the canvas to sadden us with its imperfect beauty, and goes to picture forth the whole, if it be no irreverence to say so, in the hues of heaven. But rather such incomplete designs of this life will be perfected nowhere. This so frequent abortion of man's dearest projects must be taken as a proof that the deeds of earth, however etherealized by piety or genius, are without value, except as exercises and manifestations of the spirit. In heaven, all ordinary thought is higher and more melodious than Milton's song. Then, would he add another verse to any strain that he had left unfinished here?

But to return to Owen Warland. It was his fortune, good or ill, to achieve the purpose of his life. Pass we over a long space of intense thought, yearning effort, minute toil, and wasting anxiety, succeeded by an instant of solitary triumph: let all this be imagined; and then behold the artist, on a winter evening, seeking admittance to Robert Danforth's fireside circle. There he found the man of iron, with his massive substance thoroughly warmed and attempered by domestic influences. And there was Annie, too, now transformed into a matron, with much of her husband's plain and sturdy nature, but imbued, as Owen Warland still believed, with a finer grace, that might enable her to be the interpreter between strength and beauty. It happened, likewise, that Old Peter Hovenden was a guest this evening at his daughter's fireside, and it was his well-remembered expression of keen, cold criticism that first encountered the artist's glance.

"My old friend Owen!" cried Robert Danforth, starting up and compressing the artist's delicate fingers within a hand that was accustomed to grip bars of iron. "This is kind and neighborly to come to us at last. I was afraid your perpetual motion had bewitched you out of the remembrance of old times."

"We are glad to see you," said Annie, while a blush reddened her matronly cheek. "It was not like a friend to stay from us so long."

"Well, Owen," inquired the old watchmaker, as his first greeting, "how comes on the beautiful? Have you created it at last?"

The artist did not immediately reply, being startled by the apparition of a young child of strength that was tumbling about on the carpet, — a little personage who had come mysteriously out of the infinite, but with something so sturdy and real in his composition that he seemed moulded out of the densest substance which earth could supply. This hopeful infant crawled towards the new-comer, and setting himself on end, as Robert Danforth expressed the posture, stared at Owen with a look of such sagacious observation that the mother could not help exchanging a proud glance with her husband. But the artist was disturbed by the child's look, as imagining a resemblance between it and Peter Hovenden's habitual expression. He could have fancied that the old watchmaker was compressed into this baby shape, and looking out of those baby eyes, and repeating, as he now did, the malicious question: —

"The beautiful, Owen! How comes on the beautiful? Have you succeeded in creating the beautiful?"

"I have succeeded," replied the artist, with a momentary light of triumph in his eyes and a smile of sunshine, yet steeped in such depth of thought that it was almost sadness. "Yes, my friends, it is the truth. I have succeeded."

"Indeed!" cried Annie, a look of maiden mirthfulness peeping out of her face again. "And is it lawful now, to inquire what the secret is?"

"Surely; it is to disclose it that I have come," answered Owen Warland "You shall know, and see, and touch, and possess the secret! For, Annie, — if by that name I may still address the friend of my boyish years, — Annie, it is for your bridal gift that I have wrought this spiritualized mechanism, this harmony of motion, this mystery of beauty. It comes late, indeed; but it is as we go onward in life, when objects begin to lose their freshness of hue and our souls their delicacy of perception, the spirit of beauty is most needed. If, — forgive me, Annie, — if you know how to value this gift, it can never come too late."

He produced, as he spoke, what seemed a jewel box. It was carved richly out of ebony by his own hand, and inlaid with a fanciful tracery of pearl, representing a boy in pursuit of a butterfly, which, elsewhere, had become a winged spirit, and was flying heavenward; while the boy, or youth, had found such efficacy in his strong desire that he ascended from earth to cloud, and from cloud to celestial atmosphere, to win the beautiful. This case of ebony the artist opened, and bade Annie place her finger on its edge. She did so, but almost screamed as a butterfly fluttered forth, and, alighting on her finger's tip, sat waving the ample magnificence of its purple and gold-speckled wings, as if in prelude to a flight. It is impossible to express by words the glory, the splendor, the delicate gorgeousness which were softened into the beauty of this object. Nature's ideal butterfly was here realized in all its perfection; not in the pattern of such faded insects as flit among earthly flowers, but of those which hover across the meads of paradise for child-angels and the spirits of departed infants to disport themselves with. The rich down was visible upon its wings; the lustre of its eyes seemed instinct with spirit. The firelight glimmered around this wonder — the candles gleamed upon it; but it glistened apparently by its own radiance, and illuminated the finger and outstretched hand on which it rested with a white gleam like that of precious stones. In its perfect beauty, the consideration of size was entirely lost. Had its wings overreached the firmament, the mind could not have been more filled or satisfied.

"Beautiful! beautiful!" exclaimed Annie. "Is it alive? Is it alive?"

"Alive? To be sure it is," answered her husband. "Do you suppose any mortal has skill enough to make a butterfly, or would put himself to the trouble of making one, when any child may catch a score of them in a summer's afternoon? Alive? Certainly! But this pretty box is undoubtedly of our friend Owen's manufacture; and really it does him credit."

At this moment the butterfly waved its wings anew, with a motion so absolutely lifelike that Annie was startled, and even awestricken; for, in spite of her husband's opinion, she could not satisfy herself whether it was indeed a living creature of a piece of wondrous mechanism.

"Is it alive?" she repeated, more earnestly than before.

"Judge for yourself," said Owen Warland, who stood gazing in her face with fixed attention.

The butterfly now flung itself upon the air, fluttered round Annie's head, and soared into a distant region of the parlor, still making itself perceptible to sight by the starry gleam in which the motion of its wings enveloped it. The infant on the floor followed its course with his sagacious little eyes. After flying about the room, it returned in a spiral curve and settled again on Annie's finger.

"But is it alive?" exclaimed she again; and the finger on which the gorgeous mystery had alighted was so tremulous that the butterfly was forced to balance himself with his wings. "Tell me if it be alive, or whether you created it."

"Wherefore ask who created it, so it be beautiful?" replied Owen Warland. "Alive? Yes, Annie; it may well be said to possess life, for it has absorbed my own being into itself; and in the secret of that butterfly, and in its beauty, — which is not merely outward, but deep as its whole system, — is represented the intellect, the imagination, the sensibility, the soul of an Artist of the Beautiful! Yes; I created it. But" — and here his countenance somewhat changed— "this butterfly is not now to me what it was when I beheld it afar off in the day-dreams of my youth."

"Be it what it may, it is a pretty plaything," said the blacksmith, grinning with childlike delight. "I wonder whether it would condescend to alight on such a great clumsy finger as mine? Hold it hither, Annie,"

By the artist's direction, Annie touched her finger's tip to that of her husband; and, after a momentary delay, the butterfly fluttered from one to the other. It preluded a second flight by a similar, yet not precisely the same waving of wings as in the first experiment; then, ascending from the blacksmith's stalwart finger, it rose in a gradually enlarging curve to the ceiling, made one wide sweep around the room, and returned with an undulating movement to the point whence it had started.

"Well, that does beat all nature!" cried Robert Danforth, bestowing the heartiest praise that he could find expression for; and, indeed, had he paused there, a man of finer words and nicer perception could not easily have said more. "That goes beyond men, I confess. But what then? There is more real use in one downright blow of my sledge hammer than in the whole five years' labor that our friend Owen has wasted on this butterfly."

Here the child clapped his hands and made a great babble of indistinct utterance, apparently demanding that the butterfly should be given him for a plaything.

Owen Warland, meanwhile, glanced sidelong at Annie, to discover whether she sympathized in her husband's estimate of the comparative value of the beautiful and the practical. There was, amid all her kindness towards himself, amid all the wonder and admiration with which she contemplated the marvellous work of his hands and incarnation of his idea, a secret scorn—too secret, perhaps, for her own consciousness, and perceptible only to such intuitive discernment as that of the artist. But Owen, in the latter stages of his pursuit, had risen out of the region in which such a discovery might have been torture. He knew that the world, and Annie as the representative of the world, whatever praise might be bestowed, could never say the fitting word nor feel the fitting sentiment which should be the perfect recompense of an artist who, symbolizing a lofty moral by a material trifle, — converting what was earthly to spiritual gold, — had won the beautiful into his handiwork. Not at this latest moment was he to learn that the reward of all high performance must be sought within itself, or sought in vain. There was, however, a view of the matter which Annie and her husband, and even Peter Hovenden, might fully have understood, and which would have satisfied them that the toil of years had here been worthily bestowed. Owen Warland might have told them that this butterfly, this plaything, this bridal gift of a poor watchmaker to a blacksmith's wife, was, in truth, a gem of art that a monarch would have purchased with honors and abundant wealth, and have treasured it among the jewels of his kingdom as the most unique and wondrous of them all. But the artist smiled and kept the secret to himself.

"Father," said Annie, thinking that a word of praise from the old watchmaker might gratify his former apprentice, "do come and admire this pretty butterfly."

"Let us see," said Peter Hovenden, rising from his chair, with a sneer upon his face that always made people doubt, as he himself did, in everything but a material existence. "Here is my finger for it to alight upon. I shall understand it better when once I have touched it."

But, to the increased astonishment of Annie, when the tip of her father's finger was pressed against that of her husband, on which the butterfly still rested, the bright spots of gold upon its wings and body, unless her eyes deceived her, grew dim, and the glowing purple took a dusky hue, and the starry lustre that gleamed around the blacksmith's hand became faint and vanished.

"It is dying! it is dying!" cried Annie, in alarm.

"It has been delicately wrought," said the artist, calmly. "As I told you, it has imbibed a spiritual essence — call it magnetism, or what you will, In an atmosphere of doubt and mockery its exquisite susceptibility suffers torture, as does the soul of him who instilled his own life into it. It has already lost its beauty; in a few moments more its mechanism would be irreparably injured."

"Take away your hand, father!" entreated Annie, turning pale. "Here is my child; let it rest on his innocent hand. There, perhaps, its life will revive and its colors grow brighter than ever."

Her father, with an acrid smile, withdrew his finger. The butterfly then appeared to recover the power of voluntary motion, while its hues assumed much of their original lustre, and the gleam of starlight, which was its most ethereal attribute, again formed a halo round about it. Ar first, when transferred from Robert Danforth's hand to the small finger of the child, this radiance grew so powerful that it positively threw the little fellow's shadow back against the wall. He, meanwhile, extended his plump hand as he had seen his father and mother do, and watched the waving of the insect's wings with infantine delight. Nevertheless, there was a certain odd expression of sagacity that made Owen Warland feel as if here were old Peter Hovenden, partially, and but partially, redeemed from his hard scepticism into childish faith.

"How wise the little monkey looks!" whispered Robert Danforth to his wife.

"I never saw such a look on a child's face," answered Annie, admiring her own infant, and with good reason, far more than the artistic butterfly. "The darling knows more of the mystery than we do."

As if the butterfly, like the artist, were conscious of something not entirely congenial in the child's nature, it alternately sparkled and grew dim. At length it arose from the small hand of the infant with an airy motion that seemed to bear it upward without an effort, as if the ethereal instincts with which its master's spirit had endowed it impelled this fair vision involuntarily to a higher sphere. Had there been no obstruction, it might have soared into the sky and grown immortal. But its lustre gleamed upon the ceiling; the exquisite texture of its wings brushed against that earthly medium; and a sparkle or two, as of stardust, floated downward and lay glimmering on the carpet. Then the butterfly came fluttering down, and, instead of returning to the infant, was apparently attracted towards the artist's hand.

"Not so! not so!" murmured Owen Warland, as if his handiwork could have understood him. "Thou has gone forth out of thy master's heart. There is no return for thee."

With a wavering movement, and emitting a tremulous radiance, the butterfly struggled, as it were, towards the infant, and was about to alight upon his finger; but while it still hovered in the air, the little child of strength, with his grandsire's sharp and shrewd expression in his face, made a snatch at the marvellous insect and compressed it in his hand. Annie screamed. Old Peter Hovenden burst into a cold and scornful laugh. The blacksmith, by main force, unclosed the infant's hand, and found within the palm a small heap of glittering fragments, whence the mystery of beauty had fled forever. And as for Owen Warland, he looked placidly at what seemed the ruin of his life's labor, and which was yet no ruin. He had caught a far other butterfly than this. When the artist rose high enough to achieve the beautiful, the symbol by which he made it perceptible to mortal senses became of little value in his eyes while his spirit possessed itself in the enjoyment of the reality.

___ Somatoform Disorders

Two factors characterize Somatoform Disorders. (*Soma* is the Greek word for *body*; *somatoform* refers to psychological disorders that manifest themselves in physical form.) One factor is the person's announced physical symptoms, e.g., headaches, fainting spells, abdominal pains, partial paralysis, blindness, for which there are no organic explanations. The other factor is a clinician's certainty that the symptoms spring from psychological factors rather than true organic illness.

Conversion Disorder, a subcategory of Somatoform Disorders, is characterized by the loss or alteration of a specific physical function, e.g., the sense of sight or the ability to walk, that is directly related to a psychological conflict or need. In other words, the person "converts" a psychological conflict or need into a physical symptom that resolves the conflict or satisfies the need. For example, a preadolescent boy sees a particularly horrifying event. To avoid coping with the internal conflict produced by what he saw, he becomes "blind." His physical symptom enables him to keep the conflict out of his awareness. Another example is that of a fourteen year old girl who is excessively dependent on her parents and who needs their constant presence and reassurance. To bind them to her, she becomes "blind." Her physical symptom fulfills her dependency need by eliciting support that she might not otherwise warrant.

In Paul Gallico's "The Enchanted Doll," Rose Callimit and her cousin, Essie Nolan, are seen through the writings of Dr. Samuel Amony, whose narrative has a fairy-tale quality about it. What were the psychological factors that produced Essie's Conversion Disorder and how is her hobby directly related to those factors? Furthermore, how does her disorder enable her to avoid facing those factors? In addition, some attention should be paid to Rose, especially her relationship with Essie. What explanation could account for Rose's attitudes and conduct?

THE ENCHANTED DOLL
Paul Gallico

Today is the anniversary of that afternoon in April a year ago that I first saw the strange and alluring doll in the window of Abe Sheftel's stationery, cigar, and toy shop on Third Avenue near Fifteenth Street, just around the corner from my office, where the white plate with the black lettering on my doors reads: SAMUEL AMONY, M.D.

And I feel impelled to try to set down on paper some record of the things that resulted from that meeting, though I am afraid it will be a crudely told story, for I am not a writer, but a doctor.

I remember just how it was that day: the first hint of spring wafted across the East River, mingling with the soft-coal smoke from the factories and the street smells of the poor neighborhood. The wagon of an itinerant flower seller at the curb was all gay with tulips, hyacinths, and boxes of pansies, and near by a hurdy-gurdy was playing "Some Enchanted Evening."

As I turned the corner and came abreast of Sheftel's, I was made once more aware of the poor collection of toys in the dusty window, and I remembered the approaching birthday of a small niece of mine in Cleveland, to whom I was in the habit of despatching modest gifts.

Therefore, I stopped and examined the window to see if there might be anything appropriate and browsed through the bewildering array of unappealing objects — a red toy fire engine, crudely made lead soldiers, cheap baseballs, gloves and bats, all a-jumble with boxes of withered cigars, cartons of cigarettes, bottles of ink, pens, pencils, gritty stationery, and garish cardboard cut-out advertisements for soft drinks.

And thus it was my eyes eventually came to rest upon the doll tucked away in one corner. She was overshadowed by the surrounding articles and barely visible through the grime of decades collected on Abe's window, but I could see that she was made all of rag, with a painted face, and represented a little girl with the strangest, tenderest, most alluring and winsome expression on her face.

I could not wholly make her out, due to the shadows and the film through which I was looking, but I was aware that a tremendous impression had been made upon me, that somehow a contact had been established between her and myself, almost as though she had called to me. It was exactly as though I had run into a person as one does sometimes with a stranger in a crowded room with whose personality one is indelibly impressed and which lingers on.

I went inside and replied to Abe's greeting of "Hello, Doc, what can I do for you? You out of tobacco again?" with: "Let me see that rag doll, the one in the corner by the roller skates. I've got to send something to a kid niece of mine..."

Abe's eyebrows went up into his bald head and he came around the counter, the edges of his open vest flapping. "That doll?" he said. "That doll now could cost quite a bit of money, maybe more than you would want to pay. She's special made."

Nevertheless he took her from the window and placed her in my hands and here it was that I received my second shock, for she had the most amazing and wonderful quality. No more than a foot long, she was as supple and live to the touch as though there were flesh and bones beneath the clothes instead of rag stuffing.

It was indeed, as Abe had said, hand-made, and its creator had endowed it with such lifelike features and grace that it gave one the curious feeling of an alter presence. Yet there was even more than that to her. Could a doll be said to have sex appeal in the length and proportions of her legs, the shape of her head, the swirl of her skirt over her hips? Was it possible for an emotion to have been sewn into the seams marking the contours of the tiny figure? For though I am young, I have seen too much, both in peace and war, to be either sentimental or subject to hallucination. Yet to hold this doll was to feel a contact with something warm, mysterious, feminine, and wonderful. I felt that if I did not put her down I would become moved by her in some unbearable fashion.

I laid her on the counter. "What's the price, Abe?"

"Fifteen dollars."

It was my turn to look astonished. Abe said, "I told you, didn't I? I only make a dollar on it. I don't need to make no profit on you, Doc. You can have it for fourteen. Uptown in some a them big stores she gets as much as twenny and twenny-fi dollars for 'em."

"Who is 'she'?"

"Some woman over on Thirteenth Street who makes 'em. She's been there about a couple of years. She buys her cigarettes and papers here. That's how I come to get one once in a while. They sell quick."

"What is she like? What is her name?"

Abe replied, "I dunno, exactly — something like 'Calamity.' She's a big, flashy, red-haired dame, but hard. Wears a lot of furs. Not your type, Doc."

I couldn't understand it, or make the connection between the woman Abe described and the exquisite little creature that lay on the counter. "I'll take her," I said. It was more than I could afford, for my practice is among the poor, where one goes really to learn medicine. Yet I could not leave her lying there on the counter amidst the boxes of chewing gum, matches, punchboards, and magazines, for she was a creation, and something, some part of a human soul, had gone into the making of her. I counted out $14 and felt like a fool.

I felt even more of one when I had got her home and was repacking her to send her off to Cleveland. Again I felt that powerful impact of the tiny figure and realized that I had the greatest reluctance to part with her. She filled the small bedroom I had behind my consulting room with her presence and brought an indescribable longing to my throat and a sadness to my heart. For the first time since I had come out of the Army and had taken up practice I realized that I was lonely and that sometimes the satisfaction to be derived through helping the sick is not enough.

I said to myself, "Okay, Sam, boy. That's all you need now, is to start playing with dolls. The guys with the butterfly net will be along any moment."

When I came back from posting it to my niece, I though that would be the end of it, but it wasn't. I couldn't get it out of my head. I thought about it often and tried to reconcile the emotion it had aroused with what Abe had told me of the flashy red-haired woman who had created the object, but I could not. Once I was even tempted to pursue the matter, find out who she was and perhaps see her. But just at that time Virus X hit in our neighborhood and drove everything else out of my head.

It was three months or so later that my telephone rang and a woman's voice said, "Dr. Amony?"

"Yes?"

"I passed by your place once and saw your sign. Are you expensive? Do you cost a lot for a visit?"

I was repelled by the quality of the voice and calculation in it. Nevertheless replied, "I charge a dollar. If you are really ill and cannot afford to pay, I charge nothing."

"Okay. I could pay a dollar. But no more. You can come over. Callamit is the name. Rose Callamit, 937 East Thirteenth Street, second floor."

I did not make the connection at the time.

When I pushed the button under the name plate at that address, the buzzer sounded, the latch gave way, and I mounted two narrow, musty flights of stairs, dimly lighted and creaking. A door was opened an inch or so and I felt I was being subjected to scrutiny. Then the unpleasant voice said, "Dr. Amony? You can come in. I'm Rose Callamit."

I was startled by her. She was almost six feet tall, with brick, henna-dyed hair and an overpowering smell of cheap perfume. She had dark eyes, almond-shaped and slanted slightly in an Oriental fashion, and her mouth was full, thick-lipped, and heavily made up. There was a horrible vitality and flashy beauty about her. I placed her age at somewhere between forty-five and fifty.

The deepest shock, however, I sustained when I entered the room, which was one of those front parlor-bedrooms of the old-fashioned brownstone houses, furnished femininely, but with utter vulgarity by means of cheap prints, cheap satin cushions, and cheap glass perfume bottles But hanging from the wall, lying about on the bed, or tossed carelessly onto the top of an old trunk were a dozen or so rag dolls, all of them different, yet, even at first glance, filled with the same indescribable appeal and charm as that of the similar little creature that had made such a profound impression upon me. I realized that I was in the presence of the creator of those astonishing puppets.

Rose Callamit said, "Tall, dark, and handsome, eh? Ain't you kind of young to be around doctoring people?"

I answered her sharply, for I was angry, uncomfortable, and irritated. The rediscovery of these beautiful and touching creatures in this cheap, disgusting atmosphere and in connection with this horrible woman had upset me. "I'm older than you think, and my looks are none of your business. If you don't want me to treat you I'd just as soon go."

"Now now, Doctor. Can't you take a compliment?"

"I'm not interested in compliments. Are you the patient?"

"No. It's my cousin. She's sick in the back room. I'll take you to her."

Before we went in, I had to know. I asked, "Do you make these dolls?"

"Yup. Why?"

I was filled with a sense of desolation. I mumbled, "I bought one once, for a niece..."

She laughed. "Bet you paid plenty for it. They're the rage. Okay, come on."

She led me through a connecting bath and washroom into the smaller room at the back and opened the door partly, shouting, "Essie, it's the doctor!" Then, before she pushed it wide to admit me, she cried loudly and brutally, "Don't be surprised, Doctor, she's a cripple!"

The pale girl, clad in a flannel peignoir, in the chair over by the window had a look of utter despair on her countenance. I was disgusted and angry again. The way the woman had said it was in itself crippling. She was not alone telling me that Essie was a cripple; she was reminding Essie.

I tried to observe as much and as quickly as possible, for the doctor who comes into the sickroom must hear and feel and see with his skin as well as his eyes and ears.

She could not have been more than twenty-four or twenty-five. She seemed to be nothing but a pair of huge and misery-stricken eyes and what was shocking was how low the lamp of life appeared to be burning in them. She was very ill. From that first visit I remembered the underlying sweetness of her presence, the lovely brow and shapely head, now too big for her wasted frame, the translucent, blue-veined hands, flaxen hair but limp and lusterless. She had a mouth shaped to incredible pathos, soft, pale coral, and ready to tremble.

But I saw something else that astounded me and gave my heart a great lift. She was surrounded by small tables. On one of them were paints and brushes, on others, rag material, linen, stuffing threads and needles, the paraphernalia needed for the making of dolls.

Her present illness and her deformity were two separate things, yet it was the latter that caught my attention immediately even from the door, something about the way she sat, and made me wonder. The technical name for her condition would be unintelligible to you, but if it was what it looked to me at first glance, it was curable.

I asked, "Can you walk, Essie?"

She nodded listlessly.

"Please walk to me."

"Oh don't," Essie said. "Don't make me."

The pleading in her voice touched me, but I had to be sure. I said, "I'm sorry, Essie. Please do as I ask."

She rose unsteadily from her chair and limped toward me, dragging her left leg. I was certain I was right. "That's good," I said to her, smiled encouragingly, and held out my hands to her. Something strange happened. For a moment we seemed to be caught up in one another's eyes. I felt she was being swept away and drowning in the dark pool of her misery and despair while the air all about me was shaken with the force of her silent cry to me for help. Her hands lifted toward mine for an instant in imitation of my gesture, then fell back to her side. The spell was broken.

I asked, "How long have you been this way, Essie?"

Rose Callamit said, "Oh, Essie's been a cripple for years. I didn't call you for that. She's sick. I want to know what's the matter with her."

Oh yes, she was sick. Sick unto death perhaps. I had felt that as soon as I came into the room. With my glance I invited the big, vulgar woman to leave, but she only laughed. "Not on your life, Doc. I'm staying right here. You find out what's the matter with Essie and then you can tell me."

When I had finished my examination I accompanied Rose into the front room. "Well?" she said.

I asked, "Did you know that her deformity could be cured? That with the proper treatment she could be walking normally in—"

"Shut up, you!" Her cry of rage struck like a blow against my ears. "Don't you ever dare mention that to her. I've had her looked at by people who know. I won't have any young idiot raising false hopes. If you ever do, you're through here. I want to know what's ailing her. She don't eat or sleep or work good any more. What did you find out?"

"Nothing," I replied. "I don't know. There is nothing wrong organically. But there is something terribly wrong somewhere. I want to see her again. In the meantime I'm prescribing a tonic and a stimulant. I'd like to look in again after a few days."

"You'll keep your big mouth shut about curing her cripple, you understand? Otherwise I'll get another doctor."

"All right," I said. I had to be able to return to visit Essie again. Later, we would see...

When I picked up my hat and bag to leave I said, "I thought you told me it was you who made those dolls."

She looked startled for a moment as though she had never expected the subject to come up again. "I do," she snapped. "I design 'em. I let the kid work at 'em sometimes to help take her mind off she's a cripple and won't ever have a man."

But when I walked out into the bright, hot July day with the kids playing hopscotch on the sidewalk and handball against the old brewery wall and traffic grinding by, my heart told me that Rose Callamit had lied and that I had found the sweet spirit behind the enchanted doll. But the cold, clammy messenger of doctor's instinct warned me also that unless I could determine the cause of her decline, that spirit would not be long for this earth.

Her name, I found out later, was Nolan, Essie Nolan, and she was slowly dying from no determinable cause. I was sure that Rose Callamit had something to do with it. Not that Rose was killing her consciously. The red-haired woman was actually frightened. She wanted Essie alive, not dead, for Essie was her source of revenue and meal ticket.

After I had made a number of visits, Rose did not even bother to keep up the pretense that it was she herself who made the dolls, and I was able to piece together something of the picture.

When Essie was fifteen, her parents had been killed in an accident which also resulted in her injury. A court had awarded her in guardianship to her only relative, the cousin, Rose Callamit. When Essie's inheritance proved meager, Rose vented her spite by harping on her deformity. Through the years of their association, the older woman had made her deeply sensitive to and ashamed of her lameness. Her theme was always, "You are a hopeless cripple. No man will ever look at you. You will never be married or have children."

When Essie came of age, her spirit apparently was broken and she was completely subjugated to the will of her cousin, for she continued to remain with her and under her sway, living a lonely and hopeless existence. It was about this time that Essie first began to make the rag dolls, and Rose, for all of her vulgarity, greed, and indolence, had the shrewdness to recognize their unique quality and irresistible appeal. After she had sold the first ones she kept Essie at it from morning until night. Some weeks she was able to clear as much as $300 or $400. None of this, as far as I was able to determine, went to Essie.

Essie was completely under the domination of Rose and was afraid of her, but it was not that which was killing her. It was something else, and I could not find out what. Nor was I ever allowed to see her alone. Rose was always present. Never had I been so conscious of the difference between good and evil as in that room with the girl, whose poor suppressed nature fluttered so feebly in her wasted body, and that gross, thick-lipped woman with the greedy eyes and patchouli smell who exhaled the odor of wickedness.

I did not mention my belief in the possibility of cure for Essie's lameness. It was more important to discover immediately what it was that was killing her. Rose would not let her be moved to a hospital. She would not spare the money.

For ten days I thought I had arrested the process that was destroying Essie before my eyes. I stopped her work on the dolls. I brought her some books to read, some sweets, and a bottle of sherry. When I returned for my next visit, she smiled at me for the first time, and the tremulousness, longing, hunger, the womanliness and despair of the smile would have broken a heart of stone.

"That's better," I said. "Another ten days of no work. Rest, sleep, read. Then we'll see."

But Rose Callamit glowered and there was an unpleasant expression about her mouth. Her huge, overpowering bulk seemed to fill the room with hatred.

The next time I came to call she was waiting for me in her own room. She had seven one dollar bills in her hand. She said, "Okay, Doc. That's all. We don't need you any more."

"But Essie — "

"Essie's okay. Fit as a fiddle. So long, Doc…"

My eyes wandered to the old trunk in the corner. There were three new dolls lying on top of it. Was it only my imagination, or was there yet a new quality to these mute, bewitched figurines? Was each in its way a birth and a death in one, a greeting to the beauties, desires, and pleasures of life and at the same time a farewell?

I had the most powerful impulse to push the monstrous woman aside and crash through the doors to see my patient. But the habits of medical ethics are too hard to break. When a physician is dismissed, it is his duty to go unless he has reason to suspect that his patient is meeting with foul play. I had no such reason. I had failed to determine the cause of Essie's illness; Rose was undoubtedly calling in another doctor, for she needed Essie's work for an easy living and would unquestionably try to protect such a meal ticket.

Thus, with great heaviness of heart, I departed. But I thought about Essie night and day.

It was shortly after this that I became ill myself. Imperceptibly at first, then finally noticeably: loss of appetite, loss of weight, lethargy, irritability, at nighfall a half a degree to a degree of temperature, moments of weakness when I felt as though somehow I could not go on with my work. I let Dr. Saul up at the hospital go over me. He thumped and pounded and listened, the obvious routine, and reported, "Nothing wrong with you, Sam. Take it a little easier. You've probably been overworking. Nature's protest."

But I knew it wasn't that.

I began to look shocking; my skin was losing its tone, my cheekbones were beginning to show, and I was hollow-eyed from loss of sleep. I did not like the look in my eyes, or the expression about my mouth. Sometimes my nights and my dreams were filled with fever and in them I saw Essie struggling to reach me while Rose Callamit held her imprisoned in her ugly, shapeless arms. I had never been free from worry over failure to diagnose Essie's case.

My whole faith in myself as a doctor was badly shaken. A desperately stricken human being had called upon me for help and I had failed. I could not even help myself. What right had I to call myself a doctor? All through one awful night of remorse and reproach the phrase burned through my brain as though written in fire:

"Physician, heal thyself!"

Yes, heal myself before I was fit to heal others. But heal myself from what? If anything, my symptoms resembled those of Essie Nolan. Essie! Essie! Essie! Always Essie!

Was Essie my sickness? Had she always been from the first moment that I had encountered that extension of her enchanted spirit embodied in the rag doll in Abe Sheftel's shop?

And as morning grayed my back-yard window and the elevated train thundered by in increasing tempo, I knew my disease. I was in love with Essie Nolan. When I could couple the words "love" and "Essie," when I could look up and cry "I love Essie Nolan! I want her! I need her person and her soul, forever at my side" it was as though I could feel the fire of healing medicine glowing through my veins.

It had always been Essie, the warmth and yearning need, the tenderness that she expressed with her presence, and the odd, offbeat beauty of her, too, a beauty that would only reach its full flower when I had cured and restored her in every way.

For now, as the scales fell from my eyes and my powers were released again through the acknowledging and freeing inside of me of the hunger, love, and compassion I had for her, I knew the sickness of Essie Nolan in full, to its last pitiful detail, and what I must do and why I must see her alone if only for a few minutes if she were not to be lost to me and to the world forever.

That morning I telephoned Abe Sheftel and said, "This is Dr. Amony, Abe. Will you do something for me?"

"Are you kiddin'? After what you done for my boy—you name it."

"Look here! You remember Rose Callamit? The doll woman? Yes. The next time she comes into the store, find some means of telephoning me. Then hold her there, somehow. Talk, or do something, anything to make her stay there a little. I need twenty minutes. Okay? Got it? I'll bless you the rest of my life."

I was in a sweat for fear it would happen while I was on an outside call, and each time I returned to the office that day I stopped by the store, but Abe would merely shake his head. Then, at five o'clock in the afternoon the phone rang. It was Abe. He said merely, "It could be now," and hung up.

It took me no more than a minute or two to run the few blocks to the brownstone house where Essie lived and press the buzzer under another name plate. When the door clicked open I went upstairs, two steps at a time. If the door was locked I would have to get the landlady. But I was in luck. Rose had expected to be gone only a few moments, apparently, and it was open. I hurried through the connecting bath and, entering the back room, found Essie.

There was so little of her left.

She was sitting up in bed, but now the absolute pallor had been replaced with two red fever spots that burned in the middle of her cheeks, a danger sign more deadly than the wastage of her hands and body. She was still surrounded by the paints and bits of colored cloth and threads, as though she did not wish to die before she had put together one more image, one more dream, one last reflection of the sweet self that life had apparently so cruelly doomed to wither.

She looked up when I came in, startled out of her lethargy. She had expected it to be Rose. Her hand went to her breast and she said my name. Not "Dr. Amony," but my given one — "Samuel!"

I cried, "Essie! Thank God I'm in time. I came to help you. I know what it is that has been...making you ill..."

She was in that state where nothing escaped her. She felt my hesitation and knew I had avoided saying "...that is killing you," for she whispered, "Does it matter now?"

I said, "There's still time, Essie. I know your secret. I know how to make you well. But you must listen to me while I tell you. Your life depends on it."

A change came over her She closed her eyes for an instant and murmured, "No. Don't, please. Let me go. I don't want to know. It will be over soon."

I had not thought that she might be unwilling or unable to face it. And yet I had to go on now. I sat down and took her hand.

"Essie. Please listen. Give me your mind. When a body is undernourished we give it food; when it is anemic, we supply blood; when it lacks iron or hormones we give it tonic. But you have had a different kind of leakage. You have been drained dry of something else without which the soul and body cannot be held together."

Her eyes opened and I saw that they were filled with horror and a glazing fear. She seemed about to lose consciousness as she begged, "No! Don't say it!"

I thought perhaps she might die then and there. But the only hope for her, for us both, was to go on.

"Essie! My brave, dear girl. It is nothing so terrible. You need not be afraid. It is only that you have been drained of love. Look at me, Essie!"

My eyes caught and held her. I willed her to remain alive, to stay with me, to hear me out. "See, Essie, a person has just so great a reservoir of love to expend. It is drawn upon through life and must ever be replenished with tenderness, affection, warmth, and hope. Thus the supply is always renewed. But yours has been emptied and there was nothing left."

I could not be sure that she still heard me. "It was Rose Callamit," I continued. "She took away your every hope of life, love, and fulfillment. But what she did later to you was a much blacker crime. For she took away *your children!*"

There, it was out! Had I killed her? Had it been I who loved her beyond words who had administered the death blow? And yet I thought I saw a flicker of life in those poor, stricken eyes, and even perhaps the faintest reflection of relief.

"Oh, yes, they were your children, Essie, those enchanted creatures you created. When you were convinced that you had lost your chance to be a woman, you compensated for it by embodying your hopes, your dreams, and, like every creator, whether mother or artist, a piece of your heart went into each of the dolls you made. You created them with love; you loved them like your own children and then each one was taken from you at birth by that money-hungry monster and nothing was given to you to replace them. And so you continued to take them from your heart, your tissue, and your blood until your life was being drained away from you. Persons can die from lack of love."

Essie stirred. Her head beneath the flaxen hair moved ever so slightly. The glaze passed from her eyes. I thought I felt the response of faint pressure from the cold hand in mine.

I cried, "But you won't, Essie, because I am here to tell you that I love you, to refill you to overflowing with all that has been taken from you. Do you hear me, Essie? I am not your doctor. I am a man telling you that I love you and cannot live without you."

I caught her incredulous whisper. "Love me? But I am a cripple."

"If you were a thousand times a cripple, I would only love you a thousand times more. But it isn't true. Rose Callamit lied to you. You can be cured. In a year I will have you walking like any other girl."

For the first time since I had known her I saw tears in her eyes and a tinge of color to her lovely brow. Then she lifted her arms to me with an utter and loving simplicity.

I picked her up out of the bed, with the blanket wrapped around her. She had no weight at all: she was like a bird. And she clung to me with a kind of sweet desperation, so that I wondered where the strength in her arms came from and the glow of her cheek against mine; she who but a moment ago had seemed so close to death.

A door slammed. Another crashed open. Rose Callamit stormed into the room. I felt Essie shudder with the old fear and bury her face in my shoulder.

But Rose was too late. It was all over. There was nothing she could do any more, and she knew it. There was not even a word spoken as I walked past her then and there carrying my burden held closely to me and went out the door and down into the street.

August had come to New York. Heat was shimmering from the melting pavements; no air stirred; water from the hydrants was flushing the streets and kids were bathing in the flow, screaming and shouting, as I carried Essie home.

That was three years ago and I am writing this on an anniversary. Essie is busy with our son and is preparing to welcome our second-to-be-born. She does not make dolls now. There is no need.

We have many kinds of anniversaries, but this is the one I celebrate privately and give thanks for — the day when I first saw and fell in love with the message from Essie's soul imprisoned in the enchanted doll that cried out to me from the grimy window of Abe Sheftel's shop on Third Avenue.

___ Psychosexual Disorders

Psychological factors play an important role in sexual functioning; consequently, four groups of mental disorders are classified as being psychosexual. Psychosexual Disorders include Gender Identity Disorders, Paraphilias, Psychosexual Dysfunctions, and Other Psychosexual Disorders. Only Paraphilias are introduced and illustrated in the material that follows.

Paraphilias

In some classifications, Paraphilias are called Sexual Deviations. However, the term *Paraphilia* is preferable since it emphasizes that the individual's attraction (*philia*) is considered deviant (*para*). For example, in Fetishism, Transvestism, and Zoophilia, the attraction is a nonhuman object that produces persistent, sexually arousing fantasies. In Pedophilia (attraction to a prepubertal child), Exhibitionism, and Voyeurism, the attraction is a nonconsenting partner who produces sexual arousal. In Sexual Masochism and Sexual Sadism, the attraction is physical suffering or psychological humiliation that produces sexual excitement.

Transvestism

Transvestism, as defined in DSM-III, is virtually restricted to heterosexual males who persistently cross-dress for the purpose of sexual arousal. When their cross-dressing is hindered, they become intensely frustrated.

"Scobie," from Lawrence Durrell's *Balthazar*, depicts not only the guilt and anxiety associated with Transvestism but also the risks the transvestite may run.

SCOBIE
Lawrence Durrell

He was sitting down on the bed now and staring at his shabby shoes. "Are you going to the party Nessim's giving for Mountolive tonight?" — "I suppose so," I said. He sniffed loudly. "I'm not invited. At the Yacht Club, isn't it?"

"Yes."

"He is Sir David now, isn't he? I saw it in the paper last week. Young to be a lord, isn't he? I was in charge of the Police Guard of Honour when he arrived. They all played out of tune but he didn't notice anything, thank God!"

"Not so young."

"And to be Minister?"

"I suppose he's in his late forties?"

Abruptly, without apparent premeditation (though he closed his eyes fast as if to shut the subject away out of sight forever) Scobie lay back on the bed, hands behind his head, and said:

"Before you go, there's a small confession I'd like to make to you, old man. Right?"

I sat down on the uncomfortable chair and nodded. "Right," he said emphatically and drew a breath. "Well then: sometimes at the full moon, *I'm Took*. I come under *An Influence.*"

This was on the face of it a somewhat puzzling departure from accepted form, for the old man looked quite disturbed by his own revelation. He gobbled for a moment and then went on in a small humbled voice devoid of his customary swagger. "I don't know what comes over me." I did not quite understand all this. "Do you mean you walk in your sleep or what?" He shook his head and gulped again. "Do you turn into a werewolf, Scobie?" Once more he shook his head like a child upon the point of tears. "I slip on female duds and my Dolly Varden," he said, and opened his eyes fully to stare pathetically at me.

"You *what?*" I said.

To my intense surprise he rose now and walked stiffly to a cupboard which he unlocked. Inside, hanging up, moth-eaten and unbrushed, was a suit of female clothes of ancient cut, and on a nail beside it a greasy old cloche hat which I took to be the so-called "Dolly Varden." A pair of antediluvian court shoes with very high heels and long pointed toes completed this staggering outfit. He did not know how quite to respond to the laugh which I was now compelled to utter. He gave a weak giggle. "It's silly, isn't it?" he said, still hovering somewhere on the edge of tears despite his smiling face, and still by his tone inviting sympathy in misfortune. "I don't know what comes over me. And yet, you know, it's always the old thrill. . . ."

A sudden and characteristic change of mood came over him at the words: his disharmony, his discomfiture gave place to a new jauntiness. His look became arch now, not wistful, and crossing to the mirror before my astonished eyes, he placed the hat upon his bald head. In a second he replaced his own image with that of a little old tart, button-eyed and razor-nosed — a tart of the Waterloo Bridge epoch, a veritable Tuppenny Upright. Laughter and astonishment packed themselves into a huge parcel inside me, neither finding expression. "For God's sake!" I said at last. "You don't go around like that, do you, Scobie?"

"Only," said Scobie, sitting helplessly down on the bed again and relapsing into a gloom which gave his funny little face an even more comical expression (he still wore the Dolly Varden), only when the Influence comes over me. When I'm not fully Answerable, old man."

He sat there looking crushed. I gave a low whistle of surprise which the parrot immediately copied. This was indeed serious. I understood now why the deliberations which had consumed him all morning had been so full of heart-searching. Obviously if one went around in a rig like that in the Arab quarter. . . . He must have been following my train of thought, for he said, "It's only sometimes when the Fleet's in." Then he went on with a touch of self-righteousness: "Of course, if there was any trouble, I'd say I was in disguise. I am a policeman when you come to think of it. After all, even Lawrence of Arabia wore a nightshirt, didn't he?" I nodded. "But not a Dolly Varden," I said. "You must admit, Scobie, it's most original. . ." and here the laughter overtook me.

Scobie watched me laugh, still sitting on the bed in that fantastic headpiece. "Take it off!" I implored. He looked serious and preoccupied now, but made no motion. "Now you know all," he said. "The best and the worst in the old skipper. Now what I was going to —"

At this moment there came a knock at the landing door. With surprising presence of mind Scobie leaped spryly into the cupboard, locking himself noisily in. I went to the door. On the landing stood a servant with a pitcher full of some liquid which he said was for the Effendi Skob. I took it from him and got rid of him, before returning to the room and shouting to the old man who emerged once more — now completely himself, bareheaded and blazered.

"That was a near shave," he breathed. "What was it?" I indicated the pitcher. "Oh, that — it's for the Mock Whisky. Every three hours."

"Well," I said at last, still struggling with these new and indigestible revelations of temperament, "I must be going." I was still hovering explosively between amazement and laughter at the thought of Scobie's second life at full moon — how had he managed to avoid a scandal all these years? — when he said: "Just a minute, old man. I only told you all this because I want you to do me a favour." His false eye rolled around earnestly now under the pressure of thought. He sagged again. "A thing like that could do me Untold Harm," he said, "Untold Harm, old man."

"I should think it could."

"Old man," said Scobie, "I want you to confiscate my duds. It's the only way of controlling the Influence."

"Confiscate them?"

"Take them away. Lock them up. It'll save me, old man. I know it will. The whim is too strong for me otherwise, when it comes."

"All right," I said.

"God bless you, son."

Together we wrapped his full-moon regalia in some newspapers and tied the bundle up with string. His relief was tempered with doubt. "You won't lose them?" he said anxiously.

"Give them to me," I said firmly and he handed me the parcel meekly. As I went down the stairs he called after me to express relief and gratitude, adding the words: "I'll say a little prayer for you, son." I walked back slowly through the dock area with the parcel under my arm, wondering whether I would ever dare to confide this wonderful story to someone worth sharing it with.

****

"I told you of Scobie's death" (so wrote Balthazar) "but I did not tell you in detail the manner of it. I myself did not know him very well but I knew of your affection for him. It was not a very pleasant business and I was concerned in it entirely by accident — indeed, only because Nimrod, who runs the Secretariat, and was Scobie's chief at three removes happened to be dining with me on that particularly evening.

"You remember Nimrod? Well, we had recently been competing for the favours of a charming young Athenian actor known by the delightful name of Socrates Pittakakis, and as any serious rivalry might have caused a bad feeling between us which neither could afford on the official level (I am in some sense a consultant to his department) we had sensibly decided to bury our jealousy and frankly share the youth — as all good Alexandrians should. We were therefore dining á trois at the Auberge Bleue with the young man between us like the filling in a meat sandwich. I must admit that I had a slight advantage over Nimrod whose Greek is poor, but in general the spirit of reason and measure reigned. The actor, who drank champagne in stout all evening — he was recovering he explained from a wasting malady by this method — in the last analysis refused to have anything to do with either of us, and indeed turned out to be passionately in love with a heavily moustached Armenian girl in my clinic. So all this effort was wasted — I must say Nimrod was particularly bitter as he had had to pay for this grotesque dinner. Well, as I say, here we all were when the great man was called away to the telephone.

"He came back after a while, looking somewhat grave, and said: 'It was from the Police Station by the docks. Apparently an old man has been kicked to death by the ratings of H.M.S. *Milton*. I have reason to believe that it might be one of the eccentrics of Q branch — there is an old Bimbashi employed there. . . .' He stood irresolutely on one leg. 'At any rate,' he went on, 'I must go down and make sure. You never know. Apparently,' he lowered his voice and drew me to one side in confidence, 'he was dressed in woman's clothes. There may be a scandal.' "

"Poor Nimrod! I could see that while his duty pressed him hard, he was most reluctant that I should be left alone with the actor. He hovered and pondered heavily. At last, however, my finer nature came to my rescue just when I had given up hope. I too rose. Undying sportsmanship! 'I had better come with you,' said I. The poor man broke into troubled smiles and thanked me warmly for the gesture. We left the young man eating fish (this time for brain fag) and hurried to the car park where Nimrod's official car was waiting for him. It did not take us very long to race along the Corniche and turn down into the echoing darkness of the dock-area with its cobbled alleys and the flickering gas light along the wharves which makes it seem so like a corner of Marseilles circa 1850. I have always hated the place with its smells of sea-damp and urinals and sesame.

"The police post was a red circular building like a Victorian post office consisting of a small charge-room and two dark sweating dungeons, airless and terrible in that summer night. It was packed with jabbering and sweating policemen all showing the startled whites of their eyes like horses in the gloom. Upon a stone bench in one of the cells lay the frail and ancient figure of an old woman with a skirt dragged up above the waist to reveal thin legs clad in green socks held by suspenders and black naval boots. The electric light had failed and a wavering candle on the sill above the body dripped wax on to one withered old hand, now beginning to settle with the approach of the rigor into a histrionic gesture—as of someone warding off a stage blow. It was your friend Scobie.

"He had been battered to death in ugly enough fashion. A lot of broken crockery inside that old skin. As I examined him a phone started to nag somewhere. Keats had got wind of something: was trying to locate the scene of the incident. It could only be a matter of time before his battered old Citroën drew up outside. Obviously a grave scandal might well be the up-shot and fear lent wings to Nimrod's imagination. 'He must be got out of these clothes,' he hissed and started beating out right and left with his cane, driving the policemen out into the corridor and clearing the cell. 'Right,' I said, and while Nimrod stood with sweating averted face, I got the body out of its clothes as best I could. Not pleasant, but at last the old reprobate lay there 'naked as a psalm' as they say in Greek. That was stage one. We mopped our faces. The little cell was like an oven.

" 'He must,' said Nimrod hysterically, 'be somehow got back into uniform. Before Keats comes poking around here. I tell you what, let's go to his digs and get it. I know where he lives.' So we locked the old man into his cell: his smashed glass eye gave him a reproachful, mournful look — as if he had been subjected to an amateur taxidermist's art. Anyway, we jumped into the car and raced across the docks to Tatwig Street while Nimrod examined the contents of the natty little leatherette handbag with which the old man had equipped himself before setting out on his adventure. In it he found a few coins, a small missal, a master's ticket, and a packet of those old-fashioned rice-papers (one hardly ever sees them now) resembling a roll of cigarette paper. That was all. 'The bloody old fool,' Nimrod kept saying as we went. 'The bloody old fool.' ' "

Voyeurism

A voyeur is a man who repeatedly seeks out situations in which he can gaze at an unsuspecting woman who is naked, disrobing, or engaging in sexual activity. (By definition, Voyeurism as a mental disorder is limited to men; no parallel disorder involving women peeping on men has been described.) His "peeping" causes sexual arousal, but he has no contact with the woman. Sometimes he experiences shame or guilt because of his activity. Most voyeurs are harmless.

In "The Strength of God," Sherwood Anderson depicts The Reverend Curtis Hartman's anxiety over his inability to control his voyeuristic behavior.

THE STRENGTH OF GOD

Sherwood Anderson

The Reverend Curtis Hartman was pastor of the Presbyterian Church of Winesburg, and had been in that position ten years. He was forty years old, and by his nature very silent and reticent. To preach, standing in the pulpit before the people, was always a hardship for him and from Wednesday morning until Saturday evening he thought of nothing but the two sermons that must be preached on Sunday. Early on Sunday morning he went into a little room called a study in the bell tower of the church and prayed. In his prayers there was one note that always predominated. "Give me strength and courage for Thy work, O Lord!" he plead, kneeling on the bare floor and bowing his head in the presence of the task that lay before him.

The Reverend Hartman was a tall man with a brown beard. His wife, a stout, nervous woman, was the daughter of a manufacturer of underwear at

Cleveland, Ohio. The minister himself was rather a favorite in the town. The elders of the church liked him because he was quiet and unpretentious and Mrs. White, the banker's wife, thought him scholarly and refined.

The Presbyterian Church held itself somewhat aloof from the other churches of Winesburg. It was larger and more imposing and its minister was better paid. He even had a carriage of his own and on summer evenings sometimes drove about town with his wife. Through Main Street and up and down Buckeye Street he went, bowing gravely to the people, while his wife, afire with secret pride, looked at him out of the corners of her eyes and worried lest the horse become frightened and run away.

For a good many years after he came to Winesburg things went well with Curtis Hartman. He was not one to arouse keen enthusiasm among the worshippers in his church but on the other hand he made no enemies. In reality he was much in earnest and sometimes suffered prolonged periods of remorse because he could not go crying the word of God in the highways and byways of the town. He wondered if the flame of the spirit really burned in him and dreamed of a day when a strong sweet new current of power would come like a great wind into his voice and his soul and the people would tremble before the spirit of God made manifest in him. "I am a poor stick and that will never really happen to me," he mused dejectedly and then a patient smile lit up his features. "Oh well, I suppose I'm doing well enough," he added philosophically.

The room in the bell tower of the church, where on Sunday mornings the minister prayed for an increase in him of the power of God, had but one window. It was long and narrow and swung outward on a hinge like a door. On the window, made of little leaded panes, was a design showing the Christ laying his hand upon the head of a child. One Sunday morning in the summer as he sat by his desk in the room with a large Bible opened before him, and the sheets of his sermon scattered about, the minister was shocked to see, in the upper room of the house next door, a woman lying in her bed and smoking a cigarette while she read a book. Curtis Hartman went on tiptoe to the window and closed it softly. He was horror stricken at the thought of a woman smoking and trembled also to think that his eyes, just raised from the pages of the book of God, had looked upon the bare shoulders and white throat of a woman. With his brain in a whirl he went down into the pulpit and preached a long sermon without once thinking of his gestures or his voice. The sermon attracted unusual attention because of its power and clearness. "I wonder if she is listening, if my voice is carrying a message into her soul," he thought and began to hope that on future Sunday mornings he might be able to say words that would touch and awaken the woman apparently far gone in secret sin.

The house next door to the Presbyterian Church, through the windows of which the minister had seen the sight that had so upset him, was occupied by two women. Aunt Elizabeth Swift, a grey competent-looking widow with money in the Winesburg National Bank, lived there with her daughter Kate Swift, a school teacher. The school teacher was thirty years old and had a neat trim-looking figure. She had few friends and bore a reputation of having a sharp tongue. When he began to think about her, Curtis Hartman remembered that she had been to Europe and had lived for two years in New York City. "Perhaps after all her smoking means nothing," he thought. He began to remember that when he was a student in college and occasionally read novels, good, although somewhat worldly women, had smoked through the pages of a book that had once fallen into his hands. With a rush of new determination he worked on his sermons all through the week and forgot, in his zeal to reach the ears and the soul of this new listener, both his embarrassment in the pulpit and the necessity of prayer in the study on Sunday mornings.

Reverend Hartman's experience with women had been somewhat limited. He was the son of a wagon maker from Muncie, Indiana, and had worked his way through college. The daughter of the underwear manufacturer had boarded in a house where he lived during his school days and he had married her after a formal and prolonged courtship, carried on for the most part by the girl herself. On his marriage day the underwear manufacturer had given his daughter five thousand dollars and he promised to leave her at least twice that amount in his will. The minister had thought himself fortunate in marriage and had never permitted himself to think of other women. He did not want to think of other women. What he wanted was to do the work of God quietly and earnestly.

In the soul of the minister a struggle awoke. From wanting to reach the ears of Kate Swift, and through his sermons to delve into her soul, he began to want also to look again at the figure lying white and quiet in the bed. On a Sunday morning when he could not sleep because of his thoughts he arose and went to walk in the streets. When he had gone along Main Street almost to the old Richmond place he stopped and picking up a stone rushed off to the room in the bell tower. With the stone he broke out a corner of the window and then locked the door and sat down at the desk before the open Bible to wait. When the shade of the window to Kate Swift's room was raised he could see, through the hole, directly into her bed, but she was not there. She also had arisen and had gone for a walk and the hand that raised the shade was the hand of Aunt Elizabeth Swift.

The minister almost wept with joy at this deliverance from the carnal desire to "peep" and went back to his own house praising God. In an ill moment he forgot, however, to stop the hole in the window. The piece of glass broken out at the corner of the window just nipped off the bare heel of the boy standing motionless and looking with rapt eyes into the face of the Christ.

Curtis Hartman forgot his sermon on that Sunday morning. He talked to his congregation and in his talk said that it was a mistake for people to think

of their minister as a man set aside and intended by nature to lead a blameless life. "Out of my own experience I know that we, who are the ministers of
God's word, are beset by the same temptations that assail you," he declared. "I have been tempted and have surrendered to temptation. It is only
the hand of God, placed beneath my head, that has raised me up. As he has
raised me so also will he raise you. Do not despair. In your hour of sin raise
your eyes to the skies and you will be again and again saved."

Resolutely the minister put the thoughts of the woman in the bed out of his
mind and began to be something like a lover in the presence of his wife. One
evening when they drove out together he turned the horse out of Buckeye
Street and in the darkness on Gospel Hill, above Waterworks Pond, put his
arm about Sarah Hartman's waist. When he had eaten breakfast in the
morning and was ready to retire to his study at the back of his house he went
around the table and kissed his wife on the cheek. When thoughts of Kate
Swift came into his head, he smiled and raised his eyes to the skies. "Inter-
cede for me, Master," he muttered, "keep me in the narrow path intent on
Thy work."

And now began the real struggle in the soul of the brownbearded minister.
By chance he discovered that Kate Swift was in the habit of lying in her bed
in the evenings and reading a book. A lamp stood on a table by the side of
the bed and the light streamed down upon her white shoulders and bare
throat. On the evening when he made the discovery the minister sat at the
desk in the study from nine until after eleven and when her light was put out
stumbled out of the church to spend two more hours walking and praying in
the streets. He did not want to kiss the shoulders and the throat of Kate Swift
and had not allowed his mind to dwell on such thoughts. He did not know
what he wanted. "I am God's child and he must save me from myself," he
cried, in the darkness under the trees as he wandered in the streets. By a tree
he stood and looked at the sky that was covered with hurrying clouds. He
began to talk to God intimately and closely. "Please, Father, do not forget
me. Give me power to go to-morrow and repair the hole in the window. Lift
my eyes again to the skies, Stay with me, Thy servant, in his hour of need."

Up and down through the silent streets walked the minister and for days
and weeks his soul was troubled. He could not understand the temptation
that had come to him nor could he fathom the reason for its coming. In a way
he began to blame God, saying to himself that he had tried to keep his feet in
the true path and had not run about seeking sin. "Through my days as a
young man and all through my life here I have gone quietly about my work,"
he declared. "Why now should I be tempted? What have I done that this
burden should be laid on me?"

Three times during the early fall and winter of that year Curtis Hartman
crept out of his house to the room in the bell tower to sit in the darkness
looking at the figure of Kate Swift lying in her bed and later went to walk and

pray in the streets. He could not understand himself. For weeks he would go along scarcely thinking of the school teacher and telling himself that he had conquered the carnal desire to look at her body. And then something would happen. As he sat in the study of his own house, hard at work on a sermon, he would become nervous and begin to walk up and down the room. "I will go out into the streets," he told himself and even as he let himself in at the church door he persistently denied to himself the cause of his being there. "I will not repair the hole in the window and I will train myself to come here at night and sit in the presence of this woman without raising my eyes. I will not be defeated in this thing. The Lord has devised this temptation as a test of my soul and I will grope my way out of darkness into the light of righteousness."

One night in January when it was bitter cold and snow lay deep on the streets of Winesburg Curtis Hartman paid his last visit to the room in the bell tower of the church. It was past nine o'clock when he left his own house and he set out so hurriedly that he forgot to put on his overshoes. In Main Street no one was abroad but Hop Higgins the night watchman and in the whole town no one was awake but the watchman and young George Willard, who sat in the office of the *Winesburg Eagle* trying to write a story. Along the street to the church went the minister, plowing through the drifts and thinking that this time he would utterly give way to sin. "I want to look at the woman and to think of kissing her shoulders and I am going to let myself think what I choose," he declared bitterly and tears came into his eyes. He began to think that he would get out of the ministry and try some other way of life. "I shall go to some city and get into business," he declared. "If my nature is such that I cannot resist sin, I shall give myself over to sin. At least I shall not be a hypocrite, preaching the word of God with my mind thinking of the shoulders and neck of a woman who does not belong to me."

It was cold in the room of the bell tower of the church on that January night and almost as soon as he came into the room Curtis Hartman knew that if he stayed he would be ill. His feet were wet from tramping in the snow and there was no fire. In the room in the house next door Kate Swift had not yet appeared. With grim determination the man sat down to wait. Sitting in the chair and gripping the edge of the desk on which lay the Bible he stared into the darkness thinking the blackest thoughts of his life. He thought of his wife and for the moment almost hated her. "She has always been ashamed of passion and has cheated me," he thought. "Man has a right to expect living passion and beauty in a woman. He has no right to forget that he is an animal and in me there is something that is Greek. I will throw off the woman of my bosom and seek other women. I will besiege this school teacher. I will fly in the face of all men and if I am a creature of carnal lusts I will live then for my lusts."

The distracted man trembled from head to foot, partly from cold, partly from the struggle in which he was engaged. Hours passed and a fever assailed his body. His throat began to hurt and his teeth chattered. His feet on the study floor felt like two cakes of ice. Still he would not give up. "I will see this woman and will think the thoughts I have never dared to think," he told himself, gripping the edge of the desk and waiting.

Curtis Hartman came near dying from the effects of that night of waiting in the church, and also he found in the thing that happened what he took to be the way of life for him. On other evenings when he had waited he had not been able to see, through the little hole in the glass, any part of the school teacher's room except that occupied by her bed. In the darkness he had waited until the woman suddenly appeared sitting in the bed in her white nightrobe. When the light was turned up she propped herself up among the pillows and read a book. Sometimes she smoked one of the cigarettes. Only her bare shoulders and throat were visible.

On the January night, after he had come near dying with cold and after his mind had two or three times actually slipped away into an odd land of fantasy so that he had by an exercise of will power to force himself back into consciousness, Kate Swift appeared. In the room next door a lamp was lighted and the waiting man stared into an empty bed. Then upon the bed before his eyes a naked woman threw herself. Lying face downward she wept and beat with her fists upon the pillow. With a final outburst of weeping she half arose, and in the presence of the man who had waited to look and to think thoughts the woman of sin began to pray. In the lamplight her figure, slim and strong, looked like the figure of the boy in the presence of the Christ on the leaded window.

Curtis Hartman never remembered how he got out of the church. With a cry he arose, dragging the heavy desk along the floor. The Bible fell, making a great clatter in the silence. When the light in the house next door went out he stumbled down the stairway and into the street. Along the street he went and ran in at the door of the *Winesburg Eagle*. To George Willard, who was tramping up and down in the office undergoing a struggle of his own, he began to talk half incoherently. "The ways of God are beyond human understanding," he cried. "After ten years in this town, God has manifested himself to me in the body of a woman." His voice dropped and he began to whisper. "I did not understand," he said. "What I took to be a trial of my soul was only a preparation for a new and more beautiful fervor of the spirit. God has appeared to me in the person of Kate Swift, the school teacher, kneeling naked on a bed. Do you know Kate Swift? Although she may not be aware of it, she is an instrument of God, bearing the message of truth."

Reverend Curtis Hartman turned and ran out of the office. At the door he stopped, and after looking up and down the deserted street, turned again to George Willard. "I am delivered. Have no fear." He held up a bleeding fist for the young man to see. "I smashed the glass of the window," he cried. "Now it will have to be wholly replaced. The strength of God was in me and I broke it with my fist."

Sexual Sadism

In Sexual Sadism, a person has a need to inflict physical suffering or psychological humiliation on a partner, who may be either consenting or nonconsenting. The sadist's acts are sexually stimulating, usually to orgasm.

The brief excerpt from the Marquis de Sade's *Justine* describes sadistic behavior. The passage is valuable in that it illustrates the philosophy of Donatien Alphonse Francois de Sade (1740 – 1814), whose advocation of sexual violence led to his name being associated with a Psychosexual Disorder.

The speaker, Therese, is recounting her life to Madame de Lorsange. The excerpt illustrates the abuse by sadists that Thérèse suffered throughout her life.

JUSTINE

The Marquis de Sade

While we were arguing thus, Dubois' four companions were drinking with the poacher, and as wine disposes the malefactor's heart to new crimes and causes him to forget his old, our bandits no sooner learned of my resolution than, unable to make me their accomplice, they decided to make me their victim; their principles, their manners, the dark retreat we were in, the security they thought they enjoyed, their drunkenness, my age, my innocence — everything encouraged them. They get up from table, they confer in whispers, they consult Dubois, doings whose lugubrious mystery makes me shiver with horror, and at last there comes an order to me then and there to satisfy the desires of each of the four; if I go to it cheerfully, each will give me a crown to help me along my way; if they must employ violence, the thing will be done all the same; but the better to guard their secret, once finished with me they will stab me, and will bury me at the foot of yonder tree.

I need not paint the effect this cruel proposition had upon me, Madame, you will have no difficulty understanding that I sank to my knees before Dubois, I besought her a second time to be my protectress: the low creature did but laugh at my tears:

"Oh by God!" quoth she, "here's an unhappy little one. What! you shudder before the obligation to serve four fine big boys one after another? Listen to me," she added, after some reflection, "my sway over these dear lads is sufficiently great for me to obtain a reprieve for you upon condition you render yourself worthy of it."

"Alas! Madame, what must I do?" I cried through my tears; "command me; I am ready."

"Join us, throw in your lot with us, and commit the same deeds, without show of the least repugnance; either that, or I cannot save you from the rest." I did not think myself in a position to hesitate; by accepting this cruel condition I exposed myself to further dangers, to be sure, but they were the less immediate; perhaps I might be able to avoid them, whereas nothing could save me from those with which I was actually menaced.

"I will go everywhere with you, Madame," was my prompt answer to Dubois, "everywhere, I promise you; shield me from the fury of these men and I shall never leave your side while I live."

"Children," Dubois said to the four bandits, "this girl is one of the company, I am taking her into it; I ask you to do her no ill, don't put her stomach off the *métier* during her first days in it; you see how useful her age and face can be to us; let's employ them to our advantage rather than sacrifice them to our pleasures."

But such is the degree of energy in man's passions nothing can subdue them. The persons I was dealing with were in no state to heed reason: all four surrounded me, devoured me with their fiery glances, menaced me in a still more terrible manner; they were about to lay hands on me, I was about to become their victim.

"She has got to go through with it," one of them declared, "it's too late for discussion: was she not told she must give proof of virtues in order to be admitted into a band of thieves? and once a little used, won't she be quite as serviceable as she is while a virgin?"

I am softening their expressions, you understand, Madame, I am sweetening the scene itself; alas! their obscenities were such that your modesty might suffer at least as much from beholding them unadorned as did my shyness.

A defenseless and trembling victim, I shuddered; I had barely strength to breathe; kneeling before the quartet, I raised my feeble arms as much to supplicate the men as to melt Dubois' heart. . . .

"An instant," said one who went by the name of Coeur-de-fer and appeared to be the band's chief, a man of thirty-six years, of a bull's strength and bearing the face of a satyr; "one moment, friends: it may be possible to satisfy everyone concerned; since this little girl's virtue is so precious to her and since, as Dubois states it very well, this quality otherwise put into action could become worth something to us, let's leave it to her; but we have got to be appeased; our mood is warm, Dubois, and in the state we are in, d'ye know, we might perhaps cut your own throat if you were to stand between us and our pleasures; let's have Thérèse instantly strip as naked as the day she came into the world, and next let's have her adopt one after the other all the positions we are pleased to call for, and meanwhile Dubois will sate our hungers, we'll burn our incense upon the altars' entrance to which this creature refuses us."

"Strip naked!" I exclaimed, "Oh Heaven, what is it thou doth require of me? When I shall have delivered myself thus to your eyes, who will be able to answer for me? . . ."

But Coeur-de-fer, who seemed in no humor either to grant me more or to suspend his desires, burst out with an oath and struck me in a manner so brutal that I saw full well compliance was my last resort. He put himself in Dubois' hands, she having been put by his in a disorder more or less the equivalent of mine and, as soon as I was as he desired me to be, having made me crouch down upon all fours so that I resembled a beast, Dubois took in hand a very monstrous object and led it to the peristyles of first one and then the other of Nature's altars, and under her guidance the blows it delivered to me here and there were like those of a battering ram thundering at the gates of a besieged town in olden days. The shock of the initial assault drove me back; enraged, Coeur-de-fer threatened me with harsher treatments were I to retreat from these; Dubois is instructed to redouble her efforts, one of the libertines grasps my shoulders and prevents me from staggering before the concussions: they become so fierce I am in blood and am able to avoid not a one.

"Indeed," stammers Coeur-de-fer, "in her place I'd prefer to open the doors rather than see them ruined this way, but she won't have it, and we're not far from the capitulation.... Vigorously... vigorously, Dubois...."

And the explosive eruption of this debauchee's flames, almost as violent as a stroke of lightning, flickers and dies upon ramparts ravaged without being breached.

The second had me kneel between his legs and while Dubois administered to him as she had to the other, two enterprises absorbed his entire attention: sometimes he slapped, powerfully but in a very nervous manner, either my cheeks or my breasts; sometimes his impure mouth fell to sucking mine. In an instant my face turned purple, my chest red.... I was in pain, I begged him to spare me, tears leapt from my eyes; they roused him, he accelerated his activities; he bit my tongue, and the two strawberries on my breasts were so bruised that I slipped backward, but was kept from falling. They thrust me toward him, I was everywhere more furiously harassed, and his ecstasy supervened....

The third bade me mount upon and straddle two somewhat separated chairs and, seating myself betwixt them, excited by Dubois, lying in his arms, he had me bend until his mouth was directly below the temple of Nature; never will you imagine, Madame, what this obscene mortal took it into his head to do: willy-nilly, I was obliged to satisfy his every need .... Just Heaven! what man, no matter how depraved, can taste an instant of pleasure in such things.... I did what he wished, inundated him, and my complete submission procured this foul man an intoxication of which he was incapable without this infamy.

The fourth attached strings to all parts of me to which it was possible to tie them, he held the ends in his hand and sat down seven or eight feet from my body; Dubois' touches and kisses excited him prodigiously; I was standing erect: 'twas by sharp tugs now on this string, now on some other that the

savage irritated his pleasures: I swayed, I lost balance again and again, he
flew into an ecstasy each time I tottered; finally, he pulled all the cords at
once, I fell to the floor in front of him: such was his design: and my forehead,
my breast, my cheeks received the proofs of a delirium he owed to none but
this mania.

That is what I suffered, Madame, but at least my honor was respected
even though my modesty assuredly was not. Their calm restored, the bandits spoke of regaining the road, and that same night we reached Tremblai
with the intention of approaching the woods of Chantilly, where it was
thought a few good prizes might be awaiting us.

Other Paraphilias

Other Paraphilias is a residual category for an individual whose
Paraphilia cannot be classified elsewhere.

In William Faulkner's "A Rose for Emily," Miss Emily Grierson is introduced. Does she have more than one Paraphilia? Does Miss Emily have
other mental disorders?

A ROSE FOR EMILY
William Faulkner

When Miss Emily Grierson died, our whole town went to her funeral: the
men through a sort of respectful affection for a fallen monument, the women
mostly out of curiosity to see the inside of her house, which no one save an
old manservant — a combined gardener and cook — had seen in at least ten
years.

It was a big, squarish frame house that had once been white, decorated
with cupolas and spires and scrolled balconies in the heavily lightsome style
of the seventies, set on what had once been our most select street. But
garages and cotton gins had encroached and obliterated even the august
names of that neighborhood; only Miss Emily's house was left, lifting its
stubborn and coquettish decay above the cotton wagons and the gasoline
pumps — an eyesore among eyesores. And now Miss Emily had gone to join
the representatives of those august names where they lay in the cedar-
bemused cemetery among the ranked and anonymous graves of Union and
Confederate soldiers who fell at the battle of Jefferson.

Alive, Miss Emily had been a tradition, a duty, and a care; a sort of
hereditary obligation upon the town, dating from that day in 1894 when
Colonel Sartoris, the mayor — he who fathered the edict that no Negro

woman should appear on the streets without an apron — remitted her taxes, the dispensation dating from the death of her father on into perpetuity. Not that Miss Emily would have accepted charity. Colonel Sartoris invented an involved tale to the effect that Miss Emily's father had loaned money to the town, which the town, as a matter of business, preferred this way of repaying. Only a man of Colonel Sartoris' generation and thought could have invented it, and only a woman could have believed it.

When the next generation, with its more modern ideas, became mayors and aldermen, this arrangement created some little dissatisfaction. On the first of the year they mailed her a tax notice. February came, and there was no reply. They wrote her a formal letter, asking her to call at the sheriff's office at her convenience. A week later the mayor wrote her himself, offering to call or to send his car for her, and received in reply a note on paper of an archaic shape, in a thin, flowing calligraphy in faded ink, to the effect that she no longer went out at all. The tax notice was also enclosed, without comment.

They called a special meeting of the Board of Aldermen. A deputation waited upon her, knocked at the door through which no visitor had passed since she ceased giving china-painting lessons eight or ten years earlier. They were admitted by the old Negro in a dim hall from which a stairway mounted into still more shadow. It smelled of dust and disuse — a close, dank smell. The Negro led them into the parlor. It was furnished in heavy, leather-covered furniture. When the Negro opened the blinds of one window, they could see that the leather was cracked; and when they sat down, a faint dust rose sluggishly about their thighs, spinning with slow motes in the single sun-ray. On a tarnished gilt easel before the fireplace stood a crayon portrait of Miss Emily's father.

They rose when she entered — a small, fat woman in black, with a thin gold chain descending to her waist and vanishing into her belt, leaning on an ebony cane with a tarnished gold head. Her skeleton was small and spare; perhaps that was why what would have been merely plumpness in another was obesity in her. She looked bloated, like a body long submerged in motionless water, and of that pallid hue. Her eyes, lost in the fatty ridges of her face, looked like two small pieces of coal pressed into a lump of dough as they moved from one face to another while the visitors stated their errand.

She did not ask them to sit. She just stood in the door and listened quietly until the spokesman came to a stumbling halt. Then they could hear the invisible watch ticking at the end of the gold chain.

Her voice was dry and cold. "I have no taxes in Jefferson. Colonel Sartoris explained it to me. Perhaps one of you can gain access to the city records and satisfy yourselves."

"But we have. We are the city authorities, Miss Emily. Didn't you get a notice from the sheriff, signed by him?"

"I received a paper, yes," Miss Emily said. "Perhaps he considers himself the sheriff. . . . I have no taxes in Jefferson."

"But there is nothing on the books to show that, you see. We must go by the —"

"See Colonel Sartoris. I have no taxes in Jefferson."

"But, Miss Emily —"

"See Colonel Sartoris." (Colonel Sartoris had been dead almost ten years.) "I have no taxes in Jefferson. Tobe!" The Negro appeared. "Show these gentlemen out."

II

So she vanquished them, horse and foot, just as she had vanquished their fathers thirty years before about the smell. That was two years after her father's death and a short time after her sweetheart — the one we believed would marry her — had deserted her. After her father's death she went out very little; after her sweetheart went away, people hardly saw her at all. A few of the ladies had the temerity to call, but were not received, and the only sign of life about the place was the Negro man — a young man then — going in and out with a market basket.

"Just as if a man — any man — could keep a kitchen properly," the ladies said; so they were not surprised when the smell developed. It was another link between the gross, teeming world and the high and mighty Griersons.

A neighbor, a woman, complained to the mayor, Judge Stevens, eighty years old.

"But what will you have me do about it, madam?" he said.

"Why, send her word to stop it," the woman said. "Isn't there a law?"

"I'm sure that won't be necessary," Judge Stevens said. "It's probably just a snake or a rat that nigger of hers killed in the yard. I'll speak to him about it."

The next day he received two more complaints, one from a man who came in diffident deprecation. "We really must do something about it, Judge. I'd be the last one in the world to bother Miss Emily, but we've got to do something." That night the Board of Aldermen met — three graybeards and one younger man, a member of the rising generation.

"It's simple enough," he said. "Send her word to have her place cleaned up. Give her a certain time to do it in, and if she don't. . ."

"Dammit, sir," Judge Stevens said, "will you accuse a lady to her face of smelling bad?"

So the next night, after midnight, four men crossed Miss Emily's lawn and slunk about the house like burglars, sniffing along the base of the brickwork and at the cellar openings while one of them performed a regular sowing motion with his hand out of a sack slung from his shoulder. They broke open the cellar door and sprinkled lime there, and in all the outbuildings. As they recrossed the lawn, a window that had been dark was lighted and Miss Emily sat in it, the light behind her, and her upright torso motionless as that of an idol. They crept quietly across the lawn and into the shadow of the locusts that lined the street. After a week or two the smell went away.

That was when people had begun to feel really sorry for her. People in our town, remembering how old lady Wyatt, her great-aunt, had gone completely crazy at last, believed that the Griersons held themselves a little too high for what they really were. None of the young men were quite good enough for Miss Emily and such.. We had long thought of them as a tableau: Miss Emily a slender figure in white in the background, her father a spraddled silhouette in the foreground, his back to her and clutching a horsewhip, the two of them framed by the back-flung front door. So when she got to be thirty and was still single, we were not pleased exactly, but vindicated; even with insanity in the family she wouldn't have turned down all of her chances if they had really materialized.

When her father died, it got about that the house was all that was left to her; and in a way, people were glad. At last they could pity Miss Emily. Being left alone, and a pauper, she had become humanized. Now she too would know the old thrill and the old despair of a penny more or less.

The day after his death all the ladies prepared to call at the house and offer condolence and aid, as is our custom. Miss Emily met them at the door, dressed as usual and with no trace of grief on her face. She told them that her father was not dead. She did that for three days, with the ministers calling on her, and the doctors, trying to persuade her to let them dispose of the body. Just as they were about to resort to law and force, she broke down, and they buried her father quickly.

We did not say she was crazy then. We believed she had to do that. We remembered all the young men her father had driven away, and we knew that with nothing left, she would have to cling to that which had robbed her, as people will.

III

She was sick for a long time. When we saw her again, her hair was cut short, making her look like a girl, with a vague resemblance to those angels in colored church windows — sort of tragic and serene.

The town had just let the contracts for paving the sidewalks, and in the summer after her father's death they began the work. The construction company came with niggers and mules and machinery, and a foreman named Homer Barron, a Yankee — a big, dark, ready man, with a big voice and eyes lighter than his face. The little boys would follow in groups to hear him cuss the niggers, and the niggers singing in time to the rise and fall of picks. Pretty soon he knew everybody in town. Whenever you heard a lot of laughing anywhere about the square, Homer Barron would be in the center of the group. Presently we began to see him and Miss Emily on Sunday afternoons driving in the yellow-wheeled buggy and the matched team of bays from the livery stable.

At first we were glad that Miss Emily would have an interest, because the ladies all said, "Of course a Grierson would not think seriously of a Northerner, a day laborer." But there were still others, older people, who said that even grief could not cause a real lady to forget *noblesse oblige* — without calling it *noblesse oblige*. They just said, "Poor Emily. Her kinsfolk should come to her." She had some kin in Alabama; but years ago her father had fallen out with them over the estate of old lady Wyatt, the crazy woman, and there was no communication between between the two families. They had not even been represented at the funeral.

And as soon as the old people said, "Poor Emily," the whispering began. "Do you suppose it's really so?" they said to one another. "Of course it is. What else could. . ." This behind their hands; rustling of craned silk and satin behind jalousies closed upon the sun of Sunday afternoon as the thin, swift clop-clop-clop of the matched team passed: "Poor Emily."

She carried her head high enough — even when we believed that she was fallen. It was as if she demanded more than ever the recognition of her dignity as the last Grierson; as if it had wanted that touch of earthiness to reaffirm her imperviousness. Like when she bought the rat poison, the arsenic. That was over a year after they had begun to say "Poor Emily," and while the two female cousins were visiting her.

"I want some poison," she said to the druggist. She was over thirty then, still a slight woman, though thinner than usual, with cold, haughty black eyes in a face the flesh of which was strained across the temples and about the eyesockets as you imagine a lighthouse-keeper's face ought to look. "I want some poison," she said.

"Yes, Miss Emily. What kind? For rats and such? I'd recom —"

"I want the best you have. I don't care what kind."

The druggist named several. "They'll kill anything up to an elephant. But what you want is —"

"Arsenic," Miss Emily said. "Is that a good one?"

"Is . . . arsenic? Yes, ma'am. But what you want —"

"I want arsenic."

The druggist looked down at her. She looked back at him, erect, her face like a strained flag. "Why, of course," the druggist said. "If that's what you want. But the law requires you to tell what you are going to use it for."

Miss Emily just stared at him, her head tilted back in order to look him eye for eye, until he looked away and went and got the arsenic and wrapped it up. The Negro delivery boy brought her the package; the druggist didn't come back. When she opened the package at home there was written on the box, under the skull and bones: "For rats."

IV

So the next day we all said, "She will kill herself"; and we said it would be the best thing. When she had first begun to be seen with Homer Barron, we had said, "She will marry him." Then we said, "She will persuade him yet," because Homer himself had remarked — he liked men, and it was known that he drank with the younger men in the Elks' Club — that he was not a marrying man. Later we said, "Poor Emily," behind the jalousies as they passed on Sunday afternoon in the glittering buggy, Miss Emily with her head high and Homer Barron with his hat cocked and a cigar in his teeth, reins and whip in a yellow glove.

Then some of the ladies began to say that it was a disgrace in the town and a bad example to the young people. The men did not want to interfere, but at last the ladies forced the Baptist minister — Miss Emily's people were Episcopal — to call upon her. He would never divulge what happened during that interview, but he refused to go back again. The next Sunday they again drove about the streets, and the following day the minister's wife wrote to Miss Emily's relations in Alabama.

So she had blood-kin under her roof again and we sat back to watch developments. At first nothing happened. Then we were sure that they were to be married. We learned that Miss Emily had been to the jeweler's and ordered a man's toilet set in silver, with the letters H.B. on each piece. Two days later we learned that she had bought a complete outfit of men's clothing, including a nightshirt, and we said, "They are married." We were really glad. We were glad because the two female cousins were even more Grierson than Miss Emily had ever been.

So we were not surprised when Homer Barron — the streets had been finished some time since — was gone. We were a little disappointed that there was not a public blowing-off, but we believed that he had gone on to prepare for Miss Emily's coming, or to give her a chance to get rid of the cousins. (By that time it was a cabal, and we were all Miss Emily's allies to help circumvent the cousins.) Sure enough, after another week they departed. And, as we had expected all along, within three days Homer Barron was back in town. A neighbor saw the Negro man admit him at the kitchen door at dusk one evening.

And that was the last we saw of Homer Barron. And of Miss Emily for some time. The Negro man went in and out with the market basket, but the front door remained closed. Now and then we would see her at a window for a moment , as the men did that night when they sprinkled the lime, but for almost six months she did not appear on the streets. Then we knew that this was to be expected too; as if that quality of her father which had thwarted her woman's life so many times had been too virulent and too furious to die.

When we next saw Miss Emily, she had grown fat and her hair was turning gray. During the next few years it grew grayer and grayer until it attained an even pepper-and-salt iron-gray, when it ceased turning. Up to the day of her death at seventy-four it was still that vigorous iron-gray, like the hair of an active man.

From that time on her front door remained closed, save for a period of six or seven years, when she was about forty, during which she gave lessons in china-painting. She fitted up a studio in one of the downstairs rooms, where the daughters and granddaughters of Colonel Sartoris' contemporaries were sent to her with the same regularity and in the same spirit that they were sent on Sundays with a twenty-five cent piece for the collection plate. Meanwhile her taxes had been remitted.

Then the newer generation became the backbone and the spirit of the town, and the painting pupils grew up and fell away and did not send their children to her with boxes of color and tedious brushes and pictures cut from the ladies' magazines. The front door closed upon the last one and remained closed for good. When the town got free postal delivery Miss Emily alone refused to let them fasten the metal numbers above her door and attach a mailbox to it. She would not listen to them.

Daily, monthly, yearly we watched the Negro grow grayer and more stooped, going in and out with the market basket. Each December we sent her a tax notice, which would be returned by the post office a week later, unclaimed. Now and then we would see her in one of the downstairs windows — she had evidently shut up the top floor of the house — like the carven torso of an idol in a niche, looking or not looking at us, we could never tell which. Thus she passed from generation to generation — dear, inescapable, impervious, tranquil, and perverse.

And so she died. Fell ill in the house filled with dust and shadows, with only a doddering Negro man to wait her. We did not even know she was sick; we had long since given up trying to get any information from the Negro. He talked to no one, probably not even to her, for his voice had grown harsh and rusty, as if from disuse.

She died in one of the downstairs rooms, in a heavy walnut bed with a curtain, her gray head propped on a pillow yellow and moldy with age and lack of sunlight.

V

The Negro met the first of the ladies at the front door and let them in, with their hushed, sibilant voices and their quick, curious glances, and then he disappeared. He walked right through the house and out the back and was not seen again.

The two female cousins came at once. They held the funeral on the second day, with the town coming to look at Miss Emily beneath a mass of bought flowers, with crayon face of her father musing profoundly above the bier and the ladies sibilant and macabre; and the very old men—some in their brushed Confederate uniforms—on the porch and the lawn, talking of Miss Emily as if she had been a contemporary of theirs, believing that they had danced with her and courted her perhaps, confusing time with its mathematical progression, as the old do. To whom all the past is not a diminishing road, but, instead, a huge meadow which no winter ever quite touches, divided from them now by the narrow bottleneck of the most recent decade of years.

Already we knew that there was one room in that region above stairs which no one had seen in forty years, and which would have to be forced. They waited until Miss Emily was decently in the ground before they opened it.

The violence of breaking down the door seemed to fill this room with pervading dust. A thin, acrid pall as of the tomb seemed to lie everywhere upon this room decked and furnished as for a bridal: upon the valance curtain of faded rose color, upon the roseshaded lights, upon the dressing table, upon the delicate array of crystal and the man's toilet things backed with tarnished silver, silver so tarnished that the monogram was obscured. Among them lay a collar and tie, as if they had just been removed, which, lifted, left upon the surface a pale crescent in the dust. Upon a chair hung the suit, carefully folded; beneath it the two mute shoes and the discarded socks.

The man himself lay in the bed.

For a long while we just stood there, looking down at the profound and fleshless grin. The body had apparently once lain in the attitude of an embrace, but now the long sleep that outlasts love, that conquers even the grimace of love, had cuckolded him. What was left of him, rotted beneath what was left of the nightshirt, had become inextricable from the bed in which he lay; and upon him and upon the pillow beside him lay that even coating of the patient and biding dust.

Then we noticed that in the second pillow was the indentation of a head. One of us lifted something from it, and leaning forward, that faint and invisible dust dry and acrid in the nostrils, we saw a long strand of iron-gray hair.

___ Personality Disorders

According to DSM-III, there are eleven specific Personality Disorders, and they cluster into three groups based on observable maladaptive behavior or personal distress. Paranoid, Schizoid, and Schizotypal Personality Disorders manifest themselves in odd or eccentric behavior. Histrionic, Narcissistic, Antisocial, and Borderline Personality Disorders express themselves in overly dramatic, emotional activities. Avoidant, Dependent, Compulsive, and Passive-Aggressive Personality Disorders reveal themselves as continuous anxiousness or fear. Eight of these disorders, are introduced and illustrated in the material that follows.

Each disorder is generally recognizable by the time the person reaches adolescence, and it continues throughout his or her lifetime. While any disorder results in impaired relationships and distorted perceptions, hospitalization is usually unnecessary except when the person has an additional disorder, such as Major Depression or a brief psychotic episode.

Paranoid Personality Disorder

Individuals with Paranoid Personality Disorder exhibit three dominant symptoms. Their primary symptom is a pervasive wariness toward other people that is expressed in a variety of observable activities. Here are some examples: they constantly suspect others of double-dealing; they watch incessantly for threatening or harmful signs; they are always on guard; they engage in a concentrated search for indisputable evidence of bias against them, a search that distorts the larger context of relationships; they have a preoccupation with the concealed motives that others have and with unusual meanings to usual conversations.

The paranoid personalities' second symptom is hypersensitivity that may be revealed in mannerisms. They often feel slighted and are easily offended; they may be easily excited; they sometimes counterattack quickly to perceived threats; they may be unable to relax.

Their third symptom deals with the expression of emotions. Paranoid personalities usually have restricted emotions, i.e., the range and intensity of their emotions often are severly limited. They may be perceived by others as unemotional; they may pride themselves on being unemotional, rational, and objective. They probably lack a spontaneous sense of humor. They may have few tender and sentimental feelings toward others.

Bitsy Barlow, in Carson McCuller's "The Jockey," may fulfill the diagnostic criteria for Paranoid Personality Disorder. Bitsy's long-term functioning is not presented. If, however, one assumes that the events related are representative of how Bitsy has lived, then there is evidence that suggests this disorder. Note several specific incidents of Bitsy's wariness toward others. What are some examples of his hypersensitivity? Are these indications that his emotions are limited? If Bitsy has Paranoid Personality Disorder, is it possible that his physical size is a contributing factor? Why or why not?

THE JOCKEY

Carson McCullers

The jockey came to the doorway of the dining room, then after a moment stepped to one side and stood motionless, with his back to the wall. The room was crowded, as this was the third day of the season and all the hotels in the town were full. In the dining room bouquets of August roses scattered their petals on the white table linen and from the adjoining bar came a warm, drunken wash of voices. The jockey waited with his back to the wall and scrutinized the room with pinched, crêpy eyes. He examined the room until at last his eyes reached a table in a corner diagonally across from him, at which three men were sitting. As he watched, the jockey raised his chin and tilted his head back to one side, his dwarfed body grew rigid, and his hands stiffened so that the fingers curled inward like gray claws. Tense against the wall of the dining room, he watched and waited in this way.

He was wearing a suit of green Chinese silk that evening, tailored precisely and the size of a costume outfit for a child. The shirt was yellow, the tie striped with pastel colors. He had no hat with him and wore his hair brushed down in a stiff, wet bang on his forehead. His face was drawn, ageless, and gray.

There were shadowed hollows at his temples and his mouth was set in a wiry smile. After a time he was aware that he had been seen by one of the three men he had been watching. But the jockey did not nod; he only raised his chin still higher and hooked the thumb of his tense hand in the pocket of his coat.

The three men at the corner table were a trainer, a bookie, and a rich man. The trainer was Sylvester — a large, loosely built fellow with a flushed nose and slow blue eyes. The bookie was Simmons. The rich man was the owner of a horse named Seltzer, which the jockey had ridden that afternoon. The three of them drank whiskey with soda, and a white-coated waiter had just brought on the main course of the dinner.

It was Sylvester who first saw the jockey. He looked away quickly, put down his whiskey glass, and nervously mashed the tip of his red nose with thumb. "It's Bitsy Barlow," he said. "Standing over there across the room. Just watching us."

"Oh, the jockey," said the rich man. He was facing the wall and he half turned his head to look behind him. "Ask him over."

"God no," Sylvester said.

"He's crazy," Simmons said. The bookie's voice was flat and without inflection. He had the face of a born gambler, carefully adjusted, the expression a permanent deadlock between fear and greed.

"Well, I wouldn't call him that exactly," said Sylvester. "I've known him a long time. He was O.K. until about six months ago. But if he goes on like this, I can't see him lasting another year. I just can't."

"It was what happened in Miami," said Simmons.

"What?" asked the rich man.

Sylvester glanced across the room at the jockey and wet the corner of his mouth with his red, fleshy tongue. "A accident. A kid got hurt on the track. Broke a leg and a hip. He was a particular pal of Bitsy's. A Irish kid. Not a bad rider, either."

"That's a pity," said the rich man.

"Yeah. They were particular friends," Sylvester said. "You would always find him up in Bitsy's hotel room. They would be playing rummy or else lying on the floor reading the sports page together."

"Well, those things happen," said the rich man.

Simmons cut into his beefsteak. He held his fork prongs downward on the plate and carefully piled on mushrooms with the blade of his knife. "He's crazy," he repeated. "He gives me the creeps."

All the tables in the dining room were occupied. There was a party at the banquet table in the center, and green-white August moths had found their way in from the night and fluttered about the clear candle flames. Two girls wearing flannel slacks and blazers walked arm in arm across the room into the bar. From the main street outside came the echoes of holiday hysteria.

"They claim that in August Saratoga is the wealthiest town per capita in the world." Sylvester turned to the rich man. "What do you think?"

"I wouldn't know," said the rich man. "It may very well be so."

Daintily, Simmons wiped his greasy mouth with the tip of his forefinger. "How about Hollywood? And Wall Street ——"

"Wait," said Sylvester. "He's decided to come over here."

The jockey had left the wall and was approaching the table in the corner. He walked with a prim strut, swinging out his legs in a half-circle with each step, his heels biting smartly into the red velvet carpet on the floor. On the way over he brushed against the elbow of a fat woman in white satin at the banquet table; he stepped back and bowed with dandified courtesy, his eyes quite closed. When he had crossed the room he drew up a chair and sat at a corner of the table, between Sylvester and the rich man, without a nod of greeting or a change in his set, gray face.

"Had dinner?" Sylvester asked.

"Some people might call it that." The jockey's voice was high, bitter, clear.

Sylvester put his knife and fork down carefully on his plate. The rich man shifted his position, turning sidewise in his chair and crossing his legs. He was dressed in twill riding pants, unpolished boots, and a shabby brown jacket— this was his outfit day and night in the racing season, although he was never seen on a horse. Simmons went on with his dinner.

"Like a spot of seltzer water?" asked Sylvester. "Or something like that?"

The jockey didn't answer. He drew a gold cigarette case from his pocket and snapped it open. Inside were a few cigarettes and a tiny gold penknife. He used the knife to cut a cigarette in half. When he had lighted his smoke he held up his hand to a waiter passing by the table. "Kentucky bourbon, please."

"Now, listen, Kid," said Sylvester.

"Don't Kid me."

"Be reasonable. You know you got to behave reasonable."

The jockey drew up the left corner of his mouth in a stiff jeer. His eyes lowered to the food spread out on the table, but instantly he looked up again. Before the rich man was a fish casserole, baked in a cream sauce and garnished with parsley. Sylvester had ordered eggs Benedict. There was asparagus, fresh buttered corn, and a side dish of wet black olives. A plate of French-fried potatoes was in the corner of the table before the jockey. He didn't look at the food again, but kept his pinched eyes on the center piece of full-blown lavender roses. "I don't suppose you remember a certain person by the name of McGuire," he said.

"Now, listen," said Sylvester.

The waiter brought the whiskey, and the jockey sat fondling the glass with his small, strong, callused hands. On his wrist was a gold link bracelet that clinked against the table edge. After turning the glass between his palms, the jockey suddenly drank the whiskey neat in two hard swallows. He set down the glass sharply. "No, I don't suppose your memory is that long and extensive," he said.

"Sure enough, Bitsy," said Sylvester. "What makes you act like this? You hear from the kid today?"

"I received a letter," the jockey said. "The certain person we were speaking about was taken out from the cast on Wednesday. One leg is two inches shorter than the other one. That's all."

Sylvester clucked his tongue and shook his head. "I realize how you feel."

"Do you?" The jockey was looking at the dishes on the table. His gaze passed from the fish casserole to the corn, and finally fixed on the plate of fried potatoes. His face tightened and quickly he looked up again. A rose shattered and he picked up one of the petals, bruised it between his thumb and forefinger, and put it in his mouth.

"Well, those things happen," said the rich man.

The trainer and the bookie had finished eating, but there was food left on the serving dishes before their plates. The rich man dipped his buttery fingers in his water glass and wiped them with his napkin.

"Well," said the jockey. "Doesn't somebody want me to pass them something? Or maybe perhaps you desire to re-order. Another hunk of beefsteak, gentlemen, or —— "

"Please," said Sylvester. "Be reasonable. Why don't you go on upstairs?"

"Yes, why don't I?" the jockey said.

His prim voice had risen higher and there was about it the sharp whine of hysteria.

"Why don't I go up to my god-damn room and walk around and write some letters and go to bed like a good boy? Why don't I just —— " He pushed his chair back and got up. "Oh, foo," he said. "Foo to you. I want a drink."

"All I can say is it's your funeral," said Sylvester. "You know what it does to you. You know well enough."

The jockey crossed the dining room and went into the bar. He ordered a Manhattan, and Sylvester watched him stand with his heels pressed tight together, his body hard as a lead soldier's, holding his little finger out from the cocktail glass and sipping the drink slowly.

"He's crazy," said Simmons. "Like I said."

Sylvester turned to the rich man. "If he eats a lamb chop, you can see the shape of it in his stomach a hour afterward. He can't sweat things out of him any more. He's a hundred and twelve and a half. He's gained three pounds since we left Miami."

"A jockey shouldn't drink," said the rich man.

"The food don't satisfy him like it used to and he can't sweat it out. If he eats a lamb chop, you can watch it tooching out in his stomach and it don't go down."

The jockey finished his Manhattan. He swallowed, crushed the cherry in the bottom of the glass with his thumb, then pushed the glass away from him. The two girls in blazers were standing at his left, their faces turned toward each other, and at the other end of the bar two touts had started an argument about which was the highest mountain in the world. Everyone was with somebody else; there was no other person drinking alone that night. The jockey paid with a brand-new fifty-dollar bill and didn't count the change.

He walked back to the dining room and to the table at which the three men were sitting, but he did not sit down. "No, I wouldn't presume to think your memory is that extensive," he said. He was so small that the edge of the table top reached almost to his belt, and when he gripped the corner with his wiry hands he didn't have to stoop. "No, you're too busy gobbling up dinners in dining rooms. You're too —— "

"Honestly," begged Sylvester. "You got to behave reasonable."

"Reasonable! Reasonable!" The jockey's gray face quivered, then set in a mean, frozen grin. He shook the table so that the plates rattled, and for a moment it seemed that he would push it over. But suddenly he stopped. His hand reached out toward the plate nearest to him and deliberately he put a few of the French-fried potatoes in his mouth. He chewed slowly, his upper lip raised, then he turned and spat out the pulpy mouthful on the smooth red carpet which covered the floor. "Libertines," he said, and his voice was thin and broken. He rolled the word in his mouth, as though it had a flavor and a substance that gratified him. "You libertines," he said again, and turned and walked with his rigid swagger out of the dining room.

Sylvester shrugged one of his loose, heavy shoulders. The rich man sopped up some water that had been spilled on the tablecloth, and they didn't speak until the waiter came to clear away.

Schizotypal Personality Disorder

Individuals with Schizotypal Personality Disorder have peculiarities of thinking, perceiving, communicating, and behaving. Because of these peculiarities, they have difficulty in their relationships and employment. Schizotypal personalities often think primarily about themselves. They usually evaluate everything from a self-referential base asking "How does this affect me? What will I get out of it?" By posing such questions, they express their self-centeredness and wariness of others. Furthermore, their thinking sometimes borders on clairvoyance, i. e., the ability to perceive things that are out of the range of others' senses.

In addition, schizotypal personalities misinterpret real or imagined criticism. They often perceive criticism when it is not present; if criticism is real, they may overreact to it. Their faulty perceptions contribute to their anxiety or hypersensitivity.

Because of their preoccupation with themselves in both thinking and perceiving, schizotypal personalities also usually have difficulty in face-to-face conversations. Their comments, which tend to be cold or aloof, are often vague or overly elaborate. Their odd conversational patterns are not incoherent, but they do disrupt honest communication.

Schizotypal behavior sometimes includes social isolation. These individuals may have no close friends; they may restrict their contacts with others to the minimal demands of everyday tasks.

In her story "Paul's Case," Willa Cather depicts a teenager who seems to meet the criteria for a schizotypal personality. Specific incidents of Paul's peculiarities of thinking, perceiving, communicating, and behaving should be noted.

PAUL'S CASE

Willa Cather

It was Paul's afternoon to appear before the faculty of the Pittsburgh High School to account for his various misdemeanors. He had been suspended a week ago, and his father had called at the Principal's office and confessed his perplexity about his son. Paul entered the faculty room suave and smiling. His clothes were a trifle outgrown, and the tan velvet on the collar of his open overcoat was frayed and worn; but for all that there was something of the dandy about him, and he wore an opal pin in his neatly knotted black four-in-hand, and a red carnation in his buttonhole. This latter adornment the faculty somehow felt was not properly significant of the contrite spirit befitting a boy under the ban of suspension.

Paul was tall for his age and very thin, with high, cramped shoulders and a narrow chest. His eyes were remarkable for a certain hysterical brilliancy, and he continually used them in a conscious, theatrical sort of way, peculiarly offensive in a boy. The pupils were abnormally large, as though he were addicted to belladonna, but there was a glassy glitter about them which that drug does not produce.

When questioned by the Principal as to why he was there, Paul stated, politely enough, that he wanted to come back to school. This was a lie, but Paul was quite accustomed to lying; found it, indeed, indispensable for overcoming friction. His teachers were asked to state their respective charges against him, which they did with such a rancour and aggrievedness as evinced that this was not a usual case. Disorder and impertinence were among the offences named, yet each of his instructors felt that it was scarcely possible to put into words the real cause of the trouble, which lay in a sort of hysterically defiant manner of the boy's; in the contempt which they all knew he felt for them, and which he seemingly made not the least effort to conceal. Once, when he had been making a synopsis of a paragraph at the blackboard, his English teacher had stepped to his side and attempted to guide his hand. Paul had started back with a shudder and thrust his hands violently behind him. The astonished woman could scarcely have been more hurt and embarrassed had he struck at her. The insult was so involuntary and definitely personal as to be unforgettable. In one way and another, he had made all his teachers, men and women alike, conscious of the same feeling of physical aversion. In one class he habitually sat with his hand shading his eyes; in another he always looked out of the window during the recitation; in another he made a running commentary on the lecture, with humorous intent.

His teachers felt this afternoon that his whole atitude was symbolized by his shrug and his flippantly red carnation flower, and they fell upon him without mercy, his English teacher leading the pack. He stood through it smiling, his pale lips parted over his white teeth. (His lips were continually twitching, and he had a habit of raising his eyebrows that was contemptuous and irritating to the last degree.) Older boys than Paul had broken down and shed tears under that ordeal, but his set smile did not once desert him; and his only sign of discomfort was the nervous trembling of the fingers that toyed with the buttons of his overcoat, and an occasional jerking of the other hand which held his hat. Paul was always smiling, always glancing about him, seeming to feel that people might be watching him and trying to detect something. This conscious expression, since it was as far as possible from boyish mirthfulness, was usually attributed to insolence or "smartness."

As the inquistion proceeded, one of his instructors repeated an impertinent remark of the boy's, and the Prinicipal asked him whether he thought that a courteous speech to make to a woman. Paul shrugged his shoulders slightly and his eyebrows twitched.

"I don't know," he replied. "I didn't mean to be polite or impolite, either. I guess it's a sort of way I have, of saying things regardless."

The Prinicipal asked him whether he didn't think that a way it would be well to get rid of. Paul grinned and said he guessed so. When he was told that he could go, he bowed gracefully and went out. His bow was like a repetition of the scandalous red carnation.

His teachers were in despair, and his drawing-master voiced the feeling of them all when he declared there was something about the boy which none of them understood. He added: "I don't really believe that smile of his comes altogether from insolence; there's something sort of haunted about it.

The boy is not strong, for one thing. There is something wrong about the fellow.''

The drawing-master had come to realize that, in looking at Paul, one saw only his white teeth and the forced animation of his eyes. One warm afternoon the boy had gone to sleep at his drawing-board, and his master had noted with amazement what a white, blue-veined face it was; drawn and wrinkled like an old man's about the eyes, the lips twitching even in his sleep.

His teachers left the building dissatisfied and unhappy; humiliated to have felt so vindictive toward a mere boy, to have uttered this feeling in cutting terms, and to have set each other on, as it were, in the gruesome game of intemperate reproach. One of them remembered having seen a miserable street cat set at bay by a ring of tormentors.

As for Paul, he ran down the hill whistling the Soldiers' Chorus from "Faust," looking behind him now and then to see whether some of his teachers were not there to witness his light-heartedness. As it was now late in the afternoon and Paul was on duty that evening as usher at Carnegie Hall, he decided that he would not go home to supper.

When he reached the concert hall, the doors were not yet open. It was chilly outside, and he decided to go up into the picture gallery — always deserted at this hour — where there were some of Raffelli's gay studies of Paris streets and an airy blue Venetian scene or two that always exhilarated him. He was delighted to find no one in the gallery but the old guard, who sat in the corner, a newspaper on his knee, a black patch over one eye and the other closed. Paul possessed himself of the place and walked confidently up and down, whistling under his breath. After a while he sat down before a blue Rico and lost himself. When he bethought him to look at his watch, it was after seven o'clock, and he rose with a start and ran downstairs, making a face at Augustus Caesar, peering out from the cast-room, and an evil gesture at the Venus of Milo as he passed her on the stairway.

When Paul reached the ushers' dressing-room, half a dozen boys were there already, and he began excitedly to tumble into his uniform. It was one of the few that at all approached fitting, and Paul thought it very becoming— though he knew the tight, straight coat accentuated his narrow chest, about which he was exceedingly sensitive. He was always excited while he dressed, twanging all over to the tuning of the strings and the preliminary flourishes of the horns in the music-room; but tonight he seemed quite beside himself, and he teased and plagued the boys until, telling him that he was crazy, they put him down on the floor and sat on him.

Somewhat calmed by his suppression, Paul dashed out to the front of the house to seat the early comers. He was a model usher. Gracious and smiling he ran up and down the aisles. Nothing was too much trouble for him; he carried messages and brought programmes as though it were his greatest pleasure in life, and all the people in his section thought him a charming boy, feeling that he remembered and admired them. As the house filled, he grew more and more vivacious and animated, and the colour came to his cheeks and lips. It was very much as though this were a great reception and Paul were the host. Just as the musicians came out to take their places, his English teacher arrived with cheques for the seats which a prominent manufacturer had taken for the season. She betrayed some embarrassment when she handed Paul the tickets, and a hauteur which subsequently made her feel very foolish. Paul was startled for a moment, and had the feeling of wanting to put her out; what business had she here among all these fine people and gay colours? He looked her over and decided that she was not appropriately dressed and must be a fool to sit downstairs in such togs. The tickets had probably been sent her out of kindness, he reflected, as he put down a seat for her, and she had about as much right to sit there as he had.

When the symphony began, Paul sank into one of the rear seats with a long sigh of relief, and lost himself as he had done before the Rico. It was not that symphonies, as such, meant anything in particular to Paul, but the first sigh of the instruments seemed to free some hilarious spirit within him; something that struggled there like the Genius in the bottle found by the Arab fisherman. He left a sudden zest of life; the lights danced before his eyes and the concert hall blazed into unimaginable splendour. When the soprano soloist came on, Paul forgot even the nastiness of his teacher's being there, and gave himself up to the peculiar intoxication such personages always had for him. The soloist chanced to be a German woman, by no means in her first youth, and the mother of many children; but she wore a satin gown and a tiara, and she had that indefinable air of achievement, that world-shine upon her, which always blinded Paul to any possible defects.

After a concert was over, Paul was often irritable and wretched until he got to sleep — and tonight he was even more than usually restless. He had the feeling of not being able to let down; of its being impossible to give up his delicious excitement which was the only thing that could be called living at all. During the last number he withdrew and, after hastily changing his clothes in the dressing-room, slipped out to the side door where the singer's carriage stood. Here he began pacing rapidly up and down the walk, waiting to see her come out.

Over yonder the Schenley, in its vacant stretch, loomed big and square through the fine rain, the windows of its twelve stories glowing like those of a lighted cardboard house under a Christmas tree. All the actors and singers of any importance stayed there when they were in Pittsburgh, and a number of the big manufacturers of the place lived there in the winter. Paul had often hung about the hotel, watching the people go in and out, longing to enter and leave schoolmasters and care behind him forever.

At last the singer came out, accompanied by the conductor, who helped her into her carriage and closed the door with a cordial *auf wiedersehen* —

which set Paul to wondering whether she were not an old sweetheart of his. Paul followed the carriage over to the hotel, walking so rapidly as not to be far from the entrance when the singer alighted and disappeared behind the swinging glass doors which were opened by a Negro in a tall hat and a long coat. In the moment that the door was ajar, it seemed to Paul that he, too, entered. He seemed to feel himself go after her up the steps, into the warm, lighted building, into an exotic, a tropical world of shiny, glistening surfaces and basking ease. He reflected upon the mysterious dishes that were brought into the dining-room, the green bottles in buckets of ice, as had seen them in the supper-party pictures of the Sunday supplement. A quick gust of wind brought the rain down with sudden vehemence, and Paul was startled to find that he was still outside in the slush of the gravel driveway; that his boots were letting in the water and his scanty overcoat was clinging wet about him; that the lights in front of the concert hall were out, and that the rain was driving in sheets between him and the orange glow of the windows above him. There it was, what he wanted — tangibly before him, like the fairy world of a Christmas pantomine; as the rain beat in his face, Paul wondered whether he were destined always to shiver in the black night outside, looking up at it.

He turned and walked reluctantly toward the car tracks. The end had to come sometime; his father in his clothes at the top of the stairs, explanations that did not explain, hastily improvised fictions that were forever tripping him up, his upstairs room and its horrible yellow wallpaper, the creaking bureau with the greasy plush collar-box, and over his painted wooden bed the pictures of George Washington and John Calvin, and the framed motto, 'Feed my Lambs,' which had been worked in red worsted by his mother, whom Paul could not remember.

Half an hour later, Paul alighted from the Negly Avenue car and went slowly down one of the side streets off the main thoroughfare. It was a highly respectable street, where all the houses were exactly alike, and where business men of moderate means begot and reared large families of children, all of whom went to Sabbath School and learned the shorter catechism, and were interested in arithmetic; all of whom were as exactly alike as their homes, and of a piece with the monotony in which they lived. Paul never went up Cordelia Street without a shudder of loathing. His home was next the house of the Cumberland minister. He approached it tonight with the nerveless sense of defeat, the hopeless feeling of sinking back forever into ugliness and commonness that he had always had when he came home. The moment he turned into Cordelia Street he felt the waters close above his head. After each of these orgies of living, he experienced all the physical depression which follows a debauch; the loathing of respectable beds, of common food, of a house permeated by kitchen odours; a shuddering repulsion for the flavourless, colourless mass of every-day existence; a morbid desire for cool things and soft lights and fresh flowers.

The nearer he approached the house, the more absolutely unequal Paul felt to the sight of it all: his ugly sleeping chamber; the old bathroom with the grimy zinc tub, the cracked mirror, the dripping spigots; his father, at the top of the stairs, his hairy legs sticking out from his nightshirt, his feet thrust into carpet slippers. He was so much later than usual that there would certainly be enquiries and reproaches. Paul stopped short before the door. He felt that he could not be accosted by his father to-night; that he could not toss again on that miserable bed. He would not go in. He would tell his father that he had no car-fare, and it was raining so hard he had gone home with one of the boys and stayed all night.

Meanwhile, he was wet and cold. He went around to the back of the house and tried one of the basement windows, found it open, raised it cautiously, and scrambled down the cellar wall to the floor. There he stood, holding his breath, terrified by the niose he had made, but the floor above him was silent, and there was no creak on the stairs. He found a soap-box, and carried it over to the soft ring of light that streamed from the furnace door, and sat down. He was horribly afraid of rats, so he did not try to sleep, but sat looking distrustfully at the dark, still terrified lest he might have awakened his father.

In such reactions, after one of the experiences which made days and nights one of the dreary blanks of the calendar, when his senses were deadened, Paul's head was always singlularly clear. Suppose his father had heard him getting in at the window and had come down and shot him for a burglar? Then, again, suppose his father had come down, pistol in hand, and he had cried out in time to save himself, and his father had been horrified to think how nearly he had killed him? Then again, suppose a day should come when his father would remember that night, and wish there had been no warning cry to stay his hand? With this last supposition Paul entertained himself until daybreak.

The following Sunday was fine; the sodden November chill was broken by the last flash of autumnal summer. In the morning Paul had to go to church and Sabbath School, as always. On seasonable Sunday afternoons the burghers of Cordelia Street usually sat out oin their front "stoops,"and talked to their neighbours on the next stoop, or called to those accross the street in neighbourly fashion. The men sat plaidly on gay cushions placed upon the steps that led down to the sidewalk, while the women, in their Sunday "waists," sat in rockers on the cramped porches, pretending to be greatly at their ease. The children played in the streets; there were so many of them that the place resembled the recreation grounds of a kindergarten. The men on the steps, all in their shirt-sleeves, their vests unbuttoned, sat with their legs well apart, their stomachs comfortably protruding, and talked of the prices of things, or told anecdotes of the sagacity of their various chiefs and overlords. They occasionally looked over the multitude of squabbling children, listened affectionately to their high-pitched, nasal voices, smiling to see their own proclivities reproduced in their offspring, and interspersed their legends of the iron kings with remarks about their sons' progress at school, their grades in arithmetic, and the amounts they had saved in their toy banks.

On this last Sunday of November, Paul sat all the afternoon on the lowest step of his "stoop," staring in the the street, while his sisters, in their rockers, were talking to the minister's daughters next door about how many shirtwaists they had made in the last week, and how many waffles someone had eaten at the last church supper. When the weather was warm, and his father was in a particularly jovial frame of mind, the girls made lemonade, which was always brought out in a red-glass pitcher, ornamented with forget-me-nots in blue enamel. This the girls thought very fine, and the neighbors joked about the suspicious colour of the pitcher.

To-day Paul's father, on the top step, was talking to a young man who shifted a restless baby from knee to knee. He happened to be the young man who was daily held up to Paul as model, and after whom it was his father's dearest hope that he would pattern. This young man was of a ruddy complexion, with a compressed, red mouth, and faded, nearsighted eyes over which he wore thick spectacles, with gold bows that curved about his ears. He was clerk to one of the magnates of a great steel corporation, and was looked upon in Cordelia Street as a young man with a future. There was a story that, some five years ago — he was now barely twenty-six — he had been a trifle "dissipated," but in order to curb his appetites and save the loss of time and strength that a sowing of wild oats might have entailed, he had taken his chief's advice, oft reiterated to his employees, and at twenty-one had married the first woman whom he could persuade to share his fortunes. She happened to be an angular schoolmistress, much older than he, who also wore thick glasses, and who had now borne him four children, all near-sighted like herself.

The young man was relating how his chief, now cruising in the Mediterranean, kept in touch with all the details of the business, arranging his office hours on his yacht just as though he were at home, and "knocking off work enough to keep two stenographers busy." His father told, in turn, the plan his corporation was considering, of putting in an electric railway plant at Cairo. Paul snapped his teeth; he had an awful apprehension that they might spoil it all before he got there. Yet he rather liked to hear these legends of the iron kings that were told and retold on Sundays and holidays; these stories of palaces in Venice, yachts on the Mediterranean, and high play at Monte Carlo appealed to his fancy, and he was interested in the triumphs of cash-boys who had become famous, though he had no mind for the cash-boy stage.

After supper was over, and he had helped to dry the dishes, Paul nervously asked his father whether he could go to George's to get some help in his geometry, and still more nervously asked for car-fare. This latter request he had to repeat, as his father, on principle, did not like to hear requests for money, whether much or little. He asked Paul whether he could not go to some boy who lived nearer, and told him that he ought not to leave his school work until Sunday; but he gave him the dime. He was not a poor man, but he had a worthy ambition to come up in the world. His only reason for allowing Paul to usher was that he thought a boy ought to be earning a little.

Paul bounded upstairs, scrubbed the greasy odour of the dishwater from his hands with the ill-smelling soap he hated, and then shook over his fingers a few drops of violet water from the bottle he kept hidden in his drawer. He left the house with his geometry conspicuously under his arm, and the moment he got out of Cordelia Street and boarded a downtown car, he shook off the lethargy of two deadening days, and began to live again.

The leading juvenile of the permanent stock company which played at one of the downtown theatres was an acquaintance of Paul's, and the boy had been invited to drop in at the Sunday-night rehearsals whenever he could. For more than a year Paul had spent every available moment loitering about Charley Edwards's dressing-room. He had won a place among Edwards's following not only because the young actor, who could not afford to employ a dresser, often found him useful, but because he recognized in Paul something akin to what churchmen term "vocation."

It was at the theatre and at Carnigie Hall that Paul really lived; the rest was but a sleep and a forgetting. This was Paul's fairy tale, and it had for him all the allurement of a secret love. The moment he inhaled the gassy, painty, dusty odour behind the scenes, he breathed like a prisoner set free, and felt within him the possibility of doing or saying splendid, brilliant thing. The moment the cracked orchestra beat out the overture from "Martha," or jerked at the serenade from "Rigoletto," all stupid and ugly things slid from him, and his senses were deliciously, yet delicately fired.

Perhaps it was because, in Paul's world, the natural nearly always wore the guise of ugliness, that a certain element of artificiality seemed to him necessary in beauty. Perhaps it was because his experience of life elsewhere was so full of Sabbath-School picnics, petty economies, wholesome advice as to how to succeed in life, and unescapable odours of cooking, that he found this existence so alluring, these smartly clad men and women so attractive, that he was so moved by these starry apple orchards that bloomed perennially under the limelight. It would be difficult to put it strongly enough how convincingly the stage entrance of that theatre was for Paul the actual portal of Romance. Certainly none of the company ever suspected it, least of all Charley Edwards. It was very like the old stories that used to float about

London of fabulously rich Jews, who had subterranean halls, with palms, and fountains, and soft lamps and richly apparelled women who never saw the disenchanting light of London day. So, in the midst of that smoke-palled city, enamoured of figures and grimy toil, Paul had his secret temple, his wishing-carpet, his bit of blue-and-white Mediterranean shore bathed in perpetual sunshine.

Several of Paul's teachers had a theory that his imagination had been perverted by garish fiction; but the truth was he scarcely ever read at all. The books at home were not such as would either tempt or corrupt a youthful mind, and as for reading the novels that some of this friends urged upon him — well, he got what he wanted much more quickly from music; any sort of music, from an orchestra to a barrel-organ. He needed only the spark, the indescribable thrill that made his imagination master of his senses, and he could make plots and pictures enough of his own. It was equally true that he was not stage-struck — not, at any rate, in the usual acceptation of that expression. He had no desire to become an actor, any more than he had to become a musician. He felt no necessity to do any of these things; what he wanted was to see, to be in the atmosphere, float on the wave of it, to be carried out, blue league after league, away from everything.

After a night behind the scenes, Paul found the schoolroom more than ever repulsive; the bare floors and naked walls; the prosy men who never wore frock coats, or violets in their buttonholes; the women with their dull gowns, shrill voices, and pitiful seriousness about prepositions that govern the dative. He could not bear to have the other pupils think, for a moment, that he took these people seriously; he must convey to them that he considered it all trivial, and was there only by way of a joke, anyway. He had autographed pictures of all the members of the stock company which he showed his classmates, telling them the most incredible stories of his familiarity with these people, of his acquaintance with the soloists who came to Carnegie Hall, his suppers with them and the flowers he sent them. When these stories lost their effect,and his audience grew listless, he would bid all the boys goodbye, announcing that he was going to travel for a while; going to Naples, to California, to Egypt. Then, next Monday, he would slip back, conscious and nervously smiling; his sister was ill, and he would have to defer his voyage until spring.

Matters went steadily worse with Paul at school. In the itch to let his instructors know how heartily he despised them, and how thoroughly he was appreciated elsewhere, he mentioned once or twice that he had no time to fool with theorems; adding — with a twitch of the eyebrows and a touch of that nervous bravado which so perplexed them — that he was helping the people down at the stock company; they were old friends of his.

The upshot of the matter was that the Principal went to Paul's father, and Paul was taken out of school and put to work. The manager at Carnegie Hall was told to get another usher in his stead; the doorkeeper at the theatre was warned not to admit him to the house; and Charley Edwards remorsefully promised the boy's father not to see him again.

The members of the stock company were vastly amused when some of Paul's stories reached them — especially the women. They were hard-working women, most of them supporting indolent husbands or brothers, and they laughed rather bitterly at having stirred the boy to such fervid and florid inventions. They agreed with the faculty and with his father, that Paul's was a bad case.

The east-bound train was ploughing through a January snowstorm; the dull dawn was beginning to show grey when the engine whistled a mile out of Newark. Paul started up from the seat where he had lain curled in uneasy slumber, rubbed the breath-misted window-glass with his hand, and peered out. The snow was whirling in curling eddies above the white bottom lands, and the drifts lay already deep in the fields and along the fences, while here and there the tall dead grass and dried weed stalks protruded black above it. Lights shone from the scattered houses, and gang of labourers who stood beside the track waved their lanterns.

Paul had slept very little, and he felt grimy and uncomfortable. He had made the all-night journey in a day coach because he was afraid if he took a Pullman he might be seen by some Pittsburgh business man who had noticed him in Denny and Carson's office. When the whistle woke him, he clutched quickly at his breast pocket, glancing about him with an uncertain smile. But the little, clay-bespattered Italians were still sleeping, the slatternly women across the aisle were in open-mouthed oblivion, and even the crumby, crying babies were for the time stilled. Paul settled back to struggle with his impatience as best he could.

When he arrived at the Jersey City station, he hurried through his break-fast, manifestly ill at ease and keeping a sharp eye about him. After he reached the Twenty-Third Street station, he consulted a cabman, and had himself driven to a men's furnishing establishment which was just opening for the day. He spent upward of two hours there, buying with endless recon-sidering and great care. His new street suit he put on in the fitting-room; the frock coat and dress clothes he had bundled into the cab with his new shirts. Then he drove to a hatter's and a shoe house. His next errand was at Tif-fany's, where he selected silver-mounted brushes and a scarf-pin. He would not wait to have his silver marked, he said. Lastly, he stopped at a trunk shop on Broadway, and had his purchases packed into various travelling-bags.

It was a little after one o'clock when he drove up to the Waldorf, and, after settling with the cabman, went into the office. He registered from Washington; said his mother and father had been abroad, and that he had come down to await the arrival of their steamer. He told his story plausibly and had no trouble, since he offered to pay for them in advance, in engaging his rooms; a sleeping-room, sitting-room, and bath.

Not once, but a hundred times Paul had planned this entry into New York. He had gone over every detail of it with Charley Edwards, and in his scrapbook at home there were pages of description about New York hotels, cut from the Sunday papers.

When he was shown to his sitting-room on the eighth floor, he saw at a glance that everthing was as it should be; there was but one detail in his mental picture that the place did not realize, so he rang for the bell-boy and sent him down for flowers. He moved about nervously until the boy returned, putting away his new linen and fingering it delightedly as he did so. When the flowers came, he put them hastily into water, and then tumbled into a hot bath. Presently he came out of his white bathroom, resplendent in his new silk underwear, and playing with the tassels of his red robe. The snow was whirling so fiercely outside his windows that he could scarcely see across the street; but within, the air was deliciously soft and fragrant. He put the violets and jonquils on the tabouret beside the couch, and threw himself down with a long sigh, covering himself with a Roman blanket. He was thoroughly tired; he had been in such haste, he had stood up to such a strain, covered so much ground in the last twenty-four hours, that he wanted to think how it had all come about. Lulled by the sound of the wind, the warm air, and the cool fragrance of the flowers, he sank into deep, drowsy retrospection.

It had been wonderfully simple; when they had shut him out of the theatre and concert hall, when they had taken away his bone, the whole thing was virtually determined. The rest was a mere matter of opportunity. The only thing that at all surprised him was his own courage — for he realized well enough that he had always been tormented by fear, a sort of apprehensive dread which, of late years, as the meshes of the lies he had told closed about him, had been pulling the muscles of his body tighter and tighter. Until now, he could not remember a time when he had not been dreading something. Even when he was a little boy, it was always there — behind him, or before, or on either side. There had always been the shadowed corner, the dark place into which he dared not look, but from which something seemed always to be watching him — and Paul had done things that were not pretty to watch, he knew.

But now he had a curious sense of relief, as though he had at last thrown down the gauntlet to the thing in the corner.

Yet it was but a day since he had been sulking in the traces; but yesterday afternoon that he had been sent to the bank with Denny and Carson's deposit, as usual — but this time he was instructed to leave the book to be balanced. There was above two thousand dollars in cheques, and nearly a thousand in the banknotes which he had taken from the book and quietly transferred to his pocket. At the bank he had made out a new deposit slip. His nerves had been steady enough to permit of his returning to the office, where he had finished his work and asked for a full day's holiday to-morrow, Saturday, giving a perfectly reasonable pretext. The bank book, he knew, would not be returned before Monday or Tuesday, and his father would be out of town for the next week. From the time he slipped the banknotes into his pocket until he boarded the night train for New York, he had not known a moment's hesitation.

How astonishingly easy it had all been; here he was, the thing done; and this time there would be no awakening, no figure at the top of the stairs. He watched the snowflakes whirling until he fell asleep.

When he woke, it was four o'clock in the afternoon. He bounded up with a start; one of his precious days gone already! He spent nearly an hour in dressing, watching every stage of his toilet carefully in the mirror. Everything was quite perfect; he was exactly the kind of boy he had always wanted to be.

When he went downstairs, Paul took a carriage and drove up Fifth Avenue toward the Park. The snow had somewhat abated; carriages and tradesmen's wagons were hurrying soundlessly to and fro in the winter twilight; boys in woollen mufflers were shovelling off the doorsteps; the Avenue stages made fine spots of colour against the white street. Here and there on the corners whole flower gardens blooming behind glass windows, against which the snowflakes stuck and melted; violets, roses, carnations, lilies-of-the-valley—somehow vastly more lovely and alluring that they blossomed thus unnaturally in the snow. The Park itself was a wonderful stage winter-piece.

When he returned, the pause of the twilight had ceased, and the tune of the streets had changed. The snow was falling faster, lights streamed from the hotels that reared their many stories fearlessly up into the storm, defying the raging Atlantic winds. A long, black stream of carriages poured down the Avenue, intersected here and there by other streams, tending horizontally. There were a score of cabs about the entrance of his hotel, and his driver had to wait. Boys in livery were running in and out of the awning stretched across the sidewalk, up and down the red velvet carpet laid from the door to the street. Above, about, within it all, was the rumble and roar, the hurry and toss of thousands of human beings as hot for pleasure as himself, and on every side of him towered the glaring affirmation of the omnipotence of wealth.

The boy set his teeth and drew his shoulders together in a spasm of realization; the plot of all dramas, the text of all romances, the nerve-stuff of all sensations was whirling about him like the snowflakes. He burnt like a fagot in a tempest.

When Paul came down to dinner, the music of the orchestra floated up the elevator shaft to greet him. As he stepped into the thronged corridor, he sank back into one of the chairs against the wall to get his breath. The lights, the chatter, the perfumes, the bewildering medley of colour—he had, for a moment, the feeling of not being able to stand it. But only for a moment; these were his own people, he told himself. He went slowly about the corridors, through the writing-rooms, smoking-rooms, reception-rooms, as though he were exploring the chambers of an enchanted palace, built and peopled for him alone.

When he reached the dining-room he sat down at a table near a window. The flowers, the white linen, the many-coloured wine-glasses, the gay toilettes of the women, the low popping of corks, the undulating repetitions of the "Blue Danube" from the orchestra, all flooded Paul's dream with bewildering radiance, When the roseate tinge of his champagne was added—that cold, precious, bubbling stuff that creamed and foamed in his glass—Paul wondered that there were honest men in the world at all. This was what all the world was fighting for, he reflected; this was what all the struggle was about. He doubted the reality of his past. Had he ever known a place called Cordelia Street, a place where fagged-looking business men boarded the early car? Mere rivets in a machine they seemed to Paul—sickening men, with combings of children's hair always hanging to their coats, and the smell of cooking in their clothes. Cordelia Street—Ah, that belonged to another time and country! Had he not always been thus, had he not sat here night after night, from as far back as he could remember, looking pensively over just such shimmering textures, and slowly twirling the stem of a glass like this one between his thumb and middle finger? He rather thought he had.

He was not in the least abashed or lonely. He had no especial desire to meet or to know any of these people; all he demanded was the right to look on and conjecture, to watch the pageant. The mere stage properties were all he contended for. Nor was he lonely later in the evening, in his loge at the Opera. He was entirely rid of his nervous misgivings, of his forced aggressiveness, of the imperative desire to show himself different from his surroundings. He felt now that his surroundings explained him. Nobody questioned the purple; he had only to wear it passively. He had only to glance down at his dress coat to reassure himself that here it would be impossible for anyone to humiliate him.

He found it hard to leave his beautiful sitting-room to go to bed that night, and sat long watching the raging storm from his turret window. When he went to sleep, it was with the lights turned on in his bedroom; partly because of his old timidity, and partly so that, if he should wake in the night, there would be no wretched moment of doubt, no horrible suspicion of yellow wallpaper, or of Washington and Calvin above his bed.

On Sunday morning the city was practically snowbound. Paul breakfasted late, and in the afternoon he fell in with a wild San Francisco boy, a freshman at Yale, who said he had run down for a "little flyer" over Sunday. The young man offered to show Paul the night side of the town, and the two boys went off together after dinner, not returning to the hotel until seven o'clock the next morning. They had started out in the confiding warmth of a champagne friendship, but their parting in the elevator was singularly cool. The freshman pulled himself together to make his train, and Paul went to bed. He awoke at two o'clock in the afternoon, very thirsty and dizzy, and rang for ice-water, coffee, and the Pittsburgh papers.

On the part of the hotel management, Paul excited no suspicion. There was this to be said for him, that he wore his spoils with dignity and in no way made himself conspicuous. His chief greediness lay in his ears and eyes, and his excesses were not offensive ones. His dearest pleasures were the grey winter twilights in his sitting-room; his quiet enjoyment of his flowers, his clothes, his wide divan, his cigarette, and his sense of power. He could not remember a time when he had felt so at peace with himself. The mere release from the necessity of petty lying, lying every day and every day, restored his self-respect. He had never lied for pleasure, even at school; but to make himself noticed and admired, to assert his difference from other Cordelia Street boys; and he felt a good deal more manly, more honest, even, now that he had no need for boastful pretensions, now that he could, as his actor friends used to say, "dress the part." It was characteristic that remorse did not occur to him. His golden days went by without a shadow, and he made each as perfect as he could.

On the eighth day after his arrival in New York, he found the whole affair exploited in the Pittsburgh papers, exploited with a wealth of detail which indicated that local news of a sensational nature was at a low ebb. The firm of Denny and Carson announced that the boy's father had refunded the full amount of his theft, and that they had no intention of prosecuting. The Cumberland minister had been interviewed, and expressed his hope of yet reclaiming the motherless lad, and Paul's Sabbath-School teacher declared that she would spare no effort to that end. The rumour had reached Pittsburgh that the boy had been seen in a New York hotel, and his father had gone East to find him and bring him home.

Paul had just come in to dress for dinner; he sank into a chair, weak in the knees, and clasped his head in his hands. It was to be worse than jail, even; the tepid waters of Cordelia Street were to close over him finally and forever. The grey monotony stretched before him in hopeless, unrelieved years; — Sabbath-School, Young People's Meeting, the yellow-papered room, the damp dish-towels; it all rushed back upon him with sickening vividness. He had the old feeling that the orchestra had suddenly stopped, the sinking sensation that the play was over. The sweat broke out on his face, and he sprang to his feet, looked about him with his white, conscious smile, and winked at himself in the mirror. With something of the childish belief in miracles with which he had so often gone to class, all his lessons unlearned, Paul dressed and dashed whistling down the corridor to the elevator.

He had no sooner entered the dining-room and caught the measure of the music than his remembrance was lightened by his old elastic power of claiming the moment, mounting with it, and finding it all-sufficient. The glare and glitter about him, the mere scenic accessories had again, and for the last time, their old potency. He would show himself that he was game, he would finish the thing splendidly. He doubted, more than ever, the existence of Cordelia Street, and for the first time he drank his wine recklessly. Was he not, after all, one of these fortunate beings? Was he not still himself, and in his own place? He drummed a nervous accompaniment to the music and looked about him, telling himself over and over that it had paid.

He reflected drowsily, to the swell of the violin and the chill sweetness of his wine, that he might have done it more wisely. He might have caught an outbound steamer and been well out of their clutches before now. But the other side of the world had seemed too far away and too uncertain then; he could not have waited for it; his need had been too sharp. If he had to choose over again, he would do the same thing to-morrow. He looked affectionately about the dining-room, now gilded with a soft mist. Ah, it had paid indeed!

Paul was awakened next morning by a painful throbbing in his head and feet. He had thrown himself across the bed without undressing, and had slept with his shoes on. His limbs and hands were lead heavy, and his tongue and throat were parched. There came upon him one of those fateful attacks of clear-headedness that never occurred except when he was physically exhausted and his nerves hung loose. He lay still and closed his eyes and let the tide of realities wash over him.

His father was in New York; "stopping at some joint or other," he told himself. The memory of successive summers on the front stoop fell upon him like a weight of black water. He had not a hundred dollars left; and he knew now, more than ever, that money was everything, the wall that stood between all he loathed and all he wanted. The thing was winding itelf up; he had thought of that on his first glorious day in New York, and had even provided a way to snap the thread. It lay on his dressing-table now; he had got it out last night when he came blindly up from dinner — but the shiny metal hurt his eyes, and he disliked the look of it, anyway.

He rose and moved about with a painful effort, succumbing now and again to attacks of nausea. It was the old depression exaggerated; all the world had become Cordelia Street. Yet somehow he was not afraid of anything, was absolutely calm, perhaps because he had looked into the dark corner at last, and knew. It was bad enough, what he saw there; but somehow not so bad as his long fear of it had been. He saw everything clearly now. He had a feeling that he had made the best of it, that he had lived the sort of life he was meant to live, and for half an hour he sat staring at the revolver. But he told himself that was not the way, so he went downstairs and took a cab to the ferry.

When Paul arrived at Newark, he got off the train and took another cab, directing the driver to follow the Pennsylvania tracks out of the town. The snow lay heavy on the roadways and had drifted deep in the open fields. Only here and there the dead grass or dried weed stalks projected, singularly black, above it.

Once well into the country, Paul dismissed the carriage and walked, floundering along the tracks, his mind a medley of irrelevant things. He seemed to hold in his brain an actual picture of everything he had seen that morning. He remembered every feature of both his drivers, a toothless old woman from whom he had bought the red flowers in his coat, the agent from whom he had got his ticket, all of his fellow-passengers on the ferry. His mind, unable to cope with vital matters near at hand, worked feverishly and deftly at sorting and grouping these images. They made for him a part of the ugliness of the world, of the ache in his head, and the bitter burning on his tongue. He stooped and put a handful of snow into his mouth as he walked, but that, too, seemed hot. When he reached a little hillside, where the tracks ran through a cut some twenty feet below him, he stopped and sat down.

The carnations in his coat were drooping with the cold, he noticed; their red glory over. It occurred to him that all the flowers he had seen in the show windows that first night must have gone the same way, long before this. It was only one splendid breath they had, in spite of their brave mockery at the winter outside the glass. It was a losing game in the end, it seemed, this revolt against the homilies by which the world is run. Paul took one of the blossoms carefully from his coat and scooped a little hole in the snow, where he covered it up. Then he dozed awhile, from his weak condition, seeming insensible to the cold.

The sound of an approaching train woke him and he started to his feet, remembering only his resolution, and afraid lest he should be too late. He stood watching the approaching locomotive, his teeth chattering, his lips drawn away from them in a frightened smile; once or twice he glanced nervously sidewise, as though he were being watched. When the right moment came, he jumped. As he fell, the folly of his haste occurred to him with merciless clearness, the vastness of what he had left undone. There flashed through his brain, clearer than ever before, the blue of Adriatic water, the yellow of Algerian sands.

He felt something strike his chest — his body was being thrown swiftly through the air, on and on, immeasurably far and fast, while his limbs gently relaxed. Then, because the picture-making mechanism was crushed, the disturbing visions flashed into black, and Paul dropped back into the immense design of things.

Histrionic Personality Disorder

Histrionic personalities seem to be always on stage and in the spotlight. It is as if they are "starring" in a drama that revolves around them. If observed over a long period, they display two dominant characteristics — self-centered behavior that is intensely dramatic and egocentric attitudes that interfere with meaningful personal relationships.

Histrionic personalities behave in an exaggerated, self-centered manner. They constantly draw attention to themselves. And when they get it, they become overly emotive. They may react irrationally or impulsively to minor stimuli. They often crave frenetic activity.

These individuals usually have difficulty in establishing and developing meaningful relationships because their vanity and egocentricity get in the way. Their warmth and charm may be perceived by others as superficial. They are often inconsiderate of the wishes of others. Because of the helpless, dependent role they unknowingly play, they constantly seek reassurance from others.

The context of Editha Balcom's "starring" role in W. D. Howell's story is the outbreak of the Spanish-American War. Her performance should be observed critically. Incidents of her self-centered, dramatic behavior and evidence of the egocentric attitudes that interfere with her relationship with George Gearson should be pointed out.

EDITHA

William Dean Howells

The air was thick with the war feeling, like the electricity of a storm which has not yet burst. Editha sat looking out into the hot spring afternoon, with her lips parted, and panting with the intensity of the question whether she could let him go. She had decided that she could not let him stay, when she saw him at the end of the still leafless avenue, making slowly up towards the house, with his head down and his figure relaxed. She ran impatiently out on the veranda, to the edge of the steps, and imperatively demanded greater haste of him with her will before she called aloud to him: "George!"

He had quickened his pace in mystical response to her mystical urgence, before he could have heard her; now he looked up and answered, "Well?"

"Oh, how united we are!" she exulted, and then she swooped down the steps to him. "What is it?" she cried.

"It's war," he said, and he pulled her up to him and kissed her.

She kissed him back intensely, but irrelevantly, as to their passion, and uttered from deep in her throat, "How glorious!"

"It's war," he repeated, without consenting to her sense of it; and she did not know just what to think at first. She never knew what to think of him; that made his mystery, his charm. All through their courtship, which was contemporaneous with the growth of the war feeling, she had been puzzled by his want of seriousness about it. He seemed to despise it even more than he abhorred it. She could have understood his abhorring any sort of bloodshed; that would have been a survival of his old life when he thought he would be a minister, and before he changed and took up the law. But making light of a cause so high and noble seemed to show a want of earnestness at the core of his being. Not but that she felt herself able to cope with a congenital defect of that sort, and make his love for her save him from himself. Now perhaps the miracle was already wrought in him. In the presence of the tremendous fact that he announced, all triviality seemed to have gone out of him; she began to feel that. He sank down on the top step, and wiped his forehead with his handkerchief, while she poured out upon him her question of the origin and authenticity of his news.

All the while, in her duplex emotioning, she was aware that now at the very beginning she must put a guard upon herself against urging him, by any word or act, to take the part that her whole soul willed him to take, for the completion of her ideal of him. He was very nearly perfect as he was, and he must be allowed to perfect himself. But he was peculiar, and he might very well be reasoned out of his peculiarity. Before her reasoning went her emotioning: her nature pulling upon his nature, her womanhood upon his manhood, without her knowing the means she was using to the end she was willing. She had always supposed that the man who won her would have done something to win her; she did not know what, but something. George Gearson had simply asked her for her love, on the way home from a concert, and she gave her love to him, without, as it were, thinking. But now, it flashed upon her, if he could do something worthy to *have* won her—be a hero, *her* hero—it would be even better than if he had done it before asking her; it would be grander. Besides, she had believed in the war from the beginning.

"But don't you see, dearest," she said, "that it wouldn't have come to this if it hadn't been in the order of Providence? And I call any war glorious that is for the liberation of people who have been struggling for years against the cruelest oppression. Don't you think so, too?"

"I suppose so," he returned, languidly. "But war! Is it glorious to break the peace of the world?"

"That ignoble peace! It was no peace at all, with that crime and shame at our very gates." She was conscious of parroting the current phrases of the newspapers, but it was no time to pick and choose her words. She must sacrifice anything to the high ideal she had for him, and after a good deal of rapid argument she ended with the climax: "But now it doesn't matter about the how or why. Since the war has come, all that is gone. There are no two sides any more. There is nothing now but our country."

He sat with his eyes closed and his head leant back against the veranda, and he remarked, with a vague smile, as if musing aloud, "Our country — right or wrong."

"Yes, right or wrong!" she returned, fervidly. "I'll go and get you some lemonade." She rose rustling, and whisked away; when she came back with two tall glasses of clouded liquid on a tray, and the ice clucking in them, he still sat as she had left him, and she said, as if there had been no interruption: "But there is no quesiton of wrong in this case. I call it a sacred war. A war for liberty and humanity, if ever there was one. And I know you will see it just as I do, yet."

He took half the lemonade at a gulp, and he answered as he set the glass down: "I know you always have the highest ideal. When I differ from you I ought to doubt myself."

A generous sob rose in Editha's throat for the humility of a man, so very nearly perfect, who was willing to put himself below her.

Besides, she felt, more subliminally, that he was never so near slipping through her fingers as when he took that meek way.

"You shall not say that! Only, for once I happen to be right." She seized his hand in her two hands, and poured her soul from her eyes into his. "Don't you think so?" she entreated him.

He released his hand and drank the rest of his lemonade, and she added, "Have mine, too," but he shook his head in answering, "I've no business to think so, unless I act so, too."

Her heart stopped a beat before it pulsed on with leaps that she felt in her neck. She had noticed that strange thing in men: they seemed to feel bound to do what they believed, and not think a thing was finished when they said it, as girls did. She knew what was in his mind, but she pretended not, and she said, "Oh, I am not sure," and then faltered.

He went on as if to himself, without apparently heeding her: "There's only one way of proving one's faith in a thing like this."

She could not say that she understood, but she did understand.

He went on again. "If I believed — if I felt as you do about the war — Do you wish me to feel as you do?"

Now she was really not sure; so she said: "George, I don't know what you mean."

He seemed to muse away from her as before. "There is a sort of fascination in it. I suppose that at the bottom of his heart every man would like at times to have his courage tested, to see how he would act."

"How can you talk in that ghastly way?"

"It is rather morbid. Still, that's what it comes to, unless you're swept away by ambition or driven by conviction. I haven't the conviction or the ambition, and the other thing is what it comes to with me. I ought to have been a preacher, after all; then I couldn't have asked it of myself as I must, now I'm a lawyer. And you believe it's a holy war, Editha?" he suddenly addressed her. "Oh, I know you do! But you wish me to believe so, too?"

She hardly knew whether he was mocking or not, in the ironical way he always had with her plainer mind. But the only thing was to be outspoken with him.

"George, I wish you to believe whatever you think is true, at any and every cost. If I've tried to talk you into anything, I take it all back."

"Oh, I know that, Editha. I know how sincere you are, and how — I wish I had your undoubting spirit! I'll think it over; I'd like to believe as you do. But I don't, now; I don't, indeed. It isn't this war alone; though this seems pecul-iarly wanton and needless; but it's every war — so stupid; it makes me sick. Why shouldn't this thing have been settled reasonably?"

"Because," she said, very throatily again, "God meant it to be war."

"You think it was God? Yes, I suppose that is what people will say."

"Do you suppose it would have been war if God hadn't meant it?"

"I don't know. Sometimes it seems as if God had put this world into men's keeping to work it as they pleased."

"Now, George, that is blasphemy."

"Well, I won't blaspheme. I'll try to believe in your pocket Providence," he said, and then he rose to go.

"Why don't you stay to dinner?" Dinner at Balcom's Works was at one o'clock.

"I'll come back to supper, if you'll let me. Perhaps I shall bring you a convert.

"Well, you may come back, on that condition."

"All right. If I don't come, you'll understand."

He went away without kissing her, and she felt it a suspension of their engagement. It all interested her intensely; she was undergoing a tremen-dous experience, and she was being equal to it. While she stood looking after him, her mother came out through one of the long windows onto the veranda, with a catlike softness and vagueness.

"Why didn't he stay to dinner?"

"Because — because — war has been declared," Editha pronounced, without turning.

Her mother said, "Oh my!" and then said nothing more until she had sat down in one of the large Shaker chairs and rocked herself for some time. Then she closed whatever tacit passage of thought there had been in her mind with the spoken words: "Well, I hope *he* won't go."

"And *I* hope he *will*," the girl said, and confronted her mother with a stormy exaltation that would have frightened any creature less unimpres-sionable than a cat.

Her mother rocked herself again for an interval of cogitation. What she arrived at in speech was: "Well I guess you've done a wicked thing, Editha Balcom."

The girl said, as she passed indoors through the same window her mother had come out by: "I haven't done anything—yet."

In her room, she put together all her letters and gifts from Gearson, down to the withered petals of the first flower he had offered, with that timidity of his veiled in that irony of his. In the heart of the packet she enshrined her engagement ring which she had restored to the pretty box he had brought it her in. Then she sat down, if not calmly yet strongly, and wrote:

"George:—I understood when you left me. But I think we had better emphasize your meaning that if we cannot be one in everything we had better be one in nothing. So I am sending these things for your keeping till you have made up your mind.

"I shall always love you, and therefore I shall never marry anyone else. But the man I marry must love his country first of all, and be able to say to me,

"'I could not love thee, dear, so much,
Loved I not honor more.'

"There is no honor above America with me. In this great hour there is no other honor.

"Your heart will make my words clear to you. I had never expected to say so much but it has come upon me that I must say the utmost.

Editha."

She thought she had worded her letter well, worded it in a way that could not be bettered; all had been implied and nothing expressed.

She had it ready to send with the packet she had tied with red, white, and blue ribbon, when it occurred to her that she was not just to him, that she was not giving him a fair chance. He said he would go and think it over, and she was not waiting. She was pushing, threatening, compelling. That was not a woman's part. She must leave him free, free, free. She could not accept for her country or herself a forced sacrifice.

In writing her letter she had satisfied the impulse from which it sprang; she could well afford to wait till he had thought it over. She put the packet and the letter by, and rested serene in the consciousness of having done what was laid upon her by her love itself to do, and yet used patience, mercy, justice.

She had her reward. Gearson did not come to tea, but she had given him till morning, when, late at night there came up from the village the sound of a fife and drum, with a tumult of voices, in shouting, singing, and laughing. The noise drew nearer and nearer; it reached the street end of the avenue;

there it silenced itself, and one voice, the voice she knew best, rose over the silence. It fell; the air was filled with cheers; the fife and drum struck up, with the shouting, singing, and laughing again, but now retreating; and a single figure came hurrying up the avenue.

She ran down to meet her lover and clung to him. He was very gay, and he put his arm round her with a boisterous laugh. "Well, you must call me Captain now; or Cap, if you prefer; that's what the boys call me. Yes, we've had a meeting at the town hall, and everybody has volunteered; and they selected me for captain, and I'm going to the war, the big war, the glorious war, the holy war ordained by the pocket Providence that blesses butchery. Come along: let's tell the whole family about it. Call them from their downy beds, father, mother, Aunt Hitty, and all the folks!"

But when they mounted the veranda steps he did not wait for a larger audience; he poured the story out upon Editha alone.

"There was a lot of speaking, and then some of the fools set up a shout for me. It was all going one way, and I thought it would be a good joke to sprinkle a little cold water on them. But you can't do that with a crowd that adores you. The first thing I knew I was sprinkling hell-fire on them. 'Cry havoc, and let slip the dogs of war.' That was the style. Now that it had come to the fight, there were no two parties; there was one country, and the thing was to fight to a finish as quick as possible. I suggested volunteering then and there, and I wrote my name first of all on the roster. Then they elected me — that's all. I wish I had some ice-water."

She left him walking up and down the veranda, while she ran for the ice-pitcher and a goblet, and when she came back he was still walking up and down, shouting the story he had told her to her father and mother, who had come out more sketchily dressed then they commonly were by day. He drank goblet after goblet of the ice-water without noticing who was giving it, and kept on talking, and laughing through his talk wildly. "It's astonishing," he said, "how well the worse reason looks when you try to make it appear the better. Why, I believe I was the first convert to the war in that crowd tonight! I never thought I should like to kill a man; but now I shouldn't care; and the smokeless powder lets you see the man drop that you kill. It's all for the country! What a thing it is to have a country that *can't* be wrong, but if it is, is right, anyway."

Editha had a great, vital thought, an inspiration. She set down the ice-pitcher on the veranda floor, and ran upstairs and got the letter she had written him. When at last he noisily bade her father and mother, "Well, good-night. I forgot I woke you up: I shan't want any sleep myself," she followed him down the avenue to the gate. There, after the whirling words that seemed to fly away from her thoughts and refuse to serve them, she made a last effort to solemnize the moment that seemed so crazy, and pressed the letter she had written upon him.

"What's this?" he said. "Want me to mail it?"

"No, no. It's for you. I wrote it after you went this morning. Keep it—and read it sometime—" She thought, and then her inspiration came: "Read it if ever you doubt what you've done, or fear that I regret your having done it. Read it after you've started."

They strained each other in embraces that seemed as ineffective as their words, and he kissed her face with quick, hot breaths that were so unlike him, that made her feel as if she had lost her old lover and found a stranger in his place. The stranger said: "What a gorgeous flower you are, with your red hair, and your blue eyes that look black now, and your face with the color painted out by the white moonshine! Let me hold you under the chin, to see whether I love blood, you tiger-lily!" Then he laughed Gearson's laugh, and released her, scared and giddy. Within her wilfulness she had been frightened by a sense of subtler force in him, and mystically mastered as she had never been before.

She ran all the way back to the house, and mounted the steps panting. Her mother and father were talking of the great affair. Her mother said: "Wa'n't Mr. Gearson in rather of an excited state of mind? Didn't you think he acted curious?"

"Well, not for a man who'd just been elected captain and had set 'em up for the whole of Company A," her father chuckled back.

"What in the world do you mean, Mr. Balcom? Oh! There's Editha!" She offered to follow the girl indoors.

"Don't come, mother!" Editha called, vanishing.

Mrs. Balcom remained to reproach her husband. "I don't see much of anything to laugh at."

"Well, it's catching. Caught it from Gearson. I guess it won't be much of a war, and I guess Gearson don't think so, either. The other fellows will back down as soon as they see we mean it. I wouldn't lose any sleep over it. I'm going back to bed, myself."

Gearson came again next afternoon, looking pale and rather sick, but quite himself, even to his languid irony. "I guess I'd better tell you, Editha, that I consecrated myself to your god of battles last night by pouring too many libations to him down my own throat. But I'm all right now. One has to carry off the excitement, somehow."

"Promise me," she commanded, "that you'll never touch it again!"

"What! Not let the cannikin clink? Not let the soldier drink? Well, I promise."

"You don't belong to yourself now; you don't even belong to me. You belong to your country, and you have a sacred charge to keep yourself strong and well for your country's sake. I have been thinking, thinking all night and all day long."

"You look as if you had been crying a little, too," he said, with his queer smile.

"That's all past. I've been thinking, and worshipping you. Don't you suppose I know all that you've been through, to come to this? I've followed you every step from your old theories and opinions."

"Well, you've had a long row to hoe."

"And I know you've done this from the highest motives—"

"Oh, there won't be much pettifogging to do till this cruel war is—

"And you haven't simply done it for my sake. I couldn't respect you if you had."

"Well, then we'll say I haven't. A man that hasn't got his own respect intact wants the respect of all the other people he can corner. But we won't go into that. I'm in for the thing now, and we've got to face our future. My idea is that this isn't going to be a very protracted struggle; we shall just scare the enemy to death before it comes to a fight at all. But we must provide for contingencies, Editha. If anything happens to me—"

"Oh, George!" She clung to him, sobbing.

"I don't want you to feel foolishly bound to my memory. I should hate that, wherever I happened to be."

"I am yours, for time and eternity—time and eternity." She liked the words; they satisfied her famine for phrases.

"Well, say eternity; that's all right; but time's another thing; and I'm talking about time. But there is something! My mother! If anything happens—"

She winced, and he laughed. "You're not the bold soldier-girl of yesterday!" Then he sobered. "If anything happens, I want you to help my mother out. She won't like my doing this thing. She brought me up to think war a fool thing as well as a bad thing. My father was in the Civil War; all through it; lost his arm in it." She thrilled with the sense of the arm round her; what if that should be lost? He laughed as if divining her: "Oh it doesn't run in the family as far as I know! Then he added, gravely: "He came home with misgivings about war, and they grew on him. I guess he and mother agreed between them that I was to be brought up in his final mind about it; but that was before my time. I only knew him from my mother's report of him and his opinions, I don't know whether they were hers first; but they were hers last. This will be a blow to her. I shall have to write and tell her—"

He stopped, and she asked: "Would you like me to write, too, George?"

"I don't believe that would do. No, I'll do the writing. She'll understand a little if I say that I thought the way to minimize it was to make war on the largest possible scale at once—that I felt I must have been helping on the war somehow if I hadn't helped keep it from coming, and I knew I hadn't; when it came, I had no right to stay out of it."

Whether his sophistries satisfied him or not, they satisfied her. She clung to his breast, and whispered, with closed eyes and quivering lips: "Yes, yes, yes!"

"But if anything should happen, you might go to her and see what you could do for her. You know? It's rather far off; she can't leave her chair—"

"Oh, I'll go, if it's the ends of the earth! But nothing will happen! Nothing can! I—"

She felt herself lifted with his rising, and Gearson was saying, with his arm still round her, to her father: "Well, we're off at once, Mr. Balcom. We're to be formally accepted at the capital, and then bunched up with the rest somehow, and sent into camp somewhere, and go to the front as soon as possible. We all want to be in the van, of course; we're the first company to report to the Governor. I came to tell Editha, but I hadn't got round to it."

She saw him again for a moment at the capital, in the station, just before the train started southward with his regiment. He looked well, in his uniform, and very soldierly, but somehow girlish, too, with his clean-shaven face and slim figure. The manly eyes and the strong voice satisfied her, and his preoccupation with some unexpected details of duty flattered her. Other girls were weeping and bemoaning themselves, but she felt a sort of noble distinction in the abstraction, the most unconsciousness, with which they parted. Only at the last moment he said: "Don't forget my mother. It mayn't be such a walk-over as I supposed," and he laughed at the notion.

He waved his hand to her as the train moved off—she knew it among a score of hands that were waved to other girls from the platform of the car, for it held a letter which she knew was hers. Then he went inside the car to read it, doubtless, and she did not see him again. But she felt safe for him through the strength of what she called her love. What she called her God, always speaking the name in a deep voice and with the implication of a mutual understanding, would watch over him and keep him and bring him back to her. If with an empty sleeve, then he should have three arms instead of two, for both of hers should be his for life. She did not see, though, why she should always be thinking of the arm his father had lost.

There were not many letters from him, but they were such as she could have wished, and she put her whole strength into making hers such as she imagined he could have wished, glorifying and supporting him. She wrote to his mother glorifying him as their hero, but the brief answer she got was merely to the effect that Mrs. Gearson was not well enough to write herself, and thanking her for her letter by the hand of someone who called herself "Yrs truly, Mrs. W.J. Andrews."

Editha determined not to be hurt, but to write again quite as if the answer had been all she expected. Before it seemed as if she could have written, there came news of the first skirmish, and in the list of the killed, which was telegraphed as a trifling loss on our side, was Gearson's name. There was a frantic time of trying to make out that it might be, must be, some other Gearson; but the name and the company and the regiment and the State were too definitely given.

Then there was a lapse into depths out of which it seemed as if she never could rise again; then a lift into clouds far above all grief, black clouds, that blotted out the sun, but where she soared with him, with George — George! She had the fever that she expected of herself, but she did not die in it, she was not even delirious, and it did not last long. When she was well enough to leave her bed, her one thought was of George's mother, of his strangely worded wish that she should go to her and see what she could do for her. In the exaltation of the duty laid upon her — it buoyed her up instead of burdening her — she rapidly recovered.

Her father went with her on the long railroad journey from Northern New York to Western Iowa; he had business out at Davenport, and he said he could just as well go then as any other time; and he went with her to the little country town where George's mother lived in a little house on the edge of the illimitable cornfields, under trees pushed to a top of the rolling prairie. George's father had settled there after the Civil War, as so many other old soldiers had done; but they were Eastern people, and Editha fancied touches of the East in the June rose overhanging the front door, and the garden with early summer flowers stretching from the gate of the paling fence.

It was very low inside the house, and so dim, with the closed blinds, that they could scarcely see one another: Editha tall and black in her crapes which filled the air with the smell of their dyes; her father standing decorously apart with his hat on his forearm, as at funerals; a woman rested in a deep armchair, and the woman who had let the strangers in stood behind the chair.

The seated woman turned her head round and up, and asked the woman behind the chair: "*Who* did you say?"

Editha, if she had done what she expected of herself, would have gone down on her knees at the feet of the seated figure and said, "I am George's Editha," for answer.

But instead of her own voice she heard that other woman's voice, saying: "Well, I don't know as I *did* get the name just right. I guess I'll have to make a little more light in here," and she went and pushed two of the shutters ajar.

Then Editha's father said, in his public will-now-address-a-few-remarks tone: "My name is Balcom, ma'am—Junius H. Balcom, of Balcom's Works, New York; my daughter—"

"Oh!" the seated woman broke in, with a powerful voice, the voice that always surprised Editha from Gearson's slender frame. "Let me see you. Stand round where the light can strike on your face," and Editha dumbly obeyed. "So, you're Editha Balcom," she sighed.

"Yes," Editha said, more like a culprit than a comforter.

"What did you come for?" Mrs. Gearson asked.

Editha's face quivered and her knees shook. "I came — because — because George —" She could go no further.

"Yes," the mother said, "he told me he had asked you to come if he got killed. You didn't expect that, I suppose, when you sent him."

"I would rather have died myself than done it!" Editha said, with more truth in her deep voice than she ordinarily found in it. "I tried to leave him free —"

"Yes, that letter of yours, that came back with his other things, left him free."

Editha saw now where George's irony came from.

"It was not to be read before — unless — until — I told him so," she faltered.

"Of course, he wouldn't read a letter of yours, under the circumstances, till he thought you wanted him to. Been sick?" the woman abruptly demanded.

"Very sick," Editha said, with self-pity.

"Daughter's life," her father interposed, "was almost despaired of, at one time."

Mrs. Gearson gave him no heed. "I suppose you would have been glad to die, such a brave person as you! I don't believe he was glad to die. He was always a timid boy, that way; he was afraid of a good many things; but if he was afraid he did what he made up his mind to. I suppose he made up his mind to go; but I knew what it cost him by what it cost me when I heard of it. I had been through one war before. When you sent him you didn't expect he would get killed."

The voice seemed to compassionate Editha, and it was time. "No," she huskily murmured.

"No, girls don't; women don't, when they give their men up to their country. They think they'll come marching back, somehow, just as gay as they went, or if it's an empty sleeve, or even an empty pantaloon, it's all the more glory, and they're so much the prouder of them, poor things!"

The tears began to run down Editha's face; she had not wept till then; but it was now such a relief to be understood that the tears came.

"No, you didn't expect him to get killed," Mrs. Gearson repeated, in a voice which was startlingly like George's again. "You just expected him to kill someone else, some of those foreigners, that weren't there because they had any say about it, but because they had to be there, poor wretches — conscripts, or whatever they call 'em. You thought it would be all right for my George, your George, to kill the sons of those miserable mothers and the husbands of those girls that you would never see the faces of." The woman lifted her powerful voice in a psalmlike note. "I thank my God he didn't live to do it! I thank my God they killed him first, and that he ain't livin' with their blood on his hands!" She dropped her eyes, which she had raised with her voice, and glared at Editha. "What you got that black on for?" She lifted herself by her powerful arms so high that her helpless body seemed to hang limp its full length. "Take it off, take it off, before I tear it from your back!"

The lady who was passing the summer near Balcom's Works was sketching Editha's beauty, which lent itself wonderfully to the effects of a colorist. It had come to that confidence which is rather apt to grow between artist and sitter, and Editha had told her everything.

"To think of your having such a tragedy in your life!" the lady said. She added: "I suppose there are people who feel that way about war. But when you consider the good this war has done—how much it has done for the country! I can't understand such people, for my part. And when you had come all the way out there to console her—got up out of a sickbed! Well!"

"I think," Editha said, magnanimously, "she wasn't quite in her right mind; and so did papa."

"Yes," the lady said, looking at Editha's lips in nature and then at her lips in art, and giving an empirical touch to them in the picture. "But how dreadful of her! How perfectly—excuse me—how *vulgar!*"

A light broke upon Editha in the darkness which she felt had been without a gleam of brightness for weeks and months. The mystery that had bewildered her was solved by the word; and from that moment she rose from groveling in shame and self-pity, and began to live again in the ideal.

Borderline Personality Disorder

Individuals with Borderline Personality Disorder display instability in at least four areas. First, their interpersonal relationships are often unstable and intense. For example, they may use other people to achieve personal ends, or they may perceive others as highly valuable or worthless. In fact, their attitude toward others may shift quickly from one extreme to the other.

Second, they exhibit instability in personal behavior. They may engage in impulsive activities that are potentially self-damaging, such as free-spending, gambling, sex, alcohol or drug abuse, or overeating. Furthermore, they may injure themselves through repeated accidents or fights.

Third, individuals with this disorder also often have an uncertain understanding of their identity. They may be unsure of their long-term goals, friendships, values, and loyalties.

Finally, these individuals experience difficulty with their moods. They may unable to control their anger and, consequently, are either frequently losing their temper or are always angry. Often their mood shifts quickly to one of depression or anxiety, and then just as quickly shifts back to normal. When alone, they may experience depression, so they frantically avoid being alone.

John Craig Stewart sketches the character of Malcolm Fawlks in his "The Devil Can't Look Back." What incidents point to instability in Fawlk's interpersonal relationships, behavior, identity, and mood? Is there enough evidence to classify him as having a Borderline Personality Disorder? Could the title refer to Fawlks himself? If so, why?

THE DEVIL CAN'T LOOK BACK

John Craig Stewart

Old Malcolm Fawlks sat uneasily in the rickety wicker chair before the low burning fire. Now and then he wiped his hands on his dirty wool trousers and spread them to warm before the blaze. The wrinkled, sagging flesh of his face was half covered with a greyish-brown stubble of beard. The corners of his mouth twitched and when they did, he would draw his boney hand across his mouth as if to still some restless terror coming to life inside him. He leaned forward jerkily and spat into the fire and then straightened up in the chair, holding tight to the dirt-smeared arms. But his faded blue eyes were steady. They stared at the flickering blaze without shifting. They did not have the pleasant look of daydreams in them; they burned with the restless fever of a last hour, and behind them was the jumble of ten thousand ancient and unwelcome memories.

The winter night was quiet. There was not another house within two miles of old Fawlks's place, and he never heard even the bark of a dog that night. It was only when a sudden, sighing shift of the still cold air rattled the loose window panes that he knew the past was gone and that he was sitting alone in the present.

The old house had been there on the hill for over a hundred years, and it sagged wearily and hopelessly upon wind-worn and shaky foundations. The four broad stack chimneys seemed the only part of it which held out bravely against time and neglect.

It was not easy to bear, his being alone on this barren hill farm without a neighbor to help him bury his dead wife. When Abbie was alive, he had never wanted his neighbors even speaking to him, he never wanted anything from them when she was alive. Even after all the children were gone, he never worried about things so long as Abbie was there. They managed to get along for all those years. He sold his moonshine in the next county where people did not know him. He plowed the red hill land once a year and made a small crop of cotton and corn. Abbie seemed to keep things going when he was broke and drunk for a month at a time.

But Abbie was dead now. She had died that same afternoon in that same room. He had not thought she was going to die. He had sat there watching her with a scowl on his face. A woman ought not to get sick and mess up a man's life. Then she had opened her eyes and looked at him with a cold, terrible stare. She had shuddered as if a fit were on her, closed her eyes tight and turned her head away from him. When he got over to the bedside, she was dead. That was the way it was; Abbie had turned her face away from him and died.

Old Fawlks had not stopped to think what his life would be without Abbie. He had hitched his scrawny horse to the wagon and driven into Danby, ten miles up the road, for a wooden coffin. He had done that right away because he thought it would be easier to go ahead and bury her and get it over with. The sun was down when he returned, so he did not bury her that night. He laid her body just as it was in the coffin out in the cold hallway. But every time the thought of Abbie dying came back to him, it was like a sudden cold gust of wind against a naked body, and he would shift jerkily in his chair.

He got up and stood before the fire. He stared at the hall door for a long time. She's out there now; I wish I'd gone ahead and buried her. He cleared his throat with a gutteral rasp and turned around to look at the fire. It needed another log, but there was not another log in the room and he did not want to go outside for one. He was not afraid, but he did not want to open the door into the hall.

He kicked the charred logs; sparks flew out and the blaze flared up with crackling brightness, lighting an amber wavering semicircle about the hearth. The heavy walnut bed loomed black from the far side of the room.

The old bed, big and heavy. I'se just a little boy when I first slept in that bed. It was the night Mama and me came to live here on the hill. Papa in prison. That was when everything changed. People wouldn't speak on the streets; they said, "Ol Josiah stole the whole year's offering from the church." He was a steward in the church; the people never forgave him. Papa claimed he just borrowed it, said he was gonna replace it when the cotton was picked. But the jury found him guilty. The two policemen looked sheepish when he swore at them. He drew himself up real proud when they marched him off from the old house in Leighton. The big white house full of warm rooms and laughter. That was long ago. People changed. Mama wouldn't stay in Leighton, she took me and came back here to her old girlhood home. Mama came back home.

Old Malcolm got up, took the oil lamp in his hand and went over to the big wardrobe in the corner. He took out a quart jar of light colored whiskey and a glass. He poured it half full and sat down again in the wicker chair. He set the jar on the floor beside him and held the glass of clear liquor up between his eyes and the fire and watched it. He saw his hand trembling, and he took a large, quick gulp of the whiskey.

"Damn 'em, damn 'em all to hell," he muttered and spat viciously into the fire. By God, I never had to ask anybody for anything, he thought. I've been independent; I ain't had much but I never asked anybody for anything. I've lived my life like I saw fit and I've been the master here on this hill; nobody ever got it away from me. Nobody ever told me what to do. I've been the master and I've raised nine children. They hated me, I know; I was hard on 'em, but I raised 'em right. I made 'em work, but I gave 'em a home and all I had. Then they left me, by God, everyone of 'em left me; the ones that didn't die left me. I don't even know where a one of 'em is. Abbie was the only person to stay with me. She stayed with me 'til today, but she's gone now.

He leaned back and moved his eyes slowly about the room. He held his gaze on a spot where Abbie should be sitting, sewing or bending over an ironing board or just looking out the window at the land and the encircling woods. Yeah, he thought, Abbie was a good woman. She stayed with me through good and bad times. I mighta been a little hard on her sometimes. But, hell, how else you gonna handle a woman. I've seen these henpecked husbands in the city going around with their eyes on the ground. By God, you gotta keep a woman in hand and that's how I handled Abbie.

Malcolm Fawlks squirmed in his chair. It was twenty-five years ago now and he could hear her screams that night. It was a dark night, about like this. He came home drunk, so drunk he stumbled on the front steps. Abbie heard him coming because she was standing up in the room waiting when he opened the door and lurched in. The baby, Virginia, was six months old and she was asleep in her crib by the big bed. He staggered over and picked her up. He could remember her small sleepy head falling over on her chest as he lifted her. And then Abbie was at his side clawing at him, telling him he couldn't. She had done a lot of praying in their life together but she had never told him before he could not do anything. He pushed her aside but she came back trying to tear the baby out of his hands. He remembered the hot anger exploding inside him. He remembered dropping the baby roughly back in the crib and striking out at Abbie. The broad palm of his hand struck squarely across the side of her face. Abbie put her hands up over her face and backed away screaming like she did that night her first child was born. He staggered after her and struck her again and she sank to the floor; her screams descended to choking sobs. She was still there on the floor crying when he fell into the bed in a drunken sleep. The sound of her sobs mingled with the cries of the frightened baby in the crib.

Abbie never said anything to me about that. It was just like when all the other hard things happened; Abbie just kept on doing her work. She believed that whatever happened was God's will and she made the best of it. Her family always was mighty strong for church doings and such as that.

A low groan forced itself out of old Fawlks's chest. He got up and stood near the fire. The small flame of the lamp did not give much light and the fire was the only real brightness in all the dark night. He placed his hands on the mantlepiece and leaned over, his head down between his outstretched arms. He could feel the heat from the fire on his face. He stood there, his eyes staring into the glowing red logs thinking it was time for another drink, when he remembered Roy.

It was Roy who wanted to go to school so bad. And Abbie wanted him to go; she wanted all the children to go. I finally let Roy start when he was eight. Then one afternoon I came into the room where Abbie and Roy were talking. Roy shut up quick when he saw me.

"What you saying, Roy?"

"Nothing, Papa."

"I asked you what you're saying, Roy?" I can remember Roy standing there, his eyes wide and terrified, his whole body shaking.

"The boys at school, Papa; they—tole me you was no good."

I just stood there. "And what else did they say, Roy?"

Roy looked at the floor and twisted around. "They said Grandpa Fawlks was—was a thief."

Abbie looked away; she must have known what was coming.

"Damn you, woman. Didn't I tell you. You and your high flying ideas about school. The place for our children is here, here on this farm. You're just a hill woman, you got no pride. By God, how long does a man have to take these damn insults?"

"Get your coat, Roy, get it on." Roy backed off and fumbled with his coat, a little brown coat; his mother helped him find the sleeves. "You go back. You find the boy who said that and beat him, beat him half to death; if you have to, use a stick."

Roy was scared of me. His lips quivered and he began to cry.

"But they all said it, Papa."

"Well, find the one who started it, you know who he is, and beat him. If you don't, I'll whale the life out of you. I'll—damn you, I'll kill you."

He could remember Roy scampering out the front door, sobbing as he ran across the fields. He remembered watching his small figure disappear behind the corner of the woods where the road crossed his place. That was the last time any of the children ever entered a school

The truant officer had come to tell Malcolm Fawlks about the school attendance law. He was a fat, prim man. Malcolm listened to him for a while, then he went and got his rifle.

"There's a 'No Trespassing' sign on this place," he said; "if you ever come back here again I'll kill you."

No one came after that to bother him. He had expected the sheriff for a while, but he never came either. No, no one hardly ever came out here at all, he thought. I guess Abbie was a pretty lonesome woman. Maybe I shoulda let her go to church all those years like she wanted to. But anyway, she stayed on with me — til today.

Old Fawlks straightened up in front of the mantlepiece. He sat down in the chair and poured himself another drink. The fire was getting low; he drew the chair up closer to the hearth. He could feel the chill air of the room now. He gulped the liquor and cleared his throat. The sound of it was startling in the quiet room. The liquor turned hot in his stomach.

But she stayed on with me, he thought again. Even when all the children had gone, she stayed on.

Now he moved the chair to the side, he leaned forward, he searched the dark corners of the room with intense eyes. His boney Adam's apple moved up and down in a jerky spasm. "Why," he asked, "why did she stay with me?" He stiffened in his chair. The memory of a voice like echoes in the almost empty room: "These things are God's will, Malcolm, God's will." He felt the blood rush to his face and he jumped up from the chair.

"That's not true," he said in a shaky voice. "You damned ol fool." He swaggered before the mantlepiece, lifting the drink up and leering at it through half closed eyes. He drained the glass, sat down and poured some more whiskey. The sweat was standing out on his forehead.

But she did stay with me. The children left, one by one they grew up and left. They slipped away one by one. Roy left first. He ran away from the field one afternoon when he was chopping cotton. Jim, he was the mean one, the one I had to beat because he wouldn't work, but he never did really work. He had mean eyes, that boy. It was good riddance when he left, 'cept he took my horse with him. He was fifteen years old when he stole my horse and ran away. That was a long time ago. Wonder what ever happened to that boy? I never did break him. Nobody'll ever get a bit in his teeth.

Virginia was the last one; Virginia was my baby girl. Yes, by God, she was my pretty baby girl. She used to love me. I'd bounce her on my knee, she'd squeal and holler and shake her yellow curls. Maybe I should let her go to school like she wanted to and like Abbie begged me to; maybe she's been one to stay home if I had. She stayed til she was about seventeen, then she left.

I hunted all over Danby that night but I didn't find her. I came home, and there was just Abbie and me. Abbie looked like she was going to cry. But she just sat, just sat there. The place was mighty quiet, just Abbie and me.

Old Fawlks pressed the palm of his left hand against his forehead, the finger tips dug into his temples, and he drew the tight clasped hand down over the loose flesh of his cheeks.

But Virginia, she was a pretty thing, last time I saw her bout two years after that; she looked prettier than I'd ever seen her, like a woman, her hair was long and shiny, the color of corn silk, skin was white, pretty.

It was in Memphis. I was sitting on the soft red sofa watching the heavy velvet curtains, and waiting. Maxine musta kept them pulled across the door to make the place look mysterious. I heard 'em coming, I heard Maxine's voice, then her large bare arm reached in and drew the curtain back. "Come on in, honey," Maxine said, and Virginia stepped into the room. She stood there, like a little frightened child; but she was pretty, Lord, she was pretty. I was going to kill her right then. I was going to kill her but I waited too long. I got up and took a step toward her, then I couldn't go any farther. I don't know why, maybe because I loved her, maybe because I was glad to see her at last. I tried to speak, I wanted to ask her to come back home, but she screamed and ran out of the room. I heard the sliding doors move behind the curtain; I ran, but I heard the lock click before I got there. When I got the doors open, I went all through the house. She was gone.

"She's not coming back," Maxine said. She looked tired and scared. She was right. I never did find Virginia.

Old Fawlks stood up again. He could feel the liquor hot in his stomach. The fire was burned down to red embers but he did not care. His whole body was hot, and there were so many things he did not want to think about.

He squeezed the glass tight in his hand and peered across the dim room to the window. He walked over to it and looked out. Everything was black outside; not one star shown through the thick overcast. He tilted his grizzled head up toward the sky. He had seen Abbie do it a thousand times. He looked long before he spoke. His body swayed slightly.

"Dear Heavenly Father," he said and then paused. A great emptiness of dark silence answered him. He stood there for a moment with his head tilted up like that waiting, then he turned his back on the window. "What in hell's the Lord got to do with it?" he said and lurched back across the room and slumped down in the chair.

"Fire needs wood," he said and turned his head around and faced the familiar rocking chair across the room. Abbie was out in the hall, dead. He looked at the door again. He could hardly see it as distinct from the dim wall. He looked back at the red embers dying slowly in their grey bed of ashes.

He put his elbow on the arm of the chair and rested his chin in the palm of his hand. He seemed like an old man about to doze off to sleep, but he was thinking about Abbie again.

She was sure a pretty girl, just seventeen, when I brought her out here as my bride. We were alone then; Mama was long dead, the farm was mine. She was just a girl.

Abbie had been frightened, and he could remember back over all those years how she trembled when he touched her. But he knew how a man was supposed to take a woman and that was how he took Abbie that first night.

For a moment, he almost remembered it with pleasure; Abbie had been a pretty girl. Then he recalled the look on her face that night, he had seen her face plainly in the bright firelight, that night so long ago. It came back to him like an event of the day before. Old Fawlks moved his hand away from his chin and grasped the arms of the chair. Yes, he could remember her face white against the pillow, her wide dark eyes looking up at him with a stare of terror and disbelief. Then she had closed her eyes tight and turned her face away from him.

Old Fawlks was like a wounded vulture. He sprang up from his chair. "She looked at me that same way before she died this afternoon." He swung around to face the deep shadows of the room. All her life, Abbie had said, "These things are God's will." Abbie had never belonged to him. She had been waiting there to die when God willed it.

He turned around and seized the oil lamp in one hand, with the other he grasped the liquor jar and thrust it to his lips. He drained it, the liquid he did not swallow ran out the corners of his mouth and trickled down the stubbly grey beard and onto his coat. The jar slid out of his hand and broke with a loud crash on the hearth. He lurched toward the hall door. He swung it open, the lamplight fell upon the unpainted coffin.

"Abbie, Abbie, I want to look at you," he said. "I don't mean any disrespect, Abbie, I just want to look at you. I just want to look at you again." He stood there, his body swaying beside the coffin. His long boney fingers closed over the rough edge of the coffin lid. Slowly he lifted it until he could see the white cotton gown on Abbie's body. His breath was coming in quick hoarse rasps; he was trembling. He held the lamp up close, leaned over and looked at her face. The eyes were open; the cold impersonal stare of the corpse confronted him.

"God damn you, Abbie," he shouted and slammed the lid. He set the lamp on the coffin. He staggered back and glared about him. Then he turned and ran out of the front door and down the steps. He kept on running across the dark fields and into the darker woods beyond.

Avoidant Personality Disorder

Individuals with Avoidant Personality Disorder are torn between a strong desire for affection and acceptance and an equally strong fear of rejection. Their social relationships, understandably, are severely impaired.

Because avoidant personalities are hypersensitive, they constantly fear rejection. They usually maintain vigilance over all their relationships, ever alert for social slights, ridiculing comments, or disapproving hints.

Before they enter into relationships, they require unusual guarantees of unqualified acceptance. Consequently, avoidant personalities are socially withdrawn and have only one or two friends.

Avoidant personalities usually have low self-esteem. They devalue their accomplishments and emphasize their shortcomings.

In spite of all these characteristics, they crave affection and acceptance. Consequently, they are caught in an irresolvable tension.

Helen, in "A Touch of Marble," may have Avoidant Personality Disorder. It should be easy to point out scenes in which her hypersensitivity, need for unqualified acceptance, social withdrawal, low self-esteem, and desire for affection are manifest. How do Helen's relationships with Honey, her Aunt Margaret, and Roger affect her condition?

A TOUCH OF MARBLE

Don S. Potter

TIME: Now, and the past.

PLACE: A Hotel room in a city.

SCENE 1

A soft, drowsy, bronze light filters through the faded, cheap lace curtains framing the single window of a dingy hotel room. A tall, nervous woman in her mid-thirties enters the room from the outside hall. She comes into the room hesitantly, like a stranger, frightened and tensed, ready to fly away like a bird at sudden noise, somewhat overawed by the sudden reality of the four enclosing walls. She is followed by a blond, young sailor, whose white uniform almost floods the room. This, coupled with his obvious physical magnetism, makes him a rather brilliant figure, in sharp contrast to the older-looking woman. He begins to move a duffle bag from the middle of the floor.

PHIL. I'm not very neat.
HELEN. There's something timid about being neat. I hate being timid. I was
    scared to death, walking through that lobby. It was like — like I was a
    statue, alone in a big, bare room, and everybody staring at me.
[*She laughs nervously, her voice high and cool, then continues speaking
with a girlish softness in her voice.*] I was afraid someone would recognize
me.
PHIL. It's a big city.
HELEN. I've always felt like a stranger here — in the city.
PHIL. Cigarette?
HELEN. I don't smoke—or drink. There's an old joke about the girl who went

out on a date, and first she turned down cigarettes, then liquor. But then, when her boy friend began to look unhappy, she said: "Well, you don't have to smoke and drink to have a good time!"

PHIL. Yeah...

HELEN. I've never been in a hotel room — with a man.

PHIL. Oh? Well...

HELEN. You must think I'm really *bad*.

PHIL. Why, no, I — you don't *feel* bad, do you?

HELEN. It's just that—it's November, you know. [*She looks out the window.*] November's such a lonely time. I sat in the park all afternoon, watching the leaves — faded like the pages of old books people forgot to read. Sometimes I feel like an old book. [*She laughs nervously.*] Oh, there I go again! Self-pity's such a terrible thing, isn't it? And then you came — so white and clean — and you know what I thought? I thought: if I could touch you, if I could move my hands along your body, I could feel that whiteness in my hands, and I wouldn't feel...

PHIL. [*Moving toward her.*] Helen...

HELEN. No, we mustn't hurry. Why, we've got — we've got all night.

PHIL. Sure! I don't have to be back till Monday at eight. We've got the whole week end.

HELEN. There's something sad about this little room. You can almost hear old, dusty whispers — and nothing can hide the stains...

PHIL. I wish I could've afforded something nicer.

HELEN. How old are you?

PHIL. Nineteen.

HELEN. Nineteen? He was nineteen...

PHIL. He?

HELEN. Someone I knew a long time ago: a sailor. It was during the war; I met him in the park, just like I met you. It's funny, isn't it, the way history repeats itself? I liked him very much, but he went away.

PHIL. Oh! [*He starts removing his shoes.*] Might as well get comfortable.

HELEN. Before you came, there was an old man in the park, picking up papers, with a nail on the end on a stick. I tried to talk to him. I always talk to people. I asked him about the pigeons. When I go to the park, I always feed them. They're so gentle and soft— but so easily frightened. So I asked about the pigeons, but he didn't answer. He just laughed and went away. Later he came back, and he had a dead one. He said he walked up behind it, and stuck the nail through its back. Blood was dripping off his fingers — and he laughed.

PHIL. Is that why you'd been crying?

HELEN. I suppose...

PHIL. There *are* people like that — cruel people. You can't do anything about it.

HELEN. No...

PHIL. Best thing to do is not to think about things like that!

HELEN. I'm so silly. I'm probably ruining all the fun for you.

PHIL. No you aren't.

HELEN. Why did you stop? Why did you stop to talk to an old schoolteacher like me?

PHIL. Well, I don't know. I mean: well, I liked you. I liked the way you looked. I guess I thought you were lonesome, like me, kind of a stranger...

HELEN. A stranger?

PHIL. You weren't like the girls — well, the ones you usually run across. You're different.

HELEN. I hope not too different.

PHIL. [Somewhat anxiously.] Helen...

HELEN. I want you to understand: this never happened before. I've always been afraid. I was sitting there on the park bench, like every other week end for so long, and, well, it's almost winter. No one's ever ready for winter. But when I saw you I didn't think of winter any more.

PHIL. It's all right. I understand.

[Through the opened window comes the sound of music played on a piano. It is relatively simple music, and lushly romantic, suggestive of strong but youthful melancholy.]

HELEN. Do you hear that?

PHIL. Comes from that building next door. Must be a piano studio. They woke me up this morning.

HELEN. I know that song...

PHIL. Kind of sad! Want me to get some jazz on the radio?

HELEN. No. No. I remember that song. I had a girl friend; we were room-mates at a girls' school. She was very good at the piano. She was very good at everything. She used to play that song...

PHIL. [Approaching.] Helen...

HELEN. Are you sure that...I'm awfully nervous. Could I—could we have a drink?

PHIL. I thought you didn't drink.

HELEN. Not usually. But why don't you get a bottle of whiskey—a small one. And while you're gone, I'll order ice, and we'll have a little party here, and afterwards [With mock assurance.] we'll take a cold shower — not enough to be sober, but just enough to enjoy getting warm...

PHIL. Sounds great.

HELEN. I think I read that in a book somewhere...

PHIL. I'll be right back.

HELEN. Phil, I'm sorry.

PHIL. For what?

HELEN. To be so square!

PHIL. [*With a wave of his arm.*] Aww...

[*He exits.*]

SCENE 2

The piano music swells. HELEN *takes pins out of her hair and lets it fall across her shoulders, and removes her jacket and glasses, revealing a dress of a girl in her teens. She twirls around girlishly, suddenly stops, catching a glimpse of herself in the mirror of the dresser. As if extremely conscious of the music, she turns around and goes to the window, raises the shade and the window higher. Music floods the room, and is suddenly overridden by her nervously delicate, slightly hysterical girlish laughter. The lights dim. Then* HELEN'S *laughter merges with that of* HONEY, *offstage.*

HELEN. Honey? Honey Johnson, is that you?

[HONEY *enters: a thin but beautiful girl in a black dance costume with red sash. She carries a mirror into which she frequently stares.*]

HONEY. I'm practicing for our recital, Helen. Isn't it funny?

HELEN. Why is it funny?

HONEY. Such a sad song! I don't know why I laugh. I really don't.

HELEN. Come here, Honey, please...

HONEY. Look, Helen! It's my dance costume. I'm a raven—a beautiful raven who's been hurt. A cruel little boy has hurt me. See! [*Indicating the sash.*] This is blood; it's symbolic. At the end of the dance, I die. Isn't it sad, Helen?

HELEN. Yes, Honey, listen! I took that part in the play... [HONEY *stares.*] I didn't want to, since you were trying out for it, but...

HONEY. Oh, that! I've got more interests than that silly old play! Do you think I'm pretty, Helen?

HELEN. You're very pretty. Honey, I really didn't want the part...

HONEY. I don't *care* about the play! You know I'm the best *dancer* at Miss Carroll's. And I'm the best in Miss Prentice's gym class. And I write beautiful poetry for my English class...

HELEN. And you're my very best friend, Honey. My very best...

HONEY. I'm prettier than you. Aren't I, Helen?

HELEN. Yes.

HONEY. But I'm not as happy as you.

HELEN. You should be, Honey! You should be very happy. You're pretty, and you're good at everything.

HONEY. I'll never be happy; I know it. Never!

HELEN. Oh, yes, you will, Honey.

[HELEN *embraces her;* HONEY *shrinks back violently.*]

HONEY. Why did you touch me?

HELEN. Because I like you.

HONEY. Nobody likes me. And I know why. And I don't want anyone to touch me. You're like the others: jealous...

HELEN. No.

HONEY. You're jealous; but I don't care. I'll never care about anything. I don't care how many silly plays you're in!

HELEN. Oh, Honey...

[*She lays her hand on the girl's arm.*]

HONEY. *Don't touch me!* I'll tell Miss Carroll. I'll tell her you "touched" me! You know what will happen then.

HELEN. But I didn't mean...

HONEY. I don't care! I don't care what you meant. I don't care about anything. You know why? I'm a fallen leaf, that's why. [*Liking the melodrama.*] I'm a fallen leaf — and if I'm left alone, the wind will blow me around high in the air — and I'll be safe — away from everyone. But if you touch me, I'll crumble — all to pieces. [HONEY *laughs and dances around, and then comes back to* HELEN *angrily.*] Why did you take the part in the play? *Why?* You knew I wanted it. You knew...

HELEN. Honey...

HONEY. You hate me, that's why. You're jealous, like the others.

HELEN. That's not true.

HONEY. *It is!*

HELEN. I didn't want the part; they made me take it. Miss Prentice said I was shy, and it would do me good. She made me take it.

HONEY. That's a lie.

HELEN. I wouldn't lie to you, Honey.

HONEY. You would! You're jealous of me, because I'm so pretty. That's it, isn't it?

HELEN. No, Honey, please...

HONEY. It *is* true. You took the part, and you—*you* said you were my friend.

HELEN. I *am* your friend, your very best friend.

[*She puts an arm around her.*]

HONEY. [*Hysterically.*] No, don't touch me! I told you not to touch me. I'll tell Miss Carroll... [*Running toward the back, yelling.*] Miss Carroll! Miss Carroll! I'll tell them all: I'll tell them you put your hands on me! [*She runs off.*] Miss Carroll! Miss Carroll!

[*There is a long scream, followed by a crash of glass, then darkness.*]

SCENE 3

HELEN. *is collapsed on the bed.* MISS CARROLL, *a large, brisk administrator enters.*

MISS CARROLL. I'm so sorry, Helen. We should have known...

HELEN. Miss Carroll, it was my fault...

MISS CARROLL. We must try to forget it! It's been an ordeal for all of us — especially you, Helen. But you mustn't blame yourself for Honey's death.

HELEN. I did touch her, but...

MISS CARROLL. Now, Helen, I know how you must feel; but you'll get over it. And there's no reason for you to leave. You weren't responsible for...

HELEN. I caused her...

MISS CARROLL. My dear, you're very tense! — I'm having some medicine sent to you. I want you to promise to take it, and you must promise not to run away.

HELEN. I can't stay here. Not now.

MISS CARROLL. Helen, I don't know how much you knew about Honey. We were concerned about her, and we had sent her to our psychiatrist. He said she... Helen, it wasn't your fault at all: she was very disturbed. You musn't blame yourself, or...

HELEN. Miss Carroll, please help me! I feel so guilty.

MISS CARROLL. What is it, Helen? I *want* to help you.

HELEN. My hands — I'm afraid!

MISS CARROLL. You'll get over it after a while. Come here, my dear...

HELEN. I can't.

MISS CARROLL. You musn't be frightened of people, Helen... [*The lights begin to fade.*] You musn't be frightened...

HELEN. I can't forget.

SCENE 4

There is a momentary blackout in which MISS CARROLL *is replaced by the* AUNT, *who stands coldly and resolutely before* HELEN.

AUNT. You *must;* do you understand? Helen, you've got to get hold of yourself! You can't be afraid of people all your life. You're even afraid of me. Why, Helen?

HELEN. Aunt Margaret, I. . .

AUNT. If you'd come to me, Helen, just once and. . . [*A long pause.* HELEN *makes no response.*] You must put the memory out of your mind, or it will destroy you. Do your hear? — Destroy you, just as that reckless girl destroyed herself.

HELEN. I've tried. I've tried. If I hadn't touched her. . .

AUNT. Helen, this is painful for me, but I know girls gometimes get crushes. . .

HELEN. It wasn't that! She was the best friend I ever had. I wanted to be nice to her — show her I liked her. But she was so afraid, and I. . .

AUNT. Helen, I won't have you brooding — being morbid and hating yourself! There's no sense in moping and taking on. I want you to finish school. I know you haven't had it easy: your mother dying when you were a baby, then your father. But that girl, Helen, was *doomed.* There was nothing anybody could do for her.

HELEN. Why? Why did she do it?

AUNT. There *are* people like that, and there's nothing anybody can do. . . You must *forget;* you can't live your life with fear and guilt. That way, every moment can be torture. You've got to build your life as you go, Helen, step by step. God knows, we all have our troubles.

HELEN. What if something makes me remember? This *pain* . . .

AUNT. Pain? You don't know what pain is.

[*She becomes self-absorbed.*]

HELEN. A fallen leaf. . .

AUNT. What?

HELEN. That's what she called herself: a fallen leaf.

AUNT. [*Shaking her violently.*] Now, you listen to me! I'm sick and tired of your despair and self-pity.

HELEN. Please. . .

AUNT. If there was nothing between you and that girl, then there's no reason for all this. I know it was a shock — but you haven't tried to forget. You haven't tried!

HELEN. I have. You don't understand.

AUNT. Listen to me! Do *you* understand what it is to be fifty and live in a dark, empty house? To go to a stuffy classroom day after day, and smile at rows and rows of other people's beautiful children? Pain, you say? Do you have a pain that stays in your stomach twenty-four hours a day and won't stop — won't ever stop? You're young, Helen. You still have time: time for children, your own good life. [*She begins shaking* HELEN.] I won't let you destroy yourself, do you hear? I won't let you do it! I won't; I won't. [*The* AUNT *suddenly turns away and crosses the room. After a long pause, she turns back to* HELEN.] You must promise never to mention that girl again, as long as I live.

HELEN. All right, Aunt Margaret.

AUNT. I'm going down to help the Red Cross. I think you could at least . . . Why don't you take a walk in the park, Helen? Maybe you'll meet someone . . . [*Realizes what she has said.*] A walk in the park would do you good, instead of hiding from people.

HELEN. I'm not hiding.

[*The lights fade out.*]

SCENE 5

HELEN *repeats:* I'm not hiding. *The lights come up again, and the following scene takes place in the park. A young sailor,* ROGER, *approaches* HELEN, *whose back is turned.*

ROGER. Who are you hiding from?

HELEN. What?

ROGER. The big, bad wolf?

HELEN. The big — I was just . . . I come here all the time.

ROGER. Good for you! People are dying, I get drafted, and you play games in the park.

HELEN. I was — thinking.

ROGER. Then think about me! Don't you feel sorry for me?

HELEN. Why, no.

ROGER. Why not?

HELEN. You look very strong and happy. Why should I feel sorry for you?

ROGER. I don't know. I just think somebody should . . .

HELEN. If there's something wrong, if you're in trouble . . .

ROGER. There's nothing wrong, except war and bombs and rackets and crimes — and maybe the Russians — and a few other misfits . . .

HELEN. What else?

ROGER. Aw, nothing! I don't have time to brood; this is my first liberty in two months.

HELEN. Oh!

ROGER. Two can stroll as cheap as one, can't they?

HELEN. Well, I . . .

ROGER. Why the frown? Your mother warn you about sailors?

HELEN. My mother's dead.

ROGER. Oh.

HELEN. I live with my aunt. She says she won't retire — from teaching school — until I finish college. It's like taking her place . . . She has it all planned.

ROGER. Sounds like fun.

HELEN. Am I boring you? I don't want to keep you — I mean, if you have something you'd rather do.

ROGER. I can always get drunk, unless something turns up.

HELEN. Maybe you'd better — get drunk. I'm not very interesting.

ROGER. I'll decide that. Okay?

HELEN. Okay.

ROGER. I'm Roger. What's your name?

HELEN. Helen.

ROGER. Helen. I like that. Well, Miss Helen, what are you looking for in this great big park?

HELEN. Me? Oh — should I be looking for something?

ROGER. Most people are.

HELEN. Well, I guess I'm looking for something then. I don't know what, though.

ROGER. Do you know what I'm looking for?

HELEN. No.

ROGER. No idea?

HELEN. It must be something nice. You look so white and clean. You look like — like you shouldn't be touched — you're so white.

ROGER. Yeah? I'm not *that* white.

HELEN. I don't think anybody could look like you — so white — and not be very nice.

[HELEN *moves away, walks idly off by herself, as the lights dim. When they come up, it is dusk. A street lamp glows.*]

ROGER. I was thinking about what you said about me being *nice*. You don't know much about — well — people, do you?

HELEN. No, I guess I don't.

ROGER. You learn a lot when you live with them like I do. You get too close. They're animals. They move, they act, they smell like animals. You've just got to be a better animal.

HELEN. Do you really feel that way?

ROGER. Sure

HELEN. You sound so old! And you aren't as old as I am.

ROGER. I don't feel old. I feel young as that moon, and I want to have a good time. What about you?

HELEN. Yes, I suppose I want to have a good time.

[HELEN *walks away as before.*]

ROGER. You know, this is the third time I've been here, and all you do is turn around in circles. Don't you get dizzy?

HELEN. No.

ROGER. Don't you get tired of *not* doing anything?

HELEN. We talk a lot.

ROGER. We sure do.

HELEN. I know all about you: I know you're going overseas and . . .

ROGER. I don't know anything about *you*. I can't get close enough. I haven't even touched you.

HELEN. No, you haven't.

ROGER. I don't know why in hell I come back here.

HELEN. I'm not very exciting.

ROGER. You could be, Helen.

[He moves to her; embraces her.]

HELEN. Please . . .

ROGER. What is it?

HELEN. *[Breaks away.]* I'm sorry.

ROGER. You must like me: you keep asking me back. I don't get it.

HELEN. I like you very much.

ROGER. What are you afraid of?

HELEN. Whenever I think of putting my hands near you, I . . .

ROGER. Helen, I don't want you to think, well — that you're a pick-up or something. I know how we met; but you gotta meet some way. I like you. You make me feel good. I've never felt like this since I was a kid. You're so soft-looking, like a little bird. And the way you look at me . . . But I don't come in very often, and I sort of want to do something besides talk.

HELEN. There are — other girls.

ROGER. Sometimes I go out with other girls, after I leave you.

HELEN. You do?

ROGER. Helen, I want you to know: I don't care for those other girls. I don't even like them. I do like you.

[In the distance, a clock strikes hollowly.]

HELEN. I've got to go, Roger.

ROGER. Now?

HELEN. Yes. My aunt worries.

ROGER. For God's sake!

HELEN. Will you come Saturday? Will you meet me here?

ROGER. Look, Helen: we're going to sail any day. I may not even be in this country Saturday.

HELEN. You don't really want to come back, do you?

ROGER. Sure; I'll be here.
HELEN. You're sure?
ROGER. Yes.

[*He looks disappointed, scuffs the ground with his feet, and begins walking off. He turns back to look after her as the scene slowly fades out to blackness.*]

HELEN. [*Speaking in the darkness.*] You promised, Roger. You promised! And I had something special to tell you. I was going to be different. . .

SCENE 6

The lights come up bright in the dingy hotel room. PHIL *enters with the bottle in a paper bag.*

HELEN. [*Startled.*] Roger?
PHIL. What?
HELEN. I thought . . .
PHIL. I was someone else.
HELEN. Yes, for a moment.
PHIL. Well, I got a bottle.
HELEN. You surprised me, coming in like that. Do you like surprises? Life's no fun without surprises, do you think?
PHIL. I never thought about it.
HELEN. While I waited, I—I got to thinking about things—people I've known. About the boy in the Navy I told you about! And when you came in, I . . .
PHIL. Sorry, wrong guy!
HELEN. No reason to be sorry; it isn't your fault. He just didn't come back. Vanished.
PHIL. You want a drink?
HELEN. Isn't it strange? — I almost feel like I know you.
PHIL. You do!
HELEN. You meet girls in parks and maybe under street lights and you take them home, don't you? That's what Roger did. Maybe he met someone in another park somewhere. Maybe he died.
PHIL. You want a drink now?
HELEN. He's the only one, ever! Isn't it silly?
PHIL. You never married or anything?
HELEN. Oh, no. I'll be an old maid. Can't you tell?
PHIL. I think you're — attractive.
HELEN. Oh — While you were gone, I took my hair down. I just felt like it —

letting my hair down. [*She laughs self-consciously.*] It makes me feel much younger.

PHIL. You aren't old, Helen.

HELEN. I *feel* old. I'm thirty-four.

PHIL. That isn't old. It's just right.

HELEN. Just right for what?

PHIL. Why, to enjoy yourself.

HELEN. You're very handsome. You make me feel very strange. Roger was like that: so white and clean-looking. I wanted to touch him — touch his lips and his arms. Do you like to be — touched?

PHIL. Yes, I do. [*He is about to embrace her.*]

HELEN. [*Turns toward him, instinctively responding, then turns away.*] No . . .

PHIL. What . . . ?

HELEN. It isn't your — I want so much to put my hands against your face. But I know if I tried — like the old man in the park, running a nail through the little bird. I've always felt like that little bird.

PHIL. Something's happened to you, hasn't it? Something bad.

HELEN. No, not really. That's what's so funny. Nothing's ever really happened *to me.*

PHIL. *Look, why not have a drink?*

HELEN. [*At the window.*] It's still the same, isn't it?

PHIL. What, Helen?

HELEN. All the world outside. And us — I'm still me — and it's almost winter and the leaves have fallen . . .

PHIL. Do you live alone?

HELEN. Yes.

PHIL. Maybe you'd rather go . . .

HELEN. I live in a dark, empty house. You wouldn't like it there. It's so late — and cold. Are you cold?

PHIL. No.

HELEN. No, you're very warm. I can feel you now — warm like the sun on a little clear pool. But I'm so cold. My breasts are cold — and smooth like marble — like the breasts of a statue you shrink to touch. [*He moves toward her.*]You mustn't. . . [*She picks up a leaf from the window sill.*] I guess the wind blew it here from the park. It was all alone, and the wind brought it here. [*She carefully folds his fingers around it, and then, with great effort, slowly moves her fingers up and presses them against his lips. There is something both tremendously moving and pathetic about her final attitude, as if she knew well and perversely enjoyed her lost, fragile role.*] Don't speak! — It isn't your fault. If you touch me, I'll crumble — into little pieces.

[*She exits slowly through the door.* PHIL *watches her, speechless, then looks at his closed fist, opens it, and watches the bits of leaf float gently down. He gazes once more at the door through which she disappeared, shakes his head. The same music as in* SCENE 1 *begins again. He lights a cigarette; takes a couple of puffs, then viciously puts his heel on it and crumples it into the faded carpet.*]

CURTAIN

Dependent Personality Disorder

Individuals with Dependent Personality Disorder passively allow others to assume responsibility for major areas of their lives. They give up their right to make decisions concerning place of residence, friends, politics, and the like because they often lack the ability to function as indepedent persons.

Dependent personalities generally subordinate themselves to the person who makes their decisions. They accept subordination in order to avoid being rejected and, consequently, having to assume their rightful responsibilities. For example, a dependent personality will tolerate a physically abusive spouse in order to avoid any possibility of being deserted and left to rely on herself or himself.

Often dependent personalities cannot bear being alone except for brief periods. When left alone for several days, they become anxious and depressed.

The physical size of Penny Loomis in Sally Benson's "Little Woman" underscores her psychological dependence on Ralph, her husband. What incidents illustrate her passiveness and subordination? Does Ralph "enjoy" his dominant role in their marriage? What incidents provide evidence for answering this question?

LITTLE WOMAN

Sally Benson

Penny Loomis liked to look back to the day when Ralph had first seen her. It was the day she had first seen Ralph, too, but she didn't think of that. She remembered only the delighted, incredulous look in Ralph's eyes when he caught sight of her sitting in the large wing chair in the Matsons' living room. In the short skirts and long waists of ten years ago, she had seemed just like a doll. Later in the evening he had told her so. "I can't get over you!" he exclaimed. "You're so tiny!"

"Oh, I know! And I hate it!" she answered. "It's dreadful, really! About clothes, I mean. Why, I wear size eleven!"

"You could look taller," Louise Matson said. "Naturally, those flat-heeled shoes make you look awfully little. If you *wanted* to look taller, you could wear high heels."

Penny Loomis had surveyed her strapped, patent-leather shoes thoughtfully and then her eyes had rested for a rather long instant on Louise's substantial Size 7 brocade slippers. "It's all very well for you to talk," she replied ruefully. "Your feet are a decent size, not disgraceful little Chinese feet like mine. You have nice, *big* feet."

Taking her home that night, Ralph had commented on Louise's attitude. "She was just trying to be catty," he said. "And you were swell about it. You may be little, but you aren't *small!*" .

There was nothing to it after that first evening. It was as though Ralph never knew what hit him. There were three months of being engaged, of dancing night after night, attracting attention because Ralph was so tall— over six feet—and she was so tiny. He was enchanted with her daintiness and made jokes about it. "Now where," he would ask, looking over her head and pretending he couldn't see her, "did I put that woman I had with me?"

Everybody would laugh, especially Penny. "Big silly!" she would say. "Take me home!"

Everything she did pleased and amazed him. When, the Christmas before they were married, she presented him with a scarf she had knitted, he was genuinely overwhelmed. "I don't believe it," he said, smoothing it over and over with his hands. "You're not big enough to hold the needles."

He made so much fuss about the scarf at home that his mother, who had knitted scarves, sweaters, and socks for him all his life, was inclined to be bitter. "You act as though she'd knitted that scarf with her feet," she said acidly. "And, by the way, I put those golf stockings I just finished for you in your bottom bureau drawer."

His enchantment lasted long after they were married. It amused him to see her childish, round-toed shoes lying on the floor, to see her diminutive dresses hanging in the closet. Their house was full of company, too, those first months, men mostly, who marvelled with Ralph at the sight of Penny in an apron actually being able to get dinner, carrying platters of food almost bigger than she was.

They had no children, which was a pity, as Penny had fancied the idea of herself surrounded by tall, stalwart sons, but she had Ralph to flutter over and take care of. She made few friends and was content in their small apartment. Once Ralph asked her why she didn't go out more. "Do you good," he said, "to get out and play bridge or something in the afternoon. Why don't you look up Louise? You and she used to be pretty good friends."

Penny replied scornfully. Women were all right, she supposed. But she hated bridge, really. It was such a silly game. And she felt so funny going out with Louise, who was so tall. They looked ridiculous walking together. Ralph had laughed at that. "Say, listen," he said, "I'm taller than Louise."

"You are a man," she answered. "Men are supposed to be big."

She looked so little and so pretty that Ralph agreed with her. "Louise is kind of a horse," he said.

They spent their vacations in Canada, where Ralph liked to fish. And Penny, dressed enchantingly in boy's denim trousers, checked shirt, and felt hat, lounged against cushions in the canoe while he paddled. She would scream a little, hiding her head, as he took the fish off the hooks. When they walked, Ralph carried her over the rough spots and took her arm up the hills, so that finally, although he insisted she was no trouble, he took to fishing nearer the Lodge.

Sometimes he was surprised at the number of things a man who was married to a little thing like Penny had to think of. There was the question of theatre tickets, for instance; he had to make an effort to get seats in the first row so that Penny wouldn't have to crane her neck or sit on her coat to see the stage; he must also remember to shorten his steps when they walked together or Penny got tired and out of breath; things must be left where Penny could reach them without having to stand on a chair.

Once he had spoken to her about it. "Gosh," he said, "it is kind of tough to be as little as you are! I never thought how it must be for you, not being able to do things that other people do."

The instant the words were out of his mouth, he knew he had said the wrong thing. "I'd like to know what I can't do that other women can!" she told him indignantly. "I think I manage to keep busy!"

He had to admit she did keep busy. In fact, she was never still. She was as busy, he thought, as a canary in a cage, fluttering, picking, keeping up an incessant chirping. "Sure you keep busy," he said. "Busy as a bird."

When they ahd been married almost ten years, he went on a business trip to Chicago. The thought of being left all alone frightened Penny and she made a great deal of it. He must put a chain lock on the front door and write down where he would be every night so that she could call him in case anything happened. Her anxious fluttering depressed him, and his depression lasted until he was safely on the train and seated in the warm, noisy dining car.

His second night in Chicago, the man he had come to see, a Mr. Merrick, asked him out for dinner. Mrs. Merrick went with them. She was a plain-looking woman, a little too stout, but there was something pleasing in the monotony of her solid brown hair that had no disturbing highlights, in her soft, friendly brown eyes, and her uninteresting brown felt hat. She had the appearance of a woman who had contemplatively set aside all personal vanity and turned to other things.

Ralph was surprised to find himself having a rather hilarious evening with them, and delighted to learn that Mr. Merrick had about decided to go back to New York with him and wind up their business for good and all. "And take me," Mrs. Merrick said.

"Oh, sure, take you," Mr. Merrick agreed.

And Ralph had added, "You bet!"

That night at the hotel, he wrote to Penny. It was a long, enthusiastic letter, and he wrote everything he could think of to please her. "They asked all about you," he wrote. "And I told them you were no bigger than a minute and as pretty as a picture. So we'll take them to dinner, when I get back, which should be about Friday. I'll wire exactly when. I miss you."

As he wrote "I miss you," he stopped and put his pen down on the desk. It struck him that he hadn't missed Penny at all, while she — well, he supposed that she was rattling around in the apartment not knowing what to do with herself. It occurred to him that she ought to have something to do, something better than fussing around with things at home. Not that he wanted her to work, he thought. Penny was far too helpless and little to be able to cope with a job. His heart softened when he remembered their evenings together with Penny curled up on his lap as he sat in the big chair, talking to him a mile a minute in her rather high, clear voice. He was ashamed of the many times he had wished she would read more, and recalled one dreadful evening when he had looked up from his paper at the sound of her nervous wandering about the room to say, "For the love of Pete, *light,* can't you?"

Thinking of these things and of the fine evening he had had with the Merricks, he picked up his pen again and underlined "I miss you."

The trip back to New York with the Merricks was great, but Penny was not at the station to meet him. "Unless we've missed her," he said gaily. "She's so darned little, she's easy to miss."

He assured the Merricks that he would just dash home, change his clothes, pick up Penny, and meet them at their hotel.

Penny was waiting for him at home. She was almost hysterically glad to see him, and he noticed that the house was shining and spotless, with fresh flowers in the vases and a wood fire burning in the grate. She was already dressed for the evening in a pale-pink taffeta dress with many ruffles, and stubby satin shoes tied with large bows. She wore a ribbon around her hair, and in the shaded lights of the living room she looked very young. It was only when she followed him to the bathroom to talk to him while he shaved that he noticed her more closely; the line of her mouth, always too thin, looked set and unhappy; the skin on her face looked drawn; and there was more than a sprinkling of gray in her black hair. The pink taffeta dress looked suddenly absurd on her, and he wished that she had worn something more suitable, something more her age. Why, Penny must be thirty-five!

She was curious about the Merricks, she said. "I never heard you make so much fuss over any two people in my life. What's she like?"

"Mrs. Merrick?" he asked, struggling with his stiff white shirt. "Oh, she's darned nice."

"Oh, I *know* that," Penny answered impatiently. "I know you think she's nice. What does she look like? Is she pretty?"

"No," he told her. "You couldn't call her pretty."

"Well, is she big, little, fat, thin?"

"She's not little," he said. Why, she'd make two of you."

This seemed to satisfy her and she asked no more about the Merricks.

At the hotel they were told that Mr. and Mrs. Merrick were waiting for them in the main dining room. Walking through the lobby and down the long corridor, Penny was pleasantly conscious of the stir they created. She even shortened her steps a little, so that she appeared to be keeping up with Ralph by tripping at his side.

Mrs. Merrick's first words to her were what she expected. "Why, you're tiny!"

Penny laughed sweetly and looked up at Ralph. "Yes isn't it silly?" she said. "I must look perfectly absurd beside Ralph who is so enormous."

Mrs. Merrick's eyes took in every detail of Penny, her dress, her shoes, and the ribbon around her hair, and then she said, in almost the exact words that Louise had used so many years ago, "Do you know, with heels you'd look much taller. Why, you must be five feet one or so, and with good, high heels you'd look three inches taller. That would make you five feet four, which is a nice height. A great many movie actresses are five feet four."

Penny laughed again, but she flushed slightly.

"Now, Nellie," Mr. Merrick said, "don't go to making people over the first minute you see them. Maybe Mrs. Loomis *likes* to look small."

"Nonsense!" Mrs. Merrick exclaimed heartily. "No one wants to look like a midget! That is, no one wants to look *too* different. I know I was awfully tall for my age when I was about fifteen and I felt terribly about it. I was a sight, I can tell you."

And you're a sight now, Penny thought furiously. She chose a seat next to Mrs. Merrick and during dinner she rested her small, thin hand next to Mrs. Merrick's large, square one. She picked at her food daintily and exclaimed pleasantly when the other woman ordered ice cream with chocolate sauce for dessert. "Not that I wouldn't love it, but I just haven't *room,*" she said.

Later, when the music started, she was surprised to see Ralph spring eagerly to his feet and ask Mrs. Merrick to dance.

"I haven't danced much lately," he said. "But let's go!"

He put one arm around Mrs. Merrick's waist and they started off. It was pleasant to have her face so near his own, to feel her soft, straight hair brush his forehead. She wore a dark-brown velvet dress, not very new and not very smart, but she had dignity and she moved smoothly with him across the dance floor. Over her shoulder he saw Penny dancing with Mr. Merrick. She was looking up into his face and talking brightly and animatedly. Mr. Merrick was bending down to catch what she was saying, smiling a frozen sort of smile, but he didn't look very happy.

The rest of the evening was not especially successful. Ralph tried in vain to recapture the spirit of hilarity he had felt with the Merricks in Chicago. But there was a sort of uneasiness in the air, even though Penny showed them several match tricks.

He was a little relieved, as they said good night, to learn that the Merricks had bought theatre tickets for the following evening and were leaving the day after for Chicago.

All the way home, Ralph sat in one corner of the taxi watching Penny as she talked. Her head was bent slightly to one side in the birdlike way she affected, and the white street lights flashing through the window were not kind to her. As he looked at her, she seemed to grow smaller and smaller until there was nothing much left of her but a pink taffeta dress and a pink ribbon. It had started to rain and the drops on the glass cast black dots on the pink taffeta dress, and he had the impression that it, too, might eventually disappear.

He did not notice that the cab had stopped in front of their apartment until Penny's voice gaily brought him back to earth. It was habit that made him pick her up and carry her across the wet, slippery pavement. And for such a little woman, she felt surpisingly heavy in his arms.

Compulsive Personality Disorder

Compulsive personalities are inappropriately preoccupied with trivial matters such as making lists, assigning priorities, and determining rules. Their preoccupation often inhibits their ability to perceive the total context in which they live. Their attention is narrowly focused. As a result, they often seem emotionally cold. Their inability to express warm and tender feelings generally keeps relationships on a formal, serious plane. In addition, compulsive personalities may insist on doing things their way, but they are often indecisive as to how to do them. They are fearful of making a mistake, so they procrastinate. Their insistence and indecision often cause resentment or pain in others, but compulsive personalities are rarely aware of that, they are too busy with their inconsequential matters.

Compulsive personalities often have difficulty relaxing. They delay pleasurable activities until the list is finished or the rules established. However, the list is seldom completed and the rules continue to expand, so relaxation and pleasure are postponed indefinitely.

Invariably, these traits contribute to troubled relationships and to a pervasive feeling of dread with which compulsive personalities have learned to live; they have their trivialities.

The title of Douglas Woolf's short story, "The Flyman," announces George Nader's preoccupation. How does his preoccupation inhibit his perception of his environment? It should be easy to note examples of his lack of warmth. Some attention should be paid to George's wife, Zoe. Is there enough evidence to determine whether Zoe also is a compulsive personality?

THE FLYMAN

Douglas Woolf

When the moving men had shoved and strapped the last piece, the last slippery convenience, inside the moving van, George Nader looked about him with very little sense of loss, for everything that remained, the flypaper, the swatters, and he believed the turtle bowl, was his. Had Zoe been divorcing him and taking along her legal property as dowry to another man, the division of goods would have been exactly this, except of course that she would then have been leaving George himself behind to enjoy the pure, seeming inconvenience of the house. He would never know what time it was: only sit at the back-door and watch the cactus shadows on the sand outside, perhaps noting whether the sun or the moon was moving them. With the hours thus confused there would be no prompt, rude guests to demand his silent presence in the living room, their polished mahogany cage would be gone, not to mention their electricity. He would look without commitment at the mirrorless walls, for the loathsome electric razor would be buzzing the fuzz on some other cheek or the stubble underneath Zoe's arms. He would sleep, night or day, in the built-in bathtub, and survive on grapefruit and oranges and the neighbors' eggs. Delighted with such pictures, smiling upon Zoe's swollen rear, he took up a handy swatter and brandished it enchantingly until the men returned.

What he liked about the moving men was their pride in being watched. They spoke in low rough voices, cursing only humorously when his flypaper caught them up, pausing occasionally in their work to compliment Zoe upon this piece or that but once outside tossing her furniture quite insultingly among them as though it were simply so much stuff which they alone knew the real value of. At the very first, when they had stood in the living room wondering where to begin, he had said, "Take everything with faces, or legs," and had settled in a chair to watch how nicely it worked out that way, with the exception of a few planters of ivy and the pasteboard boxes of odds and ends, until they had taken the chair itself from under him. "Easy now," he had standing said, and when they smiled expectantly as though hoping he had found some failure in their work: "Everything but me, that is." And now he stood grinning as they shoved respectfully past Zoe at the door, where she hoped her presence would urge them to use a little more care, less skill, in their wild slippery sprint to the van, but as the van door cracked shut he sobered his face for her turn to him.

"Looks different, doesn't it?" he quickly said, not in sympathy or even sincerity but only wanting to take the words from her pursing mouth. "Bleak?"

"It does, it does," she agreed, forced to it, but hastily regained herself: "We filled two-thirds of a van, you know."

"Big baby too," he shot.

"It was," said Zoe.

He looked fiercely away from her fuzzy head, to the grey, permanent shadow of the departed television-radio. What had she expected of him once, that he had not given her? He supposed that at first it had been children, although as a struggling, wild-eyed veteran his reasons had been entirely economic, plausible, and she had agreed with him. Only in time, as he progressed, had the question become less economic than eugenic, and she had agreed again. How could she not. For it had grown increasingly clear that no child of his could have the common view, or chance. Today the question was no longer asked, yet he felt that secretely, in whatever depths she had, Zoe would have welcomed the pleasures of an abortion, the living proof that in fact she could create. Few men would help her prove it now, he and time had taken care of that. So they had settled on an easier enmity, as less harrowing, more mentionable, her loss of the housewife's sweet dependence which he had so easily usurped for himself. Deprived of her empty days, Zoe had filled her nights with appliances. Looked at in this way the unwieldy procession which he had just witnessed could not be said to betoken Zoe's unfathered children so much as a bitter, accurate accounting of Zoe's paychecks, and this cynical view of it made him able to turn to her again. "Wait until we get up north," Zoe said.

"Oh, wait." He followed her zigzag course toward the kitchen, even he finding it oddly difficult to avoid the flypaper strips with the furniture no longer there to inhibit him, and he fancied he heard soft curses among Zoe's fat breaths. Watching her unwind from a gummy strip, he felt himself struck by a change in her appearance, the first he could recall in years. It was as though the moving men had carted off not only her movables but her very makeup itself, that pink, almost livid glaze with which she regularly hid from him and all the world the face he had loved twelve, maybe fifteen years before. And seeing in this abrupt way how dry and sucked of life she was, finally justifying her endeavor to look like anyone else but Zoe, he felt a sudden terror of time and reached his hand to her. "Zoe."

Zoe took his hand.

"I'm sorry, Zoe."

She patted it, and now he watched her puffy fingers drape gummed paper along the soft, freckled flesh of his outstretched arm until it clung to the hairs there securely enough for her to draw free of it. Looking up from dead and drying flies, he saw her bright black eyes twinkle with something between defiance and disgust. "Why this?"

"Because," she said. "It's yours isn't it?"

"Ah." His hand shot sidewise for a buzzing fly, caught it effortlessly in mid-flight and tossed it stunned to the floor for his ready foot to quash. There had been a time when Zoe would have watched this exhibition with genuine admiration, but today she turned sharply off as though he had belched or gassed the place. Well, as the doctor said, some men hate Mexicans and Republicans, some beat their wives.

"George, promise you'll have it all cleared out when I get back?"

"Back?"

"From the market, George."

He suddenly smiled, at the picture of them following that two-thirds van of conveniences through eighteen hundred miles of ice and snow and stopping from time to time to eat cold canned goods beside the road. Certainly he would not build a fire, and he could not imagine heat from a fire of Zoe's. This was not a new thought, but he added to it now the one that Zoe would surely have packed the can opener away in the kitchen appliance box, and he spoke hurriedly lest she too might think of it. "You hurry right along." he said. "I'll take care of everything."

"Well . . ." He followed once more as she zagged through the kitchen, the front room, the hall, somehow this time escaping entanglement but turning finally at the front door to seek her purse. With all the furniture gone, there was nowhere for Zoe to hunt. Even at best, things had been, as he thought, fuzzy around their home. For Zoe's talents were almost purely operative, or rather her affinities: she was a superlative driver of automobiles, unhampered by any comprehension of what made them run; she could twirl painful clarity from television sets, just so long as their extension cords and socket plugs were good; and of course over both their lives loomed that cryptically initialed machine, monstrously dialed, with which she made airplane parts whose names and places she did not know. Otherwise there was that fuzziness, that flapping, searching, beseeching, wasted fuss which made him grind his teeth and wince. But we do not hate people, he recalled, not even for enduring us, and grinned a wistful grin at Zoe before turning his attention to his papered arm. "Look on the mantel piece," he said, and imagining Zoe's bleak glare of thanks waved his swatter graciously.

He felt her departure in much the same way that he felt the flypaper tear free of his hair and flesh, as a paradox of pain, relief. He tensed to the chattering porch, to the car's whamming doors, to the pitiable whine of a young motor overtaxed and finally to the smothering cloud of dust that seeped through the fine-meshed screens, yet he was glad. When he turned it was almost as though Zoe had really left, scattering her own ashes behind her over the neighborhood; in twenty minutes, he knew, she would be back to stir them up again.

Meanwhile he did not mind too much what he had to do. It was the thought alone that had almost paralyzed him, when the furniture and Zoe had still been there, the thought of tearing down all his ingenious, tactically flawless stations without the possibility or necessity of ever replacing them. But now in the empty house his defenses hung like so much random paper, forlornly grouped, disorganized. What he did, quickly, was start at the front door and work his way in as nearly a straight line as possible along the south wall, yanking flypapers as he came to them and draping them in careless yet attractive disarray over the handle of the swatter which he still held. Then quickly back along the other wall and crisscross here and there about the room. When he had filled his swatter he reached for another, presently a third, but half a fourth finished the livingroom. The bedroom and kitchen yielded two swattersful apiece, one each for the bathroom, pantry, hall. Back in the livingroom he stuck his entire collection upended in the empty turtle bowl. Gathering the remaining, unused swatters, he added them one by one with flourishes to his bouquet, stood back to pass on it.

He was glad to have found some use for the turtle bowl. It had not worked at all. Despite weeks of enthusiastic experimentation, under the most favorable conditions he could devise, George had never known a turtle to catch a fly. Place twelve flies within two hungry turtles overnight in a covered bowl, and in the morning twelve unmolested flies emerge. Put syrup on a turtle's nose, a fly may eat his sweets in peace. It did not work! Only if you dropped a fly into a turtle's water would it partake, and George refused to offer such sacrifices, dead or alive, simply that a turtle might stuff himself. He donated his turtles to the neighborhood and turned his attention to new pursuits. Chronologically the gyrotraps had come next after the turtle failure, and it was these he would attend to as soon as he had disposed of the mess in the turtle bowl.

Most weekends he did not go outside, except very briefly at lizard rotation times, for these were George Ingersoll's days at home. Not that he disliked the other George, he simply did not like the sense of driving him indoors. There had been a time when their weekends had been quite otherwise, they had become almost more than neighbors, finding several dependable interests in common such as their handicaps (mostly physical for the other George), their memories of beautiful, terrible northern winters which in past years they had somehow both survived, and more particularly their memory of North Africa and its big, blood-sucking flies which a man could look down upon, whether feeding on his own sores or on a corpse of whatever nationality, and say this is Evil, it isn't the Jerries after all. They had of course also had their common dismay at finding themselves banished by doctors to another Africa, a New World Sahara, their sense of loneliness and exile in this wasted land and their exasperated fascination with its flora, fauna and insect life. Weekends they had fought the desert together side by side in their back-yards, tearing up its cactus and tumbleweed, coupling their two hoses to lay its dust, attacking its blackwidows, scorpions, flies with lethal insecticides, all the while offering bitter, gasping encouragement to one another across the fence. But soon it had become clear that their intensities were not the same, that one could be satisfied with a mere surface tidiness that the other fiercely disdained. George Ingersoll spent more and more time resting on his canvas chairs, now looking contentedly at his swept backyard, now at George, his occasional shouted encouragement grown amused, polite. A certain re-straint had grown between them as nowadays it so easily did (people no longer visited the Naders, they came in small explorative groups instead) and it ended with their reverting to a neighborly distrustfulness. George un-derstood. The other still had the so-called job, was employable, while George himself had long ago lost the benign effects of the six-day purge. He understood, yet it surely hurt him that his neighbor no longer showed sym-pathy for what he was trying to do, neither took time to inquire about his experiments nor looked at them. Thus he was surprised, or a little angry, to find George on this last day lingering outside, hanging on the fence above the rubbish cans which they had found it easiest to continue sharing stealth-ily. "Morning George... Ah morning George." They performed this cere-mony solemnly, each glancing sidewise to see if the other still smiled at it. Neither did, though with George Ingersoll it was hard to say, for pain and the desert sun had long ago combined to draw back the brittle skin around his mouth into a permanent grimace. Whenever George looked up at him he was unpleasantly aware of his own soft juiciness. "Hello, George," he said again, and falsely coughed. "How have you been?"

"Oh fine, fine." George Ingersoll said, and now he did appear to smile at a ghastly joke. "And you?"

George also smiled. "Haven't seen you around much, George," he said, at the last minute muffling the "for a year or two."

"Yes, been busy inside," was said. There was a pause, while George tugged at the stubborn garbage lid. "Well, Zoe's transfer came through at last?"

"Yes, it came through," George said, banging the lid with his free fist.

"Give it one on the other side," George Ingersoll advised, and George gave it a brutal one. "No, one on the side of the *top*," and George belabored it everywhere. He put down the turtle bowl, grasped the lid handle with both big hands and lifted the entire barrel off the ground, shaking it furiously from side to side. But we do not take out our anger on inanimate objects, and cursing he let the whole thing drop. The lid bounced off. "Ah," he said, swatters clattering in.

"I wouldn't mind having that bowl, if you're done with it."

George passed the bowl over his shoulder, over the fence. "It's no good," he said, wiping his hands of it.

"Looks like just the thing for Miriam's fish."

"Oh fish — I never did try fish."

George Ingersoll patted the bowl. "I don't suppose you'll need any of this, up north?"

"No, none of it."

Still patting, George Ingersoll glanced at his neighbor's yard, then shame-fully away again. "What about your lizards, George?"

George, who had stooped for the garbage lid, straightened quickly to the sidewise face. "You'd like them, George?"

"No no no, just curious."

"Ah." George came down hard, jamming the lid back on for George.

"I don't suppose they'd live through the winter there, even if you needed them?"

George shook his head, and it was almost as though he were shivering.

George Ingersoll too looked cold. "George, what does the doctor say?"

"The doctor? Not much — it might be good for me." Probably what the doctor had said to Zoe was that anything, even painful death, could be considered a benefice. But the doctor was no medical man, George had long ago passed them. "They say there's work up there, you know."

"I certainly hope so, George." When they looked briefly at one another now, it was almost in their old way, with common memories. George Inger-soll put out his hand. "I certainly hope the change of climate is good for you."

"Well, thanks, George," he said, taking the knotty hand reluctantly in his own soft freckled one. What he would like to have known before he took it was whether his eyes blurred at the sympathy of a friend or at the certain euphemisms of a hypocrite.

"We'll certainly miss you, George."

"Oh, well now," George said, and it almost blinded him, his dubious sentiment. He yanked free his hand to wheel away. "*Well* now, George."

"I certainly . . ." Fortunately some of the Ingersoll children were fighting now, and hugging the turtle bowl George moved to disentangle them. "I'll see you, George."

Oh oh oh, will you now, George thought, stalking quickly along the fence to the garage, the shop. He emptied the wheelbarrow of rusty tools and dragged it wickedly to the shop's locked door. He had the key, had it at all times on a string looped around his belt. Quickly inside, he swung the door on howling Ingersolls. Two years ago he had papered the ceiling and walls with flypaper (no paste, no waste, the flies make their own design) but now in the broken light of the one narrow window he noted how the ceiling curled and peeled, the walls writhed disgustingly, their glue had dried. The place smelled greyly of dust and wings, nor did the 200-watt ceiling lamp do much to clear the atmosphere. As it turned out, he would not have to redecorate.

His inventions lay everywhere, on the benches and shelves, and on the floor. These were mostly the gyrotraps, tiny razor-blade fans which he had connected in series to a motor salvaged from a Lionel train. Each fan was designed to fit snugly into a No. 2 can liberally coated with marmalade. (These had worked, although their blades required daily honing and from time to time their shafts would gum.) Then too there was the syrup door: a delicate device which the weight of three inverted flies could trip, slamming them against a red brick wall. (There were only three of these, for he had been unable to make them react to the weight of a single fly, and it had tormented him to think how many strays escaped.) There were several examples of the Infallible Fly Bath, simply a solution of molasses and hydrochloric acid (which he made himself by combining sulphuric acid with common table salt) in small glass tubes. These had worked very satisfactorily indeed, until neighbors began to understand what was happening to the noses of their cats. So it did not bother him very much to dump everything in a box and wheel it out for the garbage man. He did at the last minute leave one example of each behind, on the slim chance that some future scientist might find them a starting point, a useful groundwork for further exploration in the field. Not that this possibility greatly moved him either, for in his heart he knew that with the lizards he had come as close to a final answer to the problem as any man could, or would.

Here at last was what did hurt, having to gather his beer bottles now at the very time when he had finally perfected a formula for their rotation, a formula based on the observed frequency of flies at a given location at a given hour of a given day, as modified by such known variables as temperature, cloud covering, wind, humidity, and taking into account too such intangibles as the probable traumatic effects upon flies of his increasingly devastating war against their kind. Yet if the rotation formula was a marvel of deviousness, the trap itself was almost casual in its simplicity. Squeeze a small, vaselined lizard into an empty beer bottle, feed him just enough flies to prevent his escape; now coat the bottle mouth with almost anything at all, and wait. (No electricity, no mechanical parts, after a few days at large a lizard may be used again.) He gathered the bottles quickly but gently, arranging them in neat tiers in the wheelbarrow, and he wheeled them smoothly out over the desert to a rock he knew. There he cracked each of the forty-eight bottles with deft little taps, being careful that the lizards were not cut by the broken glass. Even at that, and despite his practice of selecting his lizards for healthiness, one lizard had succumbed. Impossible to say how many flies he had taken first, although in death he did look well-satisfied. George buried him. Now he stood for a while watching the others stagger over the desert, their bloated bodies unwieldy on their stiff short legs. Facing his wheelbarrow toward the house, he steered with care among his glutted friends. Ahead Zoe's dust was in the air, and Zoe herself waited at the kitchen door for him. "You did a nice job," she said.

"Thanks, Zoe."

"All ready now?"

Silently he looked about his experimental yard, a desert once again. He raised his eyes to an evilly buzzing fly, too high for him, and he did not move or speak until it came back again. He did not snare it at once but watched it cautiously circle his head, allowing it this last time the appearance of teasing him. When it finally settled on a freckled arm, he picked it off and held it out to view. "When you are, Zoe."

"Oh, why don't you get in the car," she said, and she followed him.

"You've remembered everything?"

"Yes."

It almost seemed she had. The canned goods lay boxed in the front seat, a shiny new opener visible. He knew their bags had been in the trunk for several days, and climbing into the car, into the back, he could smell the sweet insecticide. Despite the noonday temperature, all windows were tightly shut. He smiled at how narrowly Zoe opened the driver's door, how nearly flat she squeezed, how quickly she slammed once she was in.

"Mind if I open a window, Zoe?"

"Please, let's not."

"It's hot in here."

"It's hot everywhere."

"It smells."

"Let's wait until we're underway, at least," as the motor howled.

"Ah." Outside, George Ingersoll was leading his wife forward to see them off, and Zoe stopped the car to point the friendly neighbors out to George. All arms were raised; with the windows up the pantomimic mouths could have said anything, oh-oh-oh perhaps. Now the saving children must have yelled, for the Ingersolls turned their wagging heads and ran. Releasing brakes, Zoe gaily blotted out the farewell scene.

"Now?"

"Wait until we're on the highway, George."

So he sat waiting, his eyes closed to the dusty light, his breath almost closed off too, until he felt the car spring free of sand and heard the tires take up their gleeful howl on a highway paved with kitten fur. "Now, Zoe?"

"Oh, *wait*."

But he leaned forward anyway, not toward the window but toward the driver's seat, his hand going up. He might have slapped down on her then and there, had Zoe not caught the movement in her overhead looking glass. He hung there rigidly.

"Did you see one, George?"

"No."

"Well, please remember our frontseat rule."

"Sorry, Zoe." Leaning back again, tilting his head to rest, he continued to look at Zoe. But from the lower edges of his sight he could see his great short-sleeved spotty arms, folded across his chest, and from the fuzzy edges of his consciousness could hear his big hands slapping quietly.

"What now?" Zoe wanted to know.

"Don't worry, Zoe." He watched her shaking head. "You're happy, Zoe."

"Well?"

"No, I'm glad for you," he said. His hands were working harder now, moving rhythmically and conscientiously from freckle to freckle over his juicy arms, as Zoe turned round to him. Slap slap slap, he answered her. "I'm really glad for you."

"The temperature in St. Paul last night was two below."

"Oh, it was? Below?"

"Snow is probably falling now."

"It *is*?"

In her looking glass she smiled at him. "They say the winters are nine months long."

"That's all right," he said, and also smiled, for he would have lots to do.

Passive-Aggressive Personality Disorder

Individuals with a Passive-Aggressive Personality Disorder indirectly resist the legitimate demands of their vocation or their social responsibilities. For example, a woman may resent the demands of being a mother and housekeeper, so she fails to do the marketing, laundry, cleaning, and other chores. When confronted with her neglect, she makes excuses rather than openly expressing her resentment at these demands. Rather, she expresses her resentment through her procrastination, dawdling, stubbornness, "forgetfulness," or intentional inefficiency. Behavior of this kind in a variety of situations over a long period of time indicates her pervasive ineffectiveness. She has a Passive-Aggressive Personality Disorder.

The unnamed speaker in Robert Browning's "Soliloquy of the Spanish Cloister" hates a fellow monk, Brother Lawrence. What legitimate demands of cloistered living does the speaker resent that Brother Lawrence accepts? To what indirect act of aggression does he confess?

SOLILOQUY OF THE SPANISH CLOISTER

Robert Browning

1

Gr-r-r — there go, my heart's abhorrence!
      Water your damned flower-pots, do!
If hate killed men, Brother Lawrence,
      God's blood, would not mine kill you!
What? your myrtle-bush wants trimming?
      Oh, that rose has prior claims —
Needs its leaden vase filled brimming?
      Hell dry you up with its flames!

2

At the meal we sit together:
      Salve tibi! I must hear
Wise talk of the kind of weather,
      Sort of season, time of year:
Not a plenteous cork-crop: scarcely
      Dare we hope oak-galls, I doubt:
What's the Latin name for "parsley"?
      What's the Greek name for Swine's Snout?

3

Whew! We'll have our platter burnished,
      Laid with care on our own shelf!
With a fire-new spoon we're furnished,
      And a goblet for ourself,
Rinsed like something sacrificial
      Ere 'tis fit to touch our chaps —
Marked with L for our initial!
      (He-he! There his lily snaps!)

4

Saint, forsooth! While brown Dolores
      Squats outside the Convent bank
With Sanchicha, telling stories,
      Steeping tresses in the tank,
Blue-black, lustrous, thick like horsehairs,
      — Can't I see his dead eye glow,
Bright as 'twere a Barbary corsair's?
      (That is, if he'd let it show!)

5

When he finishes refection,
      Knife and fork he never lays

Cross-wise, to my recollection,
    As do I, in Jesu's praise.
I the Trinity illustrate,
    Drinking watered orange-pulp —
In three sips the Arian frustrate;
    While he drains his at one gulp.

6

Oh, those melons? If he's able
    We're to have a feast! so nice!
One goes to the Abbot's table,
    All of us get each a slice.
How go on your flowers? None double?
    Not one fruit-sort can you spy?
Strange! And I, too, at such trouble,
    Keep them close-nipped on the sly!

7

There's a great text in Galatians,
    Once you trip on it, entails
Twenty-nine distinct damnations,
    One sure, if another fails:
If I trip him just a-dying,
    Sure of heaven as sure can be,
Spin him around and send him flying
    Off to hell, a Manichee?

8

Or, my scrofulous French novel
    On grey paper with blunt type!
Simply glance at it, you grovel
    Hand and foot in Belial's gripe:
If I double down its pages
    At the woeful sixteenth print,
When he gathers his greengages,
    Ope a sieve and slip it in't?

9

Or, there's Satan! — one might venture
    Pledge one's soul to him, yet leave
Such a flaw in the indenture
    As he'd miss till, past retrieve,
Blasted lay that rose-acacia
    We're so proud of! *Hy, Zy, Hine*...
'St, there's Vespers! *Plena gratiâ*
    Ave, Virgo! Gr-r-r — you swine!

FURTHER
READINGS

AESCHYLUS. *The Complete Greek Tragedies*. Vol. I. Chicago: University of Chicago Press, 1959.

AGEE, J. *A Death in the Family*. New York: Avon Books, 1959.

AIKEN, C. *Among the Lost People*. New York: Charles Scribner's Sons, 1934.

—— *Blue Voyage*. New York: Charles Scribner's Sons, 1927.

ALBEE, E. "The Zoo Story." In *Three Plays*. New York: Coward-McCann, Inc., 1960.

—— *Who's Afraid of Virginia Woolf?* New York: Atheneum, 1962.

ALGREN, N. *The Man with the Golden Arm*. New York: Doubleday & Co., 1949.

ANDERSON, S. *Winesburg, Ohio*. New York: The Viking Press, 1958.

ANONYMOUS. *Go Ask Alice*. Englewood Cliffs, N.J.: Prentice-Hall, Inc., 1971.

ASWELL, M. L. *The World Within*. New York: Whittlesey House, 1947.

BALDWIN, J. *Giovanni's Room*. New York: Signet, 1959.

BARTH, J. *The End of the Road*. New York: Doubleday and Co., 1967.

BASSING, E. *Home Before Dark*. New York: Random House, 1957.

BAWDEN, N. *The Birds in the Trees*. New York: Harper & Row, 1971.

BECKETT, S. *Krapp's Last Tape*. New York: Grove Press, 1957.

BELLOW, S. *The Adventures of Augie March*. New York: The Viking Press, 1965.

—— *Herzog*. London: Weidenfeld & Nicolson, 1965.

—— *The Last Analysis*. New York: The Viking Press, 1965.

BLANKFORT, M. *The Juggler*. Boston: Little, Brown, 1952.

BOTTOME, P. *Private Worlds*. New York: Houghton, 1934.

BOWEN, E. *Death of the Heart*. New York: Knopf, 1939.

BOYLE, K. "Rest Cure." In *The First Lover, and Other Stories*. New York: Smith & Haas, 1933.

BRAND, M. *Savage Sleep*. New York: Crown, 1968.

—— *The Outward Room*. New York: Simon & Schuster, 1937.

BROWN, W. *Monkey on My Back*. New York: Greenberg, 1953.

CAMUS, A. *The Stranger*. New York: Knopf, 1946.

CAPOTE, T. *The Grass Harp and a Tree of Night, and Other Stories*. New York: Signet, 1956.

—— *In Cold Blood*. New York: Signet, 1965.

CARY, J. *The Horse's Mouth*. New York: Harper & Row, 1965.

CHEKHOV, A. *The Bet, and Other Stories*. Boston: J. W. Luce, 1915.

—— *The Black Monk, and Other Stories*. New York: Frederick A. Stokes, 1915.

—— *Chekhov: The Major Plays*. New York: New American Library, 1964.

CELA, C. *Mrs. Caldwell Speaks to Her Son*. Ithaca, N.Y.: Cornell University Press, 1968.

CELINE, L. *Castle to Castle*. New York: Delacorte, 1968.

CONRAD, J. *Heart of Darkness* and *The Secret Sharer*. New York: Signet, 1950.

DAWSON, J. *The Ha-Ha*. Boston: Little, Brown & Co., 1961.

De ASSIS, M. *Epitaph of a Small Winner*. New York: Noonday Press, 1956.

—— *The Psychiatrist and Other Stories*. Berkeley, Calif.: University of California Press, 1963.

DE VRIES, P. *Madder Music*. Boston: Little, Brown & Co., 1977.

DICK, P. *A Scanner, Darkly*. New York: Doubleday & Co., 1977.

DICKINSON, E. *The Poems of Emily Dickinson*. Cambridge, Mass: The Belknap Press of Harvard University Press, 1951.

DOSTOEVSKY, F. *The Brothers Karamazov*. New York: Modern Library, 1950.

—— *Crime and Punishment*. New York: Norton, 1964.

—— "Notes from Underground." In *Three Short Novels of Dostoevsky*. New York: Dell, 1960.

—— *The Possessed*. New York: Dell, 1961.

DURRELL, L. *The Alexandria Quartet*. New York: Dutton, 1960.

ELIOT, T. S. *The Cocktail Party*. New York: Harcourt, Brace, 1950.

ELLISON, R. *Invisible Man*. New York: Random House, 1952.

ELLIOTT, D. *Listen to the Silence*. New York: Holt, Rinehart, 1969.

FAULKNER, W. *Absalom, Absalom*. New York: Random House, 1951.

—— *Light in August*. New York: Random House, 1968.

—— *The Sound and the Fury*. New York: Random House, 1946.

FITZGERALD, F. S. *The Crack-up*. New York: New Directions, 1945.

—— *Tender Is the Night*. New York: Charles Scribner's Sons, 1933.

FOWLES, J. *The Collector*. New York: Dell, 1975.

FRAME, J. *Faces in the Water*. New York: Braziller, 1961.

—— *Scented Gardens for the Blind*. New York: Braziller, 1964.

FRANKAU, G. *Michael's Wife*. New York: Dutton, 1948.

FRISCH, M. *I'm Not Stiller*. New York: Vintage Books, 1962.

GARDNER, J. *Grendel*. New York: Ballantine Books, 1975.

GENET, J. *Our Lady of the Flowers*. New York: Grove Press, 1963.

GIBSON, W. *The Cobweb*. New York: Knopf, 1954.

GIDE, A. *The Immoralist*. New York: Knopf, 1930.

GOGOL, N. *Tales of Good and Evil*. New York: Doubleday, 1957.

GOLDBERG, G. *The Lynching of Orin Newfield*. New York: The Dial Press, 1970.

GOLDING, W. *The Lord of the Flies*. New York: Coward-McCann, 1962.

—— *The Spire*. New York: Harcourt, Brace, 1965.

GOLDMAN, W. *Magic*. New York: Delacorte, 1976.

GREENBERG JOANNE. *I Never Promised You a Rose Garden*. New York: Holt, Rinehart, and Winston, 1964.

GRUBB, D. *The Night of the Hunter*. New York: Harper & Bros., 1953.

HARWOOD, R. *The Girl in Melanie Klein*. New York: Holt, Rinehart, 1969.

HAWTHORNE, N. *Hawthorne's Short Stories*. New York: Vintage Books, 1955.

—— *The Scarlet Letter*. New York: Norton, 1978.

HAYES, J. *Like Any Other Fugitive*. New York: The Dial Press, 1971.

HELLER, J. *Catch-22*. New York: Simon & Schuster, 1961.

HELLMAN, L. "The Children's Hour." In *Four Plays by Lillian Hellman*. New York: Modern Library, 1940.

HEMINGWAY, E. *"The Battler" and "Soldier's Home."* In *In Our Time*. New York; Charles Scribner's Sons, 1953.

HESSE, H. *Magister Ludi*. New York: Holt, Rinehart, 1969.

—— *Steppenwolf*. New York: Holt, Rinehart, 1949.

HUTCHINSON, R. *The Inheritor*. New York: Harper & Row, 1961.

HUXLEY, A. *After Many a Summer Dies the Swan*. New York: Harper & Row, 1939.

—— *Point Counter Point*. New York: Doubleday, 1930.

IBSEN, H. *Eleven Plays of Henrik Ibsen*. New York: Modern Library, 1935.

INGE, W. *Picnic*. New York: Random House, 1953.

JACKSON, C. *The Lost Weekend*. New York: Noonday Press, 1960.

JACKSON, S. *The Bird's Nest*. New York: Farrar, Straus & Giroux, 1954.

JAMES, H. *The Turn of the Screw, and Other Short Novels*. New York: The New American Library, 1962.

JOYCE, J. *"An Encounter."* In *Dubliners*. New York: The Viking Press, 1967.

KAFKA, F. *The Castle*. New York: Knopf, 1954.

—— "A Huger Artist." In *The Penal Colony*. New York: Schicken Books, 1948

—— *The Trial*. New York: Knopf, 1957.

KESEY, K. *One Flew Over the Cuckoo's Nest*. New York: The Viking Press, 1962.

KOESTLER, A. *Arrival and Departure*. New York: Macmillan, 1943.

KRAMM, J. *The Shrike*. New York: Random House, 1952.

LAURENTS, A. *A Clearing in the Woods*. New York: Random House, 1956.

—— *Home of the Brave*. New York: Random House, 1946.

LAWRENCE, D. H. *The Complete Short Stories*. London: Heinemann, 1957.

—— *Sons and Lovers*. London: Duckworth, 1913.

LESSING, D. *Briefing for a Descent into Hell*. The Viking Press, 1971.

LEVIN, M. *Compulsion*. New York: Pocket Books, 1959.

LIPSKY, E. *The Kiss of Death*. New York: New American Library, 1947.

MAIER, H. *Undertow*. New York: Doubleday, 1945.

MAILER, N. *An American Dream*. New York: The Dial Press, 1965.

—— *The Deer Park*. New York: Putnam, 1955.

MALAMUD, B. *The Assistant*. New York: Farrar, Straus & Giroux, 1957.

—— *The Tenants*. New York: Farrar, Straus, & Giroux, 1971.

MANN, T. *Doctor Faustus*. New York: Knopf, 1948.

—— *The Magic Mountain*. New York: Knopf, 1961.

—— *Stories of Three Decades*. New York: Modern Library, 1936.

MARCH, W. *The Bad Seed*. New York: Holt, Rinehart, 1954.

MAUGHAM, S. *Best Short Stories*. New York: Modern Library, 1957.

McCARTHY, M. *The Company She Keeps*. New York: Dell, 1955.

McCULLERS, C. *The Ballad of the Sad Cafe*. New York: Houghton-Mifflin, 1941.

—— *The Heart Is a Lonely Hunter*. New York: Houghton-Mifflin, 1940.

—— *The Member of the Wedding*. New York: Houghton-Mifflin, 1946.

—— *Reflections in a Golden Eye*. New York: Houghton-Mifflin, 1941.

MELVILLE, H. *Moby Dick*. New York: Norton, 1967.

MILLER, A. *Collected Plays*. New York: The Viking Press, 1957.

MORTIMER, P. *The Pumpkin Eater*. New York: Farrar, Straus & Giroux, 1977.

NABOKOV, V. *Lolita*. New York: Putnam, 1955.

—— *Nabokov's Dozen*. Garden City, N.Y.: Doubleday, 1958.

NIN, A. *Under a Glass Bell, and Other Stories*. Chicago: Swallow Press, 1968.

O'CONNOR, F. "Good Country People." In *A Good Man Is Hard to Find and Other Stories*. New York: Harcourt, Brace, 1955.

O'NEILL, E. *Long Day's Journey into Night*. New Haven, Conn.: Yale University Press, 1956.

—— *The Plays of Eugene O'Neill* (3 vols.). New York: Random House, 1948.

PARKER, D. *Laments for the Living*. New York: The Viking Press, 1930.

PERCY W. *Lancelot*. New York: Farrar, Straus & Giroux, 1977.

—— *The Movie Goer*. New York: Knopf, 1961.

PETERS, F. *The World Next Door*. New York: Farrar, Straus & Giroux, 1949.

PINTER, H. *The Birthday Party*. New York: Grove Press, 1961.

PIRANDELLO, L. *Naked Masks*. New York: Dutton, 1957.

—— *One, None and a Hundred Thousand*. New York: Dutton, 1933.

—— *Short Stories*. New York: Oxford University Press, 1965.

PLATH, S. *Ariel*. New York: Harper & Row, 1961

—— *The Bell Jar*. New York: Harper & Row, 1971.

POE, E. A. *Tales of Edgar Allan Poe*. New York: Random House, 1944.

POTOK, C. *The Promise*. New York: Knopf, 1969.

RENDELL, R. *A Demon in My View*. Garden City, N.Y.: Doubleday & Co., 1977.

ROBINSON, E. A. *Collected Poems*. New York: Macmillan, 1952.

ROSSNER, J. *Looking for Mr. Goodbar*. New York: Simon & Schuster, 1975.

ROTH, P. *Letting Go*. New York: Random House, 1962.

—— *Portnoy's Complaint*. New York: Random House, 1969.

ROSTEN, L. *Captain Newman, M.D.* New York: Harper & Row, 1961.

RUBENS, B. *Chosen People*. New York: Atheneum, 1961.

RUBIN, T. *Lisa and David*. New York: Macmillan, 1961.

SALINGER, J. D. *The Catcher in the Rye*. Boston: Little, Brown & Co., 1951.

—— *Nine Stories*. Boston: Little, Brown & Co., 1953.

SARTRE, J. P. *Nausea*. Norfolk, Conn.: New Directions, 1949.

—— *No Exit and Three Other Plays*. New York: Vintage Books, 1955.

SCHREIBER, F. R. *Sybil*. New York: Warner Paperback Library, 1974.

SCHULBERG, B. *What Makes Sammy Run?* New York: Random House, 1941.

SEXTON, A. *To Bedlam and Part Way Back*. Cambridge, Mass.: The Riverside Press, 1960.

SHAFFER, P. *Equus*. New York: Avon Books, 1975.

SOPHOCLES. *Sophocles. The Seven Plays in English Verse*. London: Oxford University Press, 1928.

SOUBIRAN, A. *Bedlam*. New York: Putnam, 1957.

STRINDBERG, A. *Six Plays of Strindberg*. New York: Anchor Books, 1957.

STYRON, W. *Lie Down in Darkness*. Indianapolis and New York: Bobbs-Merrill, 1951.

TARSIS, V. *Ward 7*. New York: Dutton, 1965.

TELFER, D. *The Caretakers*. New York: Simon & Schuster, 1959.

UPDIKE, J. *A Month of Sundays*. Greenwich, Conn.: Fawcett, 1976.

VESAAS, T. *The Birds*. New York: William Morrow, 1969.

VONNEGUT, K. *Breakfast of Champions*. New York: Dell, 1975.

WARD, M. J. *The Snake Pit*. New York: Random House, 1946.

WEISS, P. *Marat Sade*. New York: Atheneum, 1973.

WELTY, E. "Why I Live at the P.O." In *A Curtain of Green*. New York: Doubleday, 1941.

WERTHAM, F. *Dark Legend*. New York: Doubleday, 1949.

WEST, N. *The Day of the Locust*. New York: New Directions, 1939.

—— *Miss Lonelyhearts*. New York: New Directions, 1933.

WILDE, O. *The Picture of Dorian Gray*. New York: Modern Library, 1926.

WILLIAMS, T. *Cat on a Hot Tin Roof*. New York: New Directions, 1955.

—— *The Glass Menagerie*. New York: New Directions, 1949.

—— *A Streetcar Named Desire*. New York: New American Library, 1973.

—— *Summer and Smoke*. New York: New American Library, 1976.

WILLIAMS, W. *The Farmers' Daughters*. New York: New Directions, 1961.

WOOLF, V. *To the Lighthouse*. New York: Harcourt, Brace, 1927.

—— *Mrs. Dalloway*. New York: Modern Library, 1928.

WOUK, H. *The Caine Mutiny*. Garden City, N.Y.: Doubleday, 1951.

WRIGHT, R. *Native Son*. New York: Harper & Bros., 1940.

ZINDEL, P. *Effect of Gamma Rays on Man-in-the-Moon Marigolds*. New York: Harper & Row, 1971.